3rd International Workshop on Computational Approaches to Historical Language Change (LChange 2022)

Held online due to COVID-19

Dublin, Ireland
26 – 27 May 2022

ISBN: 978-1-7138-6744-9

Printed from e-media with permission by:

Curran Associates, Inc.
57 Morehouse Lane
Red Hook, NY 12571

Some format issues inherent in the e-media version may also appear in this print version.

Printed with permission by Curran Associates, Inc. (2023)

Association for Computational Linguistics
209 N. Eighth Street
Stroudsburg, Pennsylvania 18360

Phone: 1-570-476-8006
Fax: 1-570-476-0860

acl@aclweb.org

Additional copies of this publication are available from:

Curran Associates, Inc.
57 Morehouse Lane
Red Hook, NY 12571 USA
Phone: 845-758-0400
Fax: 845-758-2633
Email: curran@proceedings.com
Web: www.proceedings.com

LChange 2022

3rd International Workshop on Computational Approaches to Historical Language Change 2022

Proceedings of the Workshop

May 26-27, 2022

The LChange organizers gratefully acknowledge the support from the following sponsors.

Gold

Preface by the General Chair

Welcome to the 3rd International Workshop on Computational Approaches to Historical Language Change (LChange'22) co-located with ACL 2022. This year, LChange is held over two days, May 26–27 2022, as a hybrid event with participation possible both virtually and on-site in Dublin, Ireland. To support efforts in evaluation of computational methodologies for uncovering language change, LChange'22 features a shared task on semantic change detection for Spanish as one track of the workshop.

Characterizing the time-varying nature of language will have broad implications and applications in multiple fields including linguistics, artificial intelligence, digital humanities, computational cognitive and social sciences. In this workshop, we bring together the world's pioneers and experts in **computational approaches to historical language change with focus on digital text corpora**. In doing so, this workshop carries out the triple goals of disseminating the state-of-the-art research on diachronic modelling of language change, fostering cross-disciplinary collaborations, and exploring the fundamental theoretical and methodological challenges in this growing niche of computational linguistic research.

In response to the call we received 21 submissions. Each of them was carefully evaluated by at least two members of the Program Committee, whom we believed to be most appropriate for each paper. Based on the reviewers' feedback we accepted 15 full and short papers as oral or poster presentations. We had two distinguished keynote presentations: the first by Dirk Geeraerts (KU Leuven/University of Gothenburg) who presented a talk entitled "Can historical semantics save lives? (And other questions for computational diachronic semantics)", and the second by Dominik Schlechtweg (University of Stuttgart) with the talk "Human and Computational Measurement of Lexical Semantic Change". Finally, we invited two additional papers to be presented as posters, one published at the ACL 2022 conference and one in *Findings of NAACL*, which are not included in the workshop proceedings.

The shared task on semantic change discovery and detection in Spanish was divided in two phases: (1) graded change discovery; and (2) binary change detection. The main novelty with respect to the previous tasks consisted in predicting and evaluating changes for all vocabulary words in the corpus. Six teams participated in phase 1 and seven teams in phase 2.

To further support the community, we offered two student scholarships for the main conference in addition to the workshop, as well as mentoring for young researchers. Five researchers were offered mentoring on a topic of their choice, either during the workshop or virtually.

We hope that you will find the workshop papers insightful and inspiring. We would like to thank the keynote speakers for their stimulating talks, the authors of all papers for their interesting contributions and the members of the Program Committee for their insightful reviews. Our special thanks go to the emergency reviewers who stepped in to provide their expertise. We also express our gratitude to the ACL 2022 workshop chairs for their kind assistance during the organization process. Finally, our thanks go to our gold sponsor iguanodon.ai, as well as the research project "Towards Computational Lexical Semantic Change Detection" (Swedish Research Council, contract 2018-01184) and the research program "Change is Key!" (Riksbankens Jubileumsfond, contract M21-0021).

Nina Tahmasebi, workshop chair, University of Gothenburg (Sweden)
Syrielle Montariol, INRIA Paris (France)
Andrey Kutuzov, University of Oslo (Norway)
Simon Hengchen, University of Gothenburg (Sweden)
Haim Dubossarsky, University of Cambridge (United Kingdom)
Lars Borin, University of Gothenburg (Sweden)

LChange'22 Workshop Chairs

Organizing Committee

General Chair

Nina Tahmasebi, University of Gothenburg, Sweden

Program Chairs

Lars Borin, University of Gothenburg, Sweden
Simon Hengchen, University of Gothenburg, Sweden
Syrielle Montariol, INRIA Paris, France
Haim Dubossarsky, University of Cambridge, United Kingdom
Andrey Kutuzov, University of Oslo, Norway

Program Committee

Program Committee

Aleksandrs Berdicevskis, University of Gothenburg
Animesh Mukherjee, Indian Institute of Technology Kharagpur
Annalina Caputo, Dublin City University
Barbara McGillivray, King's College London, University of London
Barend Beekhuizen, University of Toronto
Clémentine Fourrier, INRIA Paris
Ekaterina Vylomova, University of Melbourne
Ella Rabinovich, University of Toronto
Enrique Manjavacas, Leiden University
Eyal Sagi, University of St. Francis
Filip Miletic, University of Toulouse
Ian Stewart, University of Michigan
Karlien Franco, KU Leuven
Lidia Pivovarova, University of Helsinki
Ludovic Tanguy, University of Toulouse
Maike Park, Leibniz-Institute for the German Language
Mario Giulianelli, University of Amsterdam
Martin Pömsl, McGill University
Matej Martinc, Jozef Stefan Institute
Mauricio Gruppi, Rensselaer Polytechnic Institute
Michael Färber, Karlsruhe Institute of Technology
Paul Cook, University of New Brunswick
Paul Nulty, University College Dublin
Pierluigi Cassotti, University of Bari
Pierpaolo Basile, University of Bari
Péter Jeszenszky, Universität Bern
Samia Touileb, University of Bergen
Stefano De Pascale, Vrije Universiteit Brussel
Taraka Rama, University of North Texas
Vaibhav Jain, Delhi Technological University, Dhirubhai Ambani Institute Of Information and Communication Technology
Valentin Hofmann, University of Oxford
Yijun Duan, AIST
Ying Li, Max Planck Institut

Keynote Talk: Can historical semantics save lives? (And other questions for computational diachronic semantics)

Dirk Geeraerts
KU Leuven/University of Gothenburg

Abstract: Drawing on a number (methodologically non-computational) diachronic semantic studies that I have carried out at various points over the past decades, I would like to draw the attention to three issues that have so far played only a secondary role in the booming field of computational diachronic semantics but that might provide some inspiration for a further expansion: first, the double-sided status of textual interpretation, which can feature both as a descriptive target and as a methodological source in historical semantics; second, the relevance of incorporating an onomasiological dimension in the definition of semantic change; and third, the distinction between generalizations about semantic change that are formulated in terms of structural and functional features (like isomorphism or frequency) and generalizations that correlate semantic changes with external phenomena (like societal changes).

Bio: Dirk Geeraerts is professor emeritus of linguistics at the University of Leuven. His main research focus involves the fields of lexical semantics and lexicology, with specific attention for social variation and diachronic change of meaning and vocabulary. He is the founder of the journal *Cognitive Linguistics*, and editor of *The Oxford Handbook of Cognitive Linguistics* (2007). Publications include *The Structure of Lexical Variation* (Mouton De Gruyter 1994), *Diachronic Prototype Semantics* (OUP 1997), *Words and Other Wonders* (Mouton De Gruyter 2006), *Theories of Lexical Semantics* (OUP 2010), and *Ten Lectures on Cognitive Sociolinguistics* (Brill 2018).

Keynote Talk: Human and Computational Measurement of Lexical Semantic Change

Dominik Schlechtweg
University of Stuttgart/University of Texas, Austin

Abstract: Human language changes over time. This change occurs on several linguistic levels such as grammar, sound or meaning. The study of meaning changes on the word level is often called Lexical Semantic Change (LSC) and is traditionally either approached from an onomasiological perspective asking by which words a meaning can be expressed, or a semasiological perspective asking which meanings a word can express over time. In recent years, the task of automatic detection of semasiological LSC from textual data has been established as a proper field of computational linguistics under the name of Lexical Semantic Change Detection (LSCD). Two main factors have contributed to this development: (i) the *digital turn* in the humanities has made large amounts of historical texts available in digital form. (ii) New *computational models* have been introduced efficiently learning semantic aspects of words solely from text. One of the main motivations behind the work on LSCD are their applications in historical semantics and historical lexicography where researchers are concerned with the classification of words into categories of semantic change. Automatic methods have the advantage to produce semantic change predictions for large amounts of data in small amounts of time and could thus considerably decrease human efforts in the mentioned fields, while being able to scan more data and thus to uncover more semantic changes which are at the same time less biased towards ad hoc sampling criteria used by researchers. On the other hand, automatic methods may also be hurtful when their predictions are biased, i.e., they may miss numerous semantic changes or label words as changing which are not. Results produced in this way may then lead researchers to make empirically inadequate generalizations on semantic change. Hence, automatic change detection methods should not be trusted until they have been evaluated thoroughly and their predictions have been shown to reach an acceptable level of correctness.

Despite the rapid growth of LSCD as a field a solid evaluation of the wealth of proposed models was still missing in 2017. The reasons were multiple, but most importantly there was no annotated benchmark test set available. In this talk I will describe the work done for my PhD from the last five years aimed at standardizing the evaluation of LSCD models.

Bio: Dominik Schlechtweg did his PhD at the IMS (University of Stuttgart) working together with Sabine Schulte im Walde on automatic detection of lexical semantic change. He held a PhD scholarship from Konrad Adenauer Foundation. Since February 2022 he is a post-doctoral researcher at the IMS (University of Stuttgart), working in the 6-year research program *Change is Key!* and in the research project *Towards computational lexical semantic change detection*. Currently, he is doing a research internship with Katrin Erk at the University of Texas, Austin.

Table of Contents

Program

Thursday, May 26, 2022

09:00 - 09:15 *Introduction*

09:15 - 10:35 *Session 1*

Low Saxon dialect distances at the orthographic and syntactic level
Janine Siewert, Yves Scherrer and Martijn Wieling

A New Framework for Fast Automated Phonological Reconstruction Using Trimmed Alignments and Sound Correspondence Patterns
Johann-Mattis List, Robert Forkel and Nathan Hill

What is Done is Done: an Incremental Approach to Semantic Shift Detection
Francesco Periti, Alfio Ferrara, Stefano Montanelli and Martin Ruskov

10:35 - 11:05 *BREAK*

11:05 - 12:30 *Session 2*

Lexicon of Changes: Towards the Evaluation of Diachronic Semantic Shift in Chinese
Jing Chen, Emmanuele Chersoni and Chu-ren Huang

Deconstructing destruction: A Cognitive Linguistics perspective on a computational analysis of diachronic change
Karlien Franco, Mariana Montes and Kris Heylen

Using Cross-Lingual Part of Speech Tagging for Partially Reconstructing the Classic Language Family Tree Model
Anat Samohi, Daniel Weisberg Mitelman and Kfir Bar

12:30 - 14:00 *LUNCH / BREAK*

14:00 - 15:00 *Keynote 1 - Dirk Geeraerts*

15:00 - 15:30 *Session 3*

Do Not Fire the Linguist: Grammatical Profiles Help Language Models Detect Semantic Change
Mario Giulianelli, Andrey Kutuzov and Lidia Pivovarova

Thursday, May 26, 2022 (continued)

15:30 - 17:00 *Poster session + COFFEE*

From qualifiers to quantifiers: semantic shift at the paradigm level
Quentin Feltgen

Explainable Publication Year Prediction of Eighteenth Century Texts with the BERT Model
Iiro Rastas, Yann Ciarán Ryan, Iiro Tiihonen, Mohammadreza Qaraei, Liina Repo, Rohit Babbar, Eetu Mäkelä, Mikko Tolonen and Filip Ginter

Caveats of Measuring Semantic Change of Cognates and Borrowings using Multilingual Word Embeddings
Clémentine Fourrier and Syrielle Montariol

Vaderland, Volk and Natie: Semantic Change Related to Nationalism in Dutch Literature Between 1700 and 1880 Captured with Dynamic Bernoulli Word Embeddings
Marije Timmermans, Eva Vanmassenhove and Dimitar Shterionov

Language Acquisition, Neutral Change, and Diachronic Trends in Noun Classifiers
Aniket Kali and Jordan Kodner

A Multilingual Benchmark to Capture Olfactory Situations over Time
Stefano Menini, Teresa Paccosi, Sara Tonelli, Marieke Van Erp, Inger Leemans, Pasquale Lisena, Raphael Troncy, William Tullett, Ali Hürriyetoğlu, Ger Dijkstra, Femke Gordijn, Elias Jürgens, Josephine Koopman, Aron Ouwerkerk, Sanne Steen, Inna Novalija, Janez Brank, Dunja Mladenic and Anja Zidar

Using neural topic models to track context shifts of words: a case study of COVID-related terms before and after the lockdown in April 2020
Olga Kellert and Md Mahmud Uz Zaman

Roadblocks in Gender Bias Measurement for Diachronic Corpora
Saied Alshahrani, Esma Wali, Abdullah R Alshamsan, Yan Chen and Jeanna Matthews

[LSCDISCOVERY SHARED TASK] *UAlberta at LSCDiscovery: Lexical Semantic Change Detection via Word Sense Disambiguation*
Daniela Teodorescu, Spencer von der Ohe and Grzegorz Kondrak

Friday, May 27, 2022

09:30 - 09:45 *Introduction day 2*

09:40 - 10:40 *Keynote 2 - Dominik Schlechtweg*

10:40 - 11:05 *BREAK*

11:05 - 11:25 *Task description paper*

[LSCDISCOVERY SHARED TASK] *LSCDiscovery: A shared task on semantic change discovery and detection in Spanish*
Frank D. Zamora-Reina, Felipe Bravo-Marquez and Dominik Schlechtweg

11:25 - 12:45 *Best task paper 1*

[LSCDISCOVERY SHARED TASK] *DeepMistake at LSCDiscovery: Can a Multilingual Word-in-Context Model Replace Human Annotators?*
Daniil Homskiy and Nikolay Arefyev

11:45 - 12:05 *Best task paper 2*

[LSCDISCOVERY SHARED TASK] *GlossReader at LSCDiscovery: Train to Select a Proper Gloss in English – Discover Lexical Semantic Change in Spanish*
Maxim Rachinskiy and Nikolay Arefyev

12:05 - 13:30 *LUNCH / BREAK*

13:30 - 15:00 *Virtual poster session + COFFEE*

[LSCDISCOVERY SHARED TASK] *BOS at LSCDiscovery: Lexical Substitution for Interpretable Lexical Semantic Change Detection*
Artem Kudisov and Nikolay Arefyev

[LSCDISCOVERY SHARED TASK] *UAlberta at LSCDiscovery: Lexical Semantic Change Detection via Word Sense Disambiguation*
Daniela Teodorescu, Spencer von der Ohe and Grzegorz Kondrak

[LSCDISCOVERY SHARED TASK] *CoToHiLi at LSCDiscovery: the Role of Linguistic Features in Predicting Semantic Change*
Ana Sabina Uban, Alina Maria Cristea, Anca Daniela Dinu, Liviu P Dinu, Simona Georgescu and Laurentiu Zoicas

[LSCDISCOVERY SHARED TASK] *HSE at LSCDiscovery in Spanish: Clustering and Profiling for Lexical Semantic Change Discovery*
Kseniia Kashleva, Alexander Shein, Elizaveta Tukhtina and Svetlana Vydrina

Friday, May 27, 2022 (continued)

15:00 - 16:00 *Mentoring*

16:00 - 16:30 *Closing*

A Multilingual Benchmark to Capture Olfactory Situations over Time

S. Menini[1] **T. Paccosi**[1] **S. Tonelli**[1] **M. Van Erp**[2] **I. Leemans**[2]
P. Lisena[3] **R. Troncy**[3] **W. Tullett**[4] **A. Hürriyetoğlu**[2] **G. Dijkstra**[2]
F. Gordijn[2] **E. Jürgens**[2] **J. Koopman**[2] **A. Ouwerkerk**[2] **S. Steen**[2]
I. Novalija[5] **J. Brank**[5] **D. Mladenić**[5] **A. Zidar**[5]
[1] FBK, [2] KNAW, [3] EURECOM, [4] ARU, [5] JSI,
{menini,tpaccosi,satonelli}@fbk.eu, inger.leemans@huc.knaw.nl
{marieke.van.erp, ali.hurriyetoglu}@dh.huc.knaw.nl
{lisena,troncy}@eurecom.fr, william.tullett@aru.ac.uk
{inna.koval,janez.brank,dunja.mladenic}@ijs.si

Abstract

We present a benchmark in six European languages containing manually annotated information about olfactory situations and events following a FrameNet-like approach. The documents selection covers ten domains of interest to cultural historians in the olfactory domain and includes texts published between 1620 to 1920, allowing a diachronic analysis of smell descriptions. With this work, we aim to foster the development of olfactory information extraction approaches as well as the analysis of changes in smell descriptions over time.

1 Introduction

Human experience is mediated through the senses, which we use to interact with the world. Since the perceptual world is so important to us, all languages have resources to describe the sensory perception. Nevertheless, previous research showed that, at least in Western European languages, the visual dimension is prevalent in language, with a richer terminology used to describe it, while the olfactory dimension is less represented (Winter, 2019). For example, in English, there are less unique words for the smell domain than for the other senses. They are also used less frequently and olfactory descriptions are often a target of cross-modal expressions.

Sensory terminology has been researched previously, with the goal to build resources and to analyse how the different senses are described in language (Tekiroğlu et al., 2014b,a). Some research is specifically devoted to smell (Lefever et al., 2018), but they all focus on contemporary language. One notable exception is the collection of essays published in Jędrzejowski and Staniewski (2021), where olfaction in different languages is analysed in a diachronic perspective. For example, Strik Lievers (2021) describes how the olfactory lexicon has changed from Latin to Italian.

In this work, we contribute to the diachronic analysis of olfactory language by annotating a multilingual benchmark with smell situations spanning three centuries. Compared to existing studies, our focus is not on the occurrences of single terms, but we rather capture smell events in texts, i.e. more complex structures involving different participants. The benchmark currently covers six languages (Dutch, English, French, German, Italian and Slovene). Annotation of Latin data is ongoing, but we do not include here the results for this language because they are still preliminary.

We describe the annotation guidelines and the document selection process. Our benchmark includes texts issued between 1620 and 1920 covering ten domains of olfactory interest to cultural history. We release the benchmark at `https://github.com/Odeuropa/benchmarks_and_corpora` and we present a first analysis of its content.

2 Related Work

Studies on olfactory language in cognitive science primarily focus on the verbal expressions of the odour perceived (Majid and Burenhult, 2014; Majid et al., 2018), while in historical studies, instead, they mainly deal with the textual accounts of experienced smells, as in Tullett (2019). Within the NLP community, little attention has been devoted to the automatic analysis of smell references in texts. Most works have focused on the creation of lexical databases, for example Tekiroğlu et al. (2014b,a) worked on the creation of Sensicon, representing the first systematic attempt to build a lex-

Proceedings of the 3rd Workshop on Computational Approaches to Historical Language Change, pages 1 - 10
May 26-27, 2022

icon automatically associated to the five senses. Other studies have focused on synaesthetic aspects of language, dealing with the multisensoriality of sensory words. For instance, Lievers and Huang (2016) create a controlled lexicon of perception, while Girju and Lambert (2021) propose to use word embeddings for the extraction of sensory descriptors and their interconnections in texts.

As regards smell-specific works, Brate et al. (2020) propose both a simple annotation scheme to capture odour-related experiences and two semi-supervised approaches to automatically replicate this annotation. Lefever et al. (2018) present an automated analysis of wine reviews, where olfaction plays a fundamental role, while McGregor and McGillivray (2018) introduce an approach to automatically identify smell-related sentences in a corpus of historical medical records using distributional semantic modelling. More recently, Tonelli and Menini (2021) present FrameNet-inspired guidelines to annotate smell events in texts. We consider this work the starting point upon which we build our annotation task. In particular, we aim at assessing the underlying assumptions of such guidelines: whether frames can be applied diachronically and across languages using the same annotation scheme.

3 Annotation Guidelines

Annotation of olfactory events and situations in texts is a new task that was recently introduced in Tonelli and Menini (2021). We adopt the same framework in this work, whose guidelines are summarised below.

Olfactory annotation is inspired by the FrameNet project (Ruppenhofer et al., 2006)[1] which, focusing on the semantic dimension of situations and participants, should be easily applicable to multiple languages and constructions. In FrameNet, events and situations are so-called *frames* and are used as synonyms for schemata, semantic memory or scenarios. They represent the components of the internal model of the world that language users have created by interpreting their environment (Fillmore, 1976).

According to frame semantics, a frame includes two main components: *lexical units* (LUs) and *frame elements* (FEs). The former are words, multiwords or idiomatic expressions that evoke a specific frame, while the latter are frame-specific semantic roles that, in case of verbal LUs, are usually realized by the syntactic dependents of the verb. For example, the *Commerce pay* frame includes as lexical units 'pay', 'payment', 'disburse', 'disbursement', 'shell out', and has the following frame elements: Buyer, Goods, Money, Rate, Seller.

While FrameNet aims to be a general-purpose resource, the guidelines we follow only concern olfactory situations. Therefore, the scope of our annotation considers only smell-related lexical units and a single frame of interest, the *Olfactory event*. The same structure as the original FrameNet is adopted based on lexical units and related frame elements. When necessary, domain-specific semantic roles are introduced upon discussions with experts in olfactory heritage and history. For example, the roles *Smell source*, *Evoked odorant* and *Odour carrier* were not originally in FrameNet, while some generic roles such as *Perceiver*, *Time*, *Location* and *Circumstances* are borrowed from the original resource. An overview of the frame elements included in our annotation is shown in Table 2.

The list of lexical units (LUs) was defined with the help of domain experts, choosing smell-related lexical units that evoke olfactory situations and events. The LU lists were created in six languages, namely English, Dutch, Italian, French, German and Slovenian. They include basic smell-related terms, which are generally comparable across languages (for instance the translation of words such as 'to smell', 'odour' 'odorous', 'smelly', 'perfume'). The lists were extended with language- and culture-specific terms, such as German compound nouns created with the roots '-gestank' and '-geruch', e.g. *Regengeruch* ('rain smell') or *Viehgestank* ('cattle stink'). The initial version of the list is reported in Table 1.

We consider these guidelines appropriate for our task because they have been designed following a multilingual perspective, with no language-specific adaptations. Furthermore, as we annotate documents from different time periods, LU lists are not fixed, giving the possibility to add new items as the outcome of the annotation process.

4 Document selection

In close collaboration with cultural historians, we defined ten domains of interest, where we expected to find a high number of smell-related

[1] https://framenet.icsi.berkeley.edu

English
Nouns: stink, scent, scents, smell, smells, odour, odor, odours, odors, stench, reek, aroma, aromas, aromatic, whiff, foetor, fetor, fragrance, musk, rankness, redolence, pong, pungency, niff, deodorant, olfaction **Verbs**: smelling, smelled , reeked, sniff, sniffed, sniffing, whiffed, fragrance, deodorized, deodorizing, snuffing, snuffed **Adjectives**: stinking, stank, stunk, scented, odourless, odoriferous , odorous, malodorous , reeking, aromatic , whiffy, fetid, foetid, fragrant, fragranced, redolent, frowzy, frowsy, pungent, funky, musty, niffy, unscented, scentless, deodorized, noisome , smelly, mephitic, olfactory **Adverbs**: musky, pungently **Other**: atmosphere, essence, putrid.
Dutch
Nouns: Aroma, Damp, Geur, Geurigheid, Geurstof, Geurtje , Luchtje, Miasma, Mufheid, Odeur, Parfum, Parfumerie, Reuck, Reuk, Reukeloosheid, Reukerij, Reukje, Reukloosheid, Reukorgaan, Reukstof, Reukwater, Reukwerk, Reukzin, Riecking, Rieking , Ruiker, Snuf, Stank, Stinkbok , Stinker, Stinkerd, Stinkgat, Stinknest, Vunsheid, Waesem, Walm, Wasem, Deodorisatie, Desodorisatie **Verbs**: Aromatiseren, Deodoriseren, Desodoriseren, Geuren, Meuren, Neuzen, Ontgeuren, Opsnuiven, Parfumeren, Rieken, Riecken, Ruiken, Ruycken, Snuffelen, Stinken, Uitwasemen, Vervliegen, Wasemen, Zwemen **Adjectives**: Aromatisch, Balsemachtig, Balsemiek, Geparfumeerd, Geurig, Geurloos, Heumig, Hommig, Hummig, Muf, Muffig, Neuswijze, Onwelriekend, Penetrant, Pisachtig, Reukloos, Riekelijk, Ruikbaar, Schimmelig, Soetgeurig, Soetreukig, Stankloos, Stankverdrijvend, Stankwerend, Stinkend, Stinkerig, Vervliegend, Vuns, Vunze, Weeïg, Welriekend, Zwavelig **Adverbs**: neusgierig, neuswijs, neuswijsheid, neuswijze, reuklustig, welgeneusd **Kinds of smell**: aardgeur, aardlucht, aardreuk, aaslucht, ademlucht, ambergeur, amberlucht, amberreuk, anijsgeur, balsemgeur, balsemlucht , bosgeur, braadgeur, braadlucht, brandlucht, brandreuk, dennenlucht, gaslucht , gasreuk, graflucht, harslucht, houtlucht, Huim, lijklucht, Meur, modderlucht , Muf, muskusgeur, muskusreuk, pestlucht, roetlucht, rooklucht, rotlucht, rozengeur, wierookgeur, wierookwalm, wierookwolk, wijnreuk, zweetlucht, Pekgeur, Pikreuk (and anything ending with -geur or -reuk).
Italian
Nouns: lezzo, morbo, putidore, fiatore, puzzo, puzza, fetore, miasma, putrefazione, effluvio, esalazione, estratto, odore, aroma, olezzo, fragranza, profumo, aulimento, odoramento, afrore, tanfo, tanfata, zaffata **Verbs**: odorare, puzzare, profumare, deodorare, odorizzare, aromatizzare, fiutare, annusare, nasare, olezzare, ammorbare, appestare, impestare, impuzzare, impuzzire, impuzzolentire, impuzzolire, intanfare **Adjectives**: puzzolente, fetente, fetido, deodorizzato, putrefatto, odorato, odoroso, odorifero, aromatizzato, profumante, profumato, suave, soave, olfattivo, olfattorio, maleodorante, aromatico, pestilenziale, puzzoso, fragrante **Adverbs**: profumatamente, odorosamente **Other**: essenza, atmosfera, sentire
French
Nouns: puanteur, flair, odeur, odorat, parfum, arôme, déodorant, nez, narine, gaz, baume, senteur, fragrance, musc, senteur, aigreur, olfaction, odorat, effluve, exhalaison, fumet, relent, pestilence, fétidité, remugle **Verbs**: puer, flairer, exhalter, odoriser, renifler, schlinguer, chlinguer, empester, parfumer, désodoriser, humer, renifler, embaumer **Adjectives**: puant, odorant, fétide, aromatique, olfactif, odorifère, odoriférant, nasal, pestilentiel, infect, malodorant, parfumé, inodore, piquant, désodorisé, méphitique, olfactif, empesté, infect, nauséabond **Other**: émanation, bouquet (about wine), sentir, sniffer, dégoûtant, dégoutant, écoeurant, percevoir
German
Nouns: Geruch, Gestank, Aroma, Parfum, Parfüm, Parfümöl, Duft, Dampf, Dunst, Duftstoff, Riechwasser, Duftwasser, Riechorgan, Geruchsorgan, Nase, Riechstoff, Aromastoff, Riechwasser, Duftwasser, Riecher, Qualm, Zigarettenqualm Anything ending on -geruch / -gestank / -duft **Verbs**: aromatisieren, riechen, stinken, schnüffeln, schnuppern, beschnuppern, parfümieren, ausdünsten, duften, qualmen, einatmen, inhalieren, ausdünsten, exhalieren, verfliegen, verdampfen, evaporieren, sich verflüchtigen **Adjectives**: parfümiert, olfaktorisch, wohlriechend, stinkend, duftend, riechend, muffig, modrig, aromatisch, blumig, geruchlos, penetrant, durchdringend, schimmlig, schimmelig Anything ending on -duft / - duftig / -riechend **Kinds of smell**: Aasgestank, Abgasgeruch, alkoholisch, angebrannt, angenehm, anregend, Apfelduft, beißend, Babygeruch, blumig, brennend, durchdringend, dominant, ekelerregend, ekelhaft, erdig, erfrischend, erregend, fade, faul, frisch, fruchtig, harzduftend, harzig, herb, herbstlich, holzig, intensiv, kamillig, käsig, klinisch, ländlich, Lavendelduft, Lebkuchenduft, ledrig, Leichengeruch, Leichengestank, metallisch, mild, minzig, mosig, Moschusgeruch, muffig, muffelig, nussig, Pfefferminzgeruch, pilzig, Puderduft, ranzig, rauchig, Regengeruch, salbeiartig, salzig, Sandelholzduft, säuerlich, schal, schwefelig, schweißig, Schweißfußgeruch, sommerlich, schwer, seifig, staubig, stechend, steril, stickig, streng, süßlich, Tabakgeruch, unangenehm, Uringeruch, verbrannt, verfault, Viehgestank, Weihrauchduft, Wundgestank, würzig, zimtig, zitronig. Anything ending on - duft / -geruch
Slovenian
Nouns: vonj, smrad, duh, voh, vonjava, dišava, umetna dišava, parfum, aroma, dišavina, priduh, vzduh, aromatičnost, pookus, pikantnost, zatohlost, deodorant, dezodorant, zadah, zaudarjanje **Verbs**: smrdeti, zaudarjati, dišati, zadišati, zavonjati, zadehteti, zaduhteti, vohati, duhati, vonjati, ovohati **Adjectives**: gnil, smrdljiv, smrdeč, umazan, usmrajen, prijeten, dišeč, aromatičen, dišaven, zaudarjajoč, postan, zatohel, opojen, brez vonja, vohalen, žaltav, strupen, toksičen, ogaben, oster, pikanten, vohalen, odišavljen **Other**: plesniv, pokvarjen, zadušljiv, zadušen, čuten, zavdajati, buket

Table 1: Initial list of possible lexical units for each language of interest. We list under *Other* the terms that were initially not included because they are ambiguous, but that were annotated as lexical units during benchmark creation.

documents. These domains are: *Household & Recipes*, *Law and Regulations*, *Literature*, *Medicine & Botany*, *Perfumes & Fashion*, *Public health*, *Religion*, *Science & Philosophy*, *Theatre*, *Travel & Ethnography*. The additional category *Other* was included in the list for documents which are relevant to the olfactory dimension but do not fall within any of the previously mentioned categories. Ideally, the benchmark should contain 10 documents for each category, distributed evenly over the time period between 1620 and 1920, for a total of 100 documents. However, no strict length requirements were defined for each document, because their availability and characteristics change drastically across languages. In some cases, a document may be few pages with dense olfactory in-

Frame Element	Example Sentence
Smell Source	The person, object or place that has a specific smell. *The odour [of tar] and [pitch] was so strong.*
Odour Carrier	The carrier of an odour, either an object (e.g. handkerchief) or atmospheric elements (wind, air) *The unpleasant smell [of the vapour] of linseed oil extended for a considerable distance.*
Quality	A quality associated with a smell and used to describe it. *Earth has a [strong], [aromatic] odour.*
Perceiver	The being that perceives an odour, who has a perceptual experience, not necessarily on purpose. *The scent is described by [Dr. Muller] as delicious.*
Evoked Odorant	The object, place or similar that is evoked by the odour, even if it is not in the scene. *In offensive perspiration of the feet [a peculiar cabbage-like] stench is given off.*
Location	The location where the smell event takes place. *And, particularly, [at the foot of the garden], where he felt so very offensive a smell that has sickened him.*
Time	An expression describing when the smelling event occurred. *Galeopsis smells fetid [at first handling], [afterwards] aromatic.*
Circumstances	The state of the world under which the smell event takes place. *[When stale] the lobster has a rank stench.*
Effect	An effect or reaction caused by the smell. *An ill smell [gives a nauseousness].*
Creator	The person that creates a (usually pleasant) smell. *The origin of perfume is commonly attributed [to the ancient Egyptians].*

Table 2: Overview of the Frame Elements (FEs) related to Olfactory situations and events with corresponding examples. Lexical units are underlined and the FE of interest is in square brackets. The same definitions hold for all languages included in the benchmark. For more details on FEs descriptions see (Tonelli and Menini, 2021).

formation, while in some other cases a book could contain smell references scattered throughout the volume. Therefore, each of the six annotation teams was free to apply the most appropriate criteria for the selection of documents to annotate. For example, Dutch annotators decided to focus on short text snippets of around 20 sentences. For Italian and English, longer passages up to a few hundred sentences are included. Other differences across languages concern the quality and variety of available documents in digital format. While for some languages, such as Dutch and English, large online repositories exist and it was possible to find documents belonging to each of the 10 domains and covering the time span of interest, the limited availability of digital repositories of Slovenian texts does not allow the collection of the full set of documents. This is the main reason why there are some qualitative and quantitative differences among languages.

Annotations were performed using INCEpTION (Klie et al., 2018), a web-based platform which allows three levels of authorisations (administrator, curator, annotator) and is therefore particularly suitable to support large annotation efforts like ours. A screenshot of the interface is shown in Figure 1.

5 Quality control

We implement two quality control measures: 1) a web-based consistency checker, and 2) double annotation of a set of documents for each language to compute inter-annotator agreement and discuss difficult cases.

5.1 Quality Consistency Check

Given the complexity of the annotation process, which is carried out by multiple annotators for each of the six languages, it is important to ensure that the different annotations are consistent with the instructions provided in the guidelines.

To facilitate a consistency check, we developed a web-based tool to automatically find when annotations are not compliant with the guidelines. The tool takes an exported WebAnno file from INCEpTION as input and outputs a report describing

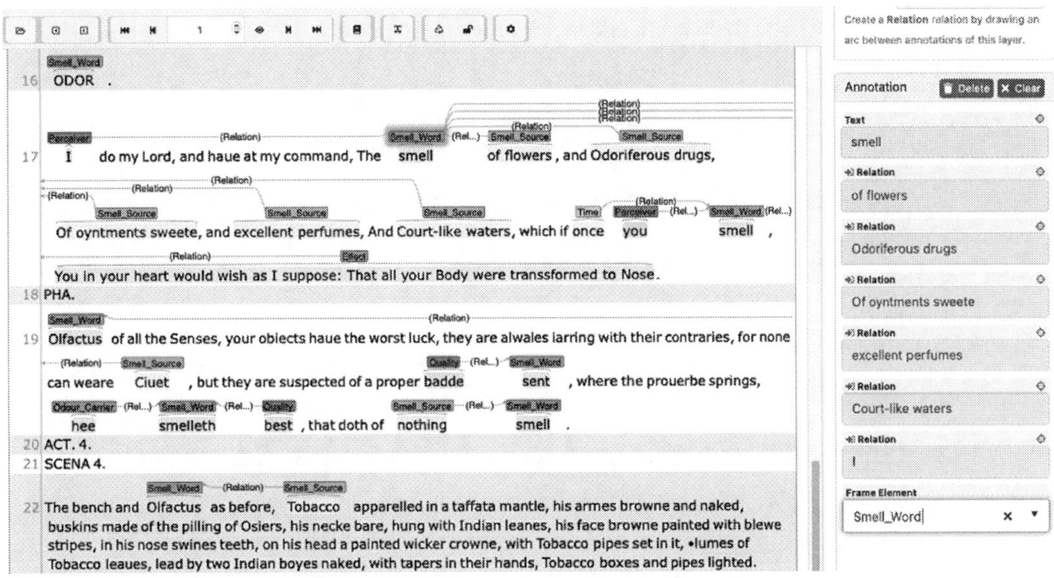

Figure 1: Screenshot of the INCEpTION annotation tool

which inconsistencies are found and where (with document ID, sentence number and string). This makes it straightforward to find the mistake and fix it quickly.

The inconsistencies identified in the files are related to both incorrect and missing annotations, focusing on the annotation procedure and not the content of the annotations. For instance, it checks if every frame element is properly connected to a smell word and if all selected spans have been assigned to a corresponding label. Operating at the level of labels and relations, that are the same for every language, and not considering the text content, the tool is language-independent.

After analysing the annotation output, the quality checker returns details about five error types:

- Spans that have been selected but not labeled;
- Smell words with double annotation, which have not been linked to themselves;[2]
- Frame elements that despite being annotated are not linked to any other element in text;
- A *Smell_Word* is the starting point of a relation instead of the ending point;
- Frame elements connected to something other than a *Smell_Word*.

Given the complexity of the annotation, for all languages involved the quality check step has been very useful to identify formal mistakes, allowing the removal of dozens of inconsistencies.

5.2 Inter-Annotator Agreement

Having at least two annotators for each language is necessary to obtain a double annotation of a subset of the benchmark and compute inter-annotator agreement, which is commonly considered a measure of annotation quality (Artstein and Poesio, 2008).

INCEpTION contains an integrated set of tools to compute inter-annotator agreement.[3] Among the proposed metrics, the most suitable for our task is Krippendorff's alpha (Krippendorff, 2011), as it supports more than two annotators (that is the case for some of the languages). This measure considers also partial overlaps, e.g. one annotator labelled only a noun while the other included also its article.

Inter-annotator agreement between two raters was computed, usually over a set of around 200 annotations (both FEs and smell words). In general, this was carried out after an extensive ini-

[2]There are instances where the same token can be at the same time a *Smell_Word* and another frame element related to the *Smell_Word* itself. For instance, 'odoriferous' may be both a *Smell_Word* and a *Quality*. In these cases, a relation should be set between the FE label and the smell word. This error notifies the absence of this relation.

[3]More details about this function are documented at `https://inception-project.github.io/releases/20.2/docs/user-guide.html#sect_monitoring_agreement`

	Dutch	English	French	German	Italian	Slovenian
Smell words	1,788	1,530	845	2,659	1,254	1,973
Total FEs	4,962	4,023	1,876	5,885	2,664	4,445
Source	1,922	1,313	710	2,297	952	1,638
Quality	1,071	1,084	450	1,730	707	936
Perceiver	336	362	140	399	153	266
Circumstances	399	248	88	274	202	228
Odour carrier	351	310	106	170	195	408
Effect	243	187	53	425	104	214
Evoked Odorant	228	91	103	258	74	285
Place	255	302	172	200	158	394
Time	127	126	49	131	119	75
Creator	30	0	5	1	0	1

Table 3: Overview of benchmark content for each language.

tial training of annotators. Agreement is 0.68 for English, 0.56 for Slovenian, 0.62 for French and 0.74 for Italian. For the other languages the process is still ongoing. In general, the major sources of disagreement are the extent of FE spans, a rather long distance between a FE and a smell word and possible different interpretations of some roles, in particular Location vs. Circumstances and Smell source vs. Odour carrier. While annotation guidelines were updated to make these distinctions clearer, some cases of disagreement are still very much dependent on annotators' preferences and interpretation.

6 Benchmark statistics

In this section, we detail the content of our benchmark in each language. Table 3 shows the number of occurrences of smell words and frame elements. Overall, for each language a good number of smell-related events and situations were annotated.

The average number of frame elements (FEs) associated with each smell event is between 2.1 and 2.7 for all languages, showing an interesting common feature. Furthermore, the most frequent FE is the *Smell Source*, followed by the *Quality* for all languages. This shows a pattern in the way smell situations and events are typically described, where the source and the quality are clearly core elements that are necessary to characterise the scene.

The FE element with the least annotations is instead 'Creator'. This is due to the fact that this role was added at a later stage in the annotation process, mainly to cover documents related to perfumery. It is therefore present only in the benchmarks that contain this kind of documents. For further discussion see Section 8.

In Figure 2, we report the number of documents per domain in each language-specific benchmark (see list of domains in Section 4). Overall, we observe a prevalence of literary texts (LIT), probably because this is the most represented domain in large repositories such as Wikisource and Project Gutenberg. Travel literature and medical texts are also well-represented in all languages. Despite the effort to have a balanced benchmark covering the same domains in all languages, however, results are mixed. For some languages, well-represented in large digital repositories, this balance was possible to some extent, with English being the only one covering all domains. For other languages, the benchmarks are affected by the limited variety of resources available in digital format, see for example Slovenian. Availability is a major obstacle when trying to create historical corpora that cover different domains.

In Figure 3, we report the temporal distribution of the documents present in the benchmark for each language. All languages overlap in the time period of interest, with the Dutch benchmark including some earlier texts but no data after 1880, and the Italian dataset going beyond 1930. Similar to the above remarks, also in this case we observe that, due to different data availability, not all time periods are covered equally.

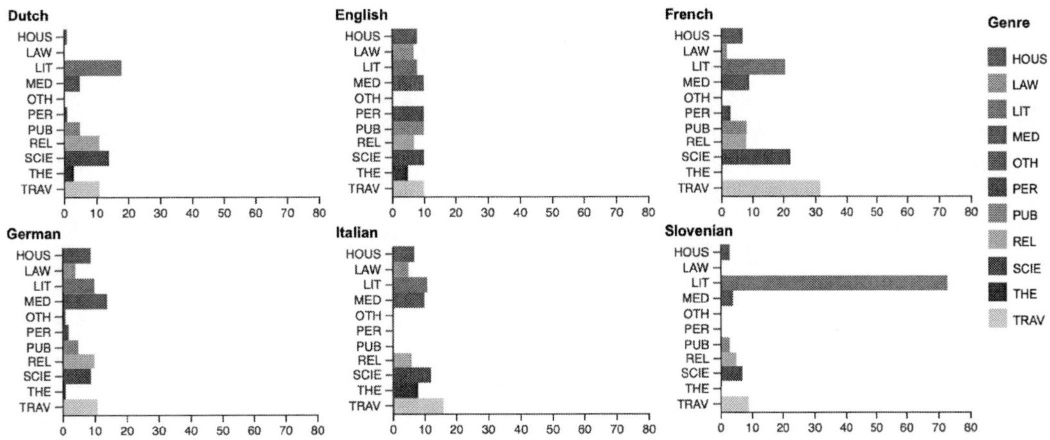

Figure 2: Number of documents per domain in each language-specific benchmark. HOUS = Household & Recipes, LAW = Law, LIT = Literature, MED = Medicine & Botany, OTH = Other, PER = Perfumes & Fashion, PUB = Public health, REL = Religion, SCIE = Science & Philosophy, THE = Theatre, TRAV = Travel & Ethnography.

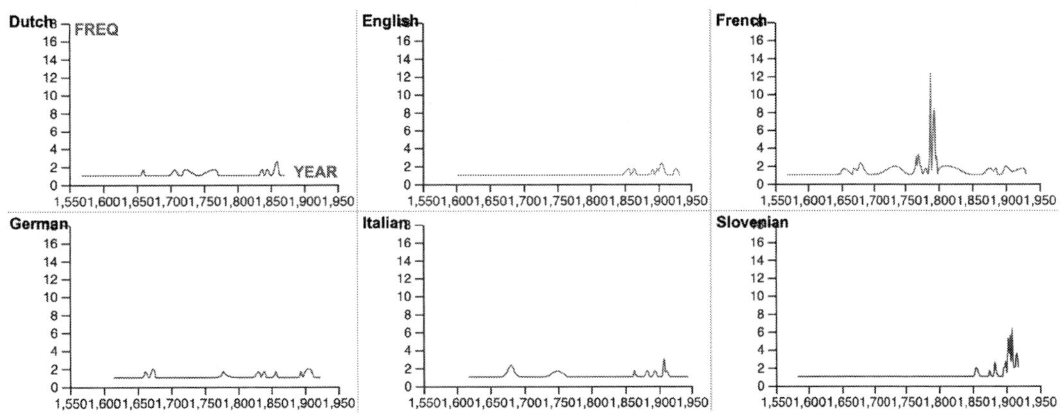

Figure 3: Temporal distribution of documents in each language-specific benchmark

7 Towards smell related information extraction

One of the goals of this benchmark is to enable temporal-aware information extraction tasks related to the olfactory domain. As a first step in this direction, we explore sentence classification using the English benchmark. Since our corpus consists of historical documents, we evaluate performance of a transformer model that is pre-trained using historical corpora, in light of Lai et al. (2021)'s proposal.

We focus on the task of classifying sentences as smell-related or not. Since the corpus is annotated at token level, we first label the sentences that contain any smell event annotation as smell-related, which are 897 out of the total 3,141 sentences. We randomly choose 650 (190 smell-related, 460 not smell-related) sentences as a held-out to measure the performance of fine-tuning on the remaining 2,491 sentences.

We compare the performance obtained using BERT base uncased with sequence length 128[4] (Devlin et al., 2019), RoBERTa base case-sensitive with sequence length 512[5] (Liu et al., 2019), and MacBERTh (Manjavacas and Fonteyn, 2021)[6] to identify sentences that are smell-related in English. MacBERTh is a BERT variant that is uncased with sequence length 128 and pre-trained from scratch using historical corpora. Each model was fine-tuned five times using five different ran-

[4]`https://huggingface.co/bert-base-uncased`, accessed on February 27, 2022

[5]`https://huggingface.co/roberta-base`, accessed on February 27, 2022

[6]`https://www.github.com/emanjavacas/macberth-eval`, accessed on February 27, 2022.

dom seeds (42, 43, 44, 45, 46) for all random aspects of the fine-tuning, batch size of 64, sequence length of 64, learning rate (2e-5), epochs (30), and random splitting for obtaining a development set from the training set (.15). Table 4 demonstrates the median performance of each fine-tuned model in terms of Matthews Correlation Coefficient (MCC), Precision, Recall, and F1-macro on the held-out dataset. We observe that macBERTh, which was pretrained using historical data, outperforms the base transformer models BERT and RoBERTa. This confirms the need to build models that are temporal-aware when dealing with historical corpora. Furthermore, the performance achieved by all models is above 0.90, showing that it is possible to yield good results in the task even if using relatively few training data.

Model	MCC	Precision	Recall	F1-macro
BERT	81.44	92.82	90.17	90.43
MacBERTh	85.66	94.08	91.91	92.72
RoBERTa	84.51	93.43	91.43	92.11

Table 4: Median scores in terms of Mathews Correlation coefficient (MCC) and macro precision, recall, and F1 over five runs

We analyzed the predictions of the best RoBERTa and MacBERTh models on 300 test sentences divided into two groups: the first one includes test sentences from documents published between 1619 and 1846, while the second covers the time period between 1847 and 1925. The F1-macro obtained with the MacBERTh model is 95.40 and 90.46 for the earlier (1619-1846) and later periods (1847-1925) respectively. The RoBERTa model achieves 92.46 and 91.42 F1-macro in the same setting. Although the MacBERTh model yields significantly better results for data published in the earlier period, the RoBERTa model yields a balanced performance across periods.

8 Discussion

During the creation of the benchmark, we have encountered two major issues related to working with historical data. The first, already mentioned in Section 6, is the limited availability of documents for some languages, domains and time spans. This has affected the possibility to create balanced benchmarks for all six languages, although a remarkable effort was put in manually looking for digital collections and selecting relevant documents.

Another major issue was the need to clean or correct some of the texts before the annotation, mostly due to the limits of OCR applied to old documents. Problematic transcriptions can be connected in part to stains or other imperfections in the paper, and in part to the evolution of language, with older documents presenting letters that have fallen into disuse in contemporary language. For instance, in French, Italian and English we found lost characters (e.g. long s "ſ", often confused with "f" as in "perfumes", misspelled as "persumes" in English), characters used differently (v instead of u, like in "vne" for French, or "vlcers" for English), changes in word spelling ("pourquoy" instead of "pourquoi" in French), and abandoned words.

Another interesting element is that annotation guidelines were adapted several times during the benchmark creation process, because it was not possible to foresee all potential issues we encountered during annotation. Indeed, domain specificity of some texts and the different use of language in historical documents made it difficult to straightforwardly follow annotation instructions. For example, frame element definitions have been adjusted and the 'Creator' element was added. Furthermore, the initial list of lexical units (Table 1) was extended in the process, enabling annotators to add new terms encountered during manual labelling.

9 Conclusion and Future Work

In this paper, we presented a multilingual benchmark annotated with smell-related information and covering six languages, which we make available to the research community. We have described the document selection rationale, the annotation process and the main challenges related to the creation of a multilingual benchmark containing historical documents. Annotation of Latin is in progress, and it will be added to the benchmark as soon as it is complete.

The benchmark is only a first step towards the analysis and extraction of olfactory information from historical documents. The work introduced in Section 7 will be extended to all six languages, using historical BERTs when available. Furthermore, we will go beyond simple sentence classification, training multilingual classifiers to identify lexical units and frame elements. Since the size of the benchmark is rather limited, we will try to expand it in the future but also explore semi-supervised, few-shot and cross-lingual approaches to olfactory information extraction.

Acknowledgements

This research has been supported by the European Union's Horizon 2020 program project ODEUROPA[7] under grant agreement number 101004469.

References

Ron Artstein and Massimo Poesio. 2008. Survey article: Inter-coder agreement for computational linguistics. *Computational Linguistics*, 34(4):555–596.

Ryan Brate, Paul Groth, and Marieke van Erp. 2020. Towards olfactory information extraction from text: A case study on detecting smell experiences in novels. In *Proceedings of the The 4th Joint SIGHUM Workshop on Computational Linguistics for Cultural Heritage, Social Sciences, Humanities and Literature*, pages 147–155, Online. International Committee on Computational Linguistics.

Jacob Devlin, Ming-Wei Chang, Kenton Lee, and Kristina Toutanova. 2019. BERT: Pre-training of deep bidirectional transformers for language understanding. In *Proceedings of the 2019 Conference of the North American Chapter of the Association for Computational Linguistics: Human Language Technologies, Volume 1 (Long and Short Papers)*, pages 4171–4186, Minneapolis, Minnesota. Association for Computational Linguistics.

C. Fillmore. 1976. Frame semantics and the nature of language *. *Annals of the New York Academy of Sciences*, 280.

Roxana Girju and Charlotte Lambert. 2021. Intersense: An investigation of sensory blending in fiction. *CoRR*, abs/2110.09710.

Łukasz Jędrzejowski and Przemysław Staniewski. 2021. *The Linguistics of Olfaction. Typological and Diachronic Approaches to Synchronic Diversity*. John Benjamins, Amsterdam.

Jan-Christoph Klie, Michael Bugert, Beto Boullosa, Richard Eckart de Castilho, and Iryna Gurevych. 2018. The inception platform: Machine-assisted and knowledge-oriented interactive annotation. In *Proceedings of the 27th International Conference on Computational Linguistics: System Demonstrations*, pages 5–9. Association for Computational Linguistics.

[7] `https://odeuropa.eu/`

Klaus Krippendorff. 2011. Computing krippendorff's alpha-reliability. `https://repository.upenn.edu/asc_papers/43/`.

Viet Lai, Minh Van Nguyen, Heidi Kaufman, and Thien Huu Nguyen. 2021. Event Extraction from Historical Texts: A New Dataset for Black Rebellions. In *Findings of the Association for Computational Linguistics: ACL-IJCNLP 2021*, pages 2390–2400, Online. Association for Computational Linguistics.

Els Lefever, Iris Hendrickx, Ilja Croijmans, Antal van den Bosch, and Asifa Majid. 2018. Discovering the language of wine reviews: A text mining account. In *Proceedings of the Eleventh International Conference on Language Resources and Evaluation (LREC 2018)*, Miyazaki, Japan. European Language Resources Association (ELRA).

Francesca Strik Lievers and Chu-Ren Huang. 2016. A lexicon of perception for the identification of synaesthetic metaphors in corpora. In *Proceedings of the Tenth International Conference on Language Resources and Evaluation (LREC'16)*, pages 2270–2277, Portorož, Slovenia. European Language Resources Association (ELRA).

Yinhan Liu, Myle Ott, Naman Goyal, Jingfei Du, Mandar Joshi, Danqi Chen, Omer Levy, Mike Lewis, Luke Zettlemoyer, and Veselin Stoyanov. 2019. Roberta: A robustly optimized bert pretraining approach. *ArXiv*, abs/1907.11692.

Asifa Majid and Niclas Burenhult. 2014. Odors are expressible in language, as long as you speak the right language. *Cognition*, 130(2):266–270.

Asifa Majid, Niclas Burenhult, Marcus Stensmyr, Josje De Valk, and Bill S Hansson. 2018. Olfactory language and abstraction across cultures. *Philosophical Transactions of the Royal Society B: Biological Sciences*, 373(1752):20170139.

Enrique Manjavacas and Lauren Fonteyn. 2021. Macberth: Development and evaluation of a historically pre-trained language model for english (1450-1950). In *Proceedings of the Workshop on Natural Language Processing for Digital Humanities (NLP4DH)*.

Stephen McGregor and Barbara McGillivray. 2018. A distributional semantic methodology for enhanced search in historical records: A case study on smell. In *Proceedings of the 14th Conference on Natural Language Processing, KONVENS 2018, Vienna, Austria, September 19-21, 2018*, pages 1–11. Österreichische Akademie der Wissenschaften.

Josef Ruppenhofer, Michael Ellsworth, Myriam Schwarzer-Petruck, Christopher R. Johnson, and Jan Scheffczyk. 2006. Framenet ii: Extended theory and practice. Working paper, International Computer Science Institute, Berkeley, CA.

Francesca Strik Lievers. 2021. Smelling over time. the lexicon of olfaction from latin to italian. In (Jędrzejowski and Staniewski, 2021), pages 369–397.

Serra Sinem Tekiroğlu, Gözde Özbal, and Carlo Strapparava. 2014a. A computational approach to generate a sensorial lexicon. In *Proceedings of the 4th Workshop on Cognitive Aspects of the Lexicon (CogALex)*, pages 114–125, Dublin, Ireland. Association for Computational Linguistics and Dublin City University.

Serra Sinem Tekiroğlu, Gözde Özbal, and Carlo Strapparava. 2014b. Sensicon: An automatically constructed sensorial lexicon. In *Proceedings of the 2014 Conference on Empirical Methods in Natural Language Processing (EMNLP)*, pages 1511–1521, Doha, Qatar. Association for Computational Linguistics.

Sara Tonelli and Stefano Menini. 2021. FrameNet-like annotation of olfactory information in texts. In *Proceedings of the 5th Joint SIGHUM Workshop on Computational Linguistics for Cultural Heritage, Social Sciences, Humanities and Literature*, pages 11–20, Punta Cana, Dominican Republic (online). Association for Computational Linguistics.

William Tullett. 2019. *Smell in Eighteenth-Century England: A Social Sense*. Oxford University Press.

Bodo Winter. 2019. *Sensory linguistics: Language, perception and metaphor*, volume 20. John Benjamins Publishing Company.

Language Acquisition, Neutral Change, and Diachronic Trends in Noun Classifiers

Aniket Kali
University of Toronto
Department of Computer Science
Toronto, ON, Canada
aniket.kali@mail.utoronto.ca

Jordan Kodner
Stony Brook University
Department of Linguistics &
Institute for Advanced Computational Science
Stony Brook, NY, USA
jordan.kodner@stonybrook.edu

Abstract

Languages around the world employ classifier systems as a method of semantic organization and categorization. These systems are rife with variability, violability, and ambiguity, and are prone to constant change over time. We explicitly model change in classifier systems as the population-level outcome of child language acquisition over time in order to shed light on the factors that drive change to classifier systems. Our research consists of two parts: a contrastive corpus study of Cantonese and Mandarin child-directed speech to determine the role that ambiguity and homophony avoidance may play in classifier learning and change followed by a series of population-level learning simulations of an abstract classifier system. We find that acquisition without reference to ambiguity avoidance is sufficient to drive broad trends in classifier change and suggest an additional role for adults and discourse factors in classifier death.

1 Introduction

Classifier and measure word systems are common across the world's languages. While they are the most common and most associated with Southeast and East Asia, they are also present in some languages of South Asia, Australia, the Pacific, and the Americas among others (Aikhenvald, 2000). Systems vary language-to-language, but share some general properties. They divide up the space of nouns along some semantic space, often encoding lexical semantic information including animacy, concreteness, and size and shape categories. For example, Mandarin has classifiers for long objects (e.g., *tiáo* 條), some animals (*zhī* 隻), and vehicles (*liàng* 輛). On the other hand, some classifiers like the Mandarin general classifier *gè* 個 do not seem to pick out anything in particular, or they instead pick out extremely narrow, almost lexicalized classes, such as *zūn* 尊, which as a classifier applies only to certain colossal metal objects such as cannons and Buddhist statues (Gao and Malt, 2009).

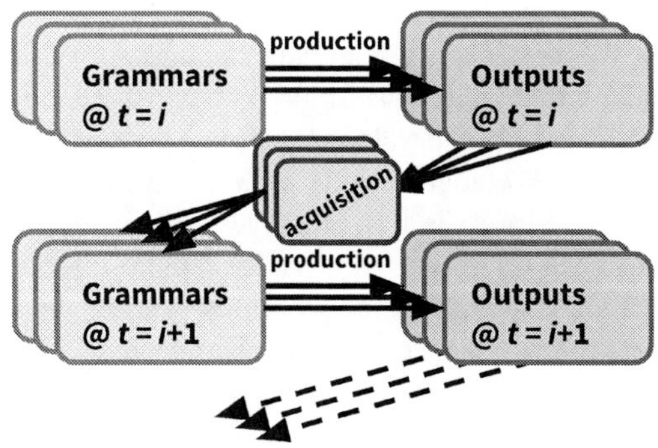

Figure 1: The Z-model of change extended to a population setting

Compared to most inflectional noun class systems, classifiers are more subject to variable discourse conditions. Several classifiers may be used grammatically with a given noun as conditions allow. For example, 'a goat' may be expressed with the animal classifier *zhī* or general classifier *gè*, but also *tiáo* or *tóu* 頭 used for livestock (Erbaugh, 1986). The balance of semantic specificity, arbitrariness, and variability presents a challenge for native learners. How do individuals acquire both the semantic conditions and arbitrary lexical patterns of classifier systems?

Parallel to this, classifier systems are subject to constant change, both for language-internal reasons (e.g., grammaticalization of new classifiers, word death of old classifiers) and external ones, particularly contact (Aikhenvald, 2000). Erbaugh (1986) illustrates a few cases of changes in classifier usage in Mandarin and its ancestors over the past 3500 years. *Gè* 個, the overwhelming majority catch-all classifier in the modern language only gained this status during the Qing Dynasty (CE 1644-1912). For the millennium prior since the Tang dynasty, *méi* 枚 had been the default, but it has since been relegated to a niche classifier for small needle and

Proceedings of the 3rd Workshop on Computational Approaches to Historical Language Change, pages 11 - 22
May 26-27, 2022 ©2022 Association for Computational Linguistics

badge-like objects. Both *gè* and *méi* began as niche classifiers in their respective eras before gradually generalizing. In a similar vein, Habibi et al. (2020) explore how linguistic categories change through chaining, via the usage of Mandarin Chinese classifiers in the past half century. The latter two studies discuss the development of Mandarin classifiers over time. They are based on careful research, but they are also limited to a single language. Erbaugh (1986) in particular stops short of a quantitative assessment.

We provide a computational analysis of diachronic trends in classifier systems which complements prior developmental and historical research. We approach the problem in two ways. First, we present a quantitative analysis of classifiers in Cantonese and Mandarin child-directed speech to investigate the possibility of a functional role for classifiers as disambiguators which could influence the direction of child-driven change. Second, we model a simulated classifier system using a population-level transmission model to determine how language acquisition may drive trends in classifier patterns over time. We find support for input sparsity and learning, without reference to specific functional concerns, as a primary driver for gradual classifier generalization over time.

1.1 Outline

The paper is organized as follows. Section 2 surveys cross-linguistic patterns in classifier acquisition and summarizes work connecting language acquisition to change. Section 3 is a comparative study of adult classifier use in Cantonese and Mandarin child-directed speech corpora. This motivates our simulation. We show that the historical development of classifiers is unlikely to be driven by functional communicative concerns such as ambiguity avoidance on behalf of the learner. Section 4 describes our simulation, which falls under the umbrella of *neutral* or *drift*-based models of change. We find that classifiers tend to generalize, fail to maintain distinct semantic features, and also cannot go out of use randomly. Section 5 discusses the implications of our simulation in reference to Chinese in particular and provides suggestions for future extensions to this line of work.

2 Classifier Learning and Change

Language acquisition has long been implicated as a driver of language change (Paul, 1880; Halle, 1962; Andersen, 1973; Baron, 1977; Lightfoot, 1979; Niyogi and Berwick, 1997; Yang, 2002; Kroch, 2005; van Gelderen, 2011; Yang, 2016; Cournane, 2017; Kodner, 2020, *i.a.*), and this has particularly been true for morphology, where child overproductivity errors (Marcus et al., 1992; Mayol, 2007) quite often mirror the processes of analogical change, which is itself closely connected to productivity (Hock, 2003, p.446).

Classifier systems are not structurally morphological and do not trigger syntactic agreement like inflectional noun class systems, but they share some key properties in both their use and acquisition. Both often encode lexical semantic information including animacy, concreteness, and size and shape categories. For example, the Bantu language Shona has noun classes for mostly long-skinny things (e.g., class 11 *ru-*), classes for animals (e.g., class 9 *(i)-*), and miscellaneous classes (e.g., class 7 *chi-*) which correspond broadly to the Mandarin classifiers described in Section 1. Both noun classes and classifiers may be semantically porous with many lexical exceptions. And while classifiers are generally more variable than inflectional classes, the later may also show variability. In Shona again, people usually take the class 1 *mu-* prefix (*mu-nhu* 'person'), but if a speaker wishes to highlight that a person is particularly tall and thin, they may employ the long-skinny class 11 prefix (*ru*-nhu).

Learners of classifier languages exhibit generally competent classifier use by age 4 or 5, though they show some command over their syntax much earlier (Chien et al., 2003; Tse et al., 2007; Liu, 2008). Children are prone to overusing the general or default classifier in Japanese (Uchida and Imai, 1999), Mandarin (Liu, 2008), Cantonese (Tse et al., 2007), and Vietnamese (Tran, 2011), similar to the over-extension of default patterns in morphology (Pinker and Prince, 1994). They take longer to acquire rare classifiers and those with complex semantic restrictions (Yamamoto and Keil, 2000).

A division of classifiers into semantically well-defined and arbitrary features is well-motivated by a series of experiments carried out by Gao and Malt (2009) on Mandarin. This further clarifies what the learning task entails. Children must work out whether classifiers are lexically defined or apply generally to a given semantic class and is consistent with observed developmental trajectories: young learners pass through an early lexicalized stage in which classifiers are defined narrowly by which lexical items they match with rather than their general semantics. This is by a higher than adult-rate use of generic classifiers, before they settle on an adult-like distribution (Erbaugh, 1986). This is parallel to the classic inflectional learning trajectory, a pre-generalization period, followed by over-generalization of defaults, followed by settling on an adult-like distribution.

Erbaugh (1986) explicitly connects classifier acquisition to change in Chinese and notes several parallels between Chinese classifier acquisition and change. Most relevant for the present study, classifiers are narrowly, perhaps lexically, defined when they enter the language and then trend towards generality. Furthermore, they apply to concrete objects with real-world identifiable semantics before abstract concepts, in line with children's preference for real world referents in their dialogues.

Taken together, classifier systems have enough in common with inflectional class systems that their acquisition and change can be modeled similarly. Linguistic transmission, the passing of a language from one generation to the next through native language acquisition (Weinreich et al., 1968), provides a fundamental role for acquisition in change. Andersen (1973) formalizes change as the long-term consequence of abductive processes in language acquisition through his Z-model: Speakers have some internal grammar which generates a set of linguistic examples which serve as the input to the next generation. The next generation acquires a grammar based on these finite inputs and produces outputs for the next generation. This process proceeds indefinitely. Abduction is error-prone, and differences between the grammars of the first and second generation are tantamount to change.

But language change is fundamentally a population-level process (Weinreich et al., 1968; Labov, 2001), so the Z-model must be thought of as countless parallel lines of transmission and not a single Z-shape. Additionally, transmission does not proceed through discrete generations, but rather is continuous across age cohorts in the population, so the Z-model should be staggered both across the population and across time. This view, diagrammed in Figure 1, forms the conceptual basis of our simulation.

A population-based transmission model in which what is acquired is driven primarily by the input and not additional functional factors may be described as *neutral*. This is often assumed as the baseline in biological evolution (Neutral Theory; Kimura, 1983), and may be relevant for language change as well (Kauhanen, 2017). The following section tests an alternative, that classifiers emerge to decrease homophony, before adopting a neutral approach.

3 Classifiers and Homophony

This section quantifies classifier use in Mandarin and Cantonese child-directed speech (CDS). Their systems are quite similar, both having descended from Middle Chinese. Since their divergence, the languages have undergone substantial phonological divergence resulting in much less syllable diversity in Mandarin compared to Cantonese.[1] For this reason, Mandarin is expected to show more homophony than Cantonese, though this is offset by an increase in polysyllabic words in Mandarin.

Disambiguation of homophones is one possible function of classifiers and a potential functional (i.e., non-neutral) driver of change. More elaborate classifier systems may develop in response to more rampant homophony. We compare Mandarin and Cantonese CDS to determine whether homophony avoidance is plausibly part of the child's role in the development of the Chinese classifier systems. If true, we would expect Mandarin CDS to show more noun form ambiguity than Cantonese *and* show more classifier disambiguation of homophonous word types. For comparison, we also investigated the rate of polysyllabic noun forms in Mandarin and Cantonese. The increase in polysyllabicity in Chinese varieties is traditionally taken to be a response to increased homophony due to phonemic mergers (Karlgren, 1949).

All POS-tagged Mandarin and Cantonese corpora were extracted from the R conversion (Sanchez et al., 2019) of the CHILDES database of child-directed speech corpora (MacWhinney, 2000) except for Erbaugh, which could not be retrieved. The first two data rows of Table 1 summarize the corpora, and (1)-(2) provide example utterances together with translations that we sourced from speakers of those languages. We extracted classifiers tagged `cl` from adult speech in the corpora if they preceded a noun, or preceded an adjective or adverb which preceded a noun, along with the noun itself. Sometimes transcription lines did not align with the characters, which we attempted to resolve by tracking known classifier characters and

[1]E.g., Mandarin's 4 (5) tones, and ~34 syllable rimes compared to Cantonese's 9 and 60.

Corpus	#Types (%Poly)	%Types HP	%Disamb	#Toks (%Poly)	%Toks HP	%Disamb	#Cl
Cantonese	1182 (55.6)	4.653	20.000	19880 (21.4)	7.706	6.201	76
Mandarin	2151 (71.8)	7.345	22.785	30891 (41.8)	28.558	6.506	149
Mandarin$_{type}$	1182.2 (63.0)	8.815	20.430	28066 (39.0)	28.264	6.776	140.0
Mandarin$_{tok}$	221.9 (43.0)	4.778	16.981	19880 (31.9)	23.431	3.078	98.5

Table 1: Adult Cantonese, Mandarin, avg. type freq-controlled Mandarin$_{type}$, and avg. token freq-controlled Mandarin$_{tok}$ corpus size, %nouns polysyllabic, % nouns which are homophonous (HP), the % of homophonous nouns which are disambiguated by their classifiers, and # classifiers.

examining the neighbourhood of the incongruency in the sentence. A handful of cases could not be resolved, so they were omitted. We omitted classifier pro-forms since no noun surfaces in the utterance. We define homophones as two word forms with different characters but the same transcription.

(1) **Cantonese** (HKU-70; Fletcher et al., 1996)
INV: 你 得 一 個 啤啤 zaa4 .

```
%mor:  pro|nei5=you stprt|dak1
num|jat1=one cl|go3=cl
n|bi4&DIM=baby sfp|zaa4 .
```

"You only have one baby?!"

(2) **Mandarin** (Zhou1; Zhou, 2001)
MOT: 开 这 个 盒子 .

```
%mor:  v:resc|kai1=open
det|zhe4=this cl|ge4 n|he2zi=box .
```

"Open this box."

Since corpus size could have a substantial effect on the ratios reported in the corpora, we opted to downsample the Mandarin corpus to match the size of Cantonese and compare both the downsampled and raw Mandarin. We dropped out Mandarin tokens selected uniformly at random until the corpus matched the Cantonese corpus in type or token count. This was repeated for 100 trials and the counts for each trial were averaged. The resulting Mandarin$_{type}$ matched for type count and Mandarin$_{tok}$ matched for token count are the last two rows in Table 1. When matched for types, the Mandarin corpus has substantially more polysyllabic words than Cantonese, and when matched for tokens, it has substantially more polysemous tokens. It also has a wider range of classifiers and measure words.

The table also shows the rates of homophonous word types in the corpora as well as the proportion of those which are *disambiguated.* We defined a homophonous word type as disambiguated if every homophone is attested with at least one classifier not attested with any other homophone in a set, and a disambiguated word token as any token which belongs to a disambiguated word type. Despite the increase in polysyllabicity, Mandarin is still much more ambiguous than Cantonese. Nevertheless, its homophones are not significantly more disambiguated.[2]

This analysis is consistent with (but does not prove) the idea that polysyllabicity emerged in Chinese in a response to ambiguity. In contrast, it does not support a role for homophony avoidance in adults as a motivation for the classifier system. Even though the Mandarin acquisition corpora attest more classifiers and measure words, only about 1/5 of homophonous types and 1/18 of homophonous tokens are disambiguated by classifiers. The fact that tokens are much less likely than types to be disambiguated, and that the type disambiguation rate declines as the number of types fall in Table 1, also indicates the type disambiguation rate is generous and inflated by low frequency and edge cases. Additionally, Mandarin does not exhibit more classifier disambiguation even though it is more homophonous than Cantonese. Given this, we can justify our major modeling assumption, that changes to the classifier system need not be primarily driven by communicative concerns. We consider potential alternative sources of functional pressure in Section 5.

4 A Classifier System in a Population

The empirical analysis in the previous section motivates a neutral model of change for the Chinese classifier system. In this section, we introduce a population-level model of linguistic transmission to investigate the dynamics of classifier systems over time. We describe the details of our simulation, including the algorithm and parameters, their relevance, and their specific empirical motivations. We then discuss our findings across different parameter settings, and consider their implications

[2]One-sided Z-test on Cantonese vs. Mandarin$_{type}$ types is insignificant: $Z = 1.570$ at $\alpha = 0.05$, while test on Cantonese vs. Mandarin$_{type}$ tokens shows that Cantonese has significantly *fewer* disambiguated homophones $Z = -2886.511$.

in the study of classifiers, learning, and language change.

4.1 Methodology

At a high level, our simulation consists of a population of entities sorted by age into "children" who are still acquiring a classifier system and "adults" with productive representations of classifiers. At the start of each iteration, the oldest adult "dies," a new child is "born," and every entity's age is incremented, with the eldest child maturing into an adult, as we describe later. During the iteration, adults interact with a subset of children, and children learn from these interactions. Crucially, transmission flows from the pool of adults as a whole. Ages are continuous, and children can learn from the youngest adults as well as the oldest. This admits the diffusion of innovations, thus actuating the change (Labov et al., 1972) and potentially yields significant variable input for the learners. Algorithm 1 formalizes the population model.[3]

Algorithm 1 Simulation iteration algorithm

```
CH ← List of children of size K
AD ← List of adults of size N − K
for s := 1...S do
    Delete AD[−1] as oldest adult "dies"
    Move CH[−1] to AD[0] as oldest child "matures" using productivity method PROD
    A new child is "born" at CH[0]
    for all adult ∈ AD do
        mutate_classifier_set(adult, A, D)
        for i := 1...I do
            child ← random child ∈ CH
            nouns ← J random lexical items
            interact(adult, child, nouns)
        end for
    end for
end for
```

Classifiers in the simulation are represented as abstract binary semantic features (abstract, but conceptually equivalent to ±ANIMATE, ±FLAT, etc.). These are encoded as binary vectors of size F. Lexical items are organized along a Zipfian distribution, since it is observed to fit token frequencies well across languages (Zipf, 1949; Baayen, 2001; Yang, 2013). At initialization, each adult has the same set of C classifiers. This set includes at least one "most general" classifier, while other classifiers are initialized randomly. Children are initialized so that at the first iteration it is as if the eldest child has gone through K iterations (and therefore rounds of interactions) already.

[3]Parameterized according to Table 2 in the Appendix.

Nearly all simulations run using a feature hierarchy: features are organized hierarchically with one most generic parent feature and up to B sub-features such that there are F total features. The presence of a sub-feature implies the presence of its parent features. Depending on the simulation, up to H features are assigned in this manner. A flat representation would make for ambiguous results in this already abstract simulation, since it would be unclear whether more features correspond to a more general or more specific classifier.

Children learn as follows: in each iteration, children observe many classifier-noun pairs. They add the features on the noun to a running tally of observed features for the classifier, but crucially, they do not yet know which features actually select the classifier, since nouns may contain properties that are just incidental and unrelated to the particular choice of classifier. After some K iterations, a child matures. The child evaluates whether a classifier productively expresses a feature by comparing its observations against a threshold for productivity provided by the Tolerance Principle (TP; Yang, 2016), a quantitative model of productivity learning which has been successful in accounting for developmental patterns in morphology and elsewhere.

For a given feature f observed with a noun paired with the classifier c, if the number of attested paired noun types that *do not* express that feature (the exceptions, e^c_f) is less that the tolerance threshold θ^c_f for that classifier, then that feature will be productive on the classifier. The tolerance threshold is calculated as in Eqn. 1. N^c is the total number of noun types attested with the classifier.[4]

$$\begin{aligned} e^c_f &< \theta^c_f, \text{ where} \\ \theta^c_f &= \frac{N^c}{\ln N^c} \end{aligned} \tag{1}$$

We provide a role for adults as drivers of change by introducing two additional parameters. An adult may drop a classifier with probability D by setting it to be non-productive on all features, and provided there is an opening (i.e., some classifier is non-productive on all features) add a new classifier with probability A. This is taken to represent choices available to adults in response to discourse and sociolinguistic factors. We believe that such factors affecting adults may be responsible for the death of

[4]See (Yang, 2018) for a summary of the TP's psychological motivation and mathematical derivation.

high frequency general classifiers, since no child in a neutral model of change would fail to learn something so well and so diversely attested.

There is always a worry that a highly parameterized simulation will do something akin to overfitting to the pattern that the researcher is trying to recreate. To guard against this, we test a wide range of parameter settings to confirm that the system's dynamics are inherent to the model and not driven by a convenient parameterization. To the extent possible, default parameters were motivated empirically (e.g., Zipfian token frequency distribution) or according to practical concerns (e.g., if the number of classifiers far exceeds the number of semantic features $C \gg F$, most classifiers will be synonymous and redundant). A full list of parameters available to the model are presented in Table 2 in the Appendix.

We ran five sets of simulations testing distinct hypotheses. The first set included 58 simulations, and did a broad sweep of the parameter space, testing parameter values on either side of their defaults as well as different non-numeric parameters. The second set included 37 simulations, and varied the probability that adults add or drop classifiers, since these values are internal to the simulation. The third set included 20 simulations, running 4 parameter settings in repetition 5 times to weed out uniquely random outcomes. The fourth set included 15 simulations, varying a few parameters but running and repeating settings for 5,000 iterations to observe what happens in the very long term. Finally, the fifth set included 20 simulations ran on default parameters, which we took the average of to affirm general trends. In total, we ran and examined 150 simulations.[5]

4.2 Results

We found that many parameterizations admitted complex dynamics, and successive runs with the same settings sometimes yielded different outcomes. All the same, there were particular trends which emerged. We observe three findings repeated across a range of settings which we believe characterize neutral transmission of classifiers more broadly. Figure 2 is an average of 20 simulations ran on default parameters. We chose these settings as the simplest ones that still admit interesting dynamics into the system. Figures 3-9 are select but

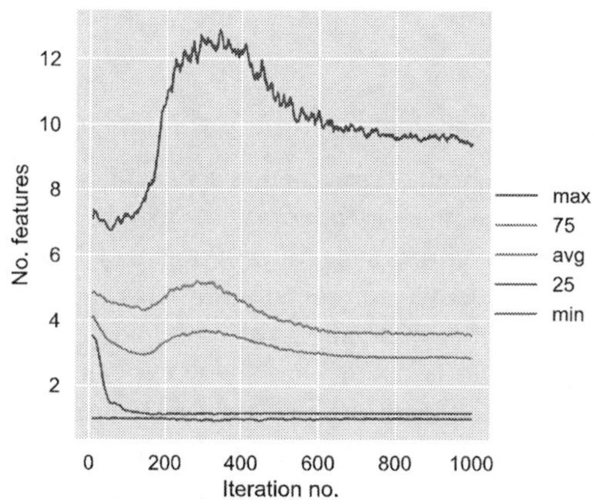

Figure 2: Average of 20 simulations run on default parameters

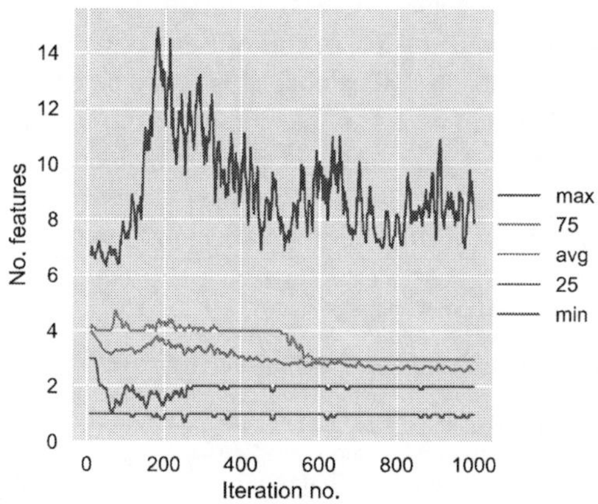

Figure 3: Typical outcome for a simulation run on default parameters

representative simulations which demonstrate particular trends.[6] They show how the maximum, minimum, and average number of features, as well as the 25th and 75th percentiles, averaged over the 10 youngest adults, change over time.

Figure 3 shows the behaviour of a typical run with default parameters. The average number of features per classifier trends downwards after a period of instability but does not do so monotonically. In contrast, Figure 4 shows a less common case where the mean number of features trending back up again. While this happens in the occasional simulation, it is an outlier. Figure 2 shows the average across 20 simulations ran on default parameters, and affirms both non-monotonicity and the general downward trend. We also introduce a further ele-

[5] All code, including the specifications of our sets of simulations, is publicly available at `https://github.com/an-k45/classifier-change`

[6] Parameterizations for each given simulation are specified in Table 4 in the Appendix.

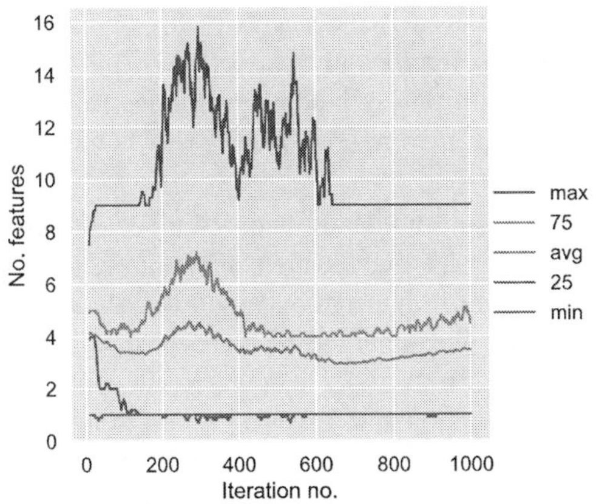

Figure 4: Atypical outcome on default parameters: mean no. features trends up

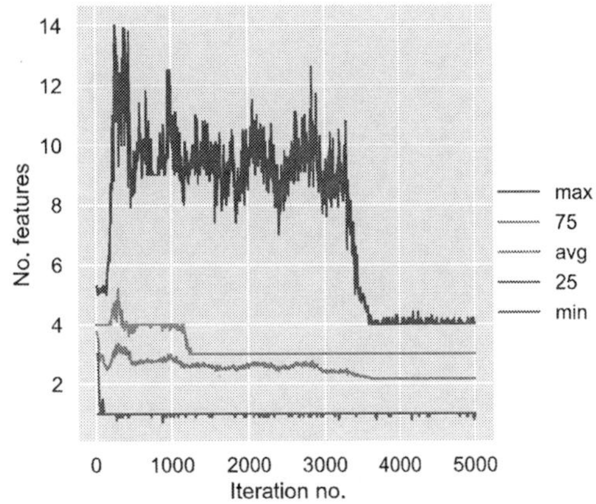

Figure 6: Simulation run for 5,000 iterations, default parameters.

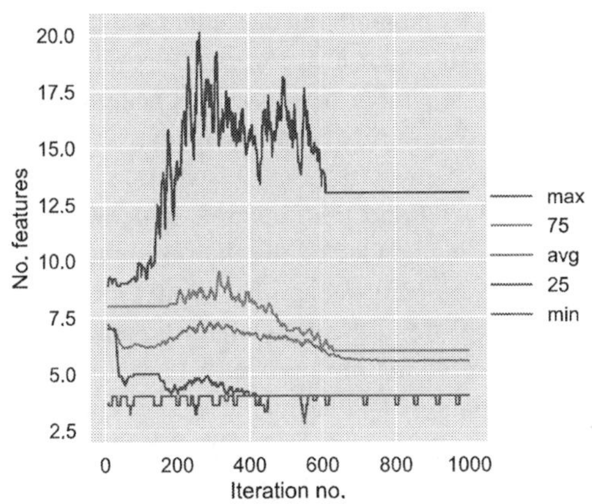

Figure 5: A simulation with variable branching in the feature hierarchy showing typical behaviour

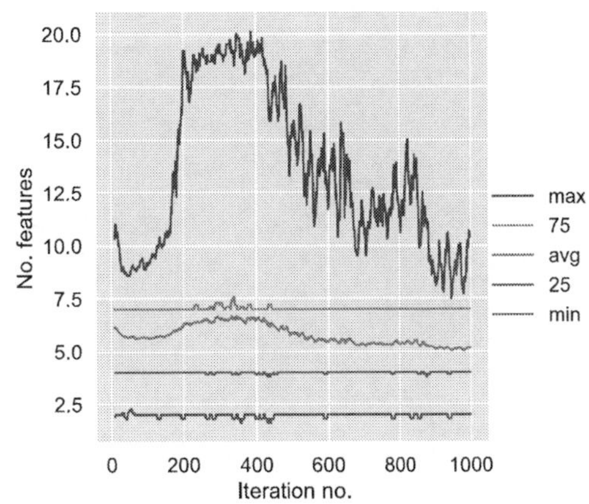

Figure 7: Simulation with variable feature initialization and 10x new classifier adding

ment of randomness in Figure 5 by allowing the branching factor of the feature hierarchy to vary, but to the same effect. This outcome is consistent with the diachronic trend observed by Erbaugh (1986) in which general classifiers emerge from more specific classifiers over time.

Our simulations often settle on a steady state after many iterations (Fig. 6). This could indicate insufficient churn in the set of available classifiers. To test this, we increased the rate of adults adding classifiers by a factor of 10, as a proxy for increased adult innovation in the classifier system. This did not have a significant effect on the average number of features over time (Fig. 7), and failed to consistently stave off the slow gradual generalization seen in earlier simulations. Robustness to this parameter choice further confirms that it is learning, and not adult innovation, to combat ambiguity, for example, that is driving the trends we observe here.

Finally, if new classifiers were initialized with a random, potentially large, number of features (Fig. 8), or if adults drop random classifiers instead of the most general ones (Fig. 9), the system rapidly and consistently devolves into one with a few more general classifiers. This outcome is inconsistent with what should happen in a classifier system, either in ordinary simulations or the diachronic data. However, it follows from the particular parameterization. A new classifier that is very semantically restricted is unlikely to be sufficiently attested for children to learn all of its features. Similarly, if classifiers are dropped randomly, highly specific classifiers will be dropped with some probability. Children will have less evidence to learn them, and they will not be acquired in their full specificity, indicating a maximum viable level of semantic specificity in

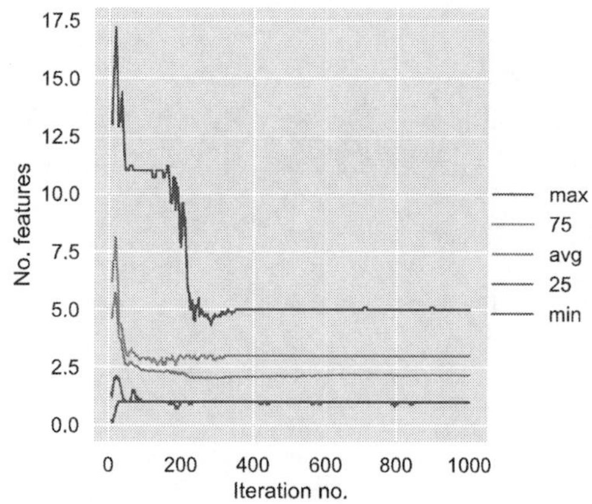

Figure 8: A simulation with multiple feature initialization showing rapid contraction

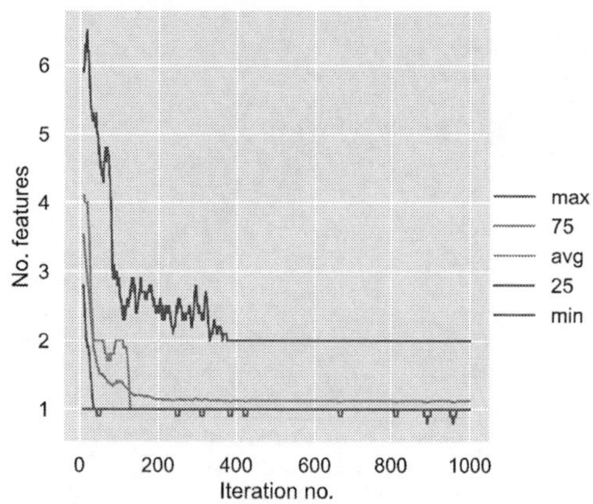

Figure 9: A simulation with random classifier dropping showing rapid contraction

classifiers over time.

5 Discussion and Conclusion

In this paper, we advocate for a view of language change as a natural outcome of language acquisition over time and across a population. This acquisition-driven view of change provides insight into the long-term dynamics of classifier systems through a cross-linguistic corpus study of modern Chinese child-directed speech and a population-level simulation of classifier change.

The cross-linguistic study (Section 3) contrasts Mandarin and Cantonese, two closely related but not mutually intelligible languages with a recent common ancestor, to test the hypothesis that classifier use is driven by homophony avoidance. We found that though Mandarin child-directed speech has substantially more homophonous types than Cantonese, its classifiers actually disambiguate homophones significantly less often. This is contrasted with polysyllabicity in Mandarin, which does show a trend consistent with homophony avoidance.

This result motivates a neutral model of classifier change driven by matters of learning and input sparsity not primarily concerned with functional pressures. We apply the Tolerance Principle (TP), a model of productivity learning, to our population-level simulation and observe general trends. The TP was chosen because it successfully models U-shaped learning trajectories in morphology where learners develop through memorization to over-generalizing phases. This is similar to the developmental pattern observed in classifier learning. Children begin by memorizing classifiers and the nouns they apply to, then move to over-use of general classifiers. A similar trend towards generalization is observed empirically in the history of Chinese classifiers. New classifiers are specific when they are introduced and tend towards generality over time. This is not a lockstep relationship along the lines of "ontogeny recapitulates phylogeny," but two parallel trends which emerge independently from the same learning process. Our population-level simulation of TP learners (Section 4) achieves this pattern under a wide range of parameter settings, providing support for the role of learning and neutral processes in this change.

5.1 Future Work

This paper opens up several avenues for future inquiry. One question that deserves more attention is the role that ambiguity and homophony avoidance play in shaping the classifier system. We show that adults (particularly in CDS) do not seem to employ classifiers as disambiguators to a greater degree in Mandarin than in Cantonese despite Mandarin showing a higher rate of ambiguity. The same question could be asked for children. Do young Mandarin-learning children use classifiers to disambiguate their speech more often than Cantonese learners? Unfortunately there is not enough child-produced speech in the Cantonese corpus to carry out a reasonable comparison.

Another question that has yet to be resolved is what could have caused the replacement of the Tang-Qing general classifier *méi* with the Qing-modern *gè*. We believe that the solution likely lies in discourse factors. Adults may choose more specific classifiers over the most general one in order to emphasize qualities of the noun being modified. This would explain why *méi* was not completely replaced when it lost its generic status and was instead reduced to a narrow semantic scope. Change here may be modeled as a sociolinguistic variable (Labov, 1994). However, such socially conditioned change is lead by young adults rather than young learners. A fully developed mechanism for changes in the classifier system would require modeling both acquisition-driven and sociolinguistic change simultaneously.

As an initial test of this hypothesis, we compared simulations in which adults drop the most generic classifier with some low probability (representing a sociolinguistic choice to prefer an innovative classifier) against simulations in which adults drop classifiers at random. We find that the former allows for the expected slow generalization of classifiers while the latter causes the system to rapidly collapse (Fig. 9). We interpret this as supportive of the discourse driven account, but sophisticated extensions would be needed to demonstrate it. Similarly, the population model could be extended to better capture sociolinguistic network topology (Milroy and Milroy, 1985; Kodner and Cerezo Falco, 2018).

Parallel to this, a complete account would incorporate more concrete semantic representations and algorithms to represent word coining into our simulations (Habibi et al., 2020; Xu and Xu, 2021). Our simulation does not meaningfully account for the creation of new classifiers, which tend to emerge through grammaticalization of nouns (Aikhenvald, 2000), nor does it provide a structured means for representing classifier semantics beyond the abstract hierarchies which we employed. Semantic chaining (Ramiro et al., 2018; Xu and Xu, 2021) is a promising candidate approach. Our population-level acquisition-driven approach provides a base upon which to develop fully featured diachronic models of classifier systems.

5.2 Conclusion

Erbaugh (2006) remarked that within noun categorization broadly, classifier systems exist somewhere in-between unmarked common nouns and grammatical systems like gender. They therefore balance semantic specificity with variance that tends toward arbitrary. We believe, and have sought to show in this paper, this follows from a view of language change that is primarily driven by children acquiring their native languages with additional changes led by adults. This dual perspective provides a place for both grammar learning and sociolinguistic discourse factors as mechanisms for change. Classifier systems are a natural juncture for these two types of change since they are both deeply embedded in the grammar and show heavy optionality, variability, and discourse sensitivity. Existing "somewhere in-between" then plausibly stems from the diffusion of innovation in learning and discourse, clarifying that child-driven change to classifier systems is neutral with respect to function.

Acknowledgements

We thank the anonymous reviewers for their critical and valuable feedback which improved this work.

References

Alexandra Y Aikhenvald. 2000. *Classifiers: A typology of noun categorization devices*. OUP Oxford.

Henning Andersen. 1973. Abductive and deductive change. *Language*, pages 765–793.

R Harald Baayen. 2001. *Word frequency distributions*, volume 18. Springer Science & Business Media.

Naomi S Baron. 1977. *Language acquisition and historical change*. North-Holland Publishing Company, Amsterdam.

Yu-Chin Chien, Barbara Lust, and Chi-Pang Chiang. 2003. Chinese children's comprehension of count-classifiers and mass-classifiers. *Journal of East Asian Linguistics*, 12(2):91–120.

Ailís Cournane. 2017. In defense of the child innovator. In Eric Mathieu and Robert Truswell, editors, *Micro Change and Macro Change in Diachronic Syntax*, pages 10–24. Oxford University Press, Oxford.

Mary S Erbaugh. 1986. Taking stock: The development of chinese noun classifiers historically and in young children. *Noun classes and categorization*, pages 399–436.

Mary S. Erbaugh. 2006. *Chinese classifiers: their use and acquisition*, volume 1, page 39–51. Cambridge University Press.

P Fletcher, T Lee, C Leung, and S Stokes. 1996. Milestones in the learning of spoken cantonese by preschool children. *Hong Kong: Language Fund.*

Ming Y. Gao and Barbara C. Malt. 2009. Mental representation and cognitive consequences of chinese individual classifiers. *Language and Cognitive Processes*, 24(7-8):1124–1179.

Amir Ahmad Habibi, Charles Kemp, and Yang Xu. 2020. Chaining and the growth of linguistic categories. *Cognition*, 202(104323).

Morris Halle. 1962. Phonology in generative grammar. *Word*, 18(1-3):54–72.

Hans Henrich Hock. 2003. Analogical change. *The handbook of historical linguistics*, pages 441–460.

Bernhard Karlgren. 1949. *The Chinese language: an essay on its nature and history*. Ronald Press Company.

Henri Kauhanen. 2017. Neutral change. *Journal of Linguistics*, 53(2):327–358.

Motoo Kimura. 1983. *The neutral theory of molecular evolution*. Cambridge University Press.

Jordan Kodner. 2020. *Language Acquisition in the Past*. Ph.D. thesis, University of Pennsylvania.

Jordan Kodner and Christopher Cerezo Falco. 2018. A framework for representing language acquisition in a population setting. In *Proc. 56th ACL*, pages 1149–1159.

Anthony Kroch. 2005. Modeling language change and language acquisition. In *Expansion of an LSA Institute forum lecture*.

William Labov. 1994. *Principles of linguistic change, volume 1: Internal factors*. John Wiley & Sons.

William Labov. 2001. *Principles of linguistic change, volume 2: Social factors*. John Wiley & Sons.

William Labov, Malcah Yaeger, and Richard Steiner. 1972. *A quantitative study of sound change in progress*, volume 1. US Regional Survey.

David W Lightfoot. 1979. *Principles of diachronic syntax*. Cambridge University Press, Cambridge.

Constantine Lignos and Charles Yang. 2018. Morphology and language acquisition. *Cambridge handbook of morphology*, pages 765–791.

Haiyong Liu. 2008. A case study of the acquisition of mandarin classifiers. *Language research*, 44(2):345–360.

Brian MacWhinney. 2000. *The CHILDES project: The database*, volume 2. Psychology Press, Abingdon-on-Thames.

Gary F Marcus, Steven Pinker, Michael Ullman, Michelle Hollander, T John Rosen, Fei Xu, and Harald Clahsen. 1992. Overregularization in language acquisition. *Monographs of the society for research in child development*.

Laia Mayol. 2007. Acquisition of irregular patterns in Spanish verbal morphology. In *Proceedings of the twelfth ESSLLI Student Session*, pages 1–11, Dublin.

James Milroy and Lesley Milroy. 1985. Linguistic change, social network and speaker innovation. *Journal of linguistics*, 21(2):339–384.

Partha Niyogi and Robert C Berwick. 1997. A dynamical systems model for language change. *Complex Systems*, 11(3):161–204.

Hermann Paul. 1880. *Prinzipien der sprachgeschichte*. T ubingen. Niemeyer.

Steven Pinker and Alan Prince. 1994. Regular and irregular morphology and the psychological status of rules of grammar. *The reality of linguistic rules*, 321:51.

Christian Ramiro, Mahesh Srinivasan, Barbara C Malt, and Yang Xu. 2018. Algorithms in the historical emergence of word senses. *Proceedings of the National Academy of Sciences*, 115(10):2323–2328.

Alessandro Sanchez, Stephan C Meylan, Mika Braginsky, Kyle E MacDonald, Daniel Yurovsky, and Michael C Frank. 2019. childes-db: A flexible and reproducible interface to the child language data exchange system. *Behavior research methods*, 51(4):1928–1941.

Jennie Tran. 2011. The acquisition of vietnamese classifiers. *Unpublished PhD Thesis at.*

Shek Kam Tse, Hui Li, and Shing On Leung. 2007. The acquisition of cantonese classifiers by preschool children in hong kong. *Journal of child language*, 34(3):495–517.

Nobuko Uchida and Mutsumi Imai. 1999. Heuristics in learning classifiers: The acquisition of the classifier system and its implications for the nature of lexical acquisition. *Japanese Psychological Research*, 41(1):50–69.

Elly van Gelderen. 2011. *The linguistic cycle: Language change and the language faculty*. Oxford University Press.

Uriel Weinreich, William Labov, and Marvin Herzog. 1968. Empirical foundations for a theory of language change. In *Directions for historical linguistics*, pages 95–195. University of Texas Press.

Aotao Xu and Yang Xu. 2021. Chaining and the formation of spatial semantic categories in childhood. *CogSci*, 43:700–706.

Kasumi Yamamoto and Frank Keil. 2000. The acquisition of japanese numeral classifiers: Linkage between grammatical forms and conceptual categories. *Journal of East Asian Linguistics*, 9(4):379–409.

Charles Yang. 2002. *Knowledge and learning in natural language*. Oxford University Press, Oxford.

Charles Yang. 2013. Who's afraid of George Kingsley Zipf? or: Do children and chimps have language? *Significance*, 10(6):29–34.

Charles Yang. 2016. *The Price of Linguistic Productivity*. MIT Press, Cambridge, MA.

Charles Yang. 2018. A user's guide to the tolerance principle. Unpublished manuscript.

Jing Zhou. 2001. Pragmatic development of mandarin-speaking young children from 14 months to 32 months. *Unpublished doctoral dissertation, The University of Hong Kong*.

George Kingsley Zipf. 1949. *Human behavior and the principle of least effort: An introduction to human ecology*.

A Appendix

Parameter	Value	Explanation
S	1000	No. simulation iterations
N	200	No. total individuals
K	40	No. children
V	1000	No. nouns in lexicon
C	25	No. classifiers in lexicon
F	50	No. features
G	4	Max no. noun features
H	3	Max no. classifier features at initialization
B	3	Max branching factor within a feature hierarchy
I	5	No. interactions by adults toward children
J	5	No. lexical items drawn per interaction
A	0.01	Prob. add classifier per iteration
D	0.01	Prob. drop classifier per iteration
PROD	TP	Method for productivity in acquisition
LEX_TYPE	Zipf	Distribution type of nouns in the lexicon
CLASS_INIT	hierarchy, single	Method for classifier initialization, including feature hierarchy
FEAT_INIT	fixed	Method for initializing a feature hierarchy, dependent on B
CLASS_DROP	general	Target for dropping classifiers

Table 2: A list of simulation parameters, their default values, and what they do. Non-numeric parameters are further described in Table 3.

Parameter	Value	Explanation
PROD	TP	Tolerance Principle (Yang, 2016)
	majority	Simple majority
LEX_TYPE	Zipf	Lexical items follow a Zipfian distribution (Zipf, 1949; Lignos and Yang, 2018)
	uniform	Lexical items follow a uniform distribution
CLASS_INIT	identity	Classifiers are initialized through an identity matrix
	random	Classifiers are initialized randomly with H features
	hierarchy, single	Classifiers are initialized with 1 feature using a feature hierarchy
	hierarchy, multiple	Classifiers are initialized with 1 to H features using a feature hierarchy
FEAT_INIT	fixed	Each feature in the hierarchy has B children
	variable	Each feature in the hierarchy has 1 to B children
CLASS_DROP	general	The classifier with the least number of features is dropped
	random	A random classifier is dropped

Table 3: A list of possible arguments for each of the non-numeric parameters in our simulation. Explanations for each of parameter's purpose are found in Table 2 and in Section 4.1.

Figure no.	Parameters
2	(used default)
3	(used default)
4	(used default)
5	FEAT_INIT = variable
6	$S = 5000$
7	$A = 0.1$, FEAT_INIT = variable
8	CLASS_INIT = hierarchy, multiple
9	CLASS_DROP = random

Table 4: The parameters that the simulation presented in each figure ran on, where they differ from the default arguments listed in Table 2.

Deconstructing destruction: A Cognitive Linguistics perspective on a computational analysis of diachronic change

Karlien Franco
KU Leuven & FWO Flanders
karlien.franco@kuleuven.be

Kris Heylen
KU Leuven & Dutch Language Institute (INT)
kris.heylen@ivdnt.org

Mariana Montes
KU Leuven
mariana.montes@kuleuven.be

Abstract

In this paper, we aim to introduce a Cognitive Linguistics perspective into a computational analysis of near-synonyms. We focus on a single set of Dutch near-synonyms, *vernielen* and *vernietigen*, roughly translated as 'to destroy', replicating the analysis from Geeraerts (1997) with distributional models. Our analysis, which tracks the meaning of both words in a corpus of 16th-20th century prose data, shows that both lexical items have undergone semantic change, led by differences in their prototypical semantic core.

1 Introduction

This paper aims to stimulate further convergence between Cognitive Linguistics approaches to language change and computational methods for semantic change. Cognitive Linguistics is a contemporary linguistic paradigm that assumes that linguistic knowledge is rooted in general cognitive capabilities, that language is shaped by usage and that meaning entails conceptualization (Dabrowska and Divjak, 2015). It pays particular attention to the interaction between semasiological change, whereby a word's meaning changes over time, and onomasiological change, whereby the semantic configuration of a set of (near-)synonyms is reorganized over time. In this paper we focus on a single set of Dutch near-synonyms, *vernielen* and *vernietigen*, roughly translated as 'to destroy'. We replicate the analysis of these verbs from Geeraerts (1997) with distributional models. The analysis, which tracks the meaning of both words in a corpus of 16th-20th century prose data, shows that both lexical items have undergone semantic change led by differences in their prototypical semantic core, as predicted by Geeraerts' work.

2 Semasiology and onomasiology in Cognitive Linguistics

Following from "The cognitive commitment", which entails that the description of human language should be congruent with what is known about cognition within and outside of linguistics (Lakoff, 1990), Cognitive Linguistics aims to be a psychologically plausible model. Language is, thus, primarily studied as a means to communicate – a way to convey and process meaning. Furthermore, a maximalist, non-reductionist perspective on linguistic knowledge is assumed. Language systems are considered to be "reflections of general conceptual organization, categorization principles, processing mechanisms, and experiential and environmental influences" (Geeraerts and Cuyckens, 2007, 3). The movement, therefore, places a large emphasis on meaning.

Geeraerts et al. (1994) examine the structure of lexical variation in the use of clothing terminology in Dutch. Crucially, it is the first study to systematically emphasize the importance of two distinctions. On the one hand, it shows that in order to obtain a full picture of the structure of lexical variation, semasiological research should be complemented with an onomasiological approach. The semasiological perspective examines the range of applications of a particular expression. Semasiology is, for this reason, often defined as research into the meaning of a particular item: given a particular word or expression, what are the referents to which the word applies? In the case of the Dutch word *monitor*, for instance, a semasiological analysis would reveal that it can refer both to a SUPERVISOR, and to a COMPUTER SCREEN (see Heylen et al., 2015). The onomasiological perspective investigates naming rather than meaning. An onomasiological approach, thus, starts from a particular

Proceedings of the 3rd Workshop on Computational Approaches to Historical Language Change, pages 23 - 32
May 26-27, 2022 ©2022 Association for Computational Linguistics

(type of) referent or concept and determines which names exist or can be used to refer to the referent. For instance, an onomasiological analysis of the concept COMPUTER SCREEN in Dutch would reveal that both *monitor* and *computerscherm* can be used to express this concept.

On the other hand, Geeraerts et al. (1994) was the first study to make the importance of the interaction between four different types of lexical variation for the structure of the lexicon explicit. First, it examines semasiological variation, the situation where a single lexical item can refer to more than one referent. For example, the lexical item *pants* can both be used to refer to a TWO-LEGGED TYPE OF OUTER GARMENT (IN GENERAL), but also to a more specific referent, viz. MEN'S UNDERWEAR. The second and third types of lexical variation that are distinguished concern two varieties of onomasiological variation: conceptual onomasiological variation and formal onomasiological variation. Conceptual onomasiological variation concerns the situation where "a referent or type of referent may be named by means of various conceptually distinct lexical categories" (Geeraerts et al., 1994, 3-4). For example, to refer to a pair of BLUE JEANS, a language user can either choose to select a lexical item belonging to the concept BLUE JEANS and use a word like *jeans* or *blue jeans*, or (s)he can conceptualize the referent as a type of PANTS, a superordinate concept, and call the denotatum *trousers* or *pants*. Formal onomasiological variation occurs when a choice has to be made between different synonymous expressions for a referent. In the blue jeans example, this would involve determining the relative frequency of the terms *jeans* versus *blue jeans* versus *trousers* versus *pants*. Finally, it shows how contextual variation can be at play both at the semasiological and onomasiological level. Contextual variation (also called speaker and situation related variation) is broadly defined: it includes both the relatively stable lectal properties of the interlocutors involved (like their gender or their nationality), but also transient situation-related features, like the register of the speech event (Geeraerts et al., 2010, 8). For the (onomasiological) blue jeans example, for instance, contextual variation may take the form of determining whether older people are more likely to refer to the concept as *blue jeans*.

The program laid out in Geeraerts et al. (1994) was applied to diachronic change in Geeraerts (1997). An important finding of this work is that semasiological and onomasiological variation and change are not independent of each other: semasiological changes also affect the onomasiological structure of a language.

3 Destructive verbs in Dutch

A classical analysis of the verbs meaning 'to destroy' in Dutch is presented in (Geeraerts, 1997, 1985, 1988). In these papers, Geeraerts analyzes *vernielen* and *vernietigen* in 19th century data taken from the citations corpus for largest historical dictionary of Dutch, the *Woordenboek der Nederlandsche taal* 'Dictionary of the Dutch Language'. Etymologically, the near-synonyms do not have the same root. *Vernielen* is a verb formed with a verbalizing prefix *ver-*, and *niel*, an obsolete Dutch adjective that roughly translates to 'down to the ground'. The literal meaning of the verb *vernielen* is then 'to throw down to the ground, to tear down'. *Vernietigen*, in contrast, is based on a verbalizing prefix *ver-*, with the adjective *nietig* (which itself comes from *niet* 'not, nothing' + a suffix *-ig*). The meaning of *vernietigen* is then 'to annihilate, to bring to naught'.

Despite these divergent sources, Geeraerts shows that the near-synonyms can be used in similar contexts by the same author in the 19th century. For instance, in examples 1 and 2 (adapted from Geeraerts, 1988, 30-31), *vernielen* and *vernietigen* occur in the context of a material artefact (a part of a building) being destroyed. He discusses many more examples that clearly show that the verbs are interchangeable in 19th century Dutch.

1. Dat huis ... werd ... tot den grond toe **vernield** (Veegens, Hist. Stud. 2, 282, 1869). [This house was demolished down to the ground.]

2. De vrijheidsmannen [hebben] ... het wapen des stichters in den voorgevel met ruwe hand **vernietigd** (Veegens, Hist. Stud. 1, 125, 1864). [The freedom fighters demolished the founder's arms in the facade with their rough hands.]

Overall, three semantic groups of uses for *vernielen* and *vernietigen* can be distinguished in his data (Table 1): concrete uses, abstract uses and personal uses. In the group of personal uses there is also a special case where an army is destroyed. This use can be considered to hold a middle position

With regard to concrete things
To demolish parts of buildings
To destroy other human artefacts
To destroy natural objects
With regard to concrete things
To annihilate existing situations, characteristics etc.
To prevent the execution of plans, intentions, etc.
With regard to persons
To kill someone
To undermine someone's physical health
To undermine someone's psychological well-being
To defeat groups of armed men or armies

Table 1: Uses of *vernielen* and *vernietigen*. Adapted from Geeraerts (1997, 191-192)

between the abstract (collective army) and personal (an individual soldier) contexts.

While the verbs are found in similar contexts, a crucial point of Geeraerts' work is that the prototypical cores of the verbs differ. More specifically, *vernielen* prototypically occurs with concrete uses, such as destroying parts of buildings. *Vernietigen* prototypically occurs in abstract contexts such as the complete annihilation of existing situations or plans. Geeraerts also notes that, while both verbs can occur with instances of partial or complete destruction, *vernielen* is prototypically used in the partial destruction sense (e.g. when a building is destroyed by a fire, parts of the structure and ashes from the fire remain), whereas *vernietigen* often implies complete annihilation to naught (e.g. when a plan is destroyed, nothing remains). In addition, the difference between the concrete and abstract uses is also visible in the context of the 'destruction' of people: while *vernielen* occurs more with the more concrete sense of to kill someone, *vernietigen* is more often found in the more abstract contexts where someone's physical or mental health is affected.

In Montes et al. (2021), the near-synonyms were analyzed in synchronic contemporary newspaper data with distributional models. The analysis showed that, since the 19th century, the prototypical cores of *vernielen* and *vernietigen* have become even stronger and the verbs are no longer easily interchangeable in every context. A highly prototypical context for *vernielen* in the 21st century data is the destruction of (parts of) buildings by fire and *vernietigen* no longer occurs in this context. In contrast, for *vernietigen*, the cancellation of decisions or ideas by a governmental body makes up a large portion of the tokens in the corpus and *vernielen* is no longer possible there. Both variants seem to have retreated to their prototypical core. In the periphery of the semantics of the verbs, some new uses have come into existence (e.g. to destroy livestock, probably as a result of the industrialization of the food industry and the regulations installed by government to keep the industry safe for consumption).

The aim of this paper is to track the diachronic change in the nearly synonymous pair *vernielen* and *vernietigen* throughout time in Dutch using distributional models. Based on the results in Geeraerts (1997, 1985, 1988) for 19th century dictionary attestations, and Montes et al. (2021) for 21st century corpus data, we expect to find in our study of continuous diachronic corpus data from the 16th to 20th century, that the overlap or interchangeability between the verbs reduces over time and that the verbs will retreat to their prototypical cores more and more over time. This finding would confirm that semasiological and onomasiological change interact and that these types of changes can be retrieved automatically from diachronic corpus data. Methodologically, we investigate the usefulness of distributional models for diachronic changes in a pair of near-synonyms.

4 Data and methods

In the analysis, we use a corpus of prose texts from DBNL, the *Digitale Bibliotheek voor de Nederlandse Letteren* 'digital library for Dutch languages and literature'. Some information about the corpus can be found in Depuydt and Brugman (2019), though the corpus is not publicly available at this time. We specifically extracted all corpus texts tagged as prose in the metadata from the 16th, 17th, 18th, 19th and 20th century. Due to data sparseness, we combine the subcorpora for the 16th and 17th century in the analysis.

As no high-quality lemmatizers or PoS-taggers are as of yet available for historical Dutch, the only preprocessing we applied to the corpus was to transform the entire corpus to lower case and to automatically indicate sentence boundaries using the pretrained nltk sentence tokenizer (Bird and Loper, 2004).

Next, we extracted all tokens for *vernielen* and *vernietigen* (including inflected forms and spelling variants) from the four subcorpora and took a random sample of N = 400 tokens for each subcorpus.

Then, we constructed a single vector space model for the tokens in each subcorpus. The models that we built are based on the procedure outlined in Schütze (1998). More specifically, we construct a vector representation for each token in the corpus, using the words in the context of the tokens to construct the vectors (first order vectors). We supplement this information by also constructing a vector for each of the relevant context words (second order vectors). An association strength measure is used rather than raw co-occurrence frequencies, namely positive pointwise mutual information or PPMI (Church and Hanks, 1989; Bullinaria and Levy, 2007; Kiela and Clark, 2014). This procedure has the advantage that both the context words for a token, as well as their semantic similarity with other context words, is taken into account (see De Pascale, 2019 and Montes, 2021). This method represents an example of a context-counting distributional model, which we opt for here (rather than for a context-predicting method) because we want to keep the results as comparable as possible to the results obtained in Montes et al. (2021) on contemporary data. One line of future research is to replicate the results obtained here with diachronic contextualized word embeddings when they become available for Dutch.

The parameters that we used are largely based on the best model found in Montes et al. (2021) for the analysis of *vernielen* and *vernietigen* in 21st century newspaper data. However, since the diachronic corpus that we use is not lemmatized or PoS-tagged, the vectors represent word forms rather than lemmas and we do not use part-of-speech filters. Additionally, we decided to decrease the window size from 15 to 10 words to the left and right of the target token for the first-order context words because preliminary analyses revealed that in models with a broader window, too many irrelevant or noisy context features were included in the analysis (also due to the fact that PoS filters cannot be applied). The parameters settings that we used are the following:

- Bag-of-words model with a window size of 10 words to the left and right of each token.

- First-order context words: all wordforms [w+] with a frequency of at least 10 in the subcorpus. First-order contextwords are subsequently filtered by their PPMI value with the target token: only words with PPMI > 2 are considered.

- Second order context words: 5000 most frequent wordforms [w+] in the subcorpus, excluding the first 100 wordforms, as these are usually function words rather than content words and therefore do not contribute a lot of semantic information.

The models were constructed with the nephosem Python library (QLVL, 2021). The result of this procedure is a token-by-context matrix with 5000 dimensions, where the dimensions represent second order context vectors, i.e. the vectors of the context words around each token. Since for some tokens no relevant context words are found with our parameter settings, these tokens are excluded from the remainder of the analysis. For clustering and visualization, we transformed this matrix into a square distance matrix by computing the cosine vector of each pair of token-level vectors, without further dimensionality reduction beforehand. Thus, this final matrix describes the dissimilarity between the vector of each token and all other token vectors in the subcorpus. As a next step, we submitted each model to a clustering procedure in R (R Core Team, 2020). We used hierarchical clustering (Ward method), distinguishing four clusters, following the procedure in Montes et al. (2021) for maximal comparability.

Finally, we analyzed each cluster per subcorpus basing ourselves on a procedure outlined in Montes (2021) that is available in the Python library semasioFlow (Montes, 2022). The procedure consists of a number of steps. First, the relevant context words, on which the token vectors are based, are extracted from the model data. Then, after each token is assigned to a cluster, we calculate how often a specific context word occurs within a particular cluster and outside of the cluster. Using this information, we can calculate which context words have an exceptionally high frequency in each cluster and therefore represent the semantics of each cluster well. In the analysis, we will only consider context words for which at least 50% of their occurrences are within the cluster of interest.

5 Results

Figure 1 (see Appendix A) shows the visualisations of the models, with one panel per subcorpus. Plot symbols show the variants (*vernielen* versus *vernietigen*) and colours indicate the clusters. The figure shows that over time, *vernielen* and *vernietigen* are distinguished more clearly by the models.

While in the 16th/17th century, there is still quite some overlap between the variants, indicating that they are still interchangeable, in the 18th century *vernielen* mostly occurs at the bottom left of the plot and *vernietigen* at the top right. In the 19th century, *vernielen* is found in the left side of the plot and *vernietigen* mostly in the bottom right. By the 20th century, the variant *vernielen* had decreased dramatically in frequency and *vernietigen* takes up most of the figure. Only one cluster remains where *vernielen* is dominant: cluster 4 at the bottom right.

Tables 2-5 show an overview of the most important context words per period and per cluster, obtained with the procedure outlined above. Only context words with a frequency of more than 2 are shown, to avoid that infrequent words get too much weight in the interpretation. The first column also shows an interpretation of each cluster. The final columns indicate the relative and absolute proportion of each variant in the cluster.

In the first subcorpus (16th-17th century, Table 2), there are three clusters where *vernielen* clearly is the major variant (clusters 2, 3 and 4). It occurs in contexts related to killing persons, a small cluster with natural objects (no context words with frequency > 2) and concrete objects like ships and cities. The first and largest cluster (N = 182 tokens) is still quite diverse and both *vernielen* and *vernietigen* are possible. Thus, in the 16th and 17th century, *vernielen* and *vernietigen* are still mostly interchangeable, although there are already a few contexts where *vernielen* is preferred.

In the 18th century subcorpus (Table 3), the variants start receding to their prototypical core more. There are two clusters where *vernielen* is more frequent and two clusters where *vernietigen* takes over. Following the hypotheses outlined above, *vernielen* mostly occurs with concrete objects like buildings (cluster 4, consisting of tokens related to fires destroying parts of buildings). In addition, it seems to occur in passive tokens (with *werden* 'became, was') where persons are destroyed: cluster 2 contains some war-related lexemes like *vijand* 'enemy', *troepen* 'troups', *leger* 'army' and some lexemes related to people, such as *hunne* 'their' and *elkaar* 'each other'. In contrast, *vernietigen* occurs in tokens with abstract objects (cluster 3) and it is also the most frequent variant in the first cluster, which does not show a clear semantic picture. In most clusters, except for 4, both variants are still possible. The context words in cluster 4 show that *vernielen* has by now become the most preferred variant for the destruction of (parts of) buildings (often by fire).

In the 19th century (Table 4), which coincides with the data analyzed in Geeraerts (1997, 1985, 1988), there are three clusters where one variant takes over, but also one cluster where the variants are interchangeable. More specifically, *vernielen* remains the most frequent variant in contexts of the destruction of (parts of) buildings (by fire, cluster 1). In contrast with the 18th century subcorpus, *vernietigen* has by now taken over contexts related to the destruction of persons, including armies (cluster 2). In this cluster *zichzelf* 'himself/herself/themselves' is the most frequent context word. This frequent use of the reflexive pronoun may indicate that the patient role for *vernietigen* in the 19th century is often the subject itself, or that it at least plays a major role. Finally, *vernietigen* also still occurs the most with abstract lexemes such as *vrijheid* 'freedom' (cluster 4). Cluster 3 only has one important context word, *waan* 'delusion', and both variants are possible in this cluster. The interpretation is not as clear as for the other clusters.

Finally, in the subcorpus for the 20th century (Table 5), *vernietigen* is much more frequent than *vernielen*. Only 108 tokens for *vernielen* occur in the complete 20th century subcorpus, but 446 are available for *vernietigen*. This may indicate that *vernielen* is on its way out, or that it is retreating to very specific contexts. The cluster analysis shows that there are still some clear contexts in which *vernietigen* is the preferred variant, but that in the 20th century data, not all clusters represent clear semantic differences. This may be partly related to the fact that *vernielen* has become very infrequent: most of the tokens that are modelled are for *vernietigen* and it is possible that the model distinguishes syntactic constructions rather than semantic contexts in which *vernietigen* can occur.

First, *vernietigen* is the most frequent variant in cluster 1, which is a diverse cluster, with the most frequent context word related to complete destruction (*geheel* 'completely'), but also consisting of other types of lexical items such as abstract concepts. In cluster 2, *vernietigen* is the most frequent variant as well. This is a semantic cluster with many war-related lexical items, although it also contains other concrete objects. The context words in cluster 3, where *vernietigen* is also the most frequent variant, are mostly function words, such as adverbs and reflexive pronouns. This cluster is not determined by semantic similarity between the tokens, but rather by the type of construction the tokens occur in. The context words in cluster 4, where both *vernielen* and *vernietigen* are possible, are mostly related to (parts of) buildings. This is a clear change compared to the earlier data, where the destruction of parts of building correlated strongly with the use of *vernielen*. However, the context words in this cluster have quite a low frequency so likely not all tokens are related to the destruction of (parts of) buildings: perhaps *vernielen* has become so infrequent that even this prototypical use is not frequent enough anymore to be distinguished by the model and clustering procedure.

6 Discussion

The models for the four subcorpora show how the relationship between the near-synonyms *vernielen* and *vernietigen* has changed over time. Semasiologically, *vernielen* was the major variant in the 16th and 17th century, occurring in tokens related to the death of persons and concrete, natural objects. Over the course of the 18th century, it developed its prototypical meaning related to the destruction of (parts of) buildings, often by fire, and this meaning remained its core usage in the 19th century. By the 20th century, the verb had decreased in frequency and its prototypical core was no longer distinguishable from the data. *Vernietigen*, in contrast, was the less frequent variant in the 16th and 17th century and at that time, there were no clear contexts yet where the verb occurred. It was mostly found in a semantically diverse cluster where its near-synonym *vernielen* was possible as well. From the 18th century onwards, the verb started to increase in frequency and it developed its prototypical sense of being used with abstract objects. In the 19th century, it also started to invade contexts where *vernielen* was preferred before (specifically related to the death of persons and to war). In the 20th century data, we also found a syntactic cluster, consisting of function words that often occur in the context of *vernietigen*.

Onomasiologically, the analysis showcased how the nuances in the concept 'to destroy' evolve over time and have become more outspoken. For instance, the clusters related to the destruction of parts of buildings are not yet visible in the oldest data but they are important clusters in the more recent datasets. Similarly, the cluster with abstract objects is not yet distinguished by the analysis for the 16th and 17th century, but these objects form a cluster on their own in the 18th and 19th century data. Moreover, the analysis also showed how these particular nuances of meaning are typically expressed by a particular verb. In the visualization, for instance, there is clearly less overlap (or interchangeability) between the verbs in the later periods (except in the 20th century data, where *vernielen* is infrequent).

Thus, this case-study showcases an example of how formal onomasiological variation and conceptual onomasiological variation can interact. On the one hand, *vernielen* and *vernietigen* serve as formal alternatives in the largest cluster from the 16th and 17th century data. However, from the 18th century onwards, each verb increasingly retreats to its prototypical core. Arguably, they should therefore be considered conceptually distinct, prototypically referring to different nuances of meaning, even though they remain nearly synonymous.

Methodologically, our usage of distributional models combined with a cluster analysis and the method, developed in Montes (2021), to analyze the context words that are good representatives for the clusters, allowed us to show how both verbs changed semantically over time. The procedure employed was quite straightforward, using a single set of parameter settings to model tokens from four diachronic subcorpora. With this procedure, we extended the analyses in Montes et al. (2021) and Geeraerts (1997) to a much longer time span. Despite the fact that we used a completely different dataset (a continuous diachronic corpus rather than dictionary citations from the 19th century only) and analysis method (an automatic procedure rather than a manual linguistic analysis), the hypotheses outlined in Geeraerts (1997) were mostly confirmed. Further, this method allowed us to track semasiological change and to investigate how this interacts with onomasiological variation over time.

One shortcoming of the approach is that the ideal settings for the parameters need not be the same for other near-synonyms or for a comparable linguistic alternation in other languages. In fact, this is one of the major findings of Montes (2021), who showed that there is no direct link between a choice of parameters and the linguistic phenomena that are revealed by a model constructed with the method proposed by Schütze (1998). Therefore, while in

Table 2: 16th & 17th century

Cluster	**Context words**	**Variants**
1 (diverse)	7: alles 'everything', geheel 'completely'; 4: natuur 'nature', geluk 'luck', duizend 'thousand', veranderingen 'changes', zonder 'without', werden 'became (pl.)', schulden 'debts', werd 'became (sg.)'; 3: gramschap 'wrath', beeld 'statue, picture', vorsten 'monarchs', oogenblik 'moment', kunt 'can', word 'become (sg.)', plantagiën 'plantations', nieuwe 'new', compagnie 'company', dezelve 'itself'	vernielen: 0.44 (80), vernietigen: 0.56 (102)
2 (TO KILL PERSONS)	10: dese 'this'; 5: doot 'death'; 4: desen 'this', t 'it'; 3: wet 'law', sulcke 'this', selve 'self', vyanden 'enemies', Christi '(of) Christ', dooden 'to kill', omme 'in order to', macht 'power', verlaten 'to leave', sonde 'sin'	**vernielen**: 0.84 (69), vernietigen: 0.16 (13)
3 (NATURAL OBJECTS)	/	**vernielen**: 0.90 (18), vernietigen: 0.10 (2)
4 (CONCRETE OBJECTS)	5: schepen 'ships'; 4: vernielen 'to destroy', steden 'cities', vloot 'fleet'; 3: zwaert 'sword', bergen 'mountains'	**vernielen**: 0.83 (45), vernietigen: 0.17 (9)

Table 3: 18th century

Cluster	**Context words**	**Variants**
1 (diverse)	5: daardoor 'because of'; 3: worde 'become (pl.)', gansch 'completely', hoop 'hope'	vernielen: 0.31 (12), **vernietigen**: 0.69 (27)
2 (TO KILL PERSONS + WAR)	12: werden 'become (pl.)'; 4: hunne 'their'; 3: elkaâr 'each other', vijand 'enemy', troepen 'troups', leger 'army', gebroken 'broken', slag 'battle', vloot 'fleet', oogst 'harvest'	**vernielen**: 0.61 (60), vernietigen: 0.39 (39)
3 (ABSTRACT OBJECTS)	5: invloed 'influence'; 4: zedelijk 'virtuous', kracht 'strength', macht 'power', revolutie 'revolution', bestaan 'existence, to exist', vrijheid 'freedom'	vernielen: 0.20 (14), **vernietigen**: 0.80 (56)
4 ((PARTS OF) BUILDINGS (FIRE))	6: brand 'fire'; 4: stad 'city'; 3: kerken 'churches', huizen 'houses', steden 'cities'	**vernielen**: 0.97 (35), vernietigen: 0.03 (1)

Table 4: 19th century

Cluster	Context words	Variants
1 ((parts of) buildings (fire))	5: huis 'house'; 4: brand 'fire'; 3: grond 'ground', boel 'things', vlammen 'flames'	**vernielen**: 0.84 (38), vernietigen: 0.16 (7)
2 (TO KILL PERSONS + WAR)	6: zichzelf 'hisself/herself/themselves', volkomen 'completely', steden 'cities'; 5: werden 'became (pl.)', leger 'army', vloot 'fleet', schepen 'ships'; 3: zorgvuldig 'carefully', gedeeltelijk 'partly', volledig 'completely', willen 'to want', brieven 'letters'	vernielen: 0.36 (35), **vernietigen**: 0.64 (63)
3 (ABSTRACT OBJECTS?)	3: waan 'delusion'	vernielen: 0.56 (15), vernietigen: 0.44 (12)
4 (ABSTRACT OBJECTS)	53: vrijheid 'freedom'	vernielen: 0.08 (3), **vernietigen**: 0.92 (37)

Table 5: 20th century

Cluster	Context words	Variants
1 (diverse)	5: geheel 'completely'; 4: bestaan 'existence, to exist'; 3: daardoor 'because of', groepen 'groups', rede 'reason', zulke 'such', schoonheid 'beauty', natuur 'nature', waarde 'value', dreigt 'threatens'	vernielen: 0.18 (19), **vernietigen**: 0.82 (87)
2 (PERSONS + WAR)	8: oorlog 'war'; 5: werden 'became (pl.)', nadat 'after', hele 'whole', gehele 'whole', oplage 'edition'; 4: documenten 'documents', moesten 'had to', volk 'people'; 3: recht 'right', kaart 'map', zouden 'would', joodse 'jewish', steden 'cities', exemplaren 'samples', geworden 'become (participle)', goden 'gods', zestig 'sixty', wereldoorlog 'world war', europese 'european'	vernielen: 0.16 (19), **vernietigen**: 0.84 (97)
3 (FUNCTION WORDS)	14: alles 'everything'; 10: zelfs 'even'; 9: zichzelf 'hisself/herself/itself'; 7: niets 'nothing'; 6: uiteindelijk 'eventually'; 4: mens 'human'; 3: waarna 'after which', god 'god', erbij 'near it', erop 'on it', definitief 'definitive', jezelf 'yourself', onmogelijk 'impossible'	vernielen: 0.18 (19), **vernietigen**: 0.82 (88)
4 ((PARTS OF) BUILDINGS)	4: huis 'house', aarde 'earth'; 3: muren 'walls', stenen 'stones'	vernielen: 0.52 (17), vernietigen: 0.48 (16)

this contribution we focus on a single set of parameters settings that were shown to be useful in analyses of the same linguistic example in another century, an alternative approach, that has been successfully employed in Montes (2021), is to consider a broader number of parameter settings to analyze linguistic phenomena.

References

Steven Bird and Edward Loper. 2004. NLTK: The natural language toolkit. In *Proceedings of the ACL Interactive Poster and Demonstration Sessions*, pages 214–217, Barcelona, Spain. Association for Computational Linguistics.

John A. Bullinaria and Joseph P. Levy. 2007. Extracting semantic representations from word co-occurrence statistics: A computational study. *Behavior Research Methods*, 39(3):510–526.

Kenneth Ward Church and Patrick Hanks. 1989. Word association norms, mutual information, and lexicography. In *ACL '89: Proceedings of the 27th Annual Meeting on Association for Computational Linguistic*, pages 76–83.

Ewa Dabrowska and Dagmar Divjak. 2015. Introduction. In Ewa Dabrowska and Dagmar Divjak, editors, *Handbook of Cognitive Linguistics*. De Gruyter Mouton, Berlin.

Stefano De Pascale. 2019. *Token-based vector space models as semantic control in lexical sociolectometry*. Doctoral dissertation, Leuven: KU Leuven.

Katrien Depuydt and Hennie Brugman. 2019. Turning Digitised Material into a Diachronic Corpus: Metadata Challenges in the Nederlab Project. In *DATeCH2019*, pages 169–173, New York.

Dirk Geeraerts. 1985. Preponderantieverschillen bij bijnasynoniemen. *De Nieuwe Taalgids*, 78:18–27.

Dirk Geeraerts. 1988. Where does prototypicality come from? In Brygida Rudzka-Ostyn, editor, *Topics in Cognitive Linguistics*, pages 207–229. John Benjamins, Amsterdam/Philadelphia.

Dirk Geeraerts. 1997. *Diachronic prototype semantics: a contribution to historical lexicology*. Oxford University Press, Oxford.

Dirk Geeraerts and Hubert Cuyckens. 2007. Introducing Cognitive Linguistics. In Dirk Geeraerts and Hubert Cuyckens, editors, *The Oxford Handbook of Cognitive Linguistics*, pages 3–21. Oxford University Press, Oxford.

Dirk Geeraerts, Stefan Grondelaers, and Peter Bakema. 1994. *The Structure of Lexical Variation: Meaning, Naming, and Context*. De Gruyter Mouton, Berlin, New York.

Dirk Geeraerts, Gitte Kristiansen, and Yves Peirsman, editors. 2010. *Advances in cognitive sociolinguistics*. Mouton de Gruyter, New York, N.Y.

K. Heylen, T. Wielfaert, D. Speelman, and D. Geeraerts. 2015. Monitoring polysemy: Word space models as a tool for large-scale lexical semantic analysis. *Lingua*, 157:153–172.

Douwe Kiela and Stephen Clark. 2014. A Systematic Study of Semantic Vector Space Model Parameters. In *Proceedings of the 2nd Workshop on Continuous Vector Space Models and Their Compositionality*, pages 21–30, Gothenburg. ACL.

George Lakoff. 1990. The invariance hypothesis. *Cognitive Linguistics*, 1(1):39–74.

Mariana Montes. 2021. *Cloudspotting. Visual analytics for distributional semantics*. Doctoral dissertation, Leuven: KU Leuven.

Mariana Montes. 2022. Montesmariana/semasioFlow: semasioFlow 0.1.0. Zenodo.

Mariana Montes, Karlien Franco, and Kris Heylen. 2021. Indestructible insights. A case study in distributional prototype semantics. In Gitte Kristiansen, Karlien Franco, Stefano De Pascale, Laura Rosseel, and Weiwei Zhang, editors, *Cognitive Sociolinguistics Revisited*, pages 251–264. De Gruyter Mouton, Berlin/Boston.

QLVL. 2021. *nephosem. Python module for type- and token-level distributional models.*

R Core Team. 2020. *R: A Language and Environment for Statistical Computing*. R Foundation for Statistical Computing, Vienna, Austria.

Hinrich Schütze. 1998. Automatic word sense discrimination. *Computational Linguistics*, 24(1):97–123.

A Appendix

Figure 1: Data in four subcorpora

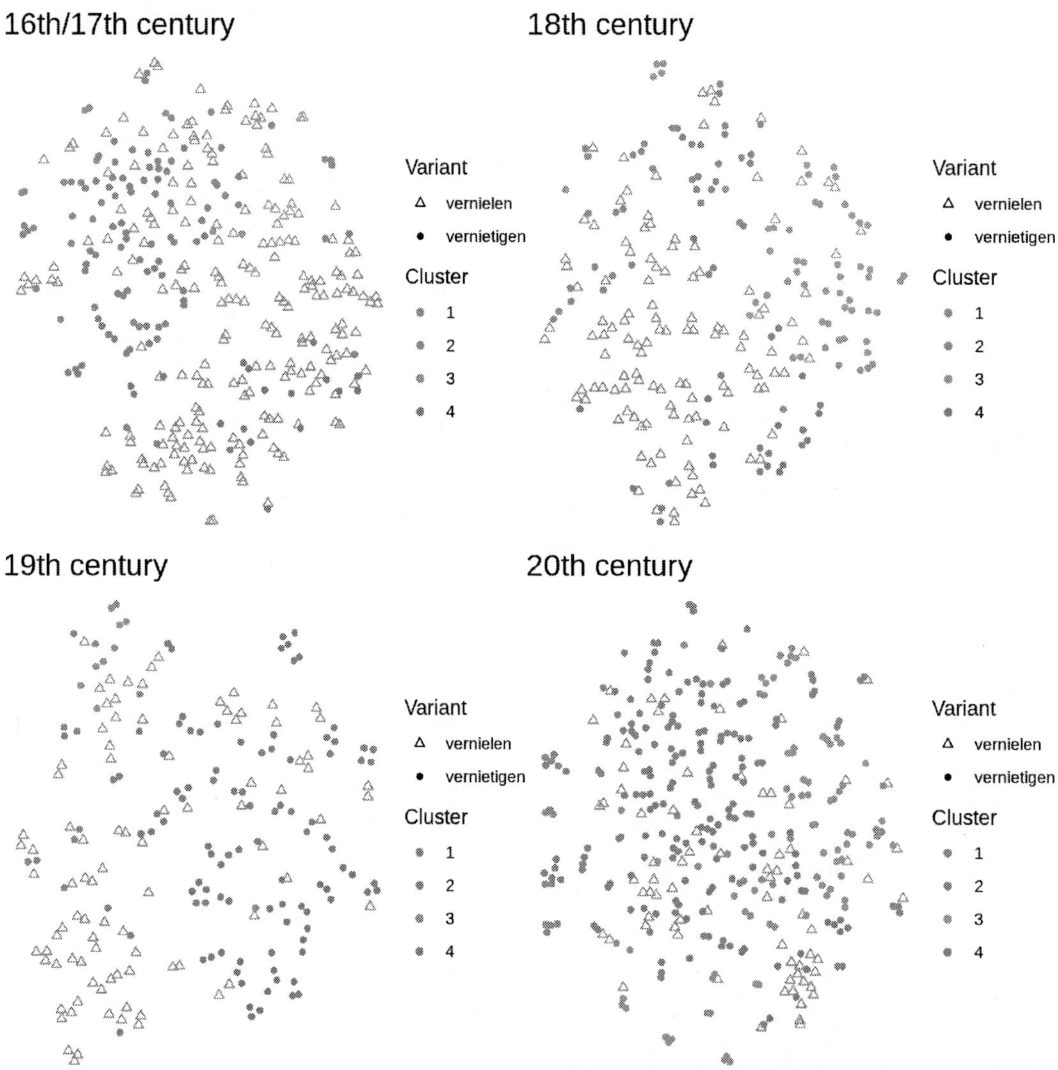

What is Done is Done: an Incremental Approach to Semantic Shift Detection

Alfio Ferrara and **Stefano Montanelli** and **Francesco Periti** and **Martin Ruskov**
Department of Computer Science - University of Milan
Via Celoria, 18 - 20133 Milano, Italy
firstname.lastname@unimi.it

Abstract

Contextual word embedding techniques for semantic shift detection are receiving more and more attention. In this paper, we present *What is Done is Done* (WiDiD), an incremental approach to semantic shift detection based on incremental clustering techniques and contextual embedding methods to capture the changes over the meanings of a target word along a diachronic corpus. In WiDiD, the word contexts observed in the past are consolidated as a set of clusters that constitute the "memory" of the word meanings observed so far. Such a memory is exploited as a basis for subsequent word observations, so that the meanings observed in the present are stratified over the past ones.

1 Introduction

The use of contextual embedding techniques is receiving more and more attention in the field of semantic shift detection. In particular, pre-trained models like BERT (Hu et al., 2019; Martinc et al., 2020a), ELMo (Kutuzov and Giulianelli, 2020; Rodina et al., 2020), and XLM-R (Cuba Gyllensten et al., 2020; Rother et al., 2020), are being proposed as promising solutions to capture the different meanings of a target word according to the different contexts in which the word appears throughout a considered diachronic corpus. Such solutions generally employ clustering techniques to aggregate embeddings of a specific word into clusters (Martinc et al., 2020a; Karnysheva and Schwarz, 2020). The idea is that each cluster denotes a specific *word meaning* that can be recognized in the considered documents. In this way, it is possible to analyze the shift of a word meaning/sense by exploiting the evolution of a cluster over time. For instance, an increasing number of elements in a cluster denotes that the associated word meaning is getting frequently adopted. On the opposite, a cluster with a decreasing number of elements over time refers to a word meaning that is getting obsolete. Usually, the corpus is static, meaning that all the documents of the considered time periods are available as one whole, and a single clustering activity is performed over the entire corpus, generating clusters of word meaning with documents of different time periods (Kutuzov et al., 2018; Tahmasebi et al., 2018, 2021). As a result, the time period in which a document is added to the corpus is not taken into account for cluster composition, and this is not completely satisfactory for an appropriate recognition of meaning changes over time. When a dynamic corpus is considered, namely time periods and documents can be progressively added, scalability issues also arise, since the clusters of word meanings need to be re-calculated or updated. As a possible solution, some recent works propose to perform clustering separately for each time period. In this case, the resulting clusters need to be aligned in order to recognize similar word meanings in different, consecutive time periods (Kanjirangat et al., 2020; Montariol et al., 2021). However, solutions based on clustering alignment are not satisfactory as well, since they do not capture the possible evolution pattern of a meaning across different time periods. A recent work proposes an average-based approach to track semantic shift via continuously evolving embeddings (Horn, 2021) computed as a weighted running average (Finch, 2009) of embeddings generated by a contextual model. This method is suitable to be applied on stream data and it is far more scalable than typically cluster-based methods. Nevertheless, it does not allow to analyse which meanings are actually changed.

In this paper, we present *What is Done is Done* (WiDiD), an incremental approach to semantic shift detection based on incremental clustering techniques and contextual embeddings to capture the changes over the meanings of a target word along a diachronic corpus. In WiDiD, we work under the assumption that the documents of the corpus become

Proceedings of the 3rd Workshop on Computational Approaches to Historical Language Change, pages 33 - 43
May 26-27, 2022 ©2022 Association for Computational Linguistics

available as a stream and they are segmented in a sequence of time periods. The word contexts observed in past time periods are consolidated as a set of clusters that constitute the "memory" of the word meanings observed so far. Such a memory is then exploited as a basis for subsequent word observations in the current time period. The idea of WiDiD is that the clusters of word meanings previously created cannot be changed (*what is done is done*), and the word meanings that are observed in the present must be stratified/integrated over the past ones. To enforce scalability, incremental clustering techniques are employed in WiDiD, so that the word embeddings extracted from the documents of the current time period are compared and assimilated into the set of consolidated clusters coming from the past time periods. A comparative evaluation of the proposed WiDiD approach against a reference benchmark is discussed in the paper according to multiple configurations characterized by different clustering algorithms and embedding methods. In particular, we present experiments based on a pretrained BERT model as well as results obtained from a trained Doc2Vec model, which has been adapted to provide pseudo-contextual word embeddings to extend the conventional static word representations of context-free embedding techniques. As a further contribution of WiDiD, different metrics for semantic shift evaluation of word meanings are defined in the paper and experimental results are provided to discuss their effectiveness.

The paper is organized as follows. In Section 2, the relevant literature is discussed. In Section 3, we present the WiDiD approach. Incremental clustering techniques and semantic shift measures of WiDiD are illustrated in Sections 4 and 5, respectively. Experimental results are discussed in Section 6. Section 7 finally provides our concluding remarks.

2 Related work

Works related to WiDiD are about the use of word embeddings for semantic shift detection by leveraging the idea that semantically-related words are close to each other in the embedding space (Mikolov et al., 2013). In approaches relying on context-free embeddings, independent word vectors defined over different "temporal" vector spaces can be compared after applying an alignment mechanism (Hamilton et al., 2016) such as the Procrustes (Schönemann, 1966). Moreover, recent contextualised architectures are proposed, like ELMo (Peters et al., 2018), BERT (Devlin et al., 2019), and XLM-R (Conneau et al., 2020), which generate dynamic word embeddings according to the use of the words in the input sequences, thus enabling the recognition of different meanings by comparing the context in which words are used throughout the text. The solution proposed in Hu et al. (2019) is one of the first examples based on BERT embeddings to track changes in word meanings and it requires lexicographic supervision, like the use of a reference dictionary (e.g., the Oxford dictionary for the English language) to list the possible word meanings beforehand, thus it is hardly applicable to low-resource languages.

A number of unsupervised approaches based on contextual embeddings are proposed to sidestep the need of lexicographic resources (Schlechtweg et al., 2020; Tahmasebi et al., 2021). In general, these kinds of approaches follow a three-step scheme: i) extraction of embeddings for each occurrence of a target word from a contextual model such as BERT (Hu et al., 2019; Martinc et al., 2020a), ELMo (Kutuzov and Giulianelli, 2020; Rodina et al., 2020), or XLM-R (Cuba Gyllensten et al., 2020; Rother et al., 2020); ii) aggregation of the embeddings with a clustering algorithm like K-Means (Giulianelli et al., 2020; Cuba Gyllensten et al., 2020), Affinity Propagation (Martinc et al., 2020a; Kutuzov and Giulianelli, 2020), or DBSCAN (Rother et al., 2020; Karnysheva and Schwarz, 2020); iii) comparison of the vector distribution over clusters according to time by using a semantic distance measure, like Jensen-Shannon divergence (Martinc et al., 2020a), Entropy Difference (Giulianelli et al., 2020), or Wasserstein Distance (Montariol et al., 2021). The main limitation of applying clustering to word embeddings is the scalability issues about memory consumption and time. As a recent contribution, in Montariol et al. (2021), a scalable and interpretable method is proposed based on merging of similar embeddings to reduce the number of representations to consider for a given word and time slice. Further solutions to overcome scalability issues are provided by Rodina et al. (2020) and Laicher et al. (2021). In particular, they propose to limit the number of embeddings by randomly sampling sentences from each period. The intrinsic time-complexity issues of applying clustering algorithms to embeddings are also addressed in Rother et al. (2020) by reducing the embedding dimensionality. In Martinc et al. (2019), the contextual embeddings of a word are averaged to generate a single word representation for each time period. In Giulianelli et al. (2020), the average pairwise distance between embeddings of different time periods is calculated. Even if these solutions are more efficient and scalable than clustering, they provide uninterpretable results since multiple word occurrences are collapsed into a single representation, like in context-free embeddings. Most of the *cluster-* and *average*-based approaches estimate the magnitude of semantic shifts ignoring the uncertainty of their estimations. As a result, estimations can be erroneously inflated since the irregularities of word frequencies over time can negatively affect the stability of word embeddings (Zhou et al., 2021; Wendlandt et al., 2018). In this respect, Liu et al. (2021) propose a solution based on the combination of BERT embeddings with permutation-based statistical test and term-frequency thresholding.

Original contribution of WiDiD. With respect to the above solutions, the WiDiD approach is based on incremental clustering techniques applied to contextual word embeddings. In WiDiD, the "memory" of word meanings observed in the past is consolidated in a set of clusters that is not re-calculated in subsequent time periods. As a result, only the word embeddings of the current time period are analyzed with the aim to measure the change with respect to the clusters of past word meanings. This way, it is possible to compare specific word meanings also from a qualitative point of view (i.e., interpretable results) without requiring any alignment mechanisim across time periods. In other words, the stratified layers of clusters over time allow to reconstruct not only the quantity of semantic shift but also the evolution of a word meaning.

3 The WiDiD approach

Consider a diachronic document corpus $\mathcal{C} = C_1 \cup C_2$ where C_2 denotes a set of documents of the time t and C_1 denotes a set of documents cumulatively collected in the $t - n$ time periods prior to t. Given a target word w, the goal of semantic shift detection is to measure how much the meaning(s) of w is changed from C_1 to C_2. The WiDiD approach relies on a contextual embedding model to represent each occurrence of the target word w in a corpus C_j (either C_1 or C_2). We keep track of the word embedding representations collected for w over time by relying on the embedding model E_1 that contains the word vectors computed over C_1.

Given this input, we process the new documents in C_2 as follows (see Figure 1).

Document selection. In this step, we select the subset of documents $C_{w,2} \subseteq C_2$ that are relevant for the word w. $C_{w,2}$ is composed by the documents containing the word w. As an alternative, any information retrieval technique suitable for finding relevant documents for a given target can be exploited for the composition of $C_{w,2}$.

Fine tuning. In this step, the model E_1 used to generate the word vectors over C_1 can be optionally updated/fine-tuned into a new model E_2 to take into account the new documents in C_2 (Kim et al., 2014; Giulianelli, 2019). When the observed time t is the initial one, the model E_1 is trained on C_2 or a pre-trained model is used. The WiDiD approach is compatible with any technique for contextual word embedding, that is any method that produces a vector embedding the meaning of a word in a specific document.

Embedding extraction. In this step, we isolate the embedding vectors representing the contextual meaning of the word w. The contextualised embedded representation of the word w in the k-th document of a corpus $C_{w,j}$ is denoted by $e^j_{w,k}$. Then, the representation of the word w in the corpus C_j is defined as:

$$\Phi^j_w = \{e^j_{w,1}, \ldots, e^j_{w,m}\},$$

with m being the number of documents in $C_{w,j}$. As the final output of this step, we have two sets of embedding vectors: Φ^1_w that is produced in the previous iterations of the WiDiD approach over the corpus $C_{w,1}$ and Φ^2_w, produced at the current time t for the corpus $C_{w,2}$.

Clustering. In this step, vectors in $\Phi^1_w \cup \Phi^2_w$ are clustered in order to group vectors representing similar meanings. The set of clusters produced in this step is denoted K_2 and the i-th cluster in K_2 is denoted $\phi_{w,i}$. A distinguishing feature of WiDiD is to perform also the clustering step in an incremental fashion, by updating the clusters K_1 computed in the previous iterations of WiDiD. A more detailed description of the incremental clustering techniques used in WiDiD is given in Section 4. The clusters of K_2 can be classified in three types (see Figure 2). Cluster types (A) and (C) contain vectors that derive from a single corpus, either the past (i.e., C_1) or the current one (i.e., C_2). The cluster type (B) is

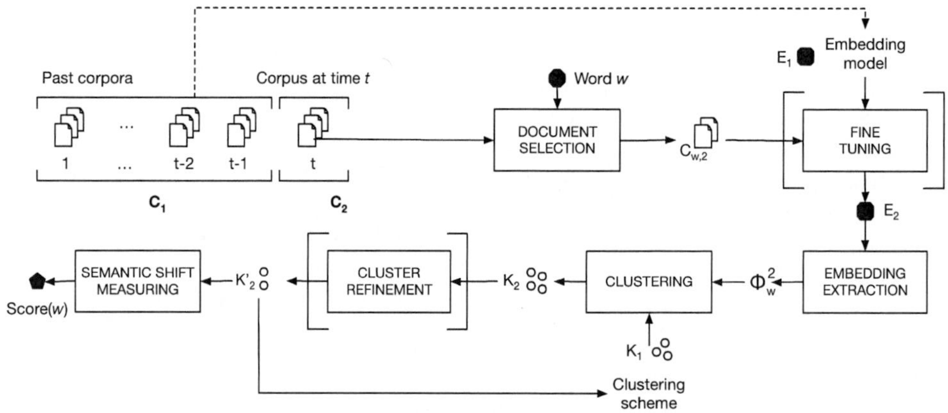

Figure 1: The WiDiD approach

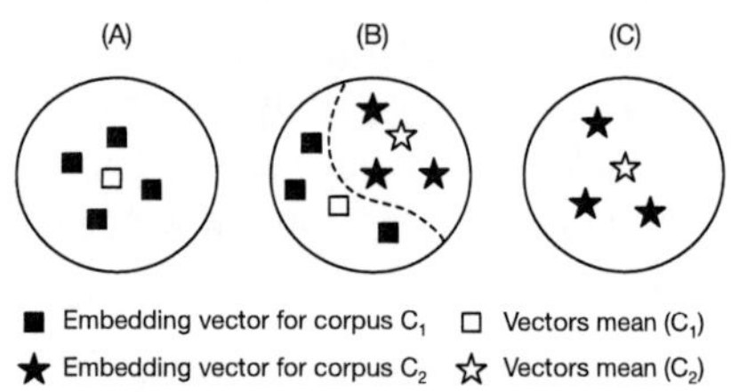

Figure 2: Types of clusters in K_2

a mixture of vectors from the past (corpus C_1) and vectors from the present time (corpus C_2). For each cluster, we compute also the mean μ_i of the vectors that are associated with the same time period (i.e., the same corpus).

Cluster refinement. The cluster set K_2 may contain poorly-informative clusters, such as clusters containing a single vector, or aged information, namely clusters that contain only vectors representing a word meaning observed a long time ago. In order to get rid of poor or aged information, in WiDiD, it is (optionally) possible to perform a cluster refinement step to drop the undesired clusters. We note that this step is also useful to reduce the information available about the past in view of a subsequent execution of WiDiD for the next time period $t + 1$. With regard to poorly-informative clusters, we enforce standard cluster pruning techniques that are typically based on a threshold over the cluster size or the average distance of vectors from the cluster centroid (Raskutti and Leckie, 1999). For aged information, the idea of WiDiD is that each cluster is associated with an aging index that measures how recently the cluster has been updated during the incremental clustering process. This index is updated each time a cluster in the cluster set K_1 is upgraded by adding vectors of Φ_w^2 (i.e., vectors deriving from the corpus C_2). A threshold over the aging index is then used to decide when an aged cluster should be pruned from K_2. As a result, this is a mechanism to regulate how much memory the WiDiD will keep about the past. The final pruned cluster set is denoted $K_2^{'}$ and will be the basis of the clustering step in the next iteration of WiDiD.

Semantic shift measuring. To evaluate whether a word w exhibits a semantic change between the two corpora C_1 and C_2, we measure the distance between the sets Φ_w^1 and Φ_w^2 using the clusters in $K_2^{'}$. Further details on how to measure semantic shift are provided in Section 5.

4 Incremental clustering

In WiDiD, we rely on incremental clustering to aggregate contextual embedding vectors that represent similar word meanings into the same cluster. We propose an incremental extension of Affinity Propagation (AP) (Frey and Dueck, 2007), called Affinity Propagation a Posteriori (APP) (see Algorithm 1). Let's call X and X_1, and L and L_1 the embeddings and the cluster labels at time t and $t-1$, respectively. At time $t = 1$ the standard AP clustering is performed. At each time $t > 1$, for each existing cluster computed at time $t - 1$, the data points $x_i \in X_1$ are packed into a single average representation, i.e. the centroid μ of each cluster. The set of the centroids for X_1 is denoted μX_1. Then, the standard AP algorithm is executed on $\mu X_1 \cup X$, with the aim to obtain a new set of temporary labels L_2, i.e., the new assignment of data points to

Algorithm 1 *The APP algorithm*

Input
t: *time step*
X: *data at time step t*
X_1: *data at time step* $t-1$
L_1: *labels at time step* $t-1$
γ: *trim factor*

Output
L, X: *at time step t*

```
if t == 1 then
    L ← AP(X)
    L, X ← Trim(L, X, γ)
    yield L, X

else if t > 1 then
    μX1 ← Pack(L1, X1)
    L2 ← AP( μX1 ∪ X )
    μL1, L ← Split(L2)
    L1 ← UnpackAndUpdate(μL1, μX1, L1, X1)
    L, X ← Trim( L1 ∪ L,  X1 ∪ X,  γ)
    yield L, X
end if
```

clusters. Such labels are then split in two subsets, μL_1 and L, which contain labels for each average representation in μX_1 and for each data point in X, respectively. Given $\mu L_1, \mu X_1, L_1, X_1$, we unpack the centroids of μL_1 into the corresponding data points X_1 mapping the previous labels L_1 into the new labels of their respective centroids μL_1. Intuitively, clusters from time step $t-1$ can't be changed, in the sense that each point from $t-1$ remain in the same cluster after running AP at time step t. However, each cluster from $t-1$ can be updated with points from t, and new clusters can be created at time step t containing no points from $t-1$. Finally, APP returns $L_1 \cup L$, which is the union of the unpacked and updated L_1 and L. APP includes the notion of aging index to use for cluster refinement, implemented through a trim factor γ. In our current implementation the idea of γ is that clusters containing less than γ percent of the whole set of embeddings $\Phi^1_w \cup \Phi^2_w$ at time t are assumed to be poorly-informative and thus they are dropped.

5 Semantic shift measuring

Clustering contextual word embeddings for a word w at time t results in a set of k clusters $K^2 = \phi_{w,1}, ..., \phi_{w,k}$ where $\phi_{w,i} \subseteq \Phi^1_w \cup \Phi^2_w$. In particular, we denote as $\phi^1_{w,i}, \phi^2_{w,i}$ the set of embeddings from Φ^1_w, and Φ^2_w respectively, enclosed in the $i-$th cluster; formally we define $\phi^1_{w,i} = \phi_{w,i} \cap \Phi^1_w$ and $\phi^2_{w,i} = \phi_{w,i} \cap \Phi^2_w$. According to this, in WiDiD, we propose three different aggregation measures to estimate semantic change. Borrowing from Giulianelli (2019), we employ the Jensen-Shannon divergence to measure semantic change leveraging cluster distributions. In addition, we adapt the methods of Martinc et al. (2019) and Kutuzov (2020) for scenarios where embeddings are clustered.

Jensen-Shannon divergence (JSD). The Jensen-Shannon divergence quantify the similarity between two probability distributions using a symmetrization of the Kullback-Leibler divergence.

$$JSD(p^1_w, p^2_w) = H\left(\frac{1}{2}\left(p^1_w + p^2_w\right)\right) - \frac{1}{2}\left(H(p^1_w) - H(p^2_w)\right) \quad (1)$$

To quantify changes between word senses we create two time-specific cluster distributions p^1_w, p^2_w as the relative number of cluster members for $t-n$, and t, respectively (Hu et al., 2019). Intuitively, we compute the value related to the $i-$th cluster as:

$$p^j_{w,i} = \frac{|\phi^j_{w,i}|}{|\Phi^j_w|} \quad (2)$$

where $j \in \{1, 2\}$.

Distance between prototype embeddings (PDIS). Recent work used the term *word prototype* to indicate a 'prototypical' representation of the word computed by averaging all its embeddings in a specific temporal sub-corpus (Rodina et al., 2020; Kutuzov, 2020; Martinc et al., 2019). In contrast to this definition, we compute (i) *sense prototypes* $\mu^1_{w,i}, \mu^2_{w,i}$ as the average embedding for each cluster partition $\phi^1_{w,i}, \phi^2_{w,i}$, respectively; and (ii) *word prototypes* M^1_w, M^2_w as the average embedding of all *sense prototypes* $\mu^1_{w,i}$, and $\mu^2_{w,i}$ respectively. The idea is that computing the average of a smaller set of more significant embeddings, i.e., the *sense prototypes*, can be beneficial to reduce noise in clusters.

The average-based method by Martinc et al. (2019) consists in computing the cosine similarity between the global average embeddings of all embeddings from $t-n$ and t, respectively. We extend this method by computing the cosine distance between M^1_w and M^2_w.

$$PDIS(M^1, M^2) = 1 - \frac{M^1 \cdot M^2}{\|M^1\| \times \|M^2\|} \quad (3)$$

Difference between prototype embedding diversities (PDIV). The method proposed by Kutuzov (2020) relies on the notion of "embedding diversity" for word prototypes (DIV). We extend this method considering sense prototypes. In particular, we estimate the degree of ambiguity for w in C_1, C_2 as the mean cosine distance d between *sense prototypes* $\mu^j_{w,i}$ and the relative *word prototype* M^j_w. The final result is the absolute difference between the relative coefficients. For the sake of simplicity, let's denote as Ψ^1_w and Ψ^2_w the set of sense prototypes of $\mu^1_{w,i}$, and $\mu^2_{w,i}$ respectively.

$$PDIV(\Psi^1_w, \Psi^2_w) = \left| \frac{\sum_{\mu^1_{w,k} \in \Psi^1_w} d(\mu^1_{w,k}, M^1_w)}{|\Psi^1_w|} - \frac{\sum_{\mu^2_{w,k} \in \Psi^2_w} d(\mu^2_{w,k}, M^2_w)}{|\Psi^2_w|} \right| \quad (4)$$

6 Evaluation of WiDiD

For evaluation of WiDiD, we rely on the Task 1 framework of SemEval-2020. SemEval is a series of international NLP workshops based on a collection of shared tasks in which computational semantic analysis systems designed by different teams are presented and compared. In particular, we focus on SemEval-2020 Subtask 2 where the goal is to consider texts from two distinct time periods and to evaluate the degree of semantic shift of a set of target words (Schlechtweg et al., 2020). In SemEval-2020, the semantic shift degree is measured by the Spearman's rank-order correlation between the semantic shift index (i.e., the ground truth) and the semantic shift assessment computed by a model for each target word in the evaluation set. Our evaluation is performed over the English and Latin corpora of SemEval-2020. A summary view of the considered corpora is provided in Table 1. As proposed in Montariol et al. (2021), in the English corpus, we removed POS tags from both the corpus and the evaluation set.

		Period	Tokens	Corpus	Target Words
SemEval English	C_1	1810 – 1860	6.5M	CCOHA	37
	C_2	1960 – 2010	6.7M		
SemEval Latin	C_1	-200 – 0	65k	LatinISE	40
	C_2	0 – 2000	253k		

Table 1: Period, size, and number of target words for English and Latin corpora of SemEval-2020

6.1 Experimental setup

In the evaluation, the following configurations of WiDiD have been adopted.

Word representations. Pre-trained BERT and trained Doc2Vec models are exploited as embedding models. We use the Transformers library by HuggingFace to extract contextual word embeddings from pre-trained BERT models without performing any fine-tuning stage (Wolf et al., 2020). We use a specific model for each language, namely *bert-base-uncased*[1] for English and *bert-base-multilingual-uncased*[2] for Latin. The models are base versions of BERT with 12 attention layers and a hidden layer of size 768. The only model available for Latin is a multilingual BERT model trained on 104 languages, including Latin.

The acquisition of contextual embeddings is done by feeding the models with text sequences from the corpora in which the target words occur. Sequence embeddings are generated one sequence at a time by summing the last 4 encoder output layers according to Devlin et al. (2019). Finally, given a sequence of size $sequence\ length \times embeddings\ size$, we cut it into pieces to get a separate contextual embedding for each token in the sequence. In this way, we extract token embeddings for each occurrence of a target word in a corpus. Due to the byte-pair input encoding scheme employed by BERT models, some tokens may not correspond to words but rather to word pieces (Sennrich et al., 2016; Wu et al., 2016). Therefore, if a word is split into more than one token, we build a single word embedding by concatenating them.

Pseudo-Word Representations. While BERT-like models generate dynamic embeddings for a word according to their belonging sequences (i.e., documents), Doc2Vec (Le and Mikolov, 2014) produces a static lookup table of word and sequence embeddings only for words and sequences seen during training. We exploit Doc2Vec by computing *pseudo*-contextual word embeddings under the assumption that word occurrences belonging to similar sequences have the same meaning. This means that, given a target word w in the corpus C_j we consider as Φ^j_w the set of sequence embeddings related to sequences where w occurs. For training

[1] `https://huggingface.co/bert-base-uncased`

[2] `https://huggingface.co/bert-base-multilingual-uncased`

Doc2Vec models, we use the Gensim library (Rehurek and Sojka, 2011). In particular, we trained word and sequence embeddings of size 100 for 15 epochs, with a window size of 10.

Clustering of embeddings. For the evaluation of WiDiD, we exploit the APP clustering algorithm described in Section 4. Since APP is an extension of the Affinity Propagation (AP) clustering algorithm, we compared the results of APP against the results of AP in the clustering step of the WiDiD approach. In addition, we tested a further incremental extension of AP called IAPNA. IAPNA is an incremental version of AP that has been proposed by Sun and Guo (2014) and it is based on the idea of computing a reasonable assignment for all the data points at the same status. Then, when new points are available, the relationships between the new points and the other points are assigned referring to their nearest neighbors and by updating the responsibility and availability indexes for those points. In particular, we use the scikit-learn (Pedregosa et al., 2011) implementation for standard AP, that we extended for implementing both IAPNA and APP.

Experiments. The following experiments have been executed. We apply the semantic shift measures illustrated in Section 5 (i.e., JSD, PDIS, PDIV) to the clusters of contextual embeddings obtained by using AP, IAPNA, and APP, respectively. Since PDIS and PDIV are extensions of the CD (*Cosine Distance over Word Prototypes*) and DIV (*Difference between Token Embedding Diversities*) measures proposed by Martinc et al. (2019) and Kutuzov (2020), we also consider them as baselines.

6.2 Experimental results

The results of our evaluation are shown in Table 2[3].

Surprisingly, Doc2Vec proved to be a suitable model for semantic shift detection, in both incremental and non-incremental clustering contexts. It performs well, while being smaller and faster than contextual models. In particular, Doc2Vec-based methods achieve the highest result in our experiments on both Latin and English, with correlation coefficient of 0.512 and 0.514, respectively. APP provides top results on both Latin and English, although AP has a slightly higher performance on English.

On average, both incremental clustering algorithms IAPNA and APP perform well in semantic shift detection compared to the conventional AP clustering. We note that IAPNA and APP have opposite behavior on Latin and English: IAPNA has higher results with BERT embeddings on Latin and Doc2Vec embeddings on English, while APP has higher results with Doc2Vec embeddings on Latin and BERT embeddings on English, respectively. The fact that IAPNA and APP perform differently on different languages is consistent with the literature results (Kutuzov and Giulianelli, 2020).

As a further remark, we note that APP produces a smaller and more reasonable number of clusters compared to both AP and IAPNA. For instance, we observed situations where both AP and IAPNA produce more than 100 clusters, that is rather unrealistic if we assume that a cluster represents a word meaning. On the opposite, in our experiments, the number of APP clusters generally varies between 0 and 30. We also note that APP is sensitive to the aging index. In Table 2, we present the top results obtained with two different values of the aging index (i.e., 0 and 5). Removing clusters containing less than 5% of the embeddings has a positive impact just in some experiments with English, but not with Latin. We plan to further investigate the effects of the aging index in our future work.

About our proposed measures for semantic shift detection (i.e., JSD, PDIS, PDIV), we note that they always perform better than the baselines CD and DIV. We also note that the CD baseline does not work well on Doc2Vec embeddings, while DIV does not work well in all our experiments. On Latin, the highest results are achieved by JSD on both Doc2Vec and BERT embeddings. On English, the top JSD and PDIS results are on Doc2Vec and BERT embeddings, respectively. More experiments are required on PDIV since it performs very differently in the various experiments we performed, and it achieves statistical significance only in four out of twelve experiments (six on Latin, six on English).

Finally, Table 3 provides the best results obtained by other literature approaches for semantic shift detection based on contextual word embeddings over the English and Latin corpora of SemEval-2020. We note that both IAPNA and APP are competitive when compared to the considered literature approaches. The WiDiD scores are above average and slightly below the maxi-

[3]The source code of our experiments is available under the MIT license at `https://github.com/umilISLab/LChange22`

Clustering	Training	Model	Latin (Spearman's coefficients) *JSD*	*PDIS*	*PDIV*	English (Spearman's coefficients) *JSD*	*PDIS*	*PDIV*
AP	trained	Doc2Vec	**0.485***	0.229	-0.023	**0.514***	0.139	0.134
	pre-trained	BERT	**0.394***	0.347*	0.236	0.356*	0.326*	**0.406***
IAPNA	trained	Doc2Vec	**0.462***	0.354*	-0.005	0.199	0.322*	**0.336***
	pre-trained	BERT	**0.411***	0.356*	-0.148	0.336*	**0.499***	0.213
APP	trained	Doc2Vec	$\mathbf{0.512_0}$*	0.337_0*	0.328_0*	$\mathbf{0.333_0}$*	0.077_0	-0.078_0
	pre-trained	BERT	$\mathbf{0.361_0}$*	0.210_0	0.036_0	0.302_0°	$\mathbf{0.512_5}$*	0.370_5*
			CD	*DIV*		*CD*	*DIV*	
	trained	Doc2Vec	0.258°	0.138	-	0.092	0.010	-
	pre-trained	BERT	0.306*	-0.017	-	0.486*	0.168	-

Table 2: Spearman's correlation coefficients over different setups with Latin and English corpora. The asterisks denote statistically significant correlations ($p \leq 0.05$), while degree symbols denote low-level correlations with ($0.05 \leq p \leq 0.1$). The subscript index indicates the value adopted for the aging index. We report in bold the highest scores for each clustering-based method considering BERT and Doc2Vec.

	Clustering	Training	Model	Latin (Spearman's coeff.)	English (Spearman's coeff.)
Beck, 2020	-	pre-trained	BERT	0.343	0.293
Karnysheva and Schwarz, 2020	K-means (English) DBSCAN (Latin)	pre-trained	ELMo	0.177	-0.155
Cuba Gyllensten et al., 2020	K-Means	**pre-trained**	XLM-R	**0.399**	0.209
Rother et al., 2020	HDBSCAN (English) GMMs (Latin)	pre-trained	BERT	0.321	0.512
Kanjirangat et al., 2020	K-means	pre-trained	BERT	0.333	0.159
Laicher et al., 2021	-	**pre-trained**	BERT	N/D	**0.571**
Arefyev and Zhikov, 2020	-	fine-tuned	XLM-R	-0.134	0.299
Kutuzov and Giulianelli, 2020	-	**fine-tuned**	ELMo (English) BERT (Latin)	**0.561**	**0.605**
Montariol et al., 2021	AP	fine-tuned	BERT	0.496	0.456
Pömsl and Lyapin, 2020	-	fine-tuned	BERT	0.464	0.246
Rosin et al., 2021	-	fine-tuned	TinyBERT (English) LatinBERT (Latin)	0.512	0.467
Martinc et al., 2020b	AP	fine-tuned	BERT	0.496	0.436
Liu et al., 2021	-	fine-tuned	BERT	0.304	0.341

Table 3: Spearman's correlation coefficients obtained by different experiments with English and Latin corpora. We report in bold the best scores for pre-trained and fine-tuned models. The hyphens indicate approaches that do not cluster contextual embeddings. N/D indicates that experimental results are not available.

mum scores (in bold). We stress that we obtained these results without fine-tuning, confirming that the idea of using incremental clustering is promising. Compared to other literature approaches based on pre-trained models without fine-tuning, we note that incremental clustering algorithms achieve the highest scores on Latin (0.512 with APP and 0.411 with IAPNA for Doc2Vec and BERT, respectively). Our results on the English corpus come second in the pre-trained ranking (0.512 with APP and 0.499 with IAPNA for Doc2Vec and BERT, respectively) after Laicher et al. (2021). All in all, excluding Laicher et al. (2021) and Kutuzov (2020), our results are the highest of all the considered literature works of Table 3, both on Latin and English.

7 Concluding remarks

In this paper, we presented the WiDiD approach characterized by incremental clustering techniques and contextual word embedding methods. Ongoing work is about the fine-tuning of adopted embedding models to further improve the quality of results. Moreover, we are working on defining cluster analysis techniques. The idea is to exploit the results of semantic shift measures to interpret possible trend patterns over clusters along the time, such as a broad meaning that forks into narrower ones, or a meaning that increases its popularity and vice versa. Further work is about the specification of aging policies to manage the memory of aged embeddings in the cluster evolution.

Acknowledgments

This paper is partially funded by the RECON project within the UNIMI-SEED research programme and by the PSR-UNIMI programme.

References

Nikolay Arefyev and Vasily Zhikov. 2020. BOS at SemEval-2020 Task 1: Word Sense Induction via Lexical Substitution for Lexical Semantic Change Detection. In *Proceedings of the Fourteenth Workshop on Semantic Evaluation*, pages 171–179, Barcelona (online). International Committee for Computational Linguistics.

Christin Beck. 2020. DiaSense at SemEval-2020 Task 1: Modeling Sense Change via Pre-trained BERT Embeddings. In *Proceedings of the Fourteenth Workshop on Semantic Evaluation*, pages 50–58, Barcelona (online). International Committee for Computational Linguistics.

Alexis Conneau, Kartikay Khandelwal, Naman Goyal, Vishrav Chaudhary, Guillaume Wenzek, Francisco Guzmán, Edouard Grave, Myle Ott, Luke Zettlemoyer, and Veselin Stoyanov. 2020. Unsupervised Cross-lingual Representation Learning at Scale. In *Proceedings of the 58th Annual Meeting of the Association for Computational Linguistics*, pages 8440–8451, Online. Association for Computational Linguistics.

Amaru Cuba Gyllensten, Evangelia Gogoulou, Ariel Ekgren, and Magnus Sahlgren. 2020. SenseCluster at SemEval-2020 Task 1: Unsupervised Lexical Semantic Change Detection. In *Proceedings of the Fourteenth Workshop on Semantic Evaluation*, pages 112–118, Barcelona (online). International Committee for Computational Linguistics.

Jacob Devlin, Ming-Wei Chang, Kenton Lee, and Kristina Toutanova. 2019. BERT: Pre-training of Deep Bidirectional Transformers for Language Understanding. In *Proceedings of the 2019 Conference of the North American Chapter of the Association for Computational Linguistics: Human Language Technologies, Volume 1 (Long and Short Papers)*, pages 4171–4186, Minneapolis, Minnesota. Association for Computational Linguistics.

Tony Finch. 2009. Incremental Calculation of Weighted Mean and Variance. *University of Cambridge*, 4(11-5):41–42.

Brendan J Frey and Delbert Dueck. 2007. Clustering by passing messages between data points. *science*, 315(5814):972–976.

Mario Giulianelli. 2019. *Lexical Semantic Change Analysis with Contextualised Word Representations*. Ph.D. thesis, University of Amsterdam - Institute for logic, Language and computation.

Mario Giulianelli, Marco Del Tredici, and Raquel Fern'andez. 2020. Analysing Lexical Semantic Change with Contextualised Word Representations. In *Proceedings of the 58th Annual Meeting of the Association for Computational Linguistics*, pages 3960–3973, Online. Association for Computational Linguistics.

William L. Hamilton, Jure Leskovec, and Dan Jurafsky. 2016. Diachronic Word Embeddings Reveal Statistical Laws of Semantic Change. In *Proceedings of the 54th Annual Meeting of the Association for Computational Linguistics (Volume 1: Long Papers)*, pages 1489–1501, Berlin, Germany. Association for Computational Linguistics.

Franziska Horn. 2021. Exploring Word Usage Change with Continuously Evolving Embeddings. In *Proceedings of the 59th Annual Meeting of the Association for Computational Linguistics and the 11th International Joint Conference on Natural Language Processing: System Demonstrations*, pages 290–297, Online. Association for Computational Linguistics.

Renfen Hu, Shen Li, and Shichen Liang. 2019. Diachronic Sense Modeling with Deep Contextualized Word Embeddings: An Ecological View. In *Proceedings of the 57th Annual Meeting of the Association for Computational Linguistics*, pages 3899–3908, Florence, Italy. Association for Computational Linguistics.

Vani Kanjirangat, Sandra Mitrovic, Alessandro Antonucci, and Fabio Rinaldi. 2020. SST-BERT at SemEval-2020 Task 1: Semantic Shift Tracing by Clustering in BERT-based Embedding Spaces. In *Proceedings of the Fourteenth Workshop on Semantic Evaluation*, pages 214–221, Barcelona (online). International Committee for Computational Linguistics.

Anna Karnysheva and Pia Schwarz. 2020. TUE at SemEval-2020 Task 1: Detecting Semantic Change by Clustering Contextual Word Embeddings. In *Proceedings of the Fourteenth Workshop on Semantic Evaluation*, pages 232–238, Barcelona (online). International Committee for Computational Linguistics.

Yoon Kim, Yi-I Chiu, Kentaro Hanaki, Darshan Hegde, and Slav Petrov. 2014. Temporal Analysis of Language through Neural Language Models. In *Proceedings of the ACL 2014 Workshop on Language Technologies and Computational Social Science*, pages 61–65, Baltimore, MD, USA. Association for Computational Linguistics.

Andrey Kutuzov. 2020. *Distributional Word Embeddings in Modeling Diachronic Semantic Change*. Ph.D. thesis, University of Oslo.

Andrey Kutuzov and Mario Giulianelli. 2020. UiO-UvA at SemEval-2020 Task 1: Contextualised Embeddings for Lexical Semantic Change Detection. In *Proceedings of the Fourteenth Workshop on Semantic Evaluation*, pages 126–134, Barcelona (online). International Committee for Computational Linguistics.

Andrey Kutuzov, Lilja Øvrelid, Terrence Szymanski, and Erik Velldal. 2018. Diachronic Word Embeddings and Semantic Shifts: a Survey. In *Proceedings of the 27th International Conference on Computational Linguistics*, pages 1384–1397, Santa Fe, New Mexico, USA. Association for Computational Linguistics.

Severin Laicher, Sinan Kurtyigit, Dominik Schlechtweg, Jonas Kuhn, and Sabine Schulte im Walde. 2021. Explaining and Improving BERT Performance on Lexical Semantic Change Detection. In *Proceedings of the 16th Conference of the European Chapter of the Association for Computational Linguistics: Student Research Workshop*, pages 192–202, Online. Association for Computational Linguistics.

Quoc Le and Tomas Mikolov. 2014. Distributed Representations of Sentences and Documents. In *Proceedings of the 31st International Conference on Machine Learning*, pages 1188–1196, Bejing, China. PMLR.

Yang Liu, Alan Medlar, and Dorota Glowacka. 2021. Statistically significant detection of semantic shifts using contextual word embeddings. *CoRR*, abs/2104.03776.

Matej Martinc, Petra Kralj Novak, and Senja Pollak. 2019. Leveraging Contextual Embeddings for Detecting Diachronic Semantic Shift. In *Proceedings of The 12th Language Resources and Evaluation Conference*, pages 4811–4819, Marseille, France. European Language Resources Association.

Matej Martinc, Syrielle Montariol, Elaine Zosa, and Lidia Pivovarova. 2020a. Capturing Evolution in Word Usage: Just Add More Clusters? *CoRR*, abs/2001.06629.

Matej Martinc, Syrielle Montariol, Elaine Zosa, and Lidia Pivovarova. 2020b. Discovery Team at SemEval-2020 Task 1: Context-sensitive Embeddings Not Always Better than Static for Semantic Change Detection. In *Proceedings of the Fourteenth Workshop on Semantic Evaluation*, pages 67–73, Barcelona (online). International Committee for Computational Linguistics.

Tomás Mikolov, Kai Chen, Greg Corrado, and Jeffrey Dean. 2013. Efficient Estimation of Word Representations in Vector Space. In *1st International Conference on Learning Representations, ICLR 2013, Scottsdale, Arizona, USA, May 2-4, 2013, Workshop Track Proceedings*.

Syrielle Montariol, Matej Martinc, and Lidia Pivovarova. 2021. Scalable and Interpretable Semantic Change Detection. In *Proceedings of the 2021 Conference of the North American Chapter of the Association for Computational Linguistics: Human Language Technologies*, pages 4642–4652, Online. Association for Computational Linguistics.

F. Pedregosa, G. Varoquaux, A. Gramfort, V. Michel, B. Thirion, O. Grisel, M. Blondel, P. Prettenhofer, R. Weiss, V. Dubourg, J. Vanderplas, A. Passos, D. Cournapeau, M. Brucher, M. Perrot, and E. Duchesnay. 2011. Scikit-learn: Machine Learning in Python. *Journal of Machine Learning Research*, 12:2825–2830.

Matthew E. Peters, Mark Neumann, Mohit Iyyer, Matt Gardner, Christopher Clark, Kenton Lee, and Luke Zettlemoyer. 2018. Deep Contextualized Word Representations. In *Proceedings of the 2018 Conference of the North American Chapter of the Association for Computational Linguistics: Human Language Technologies, Volume 1 (Long Papers)*, pages 2227–2237, New Orleans, Louisiana. Association for Computational Linguistics.

Martin Pömsl and Roman Lyapin. 2020. CIRCE at SemEval-2020 Task 1: Ensembling Context-Free and Context-Dependent Word Representations. In *Proceedings of the Fourteenth Workshop on Semantic Evaluation*, pages 180–186, Barcelona (online). International Committee for Computational Linguistics.

Bhavani Raskutti and Christopher Leckie. 1999. An evaluation of criteria for measuring the quality of clusters. In *IJCAI: Proceedings of the Sixteenth International Joint Conference on Artificial Intelligence*, volume 99, pages 905–910.

Radim Rehurek and Petr Sojka. 2011. Gensim–python framework for vector space modelling. *NLP Centre, Faculty of Informatics, Masaryk University, Brno, Czech Republic*, 3(2).

Julia Rodina, Yuliya Trofimova, Andrey Kutuzov, and Ekaterina Artemova. 2020. ELMo and BERT in Semantic Change Detection for Russian. *CoRR*, abs/2010.03481.

Guy D. Rosin, Ido Guy, and Kira Radinsky. 2021. Time masking for temporal language models. *CoRR*, abs/2110.06366.

David Rother, Thomas Haider, and Steffen Eger. 2020. CMCE at SemEval-2020 Task 1: Clustering on Manifolds of Contextualized Embeddings to Detect Historical Meaning Shifts. In *Proceedings of the Fourteenth Workshop on Semantic Evaluation*, pages 187–193, Barcelona (online). International Committee for Computational Linguistics.

Dominik Schlechtweg, Barbara McGillivray, Simon Hengchen, Haim Dubossarsky, and Nina Tahmasebi. 2020. SemEval-2020 Task 1: Unsupervised Lexical Semantic Change Detection. In *Proceedings of the Fourteenth Workshop on Semantic Evaluation*, pages 1–23, Barcelona (online). International Committee for Computational Linguistics.

Peter H Schönemann. 1966. A Generalized Solution of the Orthogonal Procrustes Problem. *Psychometrika*, 31(1):1–10.

Rico Sennrich, Barry Haddow, and Alexandra Birch. 2016. Neural Machine Translation of Rare Words with Subword Units. In *Proceedings of the 54th Annual Meeting of the Association for Computational Linguistics (Volume 1: Long Papers)*, pages 1715–1725, Berlin, Germany. Association for Computational Linguistics.

Leilei Sun and Chonghui Guo. 2014. Incremental Affinity Propagation Clustering Based on Message Passing. *IEEE Transactions on Knowledge and Data Engineering*, 26(11):2731–2744.

Nina Tahmasebi, Lars Borin, and Adam Jatowt. 2018. Survey of Computational Approaches to Lexical Semantic Change. *ArXiv e-prints*, abs/1811.06278.

Nina Tahmasebi, Lars Borin, Adam Jatowt, Yang Xu, and Simon Hengchen, editors. 2021. *Computational Approaches to Semantic Change.* Number 6 in Language Variation. Language Science Press, Berlin.

Laura Wendlandt, Jonathan K. Kummerfeld, and Rada Mihalcea. 2018. Factors Influencing the Surprising Instability of Word Embeddings. In *Proceedings of the 2018 Conference of the North American Chapter of the Association for Computational Linguistics: Human Language Technologies, Volume 1 (Long Papers)*, pages 2092–2102, New Orleans, Louisiana. Association for Computational Linguistics.

Thomas Wolf, Lysandre Debut, Victor Sanh, Julien Chaumond, Clement Delangue, Anthony Moi, Pierric Cistac, Tim Rault, Remi Louf, Morgan Funtowicz, Joe Davison, Sam Shleifer, Patrick von Platen, Clara Ma, Yacine Jernite, Julien Plu, Canwen Xu, Teven Le Scao, Sylvain Gugger, Mariama Drame, Quentin Lhoest, and Alexander Rush. 2020. Transformers: State-of-the-Art Natural Language Processing. In *Proceedings of the 2020 Conference on Empirical Methods in Natural Language Processing: System Demonstrations*, pages 38–45, Online. Association for Computational Linguistics.

Yonghui Wu, Mike Schuster, Zhifeng Chen, Quoc V. Le, Mohammad Norouzi, Wolfgang Macherey, Maxim Krikun, Yuan Cao, Qin Gao, Klaus Macherey, Jeff Klingner, Apurva Shah, Melvin Johnson, Xiaobing Liu, Lukasz Kaiser, Stephan Gouws, Yoshikiyo Kato, Taku Kudo, Hideto Kazawa, Keith Stevens, George Kurian, Nishant Patil, Wei Wang, Cliff Young, Jason Smith, Jason Riesa, Alex Rudnick, Oriol Vinyals, Greg Corrado, Macduff Hughes, and Jeffrey Dean. 2016. Google's Neural Machine Translation System: Bridging the Gap between Human and Machine Translation. *CoRR*, abs/1609.08144.

Kaitlyn Zhou, Kawin Ethayarajh, and Dan Jurafsky. 2021. Frequency-based Distortions in Contextualized Word Embeddings. *arXiv preprint arXiv:2104.08465*.

From qualifiers to quantifiers: semantic shift at the paradigm level

Quentin FELTGEN
Ghent University / Blandijnberg 2 9000 Gent Belgium
quentin.feltgen@gmail.com

Abstract

Language change has often been conceived as a competition between linguistic variants. However, language units may be complex organizations in themselves, e.g. in the case of schematic constructions, featuring a free slot. Such a slot is filled by words forming a set or 'paradigm' and engaging in inter-related dynamics within this constructional environment. To tackle this complexity, a simple computational method is offered to automatically characterize their interactions, and visualize them through networks of cooperation and competition. Applying this method to the French paradigm of quantifiers, I show that this method efficiently captures phenomena regarding the evolving organization of constructional paradigms, in particular the constitution of competing clusters of fillers that promote different semantic strategies overall.

1 Introduction

Language change is often depicted as a competition between an entrenched variant, and an innovative, rising competitor; e.g. the replacement of *of course* by *obviously* (Tagliamonte and Smith, 2021) in Present Day Canadian English, of *werðan* by *becuman* in Middle English (Petré and Cuyckens, 2008), of *moult* by *beaucoup* and *très* in Middle French (Marchello-Nizia, 2000), of *en* par *dans* as the chief locative preposition in Modern French (Fagard and Combettes, 2013), or of the former syntactic patterns for negation and interrogation by the periphrastic *do* pattern (Kroch, 1989).

Such a competition, however, is difficult to evidence. For instance, what can the *way* construction (Israel, 1996; Perek, 2018) (e.g. 'the Black Prince *plundered his way* eastward to Narbonne and back') possibly replace? Moreover, in the case of a clear replacement, the replacement is seldom total. For instance, the periphrastic *do* did not replace auxiliaries, and some verbs like *need* are still found with the older pattern; *moult* was replaced by two different words, but they both show uses that *moult* had not, and they do not cover the whole functional range that was carried by *moult*. The French *en* was replaced by *dans* in most locative contexts, but it remains more frequent than its newer counterpart (Eckart and Quasthoff, 2013; Corpus and language statistics for corpora of the Leipzig Corpora Collection, 2021). Similarly, while *be going to* can be seen as a competitor for *will*, both auxiliaries differ semantically; furthermore, it has been argued that they both feature semantic retention pertaining to their respective origins (Nicolle, 1998). The same phenomenon has been observed for discourse markers based on prepositional adverbs in French (Fagard and Charolles, 2018).

In the meanwhile, it has been posited that frequency rise evidenced by lexical items or constructions is a sign of semantic expansion (Feltgen et al., 2017). This hypothesis would provide a convenient account of the phenomena mentioned above: language change is, first and foremost, a semantic shift; if this semantic shift spills over the semantic domain of an existing form, competition arises over this overlap; if this semantic shift leads to meanings and functions that were not formerly expressed in the language, no competition occurs and there is no competitor. In this sense, lexical competitions are a sign of a semantic shift, and help identify ongoing language changes; yet language change may happen without any obvious competition.

In this paper, another perspective on the interplay between semantic change and competition is offered. Indeed, competition may arise *within* a given linguistic form dominion, especially in the case of schematic constructions, that is, constructions that feature an open slot that can be filled by different arguments (e.g. the *way too* + {ADJ/ADV} intensifier construction). These arguments can compete against one another, within the construction. Moreover, this competition needs not be one-to-one: since a large number of arguments are involved,

Proceedings of the 3rd Workshop on Computational Approaches to Historical Language Change, pages 44 - 53
May 26-27, 2022 ©2022 Association for Computational Linguistics

the competition may unfold between different clusters of arguments. Therefore, we can detect such paradigmatic competitions by looking at the correlations and anti-correlations between the frequency dynamics of the different fillers.

To give a somehow hypothetical example of this semantic shift at the paradigm level, we may consider the paradigm of classifiers (e.g. in Thai or in Korean), which categorizes nouns according to a set of principles. This categorization can, for instance, be driven by considerations of shape, or by considerations of function (Carpenter, 1992). These two broad principles may in principle both co-exist and compete over time, and individual classifiers typically fall into one or the other broad group of function-based classifiers and shape-based classifiers (things being more blurry in practice).

In this regard, we can conceive of three levels of semantic change, that are not mutually exclusive. The first is the constructional level, which corresponds to a significant change in the broad scope of the nouns to which the construction applies, for instance through the recruitment of new classifiers to operate on nouns that were previously beyond the scope of the construction, e.g. the emergence of a new classifier for the class of machines. The second level is that of the individual classifiers; e.g. the reanalysis of Thai */khan/* from a shape-based classifier to a function-based one. The third level is what I refer to as the 'paradigmatic level'. This happens when one group takes over the nouns that were classified by the other group. Nouns become then re-classified according to a new set of principles. In this case, the individual classifiers do not have to undergo semantic change; and the broad 'classifiers' construction still applies to the same nouns. Yet, these nouns are now preferentially categorized in a new way (e.g. function over shape); therefore, the properties that are made salient by the choice of a specific classifier are now different. This kind of paradigmatic reorganization is for instance illustrated by the different yet overlapping semantic roles of verb classifiers in the related Nyulnyul and Warrwa languages (McGregor, 2018).

This kind of semantic change only reveals itself at the scale of a system of linguistic units, such as constructional paradigms. As a result, traditional tools, such as word embeddings that rely on collocations (Mikolov et al., 2013), cannot be readily expected to account for it. In this paper, I offer a simple method to detect such a paradigmatic reorganization. I illustrate it on the French quantifier construction *un N de* (e.g. *une profusion de*), which exactly mirrors the English quantifier construction *a N of* (e.g. *a lot of*), whose historical development has already been studied (Traugott and Trousdale, 2013). Besides the entrenchment of the construction in Middle French, I evidence, by looking at the network of correlation between the fillers frequencies, a major paradigmatic shift occurring in Modern French. A qualitative analysis of the competing clusters is also offered.

2 Corpus and frequency profiles

2.1 The French quantifier construction

The French quantifier construction, *un Q(N) de N ('a Q(N) of N')*, is a construction in which a nominal quantifier, *Q(N)*, is used to introduce a noun, *N*, by giving an estimate of its overall count. Its structure is closely similar to a more general genitive construction *NP de NP* (similar to the English *NP of NP* from which the English quantifier construction also originates), so that automatically (and even manually) sorting the relevant occurrences from the spurious ones poses a serious challenge. To cope with this difficulty, I decided to be conservative and select only the arguments which are clear quantifiers. One useful test in this regard is that the verb may agree with the quantified noun (plural) instead of agreeing with the quantifier noun (singular), which is incompatible with a genitive reading. For one early example of it (1330): *"Tantost **une foule de** gent firent cesser leur parlement"* ("A crowd of people interrupted their discussions.")

I have retained 36 quantifier nouns for the *Q(N)* slot of the construction. Partitive constructions, which behave very similarly, have been excluded (e.g. *un morceau de*, 'a bit of'), as well as plural quantifiers, such as *des litres de vin* ('liters of wine'), which don't seem to warrant the same constructional reading.

2.2 Frantext corpus

This construction has been investigated on the Frantext database (ATILF, 1998), restricted to the 1321-2020 period. This is the longest period such that every decade is covered in the corpus with at least one text (with a minimum of 5 for the 1321-1330 decade). The selected corpus encompasses close to 300 M words. In total, I found 50k occurrences of the quantifier construction.

2.3 Frequency profile

For each decade, frequency is based on the number of tokens of the quantifier construction found in the corpus. To obtain such a count, I performed individual queries for all identified fillers, cleaned the results manually when necessary (e.g. removing from *un tas de* occurrences such as *'un tas de sable'*, 'a sandpile'), and then aggregated all fillers to get a count for the construction as a whole. Next, this number of tokens is divided by the corpus size - in number of words - associated with the decade. Finally, frequency is smoothed using a moving average over the five previous data points (e.g. the data point for the decade 1801-1810 is actually an average over the whole period 1761-1810).

The frequency profile of the quantifier construction (Figure 1) first features a pattern of latency (low frequency, slowly increasing), followed by an S-curve covering the whole sixteenth century. This pattern is commonly associated with the entrenchment of a linguistic unit (Croft, 2000; Aitchison, 2001; Blythe and Croft, 2012; Feltgen et al., 2017). That the frequency immediately decreases instead of stabilizing is a known phenomenon (Van de Velde and De Smet, 2021), but has not been associated with any semantic account so far. The subsequent and massive frequency rise does not follow a clear pattern, and is mostly due to the individual rise of three leading fillers: *nombre* ('number'), *foule* ('crowd'), and *infinité* ('infinity').

This observation is, in itself, interesting: first, during an entrenchment phase, the frequency rise of the construction is cohesive at the construction level, showing a well-formed S-curve. During this time, the functional scope of the free slot increases, but no individual filler drives the frequency profile of the construction. Next, the frequency profile of the post-S-curve period is dominated by individual fillers which become increasingly dominant over the paradigm. This clearly indicates that frequency of the construction alone, besides the well-established S-curve pattern, is not a reliable indicator of the functional changes undergone by the construction. More likely, after an early period of entrenchment, the frequency profile of the construction as a whole is mostly a by-product of the dynamics of the individual fillers. Therefore, to detect relevant changes at the constructional level, we must turn towards other quantitative measures.

3 Network of interactions

In this section, I present indicators of a major shift within the paradigmatic organization of the quantifier construction, based on the dynamical interactions between the paradigm members.

3.1 Building the network

3.1.1 Correlation matrices

The frequency profiles of the quantifiers are first extracted and computed individually. Next, we can measure the correlations between the different time series. However, it is pointless to compute the correlation over the series as a whole, since the corpus spans too long a time period: the correlation needs to be more local in time. Therefore, I decided to use a time window of 10 decades, which strikes a convenient balance between computing the correlation over a sufficiently long time series for the correlation to be meaningful, and over a sufficiently focused window to efficiently capture change phenomena. It also corresponds to the mean time of entrenchment of a form (Feltgen et al., 2017).

By computing such correlations, we can build matrices $A(t)$ for the time period t (e.g. 1451-1550), whose elements $A_{ij}(t)$ are the Pearson correlation coefficients between the frequencies of forms i and j over the corresponding time period.

Additionally, time series can show spurious correlations if they are driven by a common process, e.g. both individual forms could be driven by the frequency profile of the construction as a whole (Koplenig, 2018). Therefore, we complement this measure with a second correlation matrix, this time between the derivatives of the individual frequencies. For each time period, a matrix $B(t)$ is built for the correlations between the time series of the derivatives in the same way as $A(t)$ had been built. For a different method to compute correlation between the time series of word frequencies, the reader may refer to Koplenig (2017).

3.1.2 Filtering the matrices

At this point, the matrices need filtering, to only capture the interactions that are significant enough. Therefore, a matrix $C(t)$ is introduced, whose elements are 0 everywhere, except when both $A_{ij}(t) > \theta$ and $B_{ij}(t) > \theta$, in which case $C_{ij}(t)$ is set to 1, or when both $A_{ij}(t) < -\theta$ and $B_{ij}(t) < -\theta$, in which case $C_{ij}(t)$ is set to - 1. The threshold θ is set to 0.45. The rationale behind this choice is the following. We might want

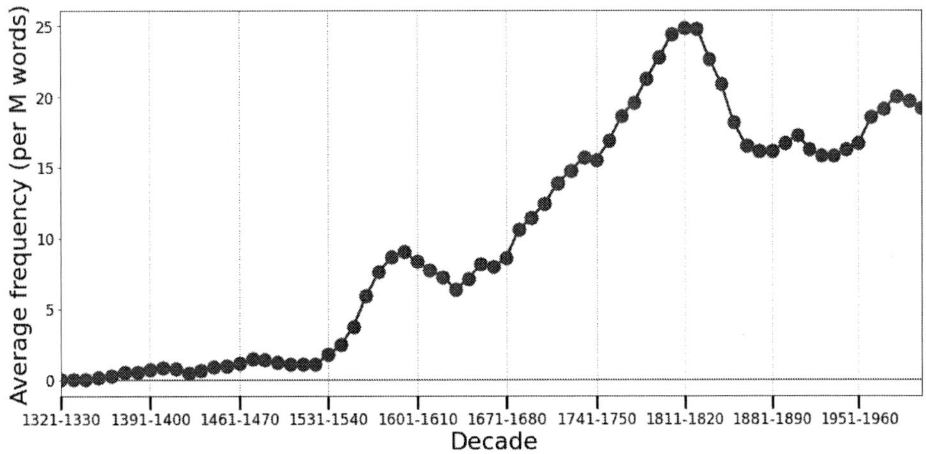

Figure 1: Smoothed frequency, per million words, of the quantifiers construction in the Frantext database.

to choose the threshold θ so that the p-value of observing such a value for the Pearson correlation coefficient is 0.05. However, if A and B are assumed to be independent, then the probability of a false positive for the joint observation of a correlation above the threshold for both quantities is $0.05^2 = 0.0025$, which is a much stricter threshold. Therefore, to set a p-value significance threshold at 0.05 for the joint observation, we must choose a Pearson correlation coefficient threshold over single quantities corresponding to a p-value of $\sqrt{0.05}$. For a Pearson correlation coefficient computed over 10 data points (our moving window covers this many points), this threshold is approximately 0.45.

From the $C(t)$ matrix, the network can be drawn by drawing two kind of links, correlation ones when $C_{ij}(t) = 1$ and anti-correlation ones when $C_{ij}(t) = -1$. In Figure 2, the latter are depicted with a thick extremity pointing towards the form whose derivative is the smaller on average over the time period considered. This way, a network of interactions between the fillers of the construction can be drawn for each time period. Note that the construction as a whole has been included among the inventory of forms, to track which cluster drives its frequency evolution; on the networks of Figure 2, the associated node is labeled 'paradigm'.

3.2 Results

The networks of earlier periods (from 1601-1610 onward) are very sparse and provide little insight into the paradigmatic dynamics. That the frequency increase over the seventeenth and eighteenth centuries is associated with the frequency rise of a few fillers that behave independently is corroborated by the sparsity of the interactions.

However, from 1791, two competing clusters are clearly emerging. On the one side, the entrenched quantifiers, with *foule* ('crowd'), *multitude* ('multitude') and *infinité* ('infinity'); on the other side, the innovative forms, with specific quantities such as *dizaine* ('dozen'), *millier* ('thousand'), etc. The cluster of entrenched quantifiers still drives the frequency profile of the construction, as evidenced by its correlation with the 'paradigm' node.

For the 1831-1930 and 1851-1950 windows, numerous anti-correlations are found between the members of the two major clusters, hinting at a competition. Since the anti-competition links point toward the members of the entrenched forms cluster, it shows that these forms are in decline relative to the forms belonging to the newly emerging cluster. The absence of anti-correlation links for the 1811-1910 network is however intriguing.

3.3 Further quantitative evidence of the cluster competition

The automated quantitative characterization of the fillers' interactions has evidenced two clusters competing against one another. However, one might argue that the identification of these two clusters only reveals that we have conflated within the same alleged quantifier construction, two separate constructions that are quite disparate in their scope and use. Therefore, we provide additional empirical evidence for the ongoing competition to stress the high level of interaction between the two groups.

Comparing the frequency profiles of the fillers

(a)

(b)

(c)

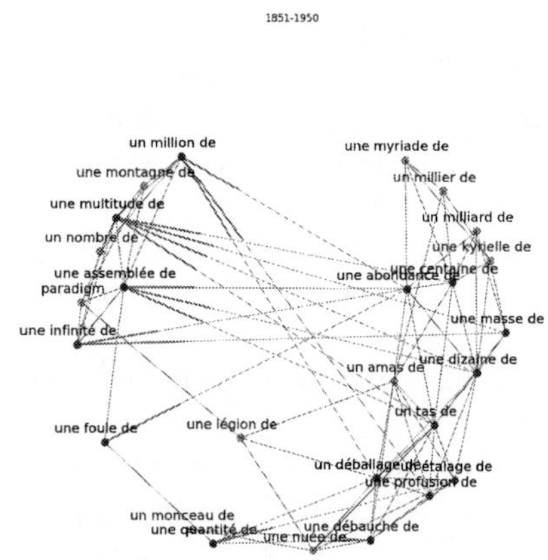

(d)

Figure 2: Network of interactions within the quantifiers construction paradigm, for four time periods: (a) 1791-1800; (b) 1811-1910; (c) 1831-1930; (d) 1851-1950. Simple edges (in blue) show correlation between nodes, edges with a wider end (in red) show an anti-correlation, and point towards the declining form.

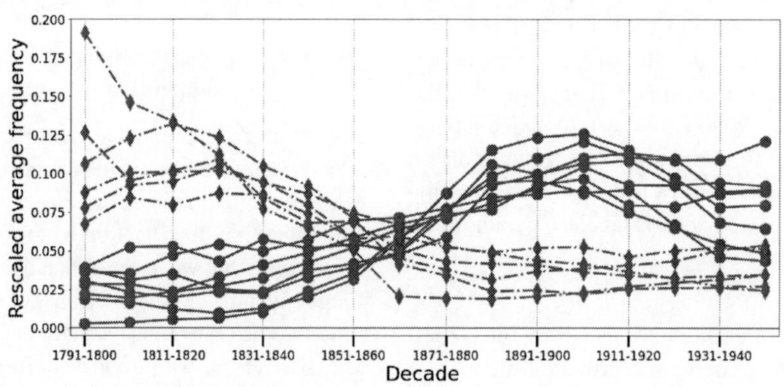

Figure 3: Rescaled frequencies of the fillers belonging to the two clusters identified through the network analysis (diamonds: entrenched members; circles: innovative members).

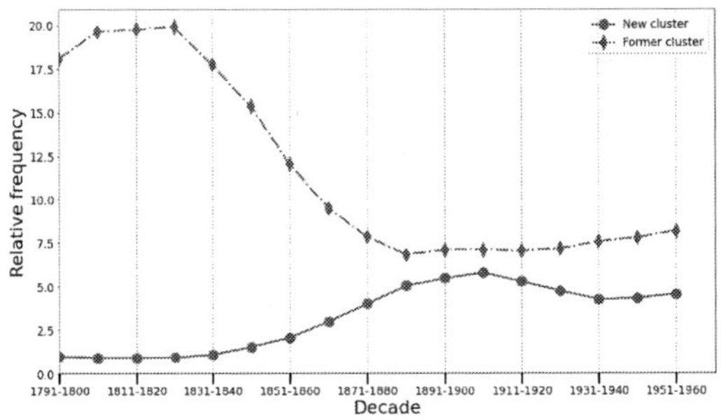

Figure 4: Frequencies, per million words, of the two clusters identified through the network analysis (diamonds: entrenched cluster; circles: innovative cluster).

is not straightforward, because different fillers can show very different magnitudes of frequency, due to the Zipfian structure of a paradigm organization (Ellis and Ogden, 2017). Therefore, we rescale each frequency profile by the mean frequency of the form for the time period under consideration (here 1791-1950, where the competition occurs). The rescaled frequencies shown in Figure 3 are clearly consistent with the competition picture.

If we furthermore plot the aggregated frequencies for each filler (Figure 4), it becomes apparent that the decline of the former cluster and the rise of the newer cluster are concomitant, even though the frequency gain of the innovative cluster does not compensate for the frequency loss of the entrenched one, which is reflected in the frequency decline of the construction as a whole. Interestingly, the outcome of this competition is a coexistence rather than an eviction of the former cluster, which remains dominant in terms of frequency.

4 Linguistic interpretation

Now that we have evidenced an ongoing competition between two different clusters of the quantifiers construction, it is worthwhile to shed light on the extent to which these clusters provide conflicting perspectives on the quantification of things. In order to better understand the functional range of each cluster, we can consider the arguments that are associated with each quantifier - that is to say, the individual paradigms of nouns attached to the single members of the construction.

Quantitative techniques based on word embeddings have been developed to automatically assess how the semantic organization of a constructional paradigm evolves diachronically Hilpert and Perek (2015); Perek (2016, 2018). An even more relevant quantitative tool to capture the semantic shift of the quantifiers is the cluster characterization based on collexeme analysis (Gries and Stefanowitsch, 2010). Since a range of methods already exist, and their application to this case study would constitute a contribution in itself, yet without any original methodology to offer, I shall remain here at a qualitative level. The more modest goal of this section is therefore to briefly illustrate how the dynamics-based methods outlined above evidence phenomena that make sense from a linguistic point of view. In what follows, I discuss the functional roles of each different fillers by simply looking at their ten most frequent collocates.

4.1 Entrenched cluster semantics

The ten most frequent arguments of the main five quantifiers of the entrenched cluster are listed on Table 1. First, generic arguments, such as *gens* ('people'), *hommes* ('men') and *choses* ('things'), are associated with most quantifiers. Next, *assemblée* ('gathering') and *quantité* ('quantity') immediately stand out from the other three quantifiers. Indeed, the former is almost exclusively used to quantify people, in agreement with its immediate lexical root, while the latter is often associated with uncountable things, like *eau* ('water') and *argent* ('money'), although its representation may be biased by its strong association with scientific texts (*quantité de chaleur* is the French name for heat energy in thermodynamics). In contrast to this, *nombre* is mostly associated with countable arguments, such as *cas* ('cases'), *fois* ('times'), *jours* ('days'), *exemplaires* ('copies'). It is also revealing that *quantité* is associated with *gens* ('people'), while *nombre* is associated with *individuals* ('individuals'): both refers to groups of persons, yet one underlines their indistinction and uncountability, while the other conceives them as separate entities.

The quantifier *foule* is often associated with abstract things, e.g. *idées* ('ideas'), *détails* ('details'), *questions* ('questions'), while *multitude* shows a surprising specialization into generic categories, as with *oiseaux* ('birds'), *insectes* ('insects'), *plantes* ('plants'), *êtres* ('beings'). After *un nombre de*, which remains the most frequent quantifier throughout the studied period, *une foule de* and *une multitude de* are respectively the second and third most frequent quantifiers of the entrenched cluster.

To summarize, the different roles of the quantifiers of this cluster are distinguished by ontological

nombre (number)	**multitude**	**foule** (crowd)	**quantité** (quantity)	**assemblée** (gathering)
hommes (men)	hommes (men)	choses (things)	chaleur (heat)	hommes (men)
heures (hours)	êtres (beings)	hommes (men)	choses (things)	femmes (women)
années (years)	faits (facts)	gens (people)	eau (water)	notables
exemplaires (copies)	choses (things)	idées (ideas)	gens (people)	gens (people)
fois (times)	idées (ideas)	détails	mots (words)	législateurs (lawmakers)
jours (days)	oiseaux (birds)	questions	lettres (letters)	médecins (doctors)
cas (cases)	objets (objects)	objets (objects)	acide (acid)	créanciers (creditors)
coups (blows)	plantes (plants)	faits (facts)	produits (products)	députés (deputies)
députés (deputies)	gens (people)	cas (cases)	argent (money)	évêques (bishops)
individus (individuals)	insectes (insects)	mots (words)	hommes (men)	poètes (poets)

Table 1: List of the ten most frequent quantified nouns for each of the five most prominent quantifiers of the entrenched cluster. I did not gloss words that are the same as their English counterparts.

considerations; they are sensitive to *what* is quantified. Furthermore, they are all impressively vague regarding the actual quantity of what they quantify: *quantité* ('quantity') and *nombre* ('number') could not be more generic, while *foule* ('crowd') and *multitude* only hints at a 'big' quantity.

4.2 Innovative cluster semantics

The arguments of the innovative cluster of quantifiers are displayed on Table 2. First of all, a lot of quantifiers become available to express the quantity in a pretty precise way: *dizaine*, *douzaine*, *vingtaine*, *centaine*, *millier*, etc. Comparing the arguments for *dizaine* and *centaine* shows that they follow very similar semantic distributions. Their arguments are items that typically need to be counted and quantified. As such, there is a significant overlap with the semantic profile of *un nombre de*.

The quantifier *nuée* ('cloud') draws on metaphoric expansion: *une nuée d'oiseaux* ('a cloud of birds'), *une nuée de flèches* ('a cloud of arrows'), are transparent, while *une nuée de solliciteurs* ('a cloud of petitioners') goes one step further on the metaphorical expansion path, and leans more towards a pure quantifier meaning. Interestingly, the arguments of *nuée* are widely different from those of the other members, while the semantic profiles of the fillers belonging to the entrenched cluster all had a more extensive overlap. This observation also applies in the case of *profusion*, whose arguments, with the exception of *détails*, are not commonly associated with the other quantifiers. Most of the arguments here indicate that *profusion* emphasizes the excess of futile or superfluous items.

Finally, *un tas de* ('a heap of') seems to take on the semantic role of *une foule de*, but its arguments are more disparate. It is remarkable that *un tas de* doubles up on the expression of indetermination; not only, as a quantifier, it expresses an uncertain quantity, but it also preferentially associates with undetermined arguments such as *choses* and *trucs*. Importantly, *un tas de* is by far the most frequent of the fillers of the innovative cluster, and as an outcome of the competition, it becomes also more frequent than *une foule de*, becoming thus the second most frequent quantifier after *un nombre de*.

The semantic pattern of quantification expressed by this innovative cluster is less clear than that of the entrenched cluster. On the one hand, a large family of quantifiers allows for an accurate assessment of the quantity in which the quantifiee is found; on the other hand, very specific quantifiers also appear, that no longer highlight which sort of things are quantified, but how the plurality comes to constitute a quantity: a lot of small things that coalesce into a whole (*nuée*), a profligate plethora of frivolities or luxury items (*profusion*), a disorganized collection of assorted stuff (*tas*). In that sense, the pragmatic coloring of these quantifiers is stronger than that of the former cluster.

Crucially, the two clusters offer two very different strategies to delineate the semantic space associated with the quantification: the first cluster focuses on the nature of what is quantified, while the second cluster focuses on how the set of items manifests itself *as a quantity*, leading to more heterogeneous semantic distributions that may span an arbitrary number of ontological categories.

5 Conclusion

Language change, as it unfolds over several, interrelated levels of the linguistic organization, is inherently complex. To understand the diachronic processes that a form or a construction participates in, tracking its frequency soon faces drastic limitations: besides the S-curve pattern of entrenchment, frequency is volatile and extremely variable, for no

profusion (multitude)	**tas** (heap)	**dizaine** (dozen)	**centaine** (hundred)	**nuée** (cloud)
fleurs (flowers)	choses (things)	années (years)	mètres (meters)	oiseaux (birds)
détails	gens (people)	jours (days)	francs	sauterelles (locusts)
colonnes (columns)	histoires (stories)	mètres (meters)	pas (steps)	moucherons (swats)
chevaux (horses)	bêtises (faults)	minutes	années (years)	solliciteurs (petitioners)
mosaïques (mosaics)	livres (books)	hommes (men)	hommes (men)	moineaux (sparrows)
ornements (ornaments)	monde (people)	pas (steps)	personnes (people)	étincelles (sparks)
couleurs (colors)	trucs (things)	personnes (people)	pieds (plants)	pierres (stones)
dentelles (laceworks)	idées (ideas)	kilomètres (kms)	millions	flèches (arrows)
mets (dishes)	questions	fois (times)	pages	hannetons (cockchafers)
roses	raisons (reasons)	pages	écus (crowns)	copeaux (shavings)

Table 2: List of the ten most frequent quantified nouns for each of the five most prominent quantifiers of the innovative cluster.

evident reason. Here, I have argued that we can achieve a fine-grained understanding of the process by looking at the interactions between the members of a constructional schema. I have offered a computational method to track and visualize such interactions, a method that can be perfected and further automatized, e.g. with the use of clustering algorithms. The picture that emerges remains highly complex, but the large cluster-to-cluster competitions that the method can evidence may lead to a fascinating linguistic insight into the fine-grained processes of language change.

When considering schematic constructions, that is, constructions that can host a variety of fillers, similarly to an ecological niche, change can occur on three levels: 1) on the level of the individual fillers (whenever they undergo functional change); 2) on the level of the construction, typically through the recruitment or loss of new fillers, that is, through changes in its syntactic productivity (Sánchez-Marco and Evert, 2011); and finally 3) in the way the fillers are organized within the construction, that is, on the paradigm level, leading to a new way to categorize the semantic space on which the construction applies. Although all three changes are expected to occur to an extent in a given process, such a process can be better characterized by one or the other of these changes.

All these changes are instances of semantic shifts; while it is clear that the first two changes affect meaning (that of the individual filler in 1, that of the construction as a whole in 2), the third kind of change is less obvious. Yet, as it redefines the categories in which the arguments of the construction are partitioned, it evidences different features of these arguments. This kind of semantic shift is especially prevalent when considering tight categories applying to a broad class of words, such as determiners, classifiers, or auxiliaries. Examples of this shift are the emergence of French demonstratives (Marchello-Nizia, 2006) or the change in the auxiliaries in Old Spanish (Mateu, 2009).

In our example of the French paradigm of quantifiers, we have shown that the construction underwent a significant paradigmatic change in the 1801-1950 period. This paradigmatic change can be related, at least on a qualitative level, to semantic considerations regarding the logic underlying the different partitioning of nouns by the two competing clusters. Individual change does not seem to play a large role in this picture, even though *un nombre de* is more versatile than the other quantifiers and is likely to have undergone a semantic shift. Constructional change does occur to some extent (the nouns covered by the innovative cluster do not all overlap with the nouns covered by the entrenched cluster). Among the innovative quantifiers, those tied to a precise quantity such as *une douzaine de* ('a dozen') are the more likely to be associated with new nouns, indicative of a semantic opening of the quantifier construction towards a 'measure' meaning, while it was more closely associated to a 'count' one (Unterbeck, 1994). This latter change may also be due to an increasing proportion of scientific texts in the corpus. Yet, the remarkable cluster competition that unfolds throughout the nineteenth century is testimony enough that the paradigm level is the most suited to understand the change phenomenon in this period.

This study is a first step, an invitation to consider more systematically language change from a systemic perspective, especially with the help of automated tools, that are most needed to deal with the intrinsic complexity of these systems. Although the analysis presented here could be refined with the use of a wider range of methods, I hope that the results are intriguing enough to foster further interest in changes unfolding on the paradigm level.

References

Jean Aitchison. 2001. *Language change: Progress or decay?* Cambridge university press.

ATILF. 1998. Base textuelle frantext (en ligne).

Richard A Blythe and William Croft. 2012. S-curves and the mechanisms of propagation in language change. *Language*, pages 269–304.

Kathie Carpenter. 1992. Two dynamic views of classifier systems: Diachronic change and individual development. *Cognitive Linguistics*, 3(2):129–150.

Corpus and language statistics for corpora of the Leipzig Corpora Collection. 2021. Corpus: fra_news_2021 - the most frequent 50 words.

William Croft. 2000. *Explaining language change: An evolutionary approach.* Pearson Education.

Thomas Eckart and Uwe Quasthoff. 2013. Statistical corpus and language comparison on comparable corpora. In *Building and using comparable corpora*, pages 151–165. Springer.

Nick C Ellis and Dave C Ogden. 2017. Thinking about multiword constructions: Usage-based approaches to acquisition and processing. *Topics in Cognitive Science*, 9(3):604–620.

Benjamin Fagard and Michel Charolles. 2018. Ailleurs, d'ailleurs, par ailleurs: De l'espace à l'humain, de l'humain au discours. *Journal of French Language Studies*, 28(3):351–375.

Benjamin Fagard and Bernard Combettes. 2013. De en à dans, un simple remplacement? une étude diachronique. *Langue française*, 178(2):93–115.

Quentin Feltgen, Benjamin Fagard, and J-P Nadal. 2017. Frequency patterns of semantic change: corpus-based evidence of a near-critical dynamics in language change. *Royal Society open science*, 4(11):170830.

Stefan Th Gries and Anatol Stefanowitsch. 2010. Cluster analysis and the identification of collexeme classes. In *Empirical and experimental methods in cognitive/functional research*, pages 73–90. CSLI Publications.

Martin Hilpert and Florent Perek. 2015. Meaning change in a petri dish: constructions, semantic vector spaces, and motion charts. *Linguistics Vanguard*, 1(1):339–350.

Michael Israel. 1996. The way constructions grow. *Conceptual structure, discourse and language*, 217:230.

Alexander Koplenig. 2017. A data-driven method to identify (correlated) changes in chronological corpora. *Journal of Quantitative Linguistics*, 24(4):289–318.

Alexander Koplenig. 2018. Using the parameters of the zipf–mandelbrot law to measure diachronic lexical, syntactical and stylistic changes–a large-scale corpus analysis. *Corpus Linguistics and Linguistic Theory*, 14(1):1–34.

Anthony S Kroch. 1989. Reflexes of grammar in patterns of language change. *Language variation and change*, 1(3):199–244.

Christiane Marchello-Nizia. 2000. Les grammaticalisations ont-elles une cause? le cas de beaucoup, moult et tres en moyen français. *L'information grammaticale*, 87(1):3–9.

Christiane Marchello-Nizia. 2006. Du subjectif au spatial: l'évolution des formes et du sens des démonstratifs en français. *Langue française*, 152(4):114–126.

Jaume Mateu. 2009. Gradience and auxiliary selection in old catalan and old spanish. In *Historical syntax and linguistic theory*, pages 176–193. Oxford University Press Oxford.

William B McGregor. 2018. The history of verb classification in nyulnyulan languages. In *The Diachrony of Classification Systems*, pages 315–351. John Benjamins Publishing Company.

Tomáš Mikolov, Wen-tau Yih, and Geoffrey Zweig. 2013. Linguistic regularities in continuous space word representations. In *Proceedings of the 2013 conference of the north american chapter of the association for computational linguistics: Human language technologies*, pages 746–751.

Steve Nicolle. 1998. A relevance theory perspective on grammaticalization. *Cognitive Linguistics*, 9(1):1–35.

Florent Perek. 2016. Using distributional semantics to study syntactic productivity in diachrony: A case study. *Linguistics*, 54(1):149–188.

Florent Perek. 2018. Recent change in the productivity and schematicity of the way-construction: A distributional semantic analysis. *Corpus Linguistics and Linguistic Theory*, 14(1):65–97.

Peter Petré and Hubert Cuyckens. 2008. The old english copula weorðan and its replacement in middle english. In *English historical linguistics 2006: selected papers from the fourteenth international conference on English historical linguistics (ICEHL 14), Bergamo 21-25 August 2006*, pages 23–48. John Benjamins Publishing Company.

Cristina Sánchez-Marco and Stefan Evert. 2011. Measuring semantic change: The case of spanish participial constructions. In *Proceedings of Quantitative Investigations in Theoretical Linguistics*, pages 79–83.

Sali A Tagliamonte and Jennifer Smith. 2021. Obviously undergoing change: Adverbs of evidentiality across time and space. *Language Variation and Change*, 33(1):81–105.

Elizabeth Closs Traugott and Graeme Trousdale. 2013. *Constructionalization and constructional changes*, volume 6. Oxford University Press.

Barbara Unterbeck. 1994. Korean classifiers. In *Theoretical issues in Korean linguistics*, pages 367–385. Center for the Study of Language (CSLI).

Freek Van de Velde and Isabeau De Smet. 2021. Markov models for multi-state language change. *Journal of Quantitative Linguistics*, pages 1–25.

Do Not Fire the Linguist: Grammatical Profiles Help Language Models Detect Semantic Change

Mario Giulianelli[*] ILLC, University of Amsterdam m.giulianelli@uva.nl

Andrey Kutuzov[*] University of Oslo andreku@ifi.uio.no

Lidia Pivovarova University of Helsinki first.last@helsinki.fi

Abstract

Morphological and syntactic changes in word usage—as captured, e.g., by grammatical profiles—have been shown to be good predictors of a word's meaning change. In this work, we explore whether large pre-trained contextualised language models, a common tool for lexical semantic change detection, are sensitive to such morphosyntactic changes. To this end, we first compare the performance of grammatical profiles against that of a multilingual neural language model (XLM-R) on 10 datasets, covering 7 languages, and then combine the two approaches in ensembles to assess their complementarity. Our results show that ensembling grammatical profiles with XLM-R improves semantic change detection performance for most datasets and languages. This indicates that language models do not fully cover the fine-grained morphological and syntactic signals that are explicitly represented in grammatical profiles.

An interesting exception are the test sets where the time spans under analysis are much longer than the time gap between them (for example, century-long spans with a one-year gap between them). Morphosyntactic change is slow so grammatical profiles do not detect in such cases. In contrast, language models, thanks to their access to lexical information, are able to detect fast topical changes.

1 Introduction

Human language is in continuous evolution. New word senses arise, and existing senses can change or disappear over time as a result of social and cultural dynamics or technological advances. NLP practitioners have become increasingly interested in this diachronic perspective of semantics. Some works focus on constructing, testing and improving psycholinguistic and sociolinguistic theories of meaning change (Xu and Kemp, 2015; Hamilton et al., 2016; Goel et al., 2016; Noble et al., 2021); others are concerned with surveying how the meaning of words has evolved historically (Garg et al., 2018; Kozlowski et al., 2019) or how it is currently transforming in public discourse (Azarbonyad et al., 2017; Del Tredici et al., 2019). Recently, we also see increased interest in more application-oriented work, with efforts to develop adaptive learning systems that can remain up-to-date with humans' continuously evolving language use (*temporal generalization*; Lazaridou et al., 2021).

An increasingly popular way to determine whether and to what degree the meaning of words has changed over time is to use 'contextualised' (or 'token-based') word embeddings extracted from large pre-trained language models (Giulianelli et al., 2020; Montariol et al., 2021) as they encode rich, context-sensitive semantic information. However, it has also been shown recently that changes in the frequency distribution of morphological and syntactic features of words, as captured by *grammatical profiles*, can also be employed for lexical semantic change detection (Giulianelli et al., 2021), with competitive performance. These are, to some extent, two opposing approaches: while language models (LMs) are largely based on word co-occurrence statistics, grammatical profiles are de-lexicalised and rely on explicit linguistic information.

Although they are superficially unaware of morphology and syntax, LMs have been shown to capture approximations of grammatical information in their deep representations (Warstadt et al., 2020). Yet are these sufficient to detect meaning shifts that are accompanied by morphosyntactic changes in word usage? We hypothesise that this is not the case, and to test this hypothesis, we combine LM-based methods and grammatical profiles into ensemble models of lexical semantic change detection.[1] If adding grammatical profiles to LMs re-

[*] Equal contribution, the authors are listed alphabetically.

[1] Throughout the paper, we refer to the systems that com-

Proceedings of the 3rd Workshop on Computational Approaches to Historical Language Change, pages 54 - 67
May 26-27, 2022 ©2022 Association for Computational Linguistics

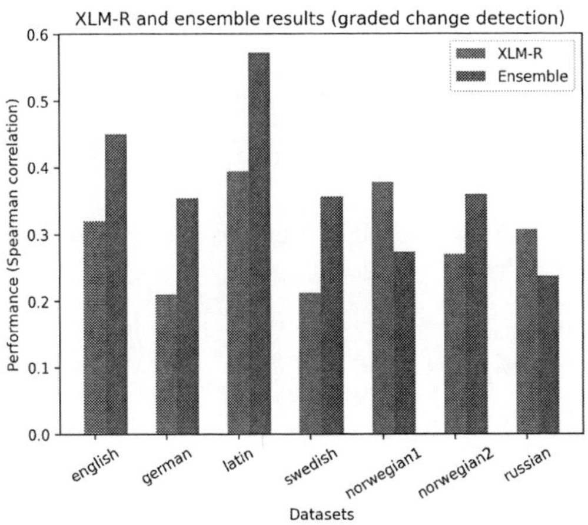

Figure 1: Performance of an XLM-R based method (PRT) and an ensemble method (PRT-MORPHSYNT) on the ranking task; see Section 3 for method descriptions. The scores for the three Russian datasets are averaged as they exhibit similar trends.

sults in a boost in performance, then this means that LMs do not capture morphosyntactic change as accurately as explicit morphological tagging and syntactic parsing (or at the very least that it is difficult to extract this type of information from the models). If we do not observe any boost, this suggests that LMs already represent all the necessary grammatical information and explicit linguistic annotation is not required. We conduct our experiments with 10 datasets, covering 7 languages. For comparability, we use the same model for all the languages. We choose XLM-R (Conneau et al., 2020), a multilingual Transformer-based masked language model which has already been successfully applied to the semantic change detection task (Arefyev and Zhikov, 2020; Arefyev et al., 2021). Although it covers the full linguistic diversity of our data, we additionally fine-tune XLM-R on monolingual diachronic corpora.

Our quantitative and qualitative evaluation of the resulting ensembles on the graded and binary semantic change detection tasks largely confirm our hypothesis. Ensembling XLM-R and grammatical profiles improves the results for 4 out of 6 languages in graded change detection (as well as for 1 of the 2 Norwegian datasets) and for 5 out of 6 languages in binary change detection. Figure 1 illustrates these improvements. The reasons why ensembles do not outperform the XLM-R baseline on some datasets are linked to the size of the gaps between the historical time periods represented in the diachronic corpora; we analyse and discuss these reasons in Section 4.3. Overall, we show that providing large language models with explicit morphosyntactic information helps them quantify semantic change.

2 Tasks and Data

The goal of lexical semantic change detection is to determine whether and to what extent a word's meaning has changed over a certain period of time. The performance of automatic systems that address this problem is typically assessed in two tasks (Schlechtweg et al., 2020). **Task 1** is a binary classification task: given a diachronic corpus and a set of target words, a system must determine whether the words lost or gained any senses between two time periods. We refer to it as the *classification task* and use accuracy as an evaluation metric. **Task 2** is a ranking task: a system must rank the target words according to the degree of their semantic change. We refer to it as the *ranking task* and use the Spearman rank-correlation with the gold rankings as an evaluation metric.

We rely on a collection of diachronic corpora and annotated target word lists covering seven languages from three Indo-European language families. Target words are annotated with binary and graded scores of semantic change, corresponding respectively to Task 1 and 2 (Schlechtweg et al., 2018). English (EN), German (DE), Latin (LA), and Swedish (SW) data are available from the SemEval 2020 Unsupervised Lexical Semantic Change Detection shared task (Schlechtweg et al., 2020). For Italian (IT), we use the data released for the EvaLita competition (Basile et al., 2020). For Norwegian (NO), we use the NorDiaChange dataset recently released by Kutuzov et al. (2022), consisting of two subsets with different target word lists and time spans. Finally, for Russian (RU), we draw from the RuShiftEval shared task (Kutuzov and Pivovarova, 2021), consisting of three subsets with different time spans and a shared target word list. Table 1 summarises the most important properties of the datasets and indicates what types of annotations are available for each language. Note that the subset splitting in Norwegian and Russian is not introduced by us, but is provided by the corresponding dataset creators.

bine LMs with grammatical profiles as 'ensembles'. These are not statistical methods of *ensemble learning* but systems that combine the predictions of different models.

	EN	DE	IT	LA	NO-1	NO-2	RU-1	RU-2	RU-3	SW
Period 1	1810-1860	1800-1899	1945-1970	-200-0	1929-1965	1980-1990	1700-1916	1918-1990	1700-1916	1790-1830
Period 2	1960-2010	1946-1990	1990-2014	0-2000	1970-2013	2012-2019	1918-1990	1992-2016	1992-2016	1895-1903
Tokens (mln)	7+7	70+72	52+197	2+9	57+175	43+649	93+122	122+107	93+107	71+110
Targets	37	48	18	40	80	80	99	99	99	32
Ranking	✓	✓	✗	✓	✓	✓	✓	✓	✓	✓
Classification	✓	✓	✓	✓	✓	✗	✗	✗	✗	✓

Table 1: Statistics for our collection of diachronic corpora and of the corresponding semantic change annotations.

3 Methods

3.1 Grammatical Profiles

Grammatical profiling is a corpus linguistic technique which allows to distinguish subtle semantic differences by measuring the distance between distributions of grammatical parameters (Gries and Divjak, 2009; Janda and Lyashevskaya, 2011). It has been shown recently that diachronic changes in grammatical profiles can serve as a strong indication of semantic change (Giulianelli et al., 2021). For our experiments we adopt this method in its best performing configuration.

First, the diachronic corpus of interest is tagged and parsed using UDPipe (Straka and Straková, 2017). We then find all occurrences of a target word in the corpus and create a count vector for each detected morphological feature. For example, a morphological profile for an English verb could look as follows:

```
Tense :  {Past 42, Pres 51}
VerbForm :  {Part 68, Fin 25, Inf 9}
Mood :  {Ind 25}
Voice :  {Pass :  17}
```

In this way, count vectors are constructed for each target word in each time period of the corpus; these are a word's grammatical profiles. The cosine distance between count vectors is computed separately for every morphological category, and the degree of semantic change between periods is measured as the maximum among the computed cosine distances. We refer to this type of grammatical profile as **MORPH**.

In addition to morphological features, a separate vector of syntactic features is created, which contains counts of dependency arc labels from a target word to its syntactic head. We refer to these grammatical profiles as **SYNT**. Semantic change is measured as the cosine distance between two syntactic vectors. Morphological and syntactic profiles can also be combined. We do this by concatenating syntactic features to the array of morphological features, and then using the maximum cosine distance as our third profile-based measure of semantic change, **MORPHSYNT**.

3.2 Static Embeddings

Static embeddings (e.g., Mikolov et al., 2013) are known to perform very well at detecting lexical semantic change (Schlechtweg et al., 2020). Therefore, although they are not directly relevant to our research question, we include them in our experiments as a point of comparison, following the common approach proposed by Hamilton et al. (2016). Further details can be found in Appendix B.

3.3 Contextualised Embeddings

Many have argued that static representations are not theoretically appropriate as a model of word meaning because they conflate all the usages of a word into a single context-independent embedding, and that contextualised representations should be used instead (e.g., Schütze, 1998; Erk and Padó, 2008; Pilehvar and Collier, 2016). This has motivated the development of semantic change detection algorithms that rely on context-dependent representations, where every usage of a word corresponds to a unique *token embedding* (Giulianelli et al., 2020; Martinc et al., 2020a). Language models produce very competitive results across languages (Kutuzov and Giulianelli, 2020), and they lead to more interpretable systems (Montariol et al., 2021).

We choose XLM-R (Conneau et al., 2020) as our pre-trained language model, since it was shown to perform well in semantic change shared tasks (Schlechtweg et al., 2020; Kutuzov and Pivovarova, 2021) and because, being multilingual, it can be applied to all languages under analysis, making evaluation more consistent. First, we finetune XLM-R on the monolingual diachronic corpora of interest. Then, we deploy it to produce token embeddings for the target words in the diachronic corpus (in both time periods, T1 and T2). Further details on these two steps can be found in Appendix A. We compute graded semantic change scores based on the extracted XLM-R embeddings and we use the scores to compile an ordered list of target words for the ranking task. Change scores are computed in four ways: 1) measuring the average pairwise cosine distance (**APD**) between embeddings collected in T1 and those in T2 (Giulianelli et al., 2020); 2) measuring the cosine distance between prototype embeddings (**PRT**)—i.e., the average contextualised word embeddings of T1 and T2 (Kutuzov and Giulianelli, 2020); 3) clustering the embeddings and then calculating the Jensen-Shannon Divergence (**JSD**) between the putative sense distributions of T1 and T2 (Martinc et al., 2020b; Giulianelli et al., 2020); 4) by taking a simple average (**APD-PRT**) of the predictions made by PRT and APD. The mathematical definitions of the metrics are given in Appendix A.4.

3.4 Change Point Detection

To solve the classification task, we transform the continuous scores produced by our three metrics into binary semantic change predictions. Following Giulianelli et al. (2021), we rank target words according to their continuous scores and classify the top n words in the ranking as 'changed' (1) and the rest of the list as 'stable' (0). To determine the change point n, we apply an offline change point detection algorithm (Truong et al., 2020) with the default settings.[2]

3.5 Ensembling

To find out whether grammatical profiles can improve the performance of embedding-based detection methods, we test all possible combinations of grammatical profile types and embedding-based metrics. Grammatical profiles come in three variants: MORPH, SYNT, and MORPHSYNT. Our embedding-based measures include APD, PRT, APD-PRT, and JSD. We compute the geometric mean $\sqrt{c_g c_e}$ between the change score c_g obtained using grammatical profiles and the score c_e output by an embedding-based metric, and use the resulting value as the ensemble semantic change score (e.g., **PRT-MORPHSYNT**).

4 Results

We assess the performance of all methods presented in Section 3 on both semantic change detection tasks using our multilingual collection of semantic change datasets (see Section 2).

[2]https://pypi.org/project/ruptures/

4.1 Ranking Task

For all methods, the Spearman rank-correlation between predicted scores and human annotations varies across languages and test sets; no method is a silver bullet for the ranking task (see Table 2). XLM-R obtains higher correlation scores in English, Swedish, Norwegian-1, and Russian (1, 2, and 3); whereas grammatical profiles outperform it in German, Latin, Swedish, and Norwegian-2. To better understand the strengths of all methods, we now first present the results of each of them individually; then we report the performance of ensembles, where each method is combined with every other to generate semantic change predictions.

Grammatical Profiles Whether morphological features, syntactic features, or a combination of both are the most effective depends on the dataset; this also varies across test sets of the same language, as can be seen in the first three rows of Table 2. The performance of the different features diverges mostly for English and Norwegian-1, where SYNT is the best approach, as well as for Norwegian-2 and Russian, where MORPH works best. Combining morphological and syntactic features helps creating better rankings for German, Latin, and Swedish.

Contextualised Embeddings The correlation scores of average pairwise distance (APD) and prototype distance (PRT) differ substantially for all datasets, with the exception of Norwegian-1 (see rows 4-7 of Table 2). APD outperforms PRT on English, Swedish, Norwegian, and Russian; PRT is better on German and Latin. Combining the two metrics in an ensemble (APD-PRT) marginally improves correlation scores for Norwegian-1 and Russian-1. Clustering contextualised embeddings (JSD) yields unstable results across datasets; it is the best contextualised method only for German.

Ensembles Whenever grammatical profiles produce better rankings than XLM-R, i.e., for German, Latin, Swedish, and Norwegian-2, combining the predictions of the two methods yields higher correlation scores than either method in isolation. The most effective contextualised method in combination with grammatical profiles is PRT, regardless of the profile type. The PRT-MORPHSYNT combination produces the overall best ranking for German and Latin, two languages with rich syntax and morphology. Which type of grammatical profile is the most complementary to XLM-R varies across datasets and it mostly corresponds to the profile type that obtains the best performance in isolation. Ensembles with JSD are outperformed by other methods, so we do not report them in Tables 2 and 3.

Static embeddings, despite their good performance in isolation, do not combine well with grammatical profiles: this type of ensemble improves correlation scores only for Latin (Table 4). As a final note, ensembles of grammatical profiles and XLM-R achieve the new best performance on the Latin ranking task of SemEval 2020 (PRT-MORPHSYNT), and establish a new SOTA for the recently released Norwegian-2 dataset (APD-MORPH).

4.2 Classification Task

Although our binary predictions for the classification task are dependent on the rankings discussed in the previous section, the overall trends of classification accuracy partly differ from the correlation trends of the ranking task. The classification results are shown in Table 3. Compared to the ranking task, ensemble methods more often produce a performance improvement with respect to grammatical profiles and contextualised embeddings used in isolation. They do so for English, German, Latin, and both Norwegian datasets. It is also more often the case that the best standalone profile and contextualised approach yield the best ensemble when combined. Another notable difference is that, when used in isolation, profiles outperform XLM-R; the opposite is true in the ranking task.

Following the structure of Section 4.1, we first present the results of each approach individually and then we report the performance of ensembles.

Grammatical Profiles At least one of the three profile types is substantially above chance performance for each language; as in the ranking task, different profile types fit different datasets. Nevertheless, SYNT is the best profile type for 4 out of 7 datasets: German, Swedish, Norwegian-1, and Italian. For the first two, it achieves the best overall scores (see Table 3). Combining morphology and syntax helps only in the case of Latin, where profiles obtain the best overall accuracy.

Contextualised Embeddings The accuracy of APD and PRT is relatively similar across test sets, with the exception of Italian, where APD has the best overall accuracy and PRT is slightly below chance. Combining APD and PRT improves results for English, German, and Norwegian. The accuracy of clustering-based JSD is either close to or below chance level for all languages.

Ensembles Ensembles of grammatical profiles and contextualised embeddings are the best performing method for Norwegian. For German and Latin they are on par with pure profiles, and for English on par with pure XLM-R. The complementarity of different profile types and contextualised metrics varies across datasets yet it is overall stronger than that between profiles and static embeddings (combining the latter two improves performance only for Latin and for Norwegian-2, see Appendix B). A more fine-grained analysis of the classification results of the ensembles reveals that 1) ensemble predictions are virtually always correct when the two standalone predictions also are, 2) ensembling tends to have positive effects on precision with respect to both standalone methods, and 3) it tends to improve the precision of contextualised methods.

4.3 Why ensembles fail

Tables 2 and 3 show that grammatical profiles are consistently worse than XLM-R on all Russian datasets, Norwegian-1 and English. This naturally extends to their ensembles, so for all these datasets, contextualised embeddings in isolation are the best approach. The explanation may seem simple for English: its poor morphology does not provide enough signal for semantic change detection. Yet this does not hold for Russian (a synthetic language with rich morphology) and, arguably, for Norwegian. Moreover, ensembles with morphology-based grammatical profiles outperform pure XLM-R on Norwegian-2, but not on Norwegian-1. Thus, the explanation is likely not language-specific.

We believe that the different nature of the diachronic corpora can be a better explaining factor. SemEval-2020 datasets feature time periods separated by at least several decades, and the same is true for Norwegian-2 (more than 20 years gap). In contrast, the gaps are much shorter for Norwegian-1 (5 years gap), Russian-1 and Russian-2 (2 years gap). We observe that when two time periods with a very short gap between them are compared, the distributions of morphosyntactic features largely overlap, negatively affecting the performance of grammatical profiles. In these cases, LM-based methods can still detect semantic change as they have access to lexical information: changes at the

Method	EN	DE	LA	SW	NO-1	NO-2	RU-1	RU-2	RU-3	AVG
					PROFILES					
MORPH	0.218	0.120	0.519	0.303	0.106	*0.409*	0.028	*0.241*	*0.293*	*0.248*
SYNT	*0.331*	0.146	0.265	0.184	*0.179*	0.006	*0.056*	0.111	0.279	0.173
MORPHSYNT	0.320	*0.298*	*0.525*	*0.334*	0.064	0.265	0.000	0.149	0.242	0.244
					CONTEXTUALISED (XLM-R)					
APD	***0.514***	0.073	0.162	*0.310*	0.389	*0.387*	0.372	***0.480***	***0.457***	*0.349*
PRT	0.320	0.210	*0.394*	0.212	0.378	0.270	0.294	0.313	0.313	0.300
APD-PRT	0.457	0.202	0.370	0.220	***0.394***	0.325	***0.376***	0.374	0.384	**0.345**
Clustering/JSD	0.127	*0.287*	0.318	-0.108	0.160	-0.137	0.247	0.267	0.362	0.169
					ENSEMBLES					
APD-MORPH	0.262	0.140	0.506	0.350	0.151	***0.503***	0.062	*0.288*	0.340	0.289
APD-SYNT	0.384	0.159	0.264	0.255	*0.262*	0.119	*0.093*	0.181	*0.354*	0.230
APD-MORPHSYNT	*0.390*	*0.290*	*0.513*	***0.397***	0.180	0.364	0.036	0.216	0.299	*0.298*
PRT-MORPH	0.278	0.204	0.528	0.305	0.236	*0.478*	0.112	*0.309*	0.336	0.309
PRT-SYNT	0.448	0.213	0.401	0.280	*0.351*	0.146	*0.186*	0.246	*0.351*	0.291
PRT-MORPHSYNT	*0.451*	***0.354***	***0.572***	*0.356*	0.273	0.360	0.117	0.269	0.326	*0.342*
APD-PRT-MORPH	0.277	0.188	0.518	0.338	0.189	*0.497*	0.092	*0.310*	0.340	0.305
APD-PRT-SYNT	0.405	0.189	0.376	0.295	*0.330*	0.121	*0.147*	0.235	*0.367*	0.274
APD-PRT-MORPHSYNT	*0.418*	*0.337*	*0.554*	*0.377*	0.236	0.359	0.092	0.255	0.328	*0.328*

Table 2: Spearman rank-correlation scores in the ranking task ('Task 2'). **Bold** indicates the best method overall (for each language); *italic* indicates the best results for a group of methods.

Method	EN	DE	LA	SW	NO-1	NO-2	IT	AVG
				PROFILES				
MORPH	*0.622*	0.479	0.625	0.581	0.486	*0.703*	0.500	0.571
SYNT	0.514	***0.625***	0.514	***0.677***	*0.622*	0.514	*0.611*	*0.582*
MORPHSYNT	0.541	0.521	***0.675***	0.581	0.486	0.432	0.444	0.526
				CONTEXTUALISED (XLM-R)				
APD	0.568	0.500	0.500	*0.613*	0.486	*0.595*	***0.667***	*0.561*
PRT	0.595	0.500	*0.550*	0.548	0.541	0.541	0.444	0.531
APD-PRT	***0.676***	*0.542*	*0.550*	*0.613*	*0.568*	0.459	0.500	0.558
Clustering/JSD	0.459	0.521	0.500	0.516	0.541	0.486	0.389	0.487
				ENSEMBLES				
APD-MORPH	*0.622*	0.500	0.575	*0.613*	0.541	***0.730***	0.500	0.583
APD-SYNT	0.568	0.479	0.550	0.581	*0.622*	0.622	*0.611*	0.576
APD-MORPHSYNT	*0.622*	***0.625***	*0.600*	*0.613*	0.514	0.703	*0.611*	***0.613***
PRT-MORPH	***0.676***	0.458	0.525	0.581	0.541	0.486	*0.500*	0.538
PRT-SYNT	0.541	*0.521*	*0.575*	*0.613*	***0.703***	*0.568*	*0.500*	*0.574*
PRT-MORPHSYNT	0.541	0.479	0.525	0.581	0.676	0.486	0.444	0.533
APD-PRT-MORPH	*0.649*	0.458	*0.650*	*0.581*	0.541	*0.676*	*0.611*	*0.595*
APD-PRT-SYNT	0.514	*0.542*	0.550	0.548	*0.676*	0.595	0.500	0.561
PRT-MORPHSYNT	0.541	0.479	0.525	*0.581*	*0.676*	0.486	0.444	0.533

Table 3: Binary accuracy scores in the classification task ('Task 1'). **Bold** indicates the best method overall (for each language); *italic* indicates the best results for a group of methods.

referential and topical level can happen much faster (consider, e.g., the words *'computer'* or *'mouse'* in English). On the other hand, when the gap between time periods is more substantial, changes in morphological and syntactic behavior of words also emerge. In these cases grammatical profiles help detect semantic shifts which LMs overlook. It is possible that adding the length of the time gap as a feature in our ensemble systems can make them less sensitive to the nature of the datasets .

Exceptions to this pattern are Latin (no gap between the time periods, but great performance of grammatical profiles) and Russian-3 (80 years gap, but profiles still lag behind XLM-R). For Latin, its extremely rich morphology can compensate for the small gap between time periods. Moreover, the second time period spans two millennia, making the short gap less problematic. Rich morphology does not help surpass XLM-R for Russian-3, but profiles do work much better for this dataset than for Russian-1 and Russian-2, where the gaps are only two years long.

5 Analysis

In this section, we analyse the predictions of all methods beyond task performance. We quantitatively evaluate their complementarity (Section 5.1), and investigate whether and how predictions made with grammatical profiles improve the performance of embedding-based metrics (Section 5.2).

5.1 Correlations between methods

To investigate whether various methods use different types of linguistic information, we compute Spearman rank-correlations between the predictions of standalone methods. The correlations, averaged over all datasets, are presented in Figure 2 (we show averaged correlations since they are highly consistent across corpora). We include the correlations of static embeddings as well (SGNS-raw and SGNS-lemma). More details about their implementations and performance can be found in Appendix B.

The two methods with the highest correlation are SGNS-raw and SGNS-lemma. This is expected, as the two methods differ only in the lemmatisation of target words. Profile-based methods (MORPH and SYNT) do not correlate with each other. Slight significant correlations are only observed for Russian-2 (0.32) and Russian-3 (0.45). Interestingly, for Russian, SYNT significantly correlates with static

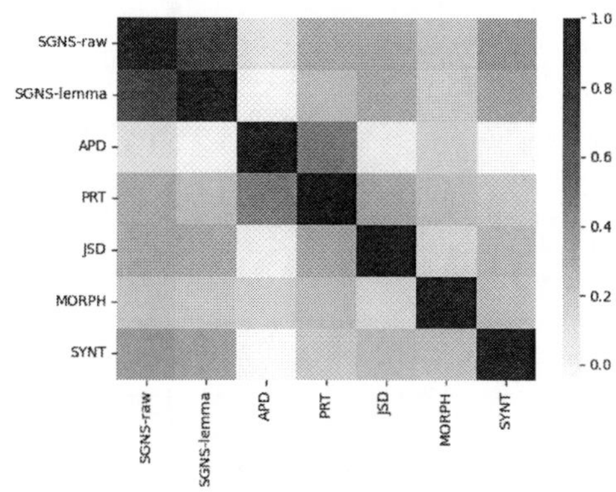

Figure 2: Averaged Spearman correlations between model predictions.

embeddings: the correlation with SGNS-raw is 0.48 for Russian-1, 0.52 for Russian-2 and 0.49 for Russian-3. Significant correlations between MORPH and static embeddings are observed for Latin (0.46) and Russian-3 (0.38).

Contextualised methods correlate weakly with grammatical profiles. Although we once again observe exceptional behaviour for the Russian datasets, the correlation between profiles and contextualized embeddings is on average weaker than between profiles and static embeddings, which might explain why combining contextualized embeddings with profiles yields notable performance improvements.

5.2 Qualitative analysis

In this section, we inspect the error patterns of our methods to find out when grammatical profiles help correct the predictions of embedding-based metrics. We frame this analysis in terms of *false positives* and *false negatives*. The definition of false positives and negatives is straightforward in the classification task. For the ranking task, we look at the signed distance between gold and predicted rankings of each word, considering a word as a false positive when the positive distance is in the highest 20% bin of the distance distribution (i.e., when the predicted rank is much higher than the true rank), and as a false negative if the negative distance is in the lowest 20% bin (i.e., when the predicted rank is much lower than the true rank). For each language, we focus on the best grammatical profile, the best contextualised method, and the best ensemble of these two.

In the English ranking task, we observe that four

of APD's five false positives are corrected by the ensemble: for example, the ranking of '*tree*' improves by 20 positions, that of '*part*' by 19, and that of '*bag*' by 17. As a result, '*tree*' and '*bag*' are only 1 position away from their respective gold ranks. For both words, the distribution of morphological features hardly vary between time period (e.g., 43.73% of the usages of '*tree*' are singular, 56.27% plural in the first time period; and in the second time period the percentages become 43.67% and 56.33%). Syntactic features vary only slightly; the most drastic change among these three words is the increase of direct object usages of '*bag*' from 33.16% to 41.40%, with all the other features remaining relatively stable—overall, a negligible change. Among APD's five false negatives, four are corrected in the best ensemble (PRT-MORPHSYNT): the strongest ranking improvements concern '*graft*' and '*plane*', whose rankings improve respectively by 18 and 15 positions. The syntactic profiles of these words vary substantially across time periods, with multiple syntactic categories increasing or decreasing their frequency of usage (e.g., usages of '*plane*' in subject and object position increase from 12.85% to 24.13% and from 13.25% to 19.67% respectively; while usages as a noun modifier decrease from 35.34% to 20.36%). The two targets that do not benefit from the ensemble are '*gas*' and '*risk*': both are false negatives for the best grammatical profile (SYNT) and they remain for the ensemble.

In the Norwegian ranking task, the best ensemble (APD-MORPH) helps pure APD mostly by fixing extreme false positives and false negatives. As an example of a fixed false positive, APD ranked '*test*' ('TEST') very high, although in fact it did not experience any semantic change at all (change score of 0). APD-MORPH decreased the change score assigned to '*test*' from 0.216 down to 0.013, returning it to its proper place at the bottom of the ranking. On the other hand, '*stryk*' changed its dominant meaning sharply in the 21st century from 'RIVER RAPIDS' to 'FAILURE', but APD failed to capture it. APD-MORPH fixed this false negative by moving '*stryk*' significantly upwards in the ranking, only 8 position away from its gold rank.

In the Latin predicted rankings, it is somewhat likely for a word to be a false positive — e.g., '*itero*' ('TO REPEAT'), '*jus*' (a 'RIGHT', the 'LAW') '*ancilla*' ('HANDMAID') — or a false negative — '*virtus*' ('STRENGTH'; 'COURAGE'; 'MANLINESS'), '*humanitas*' ('HUMAN NATURE'; 'KINDNESS'; 'CIVISILATION'), '*pontifex*' ('BISHOP'; but also, the 'POPE') — for both contextualised embeddings (PRT) and profiles (MORPHSYNT). As in the case of English, the ranking of these words does not improve with ensembling (PRT-MORPHSYNT). Overall, 7 out of 10 false negatives and 2 out of 7 false positives are corrected by the ensemble.

For German, too, ensembling (PRT-MORPHSYNT) is most effective for false negatives, 5 out of 8 are corrected. The words with the greatest improvements are '*abdecken*' ('TO UNCOVER'; but also, in financial jargon, 'TO COVER', as in *Risiko abdecken, to cover a risk*), gaining 16 positions, and '*Eintagsfliege*' ('MAYFLY', the insect; but also, metaphorically, 'FLEETING STAR') gaining 17 positions and thereby obtaining the exact gold rank. Nevertheless, out of 8 false positives, 4 are corrected; with, e.g., '*aufrechterhalten*' ('TO SUSTAIN') losing 31 rankings and '*Festspiel*' ('FESTIVAL') losing 18. As we observed for English and Latin, some words are simply difficult to rank for both methods (here, JSD and PRT-MORPHSYNT): for example, the degree of semantic change of '*Truppenteil*' ('TROOP UNIT') and '*Lyzeum*' ('LYCEUM') is overestimated whereas the change of '*packen*' ('TO PACK'; *to seize*) and '*vorliegen*' ('TO BE AVAILABLE'; 'TO BE EXISTENT'); is underestimated.

For Italian, we analyse the classification task. Among APD's 4 false positives, 2 are corrected in the ensemble's ranking (APD-SYNT), '*processare*' ('PROCESS'; 'TAKE TO TRIAL') and '*unico*' ('UNIQUE'); two nouns, '*brama*' ('YEARNING') and '*cappuccio*' ('HOOD'), remain misclassified. APD's false negatives are '*pilotato*' ('DRIVEN'; but also, metaphorically, 'PREMEDITATED') and '*rampante*' ('UNBRIDLED'; metaphorically, 'EXUBERANT'); '*pilotato*' is correctly classified by the ensemble while '*rampante*' remains undetected by all methods. Overall, the contribution of *SYNT* is not always helpful: it also leads to one changing word being labelled as stable, and three stable words being classified as changing.

6 Conclusion

We showed that providing large pre-trained language models with explicit morphosyntactic information can in many cases help detect and quantify lexical semantic change. Such 'ensemble' predictions are produced in a very straightforward way—i.e., by computing the geometric mean between semantic change scores predicted by grammatical profiles and by language models (via their contextualized embeddings). In the majority of the datasets under analysis (treating the three Russian datasets as one), the ensemble predictions outperformed single grammatical profiles or contextualised embeddings in the task of ranking words by the degree of their semantic change. The datasets where this was not true are characterized by specific properties: either languages with poor morphology or long time spans separated by narrow gaps.

We believe this means that although Transformer-based language models (like XLM-R, which we used here) are able to track morphological and syntactic properties to some extent (Warstadt et al., 2020), their encoding of grammatical features is only approximate and can therefore be improved by explicit linguistic preprocessing (morphological tagging and syntactic parsing). At any rate, we showed that this is true for the semantic change detection task, when a model has to take into account diachronic changes in morphosyntactic properties of words. The signal provided by these changes is complementary to the changes in typical lexical contexts more easily captured by distributional language models. Thus, it is still too early to fire the linguist, even if the 'linguist' is in fact an automated tagger.

As has already been said, an important limitation of grammatical profiles is their low performance when measuring semantic change across long time periods separated by very narrow gaps. This makes sense from a linguistic point of view: grammar changes slowly and gradually, sharp bursts are rare. In contrast, lexical contexts can change very quickly: for example, due to social and political events or technical progress, which is why language models excel with these datasets. The main practical take-away is therefore that diachronic grammatical profiles should be used in combination with language models especially when the gap between the compared time periods is large enough for significant grammatical changes to occur.

In the future, we plan to experiment with more sophisticated ensembling methods that go beyond simple averaging (including the usage of the information about gaps between time spans), and to perform a deeper analysis of ensemble predictions, especially in relation to distinct word senses. Finally, we also plan to evaluate ensembles formed with monolingual language models, instead of the multilingual XLM-R, as they have the potential to better capture the idiosyncrasies of specific languages.

Acknowledgements

This work has been partly supported by the European Union's Horizon 2020 research and innovation programme under grant 819455 (DREAM) and by Academy of Finland under grant numbers 333716 and 333717 (RiCEP). Our experiments were run on resources provided by UNINETT Sigma2 - the National Infrastructure for High Performance Computing and Data Storage in Norway.

References

Nikolay Arefyev, Daniil Homskiy, Maksim Fedoseev, Adis Davletov, Vitaly Protasov, and Alexander Panchenko. 2021. Deepmistake: Which senses are hard to distinguish for a wordincontext model. *Computational linguistics and intellectual technologies: Papers from the annual conference Dialogue.*

Nikolay Arefyev and Vasily Zhikov. 2020. BOS at SemEval-2020 task 1: Word sense induction via lexical substitution for lexical semantic change detection. In *Proceedings of the Fourteenth Workshop on Semantic Evaluation*, pages 171–179, Barcelona (online). International Committee for Computational Linguistics.

Hosein Azarbonyad, Mostafa Dehghani, Kaspar Beelen, Alexandra Arkut, Maarten Marx, and Jaap Kamps. 2017. Words are malleable: Computing semantic shifts in political and media discourse. In *Proceedings of the 2017 ACM on Conference on Information and Knowledge Management*, pages 1509–1518.

Pierpaolo Basile, Annalina Caputo, Tommaso Caselli, Pierluigi Cassotti, and Rossella Varvara. 2020. DIACR-Ita @ EVALITA2020: Overview of the EVALITA2020 Diachronic Lexical Semantics (DIACR-Ita) Task. *Proceedings of the Seventh Evaluation Campaign of Natural Language Processing and Speech Tools for Italian. Final Workshop (EVALITA 2020) CEUR Workshop Proceedings (CEUR-WS.org).*

Alexis Conneau, Kartikay Khandelwal, Naman Goyal, Vishrav Chaudhary, Guillaume Wenzek, Francisco Guzmán, Edouard Grave, Myle Ott, Luke Zettlemoyer, and Veselin Stoyanov. 2020. Unsupervised cross-lingual representation learning at scale. In *Proceedings of the 58th Annual Meeting of the Association for Computational Linguistics*, pages 8440–8451, Online. Association for Computational Linguistics.

Marco Del Tredici, Raquel Fernández, and Gemma Boleda. 2019. Short-term meaning shift: A distributional exploration. In *Proceedings of the 2019 Conference of the North American Chapter of the Association for Computational Linguistics: Human Language Technologies, Volume 1 (Long and Short Papers)*, pages 2069–2075, Minneapolis, Minnesota. Association for Computational Linguistics.

Katrin Erk and Sebastian Padó. 2008. A structured vector space model for word meaning in context. In *Proceedings of the 2008 Conference on Empirical Methods in Natural Language Processing*, pages 897–906, Honolulu, Hawaii. Association for Computational Linguistics.

Brendan Frey and Delbert Dueck. 2007. Clustering by passing messages between data points. *Science*, 315(5814):972–976.

Nikhil Garg, Londa Schiebinger, Dan Jurafsky, and James Zou. 2018. Word embeddings quantify 100 years of gender and ethnic stereotypes. *Proceedings of the National Academy of Sciences*, 115(16):E3635–E3644.

Mario Giulianelli, Marco Del Tredici, and Raquel Fernández. 2020. Analysing lexical semantic change with contextualised word representations. In *Proceedings of the 58th Annual Meeting of the Association for Computational Linguistics*, pages 3960–3973, Online. Association for Computational Linguistics.

Mario Giulianelli, Andrey Kutuzov, and Lidia Pivovarova. 2021. Grammatical profiling for semantic change detection. In *Proceedings of the 25th Conference on Computational Natural Language Learning*, pages 423–434, Online. Association for Computational Linguistics.

Rahul Goel, Sandeep Soni, Naman Goyal, John Paparrizos, Hanna Wallach, Fernando Diaz, and Jacob Eisenstein. 2016. The social dynamics of language change in online networks. In *International Conference on Social Informatics*, pages 41–57. Springer.

Stefan Th Gries and Dagmar Divjak. 2009. Behavioral profiles: a corpus-based approach to cognitive semantic analysis. *New directions in cognitive linguistics*, 57:75.

William L. Hamilton, Jure Leskovec, and Dan Jurafsky. 2016. Diachronic word embeddings reveal statistical laws of semantic change. In *Proceedings of the 54th Annual Meeting of the Association for Computational Linguistics (Volume 1: Long Papers)*, pages 1489–1501, Berlin, Germany. Association for Computational Linguistics.

Laura A Janda and Olga Lyashevskaya. 2011. Grammatical profiles and the interaction of the lexicon with aspect, tense, and mood in Russian. *Cognitive linguistics*, 22(4):719–763.

Austin C Kozlowski, Matt Taddy, and James A Evans. 2019. The geometry of culture: Analyzing the meanings of class through word embeddings. *American Sociological Review*, 84(5):905–949.

Andrey Kutuzov and Mario Giulianelli. 2020. UiO-UvA at SemEval-2020 task 1: Contextualised embeddings for lexical semantic change detection. In *Proceedings of the Fourteenth Workshop on Semantic Evaluation*, pages 126–134, Barcelona (online). International Committee for Computational Linguistics.

Andrey Kutuzov and Lidia Pivovarova. 2021. RuShiftEval: a shared task on semantic shift detection for Russian. *Computational linguistics and intellectual technologies: Papers from the annual conference Dialogue*.

Andrey Kutuzov, Samia Touileb, Petter Mæhlum, Tita Ranveig Enstad, and Alexandra Wittemann. 2022. NorDiaChange: Diachronic semantic change dataset for Norwegian. In *Proceedings of the 13th Language Resources and Evaluation Conference (LREC)*. European Language Resources Association.

Angeliki Lazaridou, Adhi Kuncoro, Elena Gribovskaya, Devang Agrawal, Adam Liska, Tayfun Terzi, Mai Gimenez, Cyprien de Masson d'Autume, Tomas Kocisky, Sebastian Ruder, et al. 2021. Mind the gap: Assessing temporal generalization in neural language models. *Advances in Neural Information Processing Systems*, 34.

Jianhua Lin. 1991. Divergence measures based on the Shannon entropy. *IEEE Transactions on Information theory*, 37(1):145–151.

Matej Martinc, Petra Kralj Novak, and Senja Pollak. 2020a. Leveraging contextual embeddings for detecting diachronic semantic shift. In *Proceedings of the 12th Language Resources and Evaluation Conference*, pages 4811–4819, Marseille, France. European Language Resources Association.

Matej Martinc, Syrielle Montariol, Elaine Zosa, and Lidia Pivovarova. 2020b. Capturing evolution in word usage: Just add more clusters? In *Companion Proceedings of the Web Conference 2020*, pages 343–349.

Tomas Mikolov, Ilya Sutskever, Kai Chen, Greg S Corrado, and Jeff Dean. 2013. Distributed representations of words and phrases and their compositionality. *Advances in Neural Information Processing Systems 26*.

Syrielle Montariol, Matej Martinc, and Lidia Pivovarova. 2021. Scalable and interpretable semantic change detection. In *Proceedings of the 2021 Conference of the North American Chapter of the Association for Computational Linguistics: Human Language Technologies*, pages 4642–4652, Online. Association for Computational Linguistics.

Bill Noble, Asad Sayeed, Raquel Fernández, and Staffan Larsson. 2021. Semantic shift in social networks. In *Proceedings of *SEM 2021: The Tenth Joint Conference on Lexical and Computational Semantics*, pages 26–37, Online. Association for Computational Linguistics.

Mohammad Taher Pilehvar and Nigel Collier. 2016. De-conflated semantic representations. In *Proceedings of the 2016 Conference on Empirical Methods in Natural Language Processing*, pages 1680–1690, Austin, Texas. Association for Computational Linguistics.

Dominik Schlechtweg, Anna Hätty, Marco Del Tredici, and Sabine Schulte im Walde. 2019. A wind of change: Detecting and evaluating lexical semantic change across times and domains. In *Proceedings of the 57th Annual Meeting of the Association for Computational Linguistics*, pages 732–746, Florence, Italy. Association for Computational Linguistics.

Dominik Schlechtweg, Barbara McGillivray, Simon Hengchen, Haim Dubossarsky, and Nina Tahmasebi. 2020. SemEval-2020 task 1: Unsupervised lexical semantic change detection. In *Proceedings of the Fourteenth Workshop on Semantic Evaluation*, pages 1–23, Barcelona (online). International Committee for Computational Linguistics.

Dominik Schlechtweg, Sabine Schulte im Walde, and Stefanie Eckmann. 2018. Diachronic usage relatedness (DURel): A framework for the annotation of lexical semantic change. In *Proceedings of the 2018 Conference of the North American Chapter of the Association for Computational Linguistics: Human Language Technologies, Volume 2 (Short Papers)*, pages 169–174, New Orleans, Louisiana. Association for Computational Linguistics.

Hinrich Schütze. 1998. Automatic word sense discrimination. *Computational Linguistics*, 24(1):97–123.

Milan Straka and Jana Straková. 2017. Tokenizing, POS tagging, lemmatizing and parsing UD 2.0 with UDPipe. In *Proceedings of the CoNLL 2017 Shared Task: Multilingual Parsing from Raw Text to Universal Dependencies*, pages 88–99, Vancouver, Canada. Association for Computational Linguistics.

Charles Truong, Laurent Oudre, and Nicolas Vayatis. 2020. Selective review of offline change point detection methods. *Signal Processing*, 167:107299.

Alex Warstadt, Alicia Parrish, Haokun Liu, Anhad Mohananey, Wei Peng, Sheng-Fu Wang, and Samuel R. Bowman. 2020. BLiMP: The benchmark of linguistic minimal pairs for English. *Transactions of the Association for Computational Linguistics*, 8:377–392.

Thomas Wolf, Lysandre Debut, Victor Sanh, Julien Chaumond, Clement Delangue, Anthony Moi, Pierric Cistac, Tim Rault, Remi Louf, Morgan Funtowicz, Joe Davison, Sam Shleifer, Patrick von Platen, Clara Ma, Yacine Jernite, Julien Plu, Canwen Xu, Teven Le Scao, Sylvain Gugger, Mariama Drame, Quentin Lhoest, and Alexander Rush. 2020. Transformers: State-of-the-art natural language processing. In *Proceedings of the 2020 Conference on Empirical Methods in Natural Language Processing: System Demonstrations*, pages 38–45, Online. Association for Computational Linguistics.

Yang Xu and Charles Kemp. 2015. A computational evaluation of two laws of semantic change. In *CogSci*.

Appendix

A Contextualised embeddings

Given two time periods t_1, t_2 , two corpora C_1, C_2, and a set of target words, we use a neural language model to obtain *token embeddings* of each occurrence of the target words in C_1 and C_2 and use them to compute a continuous change score. This score indicates the degree of semantic change undergone by a word between t_1 and t_2. As a language model, we choose XLM-R (Conneau et al., 2020), pre-trained multilingual transformer, in the Huggingface implementation (Wolf et al., 2020).

A.1 Target Lemmas and Word Forms

The lists of target words that we rely on contain annotations for lemmas. However, only extracting embeddings for exact matches of the lemmas would result in discarding a large number of word usages, those where the target lemma takes another form (e.g., as a result of grammatical inflection). To take all of a lemma's possible word forms into account, we parse the corpora using UDPipe (Straka and Straková, 2017) and collect a set of word forms for each target word from the UDPipe output. Furthermore, because some word forms are not present in the vocabulary of XLM-R, we add them to the vocabulary before fine-tuning.[3]

A.2 Finetuning the Language Model

As a first step, to adapt the model to the characteristics of the diachronic corpora, we finetune it, separately, on each language-specific corpus. We limit the maximum sequence length of the transformer to 256 and train the model with a batch size of 16 for an amount of epochs dependent on the corpus size: 5 epochs for English and Latin, 3 for German and Swedish, 2 for Russian, Italian and Norwegian.

A.3 Extracting contextualised embeddings

Given a target word w and its sentential context $s = (v_1, ..., v_i, ..., v_m)$ with $w = v_i$, we extract the activations of the language model's hidden layers for sentence position i. We then average over the layers (12 for XLM-R) and obtain a single vectorial representation (for XLM-R, the vector dimensionality is 768). In our experiments, the maximum context length m is set to 256 and sentences are processed in batches of size 32. The N_w contextualised embeddings collected for w can be represented as the usage matrix $\mathbf{U}_w = (\mathbf{w}_1, \ldots, \mathbf{w}_{N_w})$. The time-specific usage matrices $\mathbf{U}_w^1, \mathbf{U}_w^2$ for time periods t_1 and t_2 are used as input to a metric of semantic change.

A.4 Metrics of Semantic Change

As explained in Section 3.3, semantic change scores are computed using three metrics: 1) average pairwise distance or APD (Giulianelli et al., 2020), 2) prototype distance or PRT (Kutuzov and Giulianelli, 2020), and 3) Jensen-Shannon Divergence between embedding cluster distributions or JSD (Martinc et al., 2020b; Giulianelli et al., 2020):

APD Given two usage matrices $\mathbf{U}_w^{t_1}, \mathbf{U}_w^{t_2}$, the degree of change of w is calculated as the average cosine distance between any two embeddings from different time periods:

$$\mathrm{APD}\left(\mathbf{U}_w^{t_1}, \mathbf{U}_w^{t_2}\right) = \frac{1}{N_w^{t_1} \cdot N_w^{t_2}} \sum_{\mathbf{x}_i \in \mathbf{U}_w^{t_1},\, \mathbf{x}_j \in \mathbf{U}_w^{t_2}} cos\left(\mathbf{x}_i, \mathbf{x}_j\right) \tag{1}$$

where $N_w^{t_1}$ and $N_w^{t_2}$ are the number of occurrences of w in time periods t_1 and t_2.

PRT Here, the degree of change of w is measured as the cosine distance between the average token embeddings ('prototypes') of all occurrences of w in the two time periods:

$$\mathrm{PRT}\left(\mathbf{U}_w^{t_1}, \mathbf{U}_w^{t_2}\right) = 1 - cos\left(\frac{\sum_{\mathbf{x}_i \in \mathbf{U}_w^{t_1}} \mathbf{x}_i}{N_w^{t_1}}, \frac{\sum_{\mathbf{x}_j \in \mathbf{U}_w^{t_2}} \mathbf{x}_j}{N_w^{t_2}}\right) \tag{2}$$

JSD To compute this measure, we form a single usage matrix $[\mathbf{U}_w^{t_1}; \mathbf{U}_w^{t_2}]$ with occurrences from two corpora. We standardise it and then clustered its entries using Affinity Propagation (Frey and Dueck, 2007), a clustering algorithm which automatically selects a number of clusters for each word.[4] Finally, we define probability distributions $\mathbf{u}_w^{t_1}, \mathbf{u}_w^{t_2}$ based on the normalised counts of word embeddings in each cluster and compute a the Jensen-Shannon Divergence (Lin, 1991) between the distributions:

$$\mathrm{JSD}(\mathbf{u}_w^{t_1}, \mathbf{u}_w^{t_2}) = \mathrm{H}\left(\tfrac{1}{2}\left(\mathbf{u}_w^{t_1} + \mathbf{u}_w^{t_2}\right)\right) - \tfrac{1}{2}\left(\mathrm{H}\left(\mathbf{u}_w^{t_1}\right) - \mathrm{H}\left(\mathbf{u}_w^{t_2}\right)\right) \tag{3}$$

[3]Even after adding the word forms to the vocabulary, the Huggingface tokenizer still fails to recognise about a dozen of the target word forms and splits them into sub-tokens. For these exceptional cases, we extract the average contextualised embedding over the sub-tokens.

[4]We use the scikit-learn implementation of Affinity Propagation with default hyperparameters.

B Static Embeddings

We follow the common approach proposed by Hamilton et al. (2016), SGNS+OP, to train skip-gram negative sampling embeddings (SGNS; Mikolov et al., 2013) from scratch for each time period of the diachronic corpus, and then to align the separate vector spaces using the Orthogonal Procrustes method (OP). Semantic change is measured as the cosine distance between the embeddings of a target word in the aligned spaces (for more details, see Schlechtweg et al., 2019).

We decided not to lemmatize our corpora for these experiments to preserve as much grammatical information as it is possible but we use two preprocessing strategies for target words. In the first strategy (**SGNS-raw**) we use a raw, unlemmatized, corpus and learn embeddings for target words only in their dictionary form. All other inflected forms of the target words are ignored. In the second strategy (**SGNS-lemma**), we lemmatize target word occurrences (but not other words) and thus use all target word forms to train their embeddings.

In the ranking task, SGNS+OP confirms itself as a very competitive approach, achieving the best correlation scores on German, Swedish, and Russian 3 (see Table 4). Our results show that lemmatizing target word forms, so that they all contribute to the same static embedding, brings substantial performance improvements as well as more stability across test sets.

Our classification results again confirm the strength of static embeddings, which outperform other approaches for German, Norwegian-1, and Italian (for English and Swedish, they perform on par with the profile-contextualised ensembles). Target word form lemmatization is important but less decisive than in the ranking task (see Table 5).

Method	EN	DE	LA	SW	NO-1	NO-2	RU-1	RU-2	RU-3
STATIC									
Raw text (SNGS-raw)	0.378	0.226	0.250	-0.036	0.320	0.181	0.101	0.148	0.255
Target words lemmatized (SGNS-lemma)	0.498	**0.369**	0.106	**0.494**	0.238	0.392	0.256	0.292	**0.538**
ENSEMBLES									
SGNS-raw-MORPH	0.253	0.105	0.436	0.204	0.116	0.368	0.020	0.222	0.275
SGNS-raw-SYNT	0.341	0.159	0.234	0.158	0.250	0.024	0.019	0.113	0.248
SGNS-raw-MORPHSYNT	0.354	0.258	0.454	0.297	0.142	0.218	0.013	0.148	0.229
SGNS-lemma-MORPH	0.255	0.157	0.409	0.386	0.106	0.440	0.057	0.259	0.332
SGNS-lemma-SYNT	0.364	0.173	0.224	0.242	0.212	0.156	0.071	0.129	0.315
SGNS-lemma-MORPHSYNT	0.367	0.269	0.415	0.461	0.128	0.341	0.023	0.163	0.286

Table 4: Spearman correlation scores in the ranking task ('Task 2') with type-based static embeddings (SGNS-OP). Bold values are cases when SGNS-OP outperforms all other methods (XLM-R and grammatical profiles).

Method	EN	DE	LA	SW	NO-1	NO-2	IT
Raw (SGNS-raw)	0.514	0.542	0.400	0.548	**0.757**	0.649	0.722
Target words lemmatized (SGNS-lemma)	**0.676**	**0.646**	0.375	**0.742**	0.676	0.676	**0.778**
ENSEMBLES							
SGNS-raw-MORPH	0.622	0.562	0.600	0.484	0.486	0.622	0.500
SGNS-raw-SYNT	0.541	0.583	0.550	0.581	0.649	0.486	0.500
SGNS-raw-MORPHSYNT	0.649	0.625	0.500	0.677	0.595	0.486	0.611
SGNS-lemma-MORPH	0.622	0.438	0.625	0.484	0.514	0.703	0.500
SGNS-lemma-SYNT	0.541	0.479	0.525	0.581	0.649	0.568	0.611
SGNS-lemma-MORPHSYNT	0.649	0.604	0.600	**0.742**	0.514	0.676	0.389

Table 5: Binary accuracy scores in the classification task ('Task 1') with type-based static embeddings (SGNS-OP). Bold values are cases when SGNS-OP outperforms all other methods (XLM-R and grammatical profiles).

Explainable Publication Year Prediction of Eighteenth Century Texts with the BERT Model

Iiro Rastas[1], **Yann Ryan**[2], **Iiro Tiihonen**[2], **Mohammadreza Qaraei**[3], **Liina Repo**[1], **Rohit Babbar**[3], **Eetu Mäkelä**[2], **Mikko Tolonen**[2], **Filip Ginter**[1]

[1] TurkuNLP, University of Turku, Finland
[2] University of Helsinki, Finland
[3] Aalto University, Finland

iiro.t.rastas@utu.fi, yann.ryan@helsinki.fi
iiro.tiihonen@helsinki.fi
mohammadreza.mohammadniaqaraei@aalto.fi
tlkrep@utu.fi, rohit.babbar@aalto.fi
eetu.makela@helsinki.fi, mikko.tolonen@helsinki.fi
figint@utu.fi

Abstract

In this paper, we describe a BERT model trained on the Eighteenth Century Collections Online (ECCO) dataset of digitized documents. The ECCO dataset poses unique modelling challenges due to the presence of Optical Character Recognition (OCR) artifacts. We establish the performance of the BERT model on a publication year prediction task against linear baseline models and human judgement, finding the BERT model to be superior to both and able to date the works, on average, with less than 7 years absolute error. We also explore how language change over time affects the model by analyzing the features the model uses for publication year predictions as given by the Integrated Gradients model explanation method.

1 Introduction

Collections of historical language, such as ECCO which comprises over 180,000 titles published in the eighteenth century, are at the focus of a growing interest in the NLP community. The large quantities of raw textual data in these collections, which may cover whole centuries worth of published works, are suitable for language modelling research, a popular and highly relevant topic in NLP. The historical language itself poses new and interesting challenges, especially due to the fact that the collections span over a time frame long enough to be affected by natural language change and evolution. Furthermore, artifacts relating to the technical process – namely the OCR quality – of the works pose a whole new set of challenges rarely met in modern NLP which mostly deals with born-digital texts, for the most part devoid of such artifacts. These new developments in NLP are crucial also for historians and other humanists applying them to new research questions and ways to produce historical evidence.

The transformer model (Vaswani et al., 2017) and especially the BERT (Devlin et al., 2019) bidirectional encoder based on the transformer, form the foundation of present-day practical NLP research and are naturally also applied in the historical language domain. BERT models have already been trained with various historical data sets and languages, including at least English, German, French, Latin and classical Chinese (Ehrmann et al., 2021; Yu and Wang, 2020; Labusch et al., 2019; Bamman and Burns, 2020). The range of tasks to which it has been used in the domain is already diverse, covering at least named entity recognition, construction of word embeddings, event detection, stance detection, word sense disambiguation and the study of the animacy of target expressions (Hamdi et al., 2021; Sims et al., 2019; Coll Ardanuy et al., 2020; Hosseini et al., 2021; Beelen et al., 2021). Issues particular to the historical language domain have also produced new challenges for BERT appliers to adress, like the effect of OCR quality (Jiang et al., 2021).

In this work, we will follow two directions. Firstly, we set out to train from scratch and release a dedicated BERT model specifically on and for the ECCO dataset. Then, we establish whether such a targeted BERT model provides an advantage over other existing historical English BERT models, or even the modern English BERT. To this end we pursue a benchmark task whereby the model is trained to predict the year of publication based on the text itself. We find that the model performs much better on this task than we intuitively expected, and therefore we carry out and report on a more extensive analysis of the task including a comparison to hu-

Proceedings of the 3rd Workshop on Computational Approaches to Historical Language Change, pages 68 - 77
May 26-27, 2022 ©2022 Association for Computational Linguistics

man performance, and provide aggregated feature attributions to the BERT model predictions using the Integrated Gradients model explanation method of Sundararajan et al. (2017).

2 Data

ECCO, or Eighteenth Century Collections Online, is a set of digitized documents claimed by its publisher Gale to "contain every significant English-language and foreign-language title printed in the United Kingdom between the years 1701 and 1800" (Gale). In truth however, ECCO is a growing collection. Currently comprising the initial ECCO1 set of around 135,000 documents published in 2003 and some 47,000 further titles added as ECCO2 in 2009, the collection has recently been evaluated as containing about 54% of the works printed in the United Kingdom in the eighteenth century, and known to remain to us through time. Thus, while not complete and at points biased, it is certainly an impressive resource for eighteenth-century scholars as well as, for example, historical linguists (Tolonen et al., 2021).

For the purposes of this work, it is additionally useful to know the following information about ECCO. First, ECCO is temporally skewed toward the end of the eighteenth century, with many more works being published particularly in the final two decades of the century than in earlier ones. Second, while some non-English works are included in the collection, 94% of the documents in it are in English (the other languages with more than 1% representation are French, with 2.7% and Latin with 2.5%). Third, the print quality and thus OCR quality of the documents in ECCO correlates both with their format (pamphlet vs. book) as well as publication date, with more recent publications having a significantly better average OCR quality. Further, OCR quality also differs between ECCO1 and ECCO2, which were scanned and OCR'd using different processes. Finally, there may often be multiple editions of a single work within ECCO, and while they have been printed in the eighteenth century, they may well have originated from e.g. antiquity. Further, when the year of publication of a work has not been printed on its title page, the year has often been estimated. On the level of the whole ECCO data, this manifests itself as frequency spikes on every round fifth, tenth and fiftieth year. (Tolonen et al., 2021)

For the purposes of the year regression experiments in this work, we have dealt with the last two problems by limiting the subset of ECCO we are experimenting on to only those where the year of publication is certain, as well as only to the first editions of works that first appear in the eighteenth century. The size of this subset is approximately 40,000 documents.

3 Methods

In this section, we describe the models and methods used in this work: the pre-trained BERT model, the BERT-based year regression and feature attribution, and finally the linear baseline.

3.1 BERT pre-training

BERT model pre-training on the ECCO dataset is very similar to pre-training on any other dataset, with the structure of the dataset and the OCR noise present requiring some consideration. The sub-word vocabulary of size 50,000 is induced in the standard manner on a random sample of the dataset. For the BERT training objective which includes the next sentence prediction task, the training examples are constructed from pairs of text segments. Here each text segment is a continuous piece of text drawn from a single block of text in ECCO, where each such block of text is delimited by an empty line and corresponds to one page or one paragraph, depending on the format of the underlying work. We make an attempt to respect sentence boundaries when forming the training text segments using a simple regular expression, while keeping each segment between 128-384 tokens long, the pair subsequently trimmed to the model's maximum sequence length of 512 input tokens (sub-words and special tokens). Unlike for all other experiments, the entire ECCO dataset is used for BERT pre-training. The trained model is equal in size to the BERT Base models of Devlin et al. (2019). The final model was pre-trained for 1 million steps, with an effective batch size of 768, and learning rate 1×10^{-4}.

3.2 BERT-based year regression

As the regression model, we employ a simple linear regression layer on top of the pre-trained BERT model, as illustrated in Figure 1. The model is trained using the mean square error (MSE) objective. To ensure good model performance, the target values are z-transformed, $y' = \frac{y-\mu}{\sigma}$ where μ and σ are the mean and standard deviation of the publication years of the training set examples. The z-transformed years are centered on zero with a unit standard deviation. While this is a trivial linear transformation, it is crucial in model training: the randomly initialized output regression layer initially predicts values around 0 and a large number of training steps are needed to reach the target range of 1701–1800. During these training steps, the gradients are propagated also into the BERT model, and the combined effect turns out to be highly detrimental for the model.

The documents in our dataset, full books for the most part, are naturally considerably longer than the maximum sequence length of 512 subwords for the BERT model. We therefore split each document into a number of chunks of up to 512 sub-words in length, and subsequently average the predictions to obtain a single, document-level prediction.

Even though the ECCO works (books and pamphlets) themselves are long relative to the maximum sequence length of the model, we originally restricted the textual segments used as inputs to within a single textual block (page/paragraph) of the source document, so as to match the data on which the model was pre-trained. Many of these are relatively short, due both to the layout of the works and OCR artifacts. Unsurprisingly, though, we found during development that the prediction performance is best on long textual segments near the 512 sub-words limit. Therefore, we altered the example generation strategy and concatenated what would originally be several independent examples into a single long sequence separated by the `[SEP]` BERT control tokens. This way the model can be trained and evaluated exclusively on 512 sub-word long segments with the exception of document-ending segments and the rare cases where the entire document is shorter than 512 subwords.

3.3 Feature attributions

There are numerous methods for calculating *feature attributions*, i.e. the assignment of importance to input features with respect to the prediction made by the model. In this work, we apply the Integrated Gradients (IG) method of Sundararajan et al. (2017) to obtain attributions for the BERT-based regressor predictions. IG is a popular method specifically targeting differentiable models, assigning attributions to individual parameters of the model. In the context of BERT, the attributions would typically be calculated with respect to the input sub-word embeddings, in turn providing attributions on the level of sub-words in the input sequence. In short, the IG method defines the attribution as the integral of the gradient of the model output w.r.t. the parameter of interest, integrated on a path interpolating between a "blank" reference input sequence and the actual input sequence. This is in practice implemented by evaluating the model in N steps (here we set $N = 50$) between the reference and actual input.

In image processing, the reference input would typically be e.g. an empty image, or a white noise image. In the context of BERT, we can use the sequence `[CLS] [PAD] [PAD] ... [PAD] [SEP]`, where `[CLS]` and `[SEP]` are the special separation tokens in BERT input, and `[PAD]` is the padding token. This reference sequence has same length as the actual input and the interpolation is carried out on the input token embedding vectors.

The attribution value of each input sub-word is the sum of the scalar attributions across the dimensions of the input embeddings. A positive attribution value signals contribution *towards* the prediction made by the model, while a negative attribution value signals contribution *against* the prediction made by the model. Since the BERT model uses sub-word tokenization, splitting rare words into sub-words, to obtain word-level attributions understandable to the human reader we set the attribution of a word to be the attribution of that of its sub-words which has the highest absolute value. Thus, for instance, if an input word is divided into three sub-words with attributions of $[-0.4, 0.1, 0.21]$, the overall attribution of the word will be -0.4.

3.4 Aggregating attributions

The word attributions provided by the IG method are assigned to individual predictions, i.e. predictions on a maximum of 512 sub-words long text segments. There are therefore two levels on which the attributions may be aggregated. Firstly, relevant features aggregated across all text segments of a single long document such as a book explain the prediction the model gave to that document. And secondly, one might be interested in aggregating relevant features across all books published in a single period (e.g. one decade) so as to gain an understanding of globally relevant features for that period.

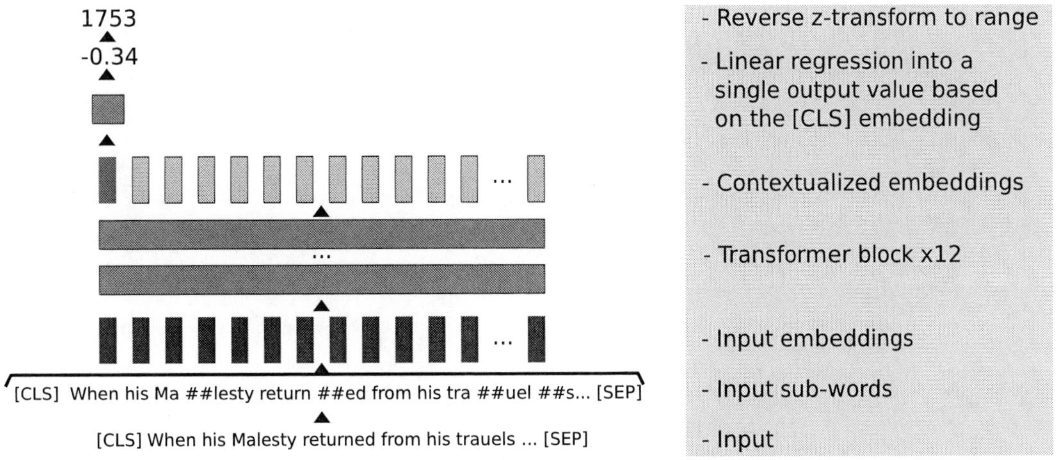

Figure 1: The regression model for a single text segment of BERT maximum sequence length, with OCR errors. Predictions across segments of a single document / book are averaged to give a final document-level prediction.

Model	**MAE**	**MSD**	**STD**
ECCO-BERT	6.32	-1.30	8.84
dbmdz/bert-base-historic-english-cased	7.27	-1.44	10.18
bert-base-cased	7.65	-0.73	10.27
MacBERTh	8.21	-1.35	11.08
Linear regression	11.88	0.26	15.38
Linear classification	12.47	-0.35	20.22

Table 1: Results for fine-tuned BERT models and the linear baseline models. MAE is mean absolute error, MSD is mean signed deviation, and STD is standard deviation, in terms of years.

There are many ways to approach this aggregation. In the simplest case, we can take the top features based on the highest attribution values across all text segments. However, this method was found to be prone to noise when the number of segments is large, such as when aggregating on a decade-level. We therefore test two additional methods. The first one counts the number of times each feature appears as a top 10 feature of a segment. To reduce the prevalence of common words, this number is further weighed with its IDF. The other method takes the average attribution value for each feature across all segments. Top features are chosen as those that have the highest average attribution value and appear in the segments more than once. Using these methods, lists of top features for each decade were qualitatively evaluated.

3.5 Linear baseline

We use a standard linear model as the baseline method, as it also allows us to compare the feature attributions, which are simple to extract from a trained linear model. As the first baseline to evaluate the performance of a linear model using support vector regression on the task of year prediction, we used the solver implemented in the Liblinear package (Fan et al., 2008). As an alternative, we also used a linear model for the direct multiclass prediction (Crammer and Singer, 2001) instead of the surrogate loss in the form of squared error.

4 Results

There are 39,429 ECCO works that have a verified year of publication during the 18th century and that constitute the earliest publication of the given work. All results are reported on the same test set of 1971 randomly selected works, which contain a total of about 225,000 text segments. A development set of the same size was reserved for hyperparameter selection, with the remaining 35,487 documents being used for training.

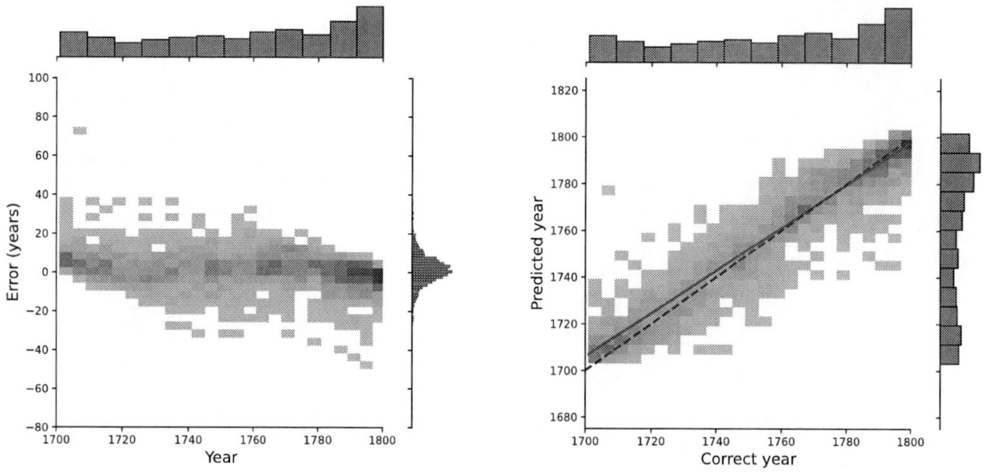

(a) (b)

Figure 2: A histogram of the errors (a) as well as a comparison between the actual years and predicted years (b) by the ECCO-BERT model.

4.1 Year regression

In addition to our pre-trained ECCO-BERT, we used three other relevant BERT models pre-trained on either historical or modern English: bert-base-cased[1], dbmdz/bert-base-historic-english-cased[2], and MacBERTh[3]. For each model, a grid search on the development set was performed to find optimal learning rate and number of training steps.

The overall results for the year regression task with the BERT models as well as the linear baseline models are summarized in Table 1. All BERT models can be fine-tuned to perform reasonably well, as the fine-tuning dataset is very large. BERT pre-trained on the ECCO dataset performs slightly better than the other models, possibly due to better fitting the OCR noise unique to the dataset. Overall, the best result of mean absolute error of 6.32 years reflects a surprisingly good performance of the BERT model on the task. To gain more insight into the predictions, the histograms of prediction errors relative to the publication year of the work are presented in Figure 2. These show no strong bias, beyond the natural fact that the publication year of older works is more likely to be overestimated and the publication year of newer works is likely to be underestimated, as the model learned the prediction range.

The impact of OCR quality on the results is worth considering. (Jiang et al., 2021) showed that pre-trained BERT on OCR'd historical books was less robust when used in a domain classification task than one trained on 'clean' text, though in that study fine-tuning significantly improved resilience to noise. Other studies on downstream NLP and language modelling tasks show that OCR quality can have a significant effect, though the extent is heavily dependant on the specific task and extent of the OCR error rate. (van Strien. et al., 2020; Hill and Hengchen, 2019) Here, we found a moderate performance difference between the ECCO1 and ECCO2 subsets of the test set, with ECCO-BERT having a mean absolute error of 6.96 years for ECCO2, but only 5.95 years for ECCO1. This is most likely due to ECCO1 having a stronger relationship between OCR quality and publication year, which could help model predictions. This suggests that a more noise-aware variant of the model, for instance a character-level version, would improve results.

4.2 Linear baseline

Contrary to the BERT model, in which the input is limited to 512 sub-words, in the linear models, the TF-IDF representation can be built over the entire corpus. For building a TF-IDF representation for each document, we used the `TfidfVectorizer` of `sklearn`. We ignored the terms that ap-

[1] `https://huggingface.co/bert-base-cased`

[2] `https://huggingface.co/dbmdz/bert-base-historic-english-cased`

[3] `https://huggingface.co/emanjavacas/MacBERTh`

pear in more than `tf-max` $= 30\%$ or less than `tf-min` $= 1\%$ of the training documents. As the data contains a significant amount of noise, the only preprocessing on token-level is removing the stop words. Furthermore, to prevent information leakage when the year of publication is explicitly stated somewhere in the document, we removed all the numbers from the documents including training and test sets[4]. The hyper-parameters of the linear models including C, `tf-max`, and `tf-min` are chosen using a validation set drawn randomly from 5% of the training data.

The histograms of the errors using linear models are depicted in Figure 3. While it seems that the classification model is more accurate in predicting the distribution of the years, having predictions with large variances leads to worse performance of this model compared to linear regression when metrics such as standard deviation are taken into account.

Overall, as can be expected, the linear baselines performs substantially worse than any of the BERT models, including modern English BERT.

4.3 Qualitative evaluation

Three approaches were used to analyse what information carried by the text tokens the BERT model might be utilising in its predictions. First, we qualitatively evaluated the predictor features of the linear regression model used as the baseline. This evaluation suggests that - even when the model is simple and features easier to interpret - there are multiple elements in the ECCO's tokens that a year predicting model can use. Some like *baptizing* (negative predictor, i.e. signalling an old publication) might relate to shifts in the composition of the ECCO during eighteenth century, others like *soveraign* and *cloath* might be related to temporal variation in spelling. Further likely information sources include language (tokens in Latin and French are prominent among negative predictors) and varying heuristics like the information that is part of the imprint [5]. For example, the term *sixpence* has high positive effect, and sixpence is a very common price printed to the imprint, but price information in ESTC is temporally varying, and mostly missing from the first years of the eighteenth century in contrast to the rest of the century (Tiihonen et al., 2021). In nearly all specific instances there is a high degree of uncertainty about the reason why a given token is or seems to be relevant for year prediction, but put together, the evaluation of the baseline model suggests that there is real information to be utilised among the noise.

In the second approach, we tried to directly evaluate the predictors relevant for the ECCO-BERT model's predictions by going through a sample of documents and interpreting three sets of predictor tokens for each. Each of these token sets relates to one of the methods of measuring the token's significance as a predictor (see section 3.4), and the motivation was to use these sets of terms to get insight into the way the model utilises information from ECCO to predict the years. In addition to the sources of variation already mentioned, the model seems to capture some very context specific terms relevant for prediction. A telling example is a work[6] on the French Revolution from 1797, that the model predicted as being published in 1794. Among the top predictor tokens for this document were *French*, *Revolution* and *Jacobins* from the second set of tokens, but also *1792*, *I792* and *r792* from the third.[7] In the third approach, the three methods were used to produce three token sets of potentially relevant predictors of the ECCO-BERT model for each decade (the approach discussed in section 3.4) of the eighteenth century. Some of the temporal development of token sets two and three might be related to significant conceptual developments that occurred during eighteenth century. For example, the term *publick* is part of the token set 2 in 1750's, and *Public* in 1790's. The emergence of the notion of a public sphere (for definition, see for example (Barker, 2004)) and the term *public(k)* during the eighteenth century are major questions both in intellectual history and political theory. The transformation from publick to public is an example of known orthographic shift where the letter *k* of words ending with *ck* drops out (Baron, 2011). Both the appearance of the term as a potentially relevant predictor for specific decades and the vari-

[4]Although the numbers are removed from the documents for the experiments with the linear models, we observed in practice that having numbers in the documents may not affect the results significantly, where the MSE metric for linear regression is 232.18 when the numbers are present and 236.71 for the other case.

[5]The text, usually at the bottom of the title page, giving the details of the book's producers a well as information on price and place of publication

[6]ESTC citation number T64288.

[7]Note that as the works are split into a large number of text segments, on average over 100 per work, whose predictions are averaged, a single segment with the correct year picked up by the model does not uniquely decide the result.

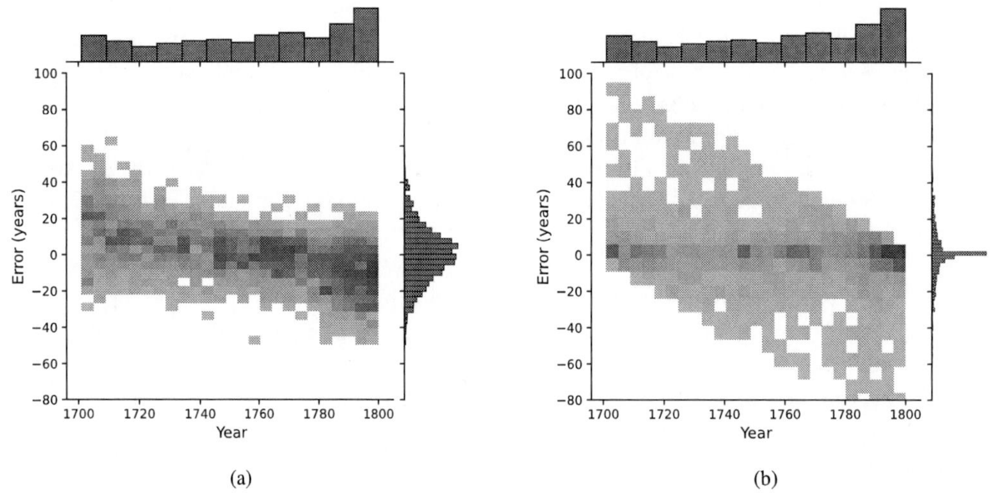

Figure 3: A histogram of the errors for linear regression (a) linear classification (b).

ation in its spelling are interesting phenomenon from the humanities perspective.

4.4 Manual annotation

As a point of comparison, a set of human-annotated predictions was also produced. Four human annotators were provided with a set of 512-token documents and asked to predict the year of publication. In addition, they were invited to label the features within each document which they determined had been most useful in making a given decision. The annotators all had some level of familiarity or expertise with early modern texts, nevertheless this is still best considered as an initial exploratory study, rather than a fully authoritative experiment. Most importantly, the human annotators did not study each work in its entirety, unlike the models.

In total 277 human predictions were gathered, from 167 distinct document snippets. Human annotators fared much worse than the BERT model predictions for the same set of documents, with a mean absolute error of 30 (27.59 if the average for multiple guesses for the same document is taken) compared with 8.73 for the model (Figure 4a, Figure 4b). Human annotators tended to over-estimate the publication year (Figure 4a). The average errors were higher for documents published towards the end of the century, though this may be partially explained by the fact, noted in section 2, that the labelled data is also biased with more occurrences towards the end (reflecting the distribution of the full dataset).

When comparing the predictive features of the model with those given by the human annotators, categorical or thematic overlap was observed. In many cases the human annotators found it difficult to articulate reasons or pick out specific words to describe how their decision was made, but where they did, it was a mixture of recognition of spelling variations (for example, the additional e in newes, or k in publick), judgements on OCR quality – which improves significantly for documents published later in the century due to improvements in print quality and subsequent digitisation – and historical evidence, for example the mention of a known historical figure or event making it possible to give the earliest possible publication date with certainty, at least. Historical clues ranged from anything from mentions of specific events (such as the resignation of Lord North which took place in 1782) to less obvious historical clues such as the mention in a document of 'hot-house grapes', a growing technique more likely to have been used at the end of the century.

By most accounts, spelling variation in English printed works had already levelled off by 1700 (Baron et al., 2009) meaning that in theory the usefulness of orthographic change as a feature is minimal. However *some* variation is still found, particularly in the earlier part of the eighteenth century, which may account for the fact that human annotators were moderately better at predicting earlier works than later. As expected, a key clue in predicting earlier dates are OCR errors and long-s words transliterated as f. This may also be part of the reason why average errors were highest towards

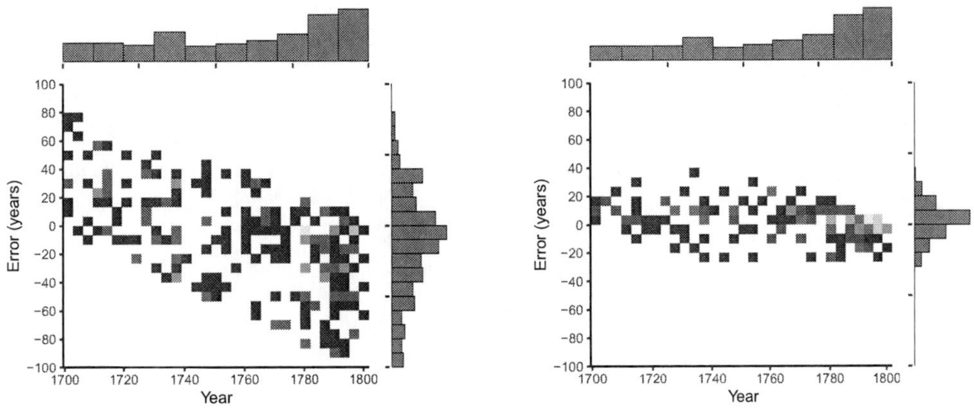

(a) (b)

Figure 4: Comparison of human annotations (a) and model predictions (b) for the same set of 167 document snippets.

the very end of the period: the use of the long s declined rapidly by 1800 and so is a less useful clue for dating a document.

The annotators reported that the task was difficult, particularly when judging a year of publication from what was usually a snippet from a much larger text. While reprints in ECCO have been removed as described in section 2, the partial re-use of text is common, for example in miscellanies, anthologies, and collected works. One consequence of this is that typical humanistic features of text such as style of writing were not always helpful in a decision about year of publication. To give one example, an incorrectly-labelled (by a human) annotation included part of a poem written by John Sheffield, Duke of Buckingham who died in 1721, but was actually in this case from a collected works published in 1780 and thus labelled with the later date in the task. Overall, spelling, OCR artifacts, and typographical changes were more useful as predictive features.

The annotation task, then, was valuable firstly as a way to understand the differences between the ways a machine model and human annotator might use features to predict years. Secondly, it shed some light on the way those with domain expertise might judge the year of publication of a particular work based on its text abstracted from the material context in which it was found. From a humanistic point of view, the task highlights the fact that human judgement of publication dates is very unreliable when dealing with extracts from larger texts, and presumably relies to a great extent on contextual information, for example font, paper, and the condition of a particular book, rather than its content.

5 Conclusions

The contributions of the paper are two-fold. Firstly, we pre-trained and openly distribute a BERT model specifically focusing on the historical English language in the Eighteenth Century Collections Online (ECCO) that is widely used in the humanities. To benchmark the model and gain understanding of its performance on historical English, we use the task of publication year prediction, in other words given the text, the task is to regress its publication year.

Our findings and analysis of the model's performance on this task then form the second contribution of the paper. We establish that the accuracy with which the model is able to predict the year of publication is well above our baseline models on full documents and also well above human performance on text snippets.

We also carried out an initial qualitative analysis of predictive features, both for our simple linear baselines and for the BERT models. We observe a degree of a useful signal among these features, intuitively understandable to a human, demonstrating the applicability of model explanation techniques also to the complex BERT model. Nevertheless, it is clear that numerous challenges still remain.

This initial study has several natural future work directions. Firstly, a further, more detailed analysis of the predictive features, and therefore of the model's predictions is clearly called for. Secondly, a more detailed comparison between human and model decisions will be carried out. And finally, as we have not specifically taken into account the OCR noise when pre-training the BERT models, more noise-aware variants of the transformer model, e.g. character-based models, will be tested on the ECCO data. The ECCO-BERT model is freely available as `TurkuNLP/eccobert-base-cased-v1` in the Hugging Face model repository.

Acknowledgements

The research was supported by the Academy of Finland under the project *High Performance Computing for the Detection and Analysis of Historical Discourses*. Computational resources were provided by CSC – IT Center for Science.

References

David Bamman and Patrick J. Burns. 2020. Latin BERT: A contextual language model for classical philology. *CoRR*, abs/2009.10053.

Chris Barker. 2004. *The SAGE dictionary of cultural studies*. Sage Publications Ltd.

Alistair Baron. 2011. *Dealing with spelling variation in Early Modern English texts*. Ph.D. thesis, Lancaster University.

Alistair Baron, Paul Rayson, and Dawn Archer. 2009. Word frequency and key word statistics in historical corpus linguistics. *Anglistik: International Journal of English Studies*, 20:41–67.

Kaspar Beelen, Federico Nanni, Mariona Coll Ardanuy, Kasra Hosseini, Giorgia Tolfo, and Barbara McGillivray. 2021. When time makes sense: A historically-aware approach to targeted sense disambiguation. In *Findings of the Association for Computational Linguistics: ACL-IJCNLP 2021*, pages 2751–2761, Online. Association for Computational Linguistics.

Mariona Coll Ardanuy, Federico Nanni, Kaspar Beelen, Kasra Hosseini, Ruth Ahnert, Jon Lawrence, Katherine McDonough, Giorgia Tolfo, Daniel CS Wilson, and Barbara McGillivray. 2020. Living machines: A study of atypical animacy. In *Proceedings of the 28th International Conference on Computational Linguistics*, pages 4534–4545, Barcelona, Spain (Online). International Committee on Computational Linguistics.

Koby Crammer and Yoram Singer. 2001. On the algorithmic implementation of multiclass kernel-based vector machines. *Journal of machine learning research*, 2(Dec):265–292.

Jacob Devlin, Ming-Wei Chang, Kenton Lee, and Kristina Toutanova. 2019. BERT: Pre-training of deep bidirectional transformers for language understanding. In *Proceedings of the 2019 Conference of the North American Chapter of the Association for Computational Linguistics: Human Language Technologies, Volume 1 (Long and Short Papers)*, pages 4171–4186, Minneapolis, Minnesota. Association for Computational Linguistics.

Maud Ehrmann, Ahmed Hamdi, Elvys Linhares Pontes, Matteo Romanello, and Antoine Doucet. 2021. Named entity recognition and classification on historical documents: A survey. *ArXiv*, abs/2109.11406.

Rong-En Fan, Kai-Wei Chang, Cho-Jui Hsieh, Xiang-Rui Wang, and Chih-Jen Lin. 2008. Liblinear: A library for large linear classification. *Journal of machine learning research*, 9(Aug):1871–1874.

Gale. Eighteenth Century Collections Online.

Ahmed Hamdi, Elvys Linhares Pontes, Emanuela Boros, Thi-Tuyet-Hai Nguyen, Günter Hackl, Jose G. Moreno, and Antoine Doucet. 2021. A multilingual dataset for named entity recognition, entity linking and stance detection in historical newspapers. *Proceedings of the 44th International ACM SIGIR Conference on Research and Development in Information Retrieval*.

Mark J Hill and Simon Hengchen. 2019. Quantifying the impact of dirty OCR on historical text analysis: Eighteenth Century Collections Online as a case study. *Digital Scholarship in the Humanities*, 34(4):825–843.

Kasra Hosseini, Kaspar Beelen, Giovanni Colavizza, and Mariona Coll Ardanuy. 2021. Neural language models for nineteenth-century english.

Ming Jiang, Yuerong Hu, Glen Worthey, Ryan C. Dubnicek, Ted Underwood, and J. Stephen Downie. 2021. Impact of ocr quality on bert embeddings in the domain classification of book excerpts. *CEUR Workshop Proceedings*, 2989:266–279. Publisher Copyright: © 2021 Copyright for this paper by its authors.; 2021 Conference on Computational Humanities Research, CHR 2021 ; Conference date: 17-11-2021 Through 19-11-2021.

Kai Labusch, Clemens Neudecker, and David Zellhöfer. 2019. Bert for named entity recognition in contemporary and historic german. In *KONVENS*.

Matthew Sims, Jong Ho Park, and David Bamman. 2019. Literary Event Detection. In *Proceedings of the 57th Annual Meeting of the Association for Computational Linguistics*, pages 3623–3634, Florence, Italy. Association for Computational Linguistics.

Mukund Sundararajan, Ankur Taly, and Qiqi Yan. 2017. Axiomatic attribution for deep networks. In *Proceedings of the 34th International Conference on Machine Learning - Volume 70*, ICML'17, page 3319–3328. JMLR.org.

Iiro Tiihonen, Mikko Tolonen, and Leo Lahti. 2021. Probabilistic analysis of early modern british book prices. volume 2989 of *CEUR Workshop Proceedings*, pages 39–48. CEUR-WS.org.

Mikko Tolonen, Eetu Mäkelä, Ali Ijaz, and Leo Lahti. 2021. Corpus linguistics and eighteenth century collections online (ecco). *Research in Corpus Linguistics*, 9(1):19–34.

Daniel van Strien., Kaspar Beelen., Mariona Ardanuy., Kasra Hosseini., Barbara McGillivray., and Giovanni Colavizza. 2020. Assessing the impact of ocr quality on downstream nlp tasks. In *Proceedings of the 12th International Conference on Agents and Artificial Intelligence - Volume 1: ARTIDIGH,*, pages 484–496. INSTICC, SciTePress.

Ashish Vaswani, Noam Shazeer, Niki Parmar, Jakob Uszkoreit, Llion Jones, Aidan N Gomez, Ł ukasz Kaiser, and Illia Polosukhin. 2017. Attention is all you need. In *Advances in Neural Information Processing Systems*, volume 30. Curran Associates, Inc.

Peng Yu and Xin Wang. 2020. Bert-based named entity recognition in chinese twenty-four histories. In *Web Information Systems and Applications*, pages 289–301, Cham. Springer International Publishing.

Using Cross-Lingual Part of Speech Tagging for Partially Reconstructing the Classic Language Family Tree Model

Anat Samohi[*]
Efi Arazi School of
Computer Science
Reichman University, Israel
anatsamohi@gmail.com

Daniel Weisberg Mitelman[*]
The Data Science Institute
Reichman University, Israel
dwmitelman@gmail.com

Kfir Bar
The Data Science Institute
Reichman University, Israel
barkfir@yahoo.com

Abstract

The tree model is well known for expressing the historic evolution of languages. This model has been considered as a method of describing genetic relationships between languages. Nevertheless, some researchers question the model's ability to predict the proximity between two languages, since it represents genetic relatedness rather than linguistic resemblance. Defining other language proximity models has been an active research area for many years. In this paper we explore a part-of-speech model for defining proximity between languages using a multilingual language model that was fine-tuned on the task of cross-lingual part-of-speech tagging. We train the model on one language and evaluate it on another; the measured performance is then used to define the proximity between the two languages. By further developing the model, we show that it can reconstruct some parts of the tree model.

1 Introduction

Language families are defined by the evolution of languages over the history, providing indications regarding the proximity between them. The tree model, which was first introduced by Augustus Schleicher (Schleicher, 1853) is considered as the consensual language-family model. For example, Figure 1 shows the Indo-European branch of the tree model; a full version of the model is nicely presented on *Ethnologue*[1]. In this paper, we refer to this source as a reference for the classic family tree model.

Concomitantly, there have been theories that question the tree model as being an indicator for language proximity, since it represents genetic relatedness rather than lexical resemblance. Loanwords, as well as other lexical influences are usually not expressed in the classic tree model. Representing historical relatedness, the tree is agnostic to various linguistic influences. Consequently, some claim that language families should be defined by alternative models (Geisler and List, 2013).

The Universal Grammar, introduced by Noam Chomsky, is usually defined as the "system of categories, mechanisms and constraints shared by all human languages and considered to be innate" (Dobrovolsky et al., 2016). In other words, a human language is derived from a set of structural rules, typically referred to as *generative grammar*, which we are usually totally unaware of. We can intuitively distinguish between nouns and verbs; children can phrase a sentence they have not heard before by ordering parts of speech they are familiar with in a valid grammatical order. A child can identify a noun without knowing what a noun is, or without even understanding the meaning of that specific noun.

It may be assumed that rather than this aspect of universal grammar being specific to language, it is more generally a part of human cognition, and there might be a common structure for different languages. Still, the ability to classify words into parts of speech requires some knowledge of the structure of the specific language.

The hypothesis we examine in this paper relies on the assumption that historically close languages, like French and Spanish, share some information that may help the classification of words into part-of-speech (POS) tags. While identifying this type of information is out of scope for this paper, we will show that this information can be used by a neural network for predicting POS tags of one language only using examples from another language.

Our goal is to redefine the proximity between languages to achieve a comparable model to the classic tree model, by considering only POS tags.

[*]Equal contribution.

[1]https://www.ethnologue.com/browse/families

Proceedings of the 3rd Workshop on Computational Approaches to Historical Language Change, pages 78 - 88
May 26-27, 2022 ©2022 Association for Computational Linguistics

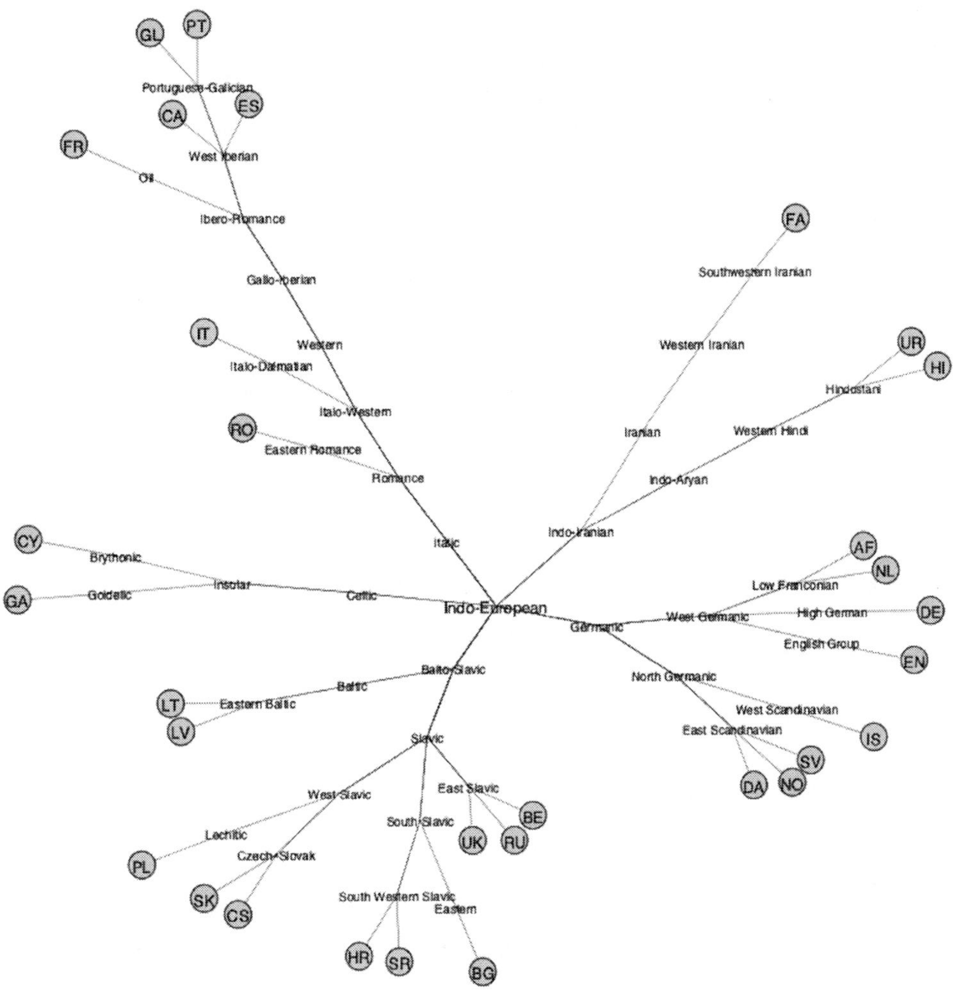

Figure 1: The Indo-European language branch; the graph was created by the `igraph` package for Python (Csardi and Nepusz, 2006). The languages are represented using their equivalent two-letter ISO 639-1 code.

To enable transferability between languages, we suggest using a multilingual pre-trained language model (MPLM), fine-tuned for the POS tagging task in a multilingual environment. Specifically, we take a multilingual zero-shot training approach by fine-tuning an MPLM to predict POS tags for texts written in one language, the source language, and evaluating it on texts written in another language, the target language. The performance metrics are then used to estimate the similarity between the source and target languages. As a final step, we generate a language-similarity graph, which we describe as an approximation for the classic tree model. We make two main contributions: (1) Reconstructing part of the classic tree model using POS-based similarity scores; and, (2) Providing some insights into the cross-lingual generalization of MPLMs.

We proceed as follows: In Section 2 we cite some related studies, following by a detailed description of our method, provided in Section 3. We end Section 3 with reporting on some results. We discuss the results in Section 4 and make some conclusions.

2 Related Work

There have been some prior studies on measuring distance between languages. In their paper, Chiswick and Miller (2005) presented some empirical observations of how rapidly speakers of a given language gained proficiency in another tongue. Specifically, they measured the speed of English acquisition by immigrants of various linguistic backgrounds in the United States and Canada. Their first languages were ranked for the distance from English, on a scale from 1.0 (very different than English) to 3.0 (closest to English). It has been found empirically that the greater the distance between an immigrant's origin language and English, the lower is the level of the immigrant's English language proficiency.

There have been many attempts to use computational tools to infer the relations between languages; the dominant approach is known as *phylogenetic linguistics*. Phylogenetic linguistics is about establishing historical relationships among languages, by considering the evolutionary nature of human languages. In computational phylogenetics, words and/or phonemes of what counts as the same language over time, are analyzed and compared among languages.

Specifically, Swadesh (1950) was first to introduce a computational phylogenetic technique called *lexicostatistics* for comparing between two languages. In lexicostatistics, the similarity between two languages is calculated by a function of the percentage of cognates found in a predefined list of words of the two languages. Swadesh's work has been followed by a number of studies that use lexicostatistics or a minor variation of it (Nakhleh et al., 2005; Holman et al., 2008; Bakker et al., 2009; Petroni and Serva, 2010; Barbançon et al., 2013).

Instead of measuring the percentage of cognates, Petroni and Serva (Petroni and Serva, 2008; Serva and Petroni, 2008) proposed to calculate a normalized Levenstein distance among words with the same meaning and then to take the average over the words contained in a cross-lingual list. Müller et al. (2010) conducted a lexical comparison using the Levenstein distance approach, between 4,350 languages of the ASJP database (Brown et al., 2008), and created a full diagram of lexical proximity. They showed that lexical resemblance is related to genetic affiliation. However, some of the languages that have been found as lexically similar, according to their technique, are not closely genetically associated.

Another computational approach for measuring language similarity is based on corpus analysis. Gamallo et al. (2017) used the known perplexity score of a probabilistic n-gram language model to measure the distance between European languages. Asgari and Mofrad (2016) compared 50 languages from different families by training a monolingual language model on each language individually, using a parallel corpus of the Bible (Christodouloupoulos and Steedman, 2015), and apply them to calculate perplexity on all the other languages. In some of the works that are mentioned above, the proximity between languages is not perfectly aligned with the classic tree model.

While the main focus has always been on lexical similarity, some attempts were made to compare languages on the syntactic level. Longobardi and Guardiano (2009) characterized 28 languages, mostly Indo-European ones, using a set of 63 predefined morpho-syntactic parameters. They calculated a normalized Hamming distance over those parametric representations, with which they were able to generate a language tree. They showed that this tree is equivalent to a tree that was generated based on a traditional lexicostatistics approach, suggesting that syntactic characteristics are sufficiently robust to reconstruct a plausible historical language tree. The same method was re-used in (Longobardi et al., 2013), which was concluded in a similar way. In a recent work, Shu et al. (2021) applied a different comparison technique on the same syntactic characteristics, using Markov models. In all of those works, the selection of the syntactic characteristics to be used for comparison, plays an important role in the creation of a language proximity model.

To the best of our knowledge, there have not been attempts to compare languages using syntactic information in a non-parametric way. In this work, we take a corpus-based approach to automatically extract part-of-speech tags from a given text in order to generate a language-proximity model. In that sense, we consider our approach as a non-parametric estimation method, since we do not need to manually define specific syntactic parameters to consider for calculating similarity between languages.

To transfer information across languages, we use mBERT, a multilingual version of BERT (Devlin et al., 2019), that was pre-trained on texts written in over 100 languages based on a shared vocabulary.[2] During pre-training, the training documents are given to mBERT without any indication on the language that they have been written with. Like

[2]Similar to BERT, mBERT's tokens are subwords.

every other pre-trained language model (PLM), the pre-trained mBERT model is typically fine-tuned on a training set of a specific downstream task, which could be either monolingual or multilingual. This unique multilingual design allows mBERT to handle multilingual tasks in a transfer-learning way. In another study, Wu and Dredze (2019) reported an impressive performance using mBERT in a zero-shot cross-lingual transfer learning setting on several NLP tasks, including POS tagging. They claimed that mBERT may learn a cross-lingual representation by generalizing and abstracting some language-specific information. A similar observation was made by Gonen et al. (2020) who claimed that mBERT learns information by two components, one that encodes the language and another that encodes some abstract information that can be used in a cross-lingual way.

3 Methodology

3.1 Language Similarity Score

For every pair of languages, source language and target language, we measure their similarity as the performance of an mBERT-based POS tagger fine-tuned on the source language, and evaluated on the target language. For training and evaluation, we use treebanks from Universal Dependencies (UD).[3] In particular, we use the Universal POS labels[4] assigned for every syntactic word in the text. The Universal POS tagset contains the following core part-of-speech categories that can be used for any UD language: adjective, adposition, adverb, auxiliary, coordinating conjunction, determiner, interjection, noun, numeral, particle, pronoun, proper noun, punctuation, subordinating conjunction, symbol, verb and other. Each treebank is divided to train and test sets. Therefore, we fine-tune mBERT on the UPOS (universal POS) tagging task using the source language's training set, and evaluate it on the target language's testing set.

Our selected evaluation metric is the micro average F1 score. Clearly, for every pair of languages we calculate two F1 scores, one for each direction. The two scores are not necessarily equivalent.

In all our experiments, we use the commonly used pre-trained language model `bert-base-multilingual-cased`, provided by the Hugging Face transformers library (Wolf et al., 2019). For every language we fine-tune the model for the standard token classification downstream task for three epochs, using a learning rate value of $5e-5$.

We include 36 languages in our study, taken from a diversity of language families and subfamilies. The full list of languages is provided in Figure 2. For each language we indicate its two-letter ISO 639-1 code, which we use throughout the paper. All the 36 languages we process are covered by mBERT.

Overall, we calculate the F1 score for every pair of languages, resulting in $36^2 = 1296$ scores. A partial list of the scores is provided in Table 1, while the full set of results is added as Appendix A. Clearly, the model that is trained on English performs better on Spanish than on Russian and Hindi.

Src/Trgt	EN	ES	RU	HI
EN	0.97	0.84	0.80	0.64
ES	0.80	0.99	0.80	0.58
RU	0.74	0.81	0.98	0.64
HI	0.61	0.57	0.67	0.97

Table 1: F1 scores for some of the language pairs. Rows represent source languages, while columns represent the target languages. For example, the first row represents the F1 scores resulted from evaluating mBERT on the UPOS tagged test sets in English, Spanish, Russian and Hindi, after previously fine-tuned on the English UPOS tagged train set.

As mentioned before, the two F1 scores that were calculated for each pair of different languages, are not necessarily equal. In fact, they are very unlikely to be equal, since the performance of the tagger is affected not only by the difference between the languages, but also by the size and the quality of the training sets, as well as the volume and quality of the texts in each relevant language, which were used for training mBERT.

The average of the absolute difference between all language pairs is 0.0874 and the standard deviation is 0.074. While some pairs have relatively similar scores in both directions, some other have significantly different ones. However, as we show later, we do not use the F1 scores directly as some sort of a distance function between the languages. Instead, we represent each language l by a vector of F1 scores calculated by all other models during evaluation on l's testing set, and use a clustering

[3] https://universaldependencies.org

[4] https://universaldependencies.org/u/pos

Romance	Germanic	Uralic	Iranian
Spanish (ES) Portuguese (PT) French (FR) Catalan (CA) Italian (IT) Galician (GL) Romanian (RO)	English (EN) German (DE) Dutch (NL) Afrikaans (AF) Icelandic (IS) Norwegian (NO) Danish (DA) Swedish (SV)	Estonian (ET) Hungarian (HU) Finnish (FI)	Persian (FA)

Slavic	Baltic	Hindustani	Semitic	Celtic
Russian (RU) Ukrainian (UK) Belarusian (BE) Polish (PL) Czech (CS) Slovak (SK) Bulgarian (BG) Croatian (HR) Serbian (SR)	Lithuanian (LT) Latvian (LV)	Hindi (HI) Urdu (UR)	Arabic (AR) Hebrew (HE)	Irish (GA) Welsh (CY)

Figure 2: The 36 languages we include in our study. We chose languages from different families and subfamilies. The two-letter ISO 639-1 code is provided in parentheses next to each language name.

algorithm to organize these vectors into language families.

Before we show how we do that, first, we argue that our cross-lingual F1 score is an important piece of information for reconstructing the classic tree model. Our argument is based on the correlation between our cross-lingual F1 score and the proximity of language pairs in the classic tree model. In order to measure the proximity between two languages in the classic tree model, we use the Wu-Palmer similarity (Wu and Palmer, 1994) metric, which was originally invented for measuring relatedness of two synsets in a WordNet taxonomy. For the context of using Wu-Palmer, the tree model has the same characteristics as WordNet; language family names are represented by intermediate nodes, while language names are represented by the leaves. Therefore, the Wu-Palmer score for two languages L_1, L_2 is calculated as follows:

$$2 \cdot \frac{depth(lcs(L_1, L_2))}{depth(L_1) + depth(L_2)}$$

with lcs representing the least common subsumer, that is, the first common ancestor of the two languages in the language-family tree. The score ranges between 0 and 1, but it can never go to zero since the depth of $lcs(L_1, L_2)$ is never zero (the model tree has a single root).

We denote the Wu-Palmer score as WP. As opposed to our cross-lingual F1 score, WP is symmetric.

We calculate WP for every language pair, and compare with our F1; the results are shown in Figure 3. Every data point in this chart represents a single language pair out of the 36^2 pairs. Overall, we learn that the F1 score increases along with WP, except maybe on relatively small WP values, representing pairs of languages taken from significantly different branches of the language-family tree.

Furthermore, we measure the correlation between the two metrics using Pearson (for linear correlation) and Spearman (for monotonic correlation) and realize that both are strongly correlated with Pearson$= 0.64$ (at $p < 0.001$), and Spearman$= 0.59$, (at $p < 0.001$).

Figure 4 visualizes the F1 scores of all language pairs as a heatmap, with target languages provided as rows and source languages as columns. For each target language, all the 36 source languages are sorted according to the F1 scores (from the highest to the lowest). The color represents the proximity, as calculated by the WP score; a lighter color is equivalent to a higher proximity. For example in the fifth row, the best performance on the Spanish test set is observed by the Spanish model, followed by other Romance languages, Catalan, Italian, Portuguese and so on. The worst performance was recorded by the Welsh model. Evidently, higher

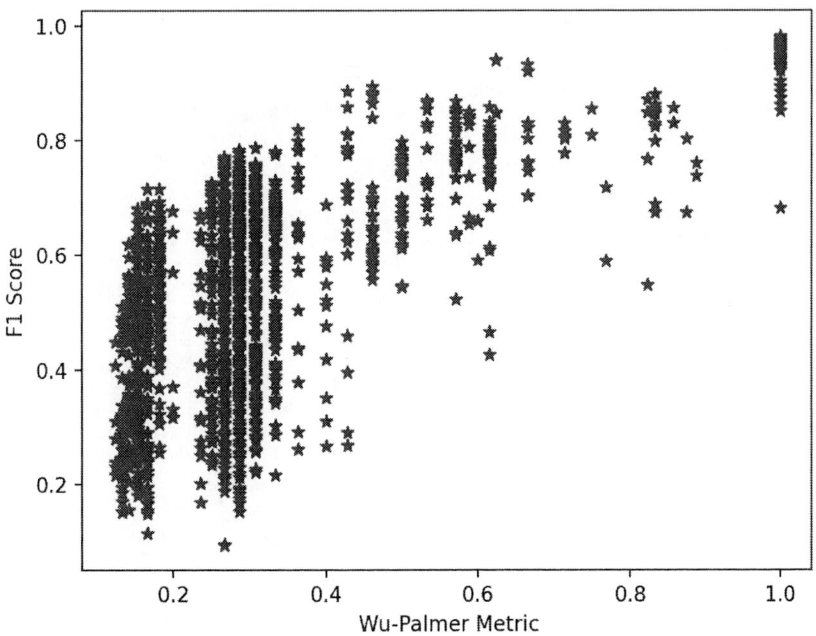

Figure 3: UPOS F1 scores compared with WP scores.

proximity values (light boxes on the left side of the heatmap) derive higher performance on the cross-lingual POS task, indicating that the closer two languages are, the encoded information in their corresponding models tends to be more helpful for POS tagging.

3.2 Reconstructing Language Families

In this section we show how we use the resulting F1 scores, calculated for every language pair, to reconstruct the language-family tree.

We represent every language l by a 36-dimensional vector consisted of the F1 scores of the models that have been trained on all other languages, evaluated on l. We generate exactly 36 vectors, one for each language. Conceptually, the vector of language l represents the similarity of l to all the other languages, by considering only cross-lingual UPOS information, as captured by mBERT.

To identify families and subfamilies of languages, we use k-means (Lloyd, 1982) to cluster the 36 vectors. In addition to the collection of vectors, k-means receives as input a parameter k that denotes the number of clusters.

According to Figure 2, the tree model organizes the 36 languages into 9 families; therefore, we run k-means with value of $k = 9$. In Figure 5 we visualize the resulting clusters. The color of the circle next to the language name marks the cluster. Note that while the k-means algorithm works with 36-dimensional vectors given as an input, we visualize the vectors on a 2-dimensional axis, which we calculate using the principal component analysis (PCA) algorithm for reducing dimensions. The clusters are summarized in Table 2. We discuss the results in the following section.

3.3 Results

The alternative partitioning for language families that we get, partially align with the classic tree model.

Cluster 1 contains only Romance languages. All languages in cluster 2, except Romanian, are considered as Germanic in the classic tree model. Cluster 3 contains all Slavic languages excluding the Baltic languages. Cluster 4 includes the Baltic languages (Lithuanian and Latvian) as well as two Uralic languages (Finnish and Estonian). Those four languages are spoken in the geographically close countries Lithuania, Latvia, Finland and Estonia, respectively, suggesting that there might be a geographical dimension in our POS-based language proximity method. We plan to further investigate this discovery as one of our future directions. Cluster 6 contains only Hindustani languages. The two Semitic languages (Hebrew and Arabic) are grouped together in cluster 7, which also includes

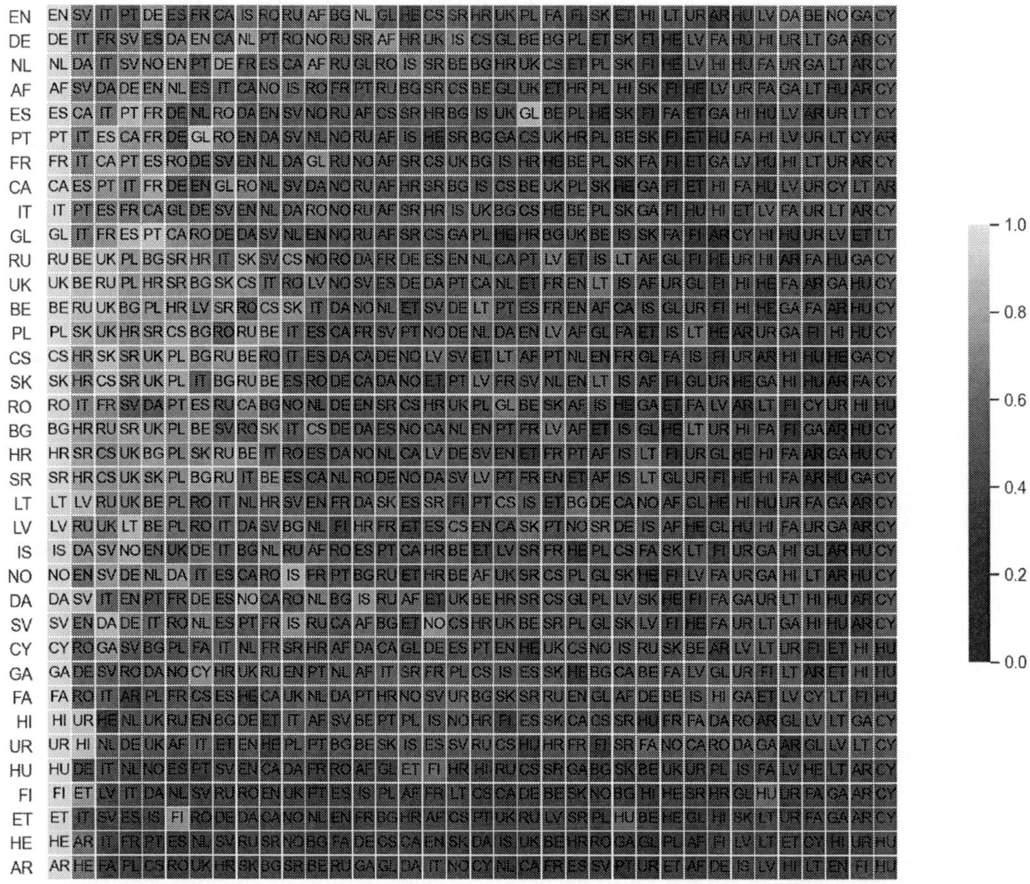

Figure 4: A heatmap of the WP scores calculated for all language pairs, sorted according to F1 scores. For more information about this arrangement see the text.

Cluster	Languages	Family
1	Spanish, Portuguese, French, Catalan, Italian, Galician	Romance
2	English, German, Dutch, Afrikaans, Icelandic, Norwegian, Danish, Swedish, Romanian	Mostly Germanic
3	Russian, Ukrainian, Belarusian, Polish, Czech, Slovak, Bulgarian, Croatian, Serbian	Slavic
4	Lithuanian, Latvian, Finnish, Estonian	Baltic and Uralic
5	Hungarian	Uralic
6	Hindi, Urdu	Hindustani
7	Persian, Hebrew, Arabic	Iranian and Semitic
8	Irish	Celtic
9	Welsh	Celtic

Table 2: The clusters obtained by running k-means with $k = 9$. We provide some information about the language families of each cluster in the third column.

Persian probably due to historical influences. Hungarian is the only language in cluster 5. Clusters 8 and 9 represents two languages of the Celtic family. They should have probably been clustered together.

Overall although there are a few misplacements, our clustering method was able to reconstruct parts of the tree model. 31 out of 36 languages were classified correctly according to the classic model.

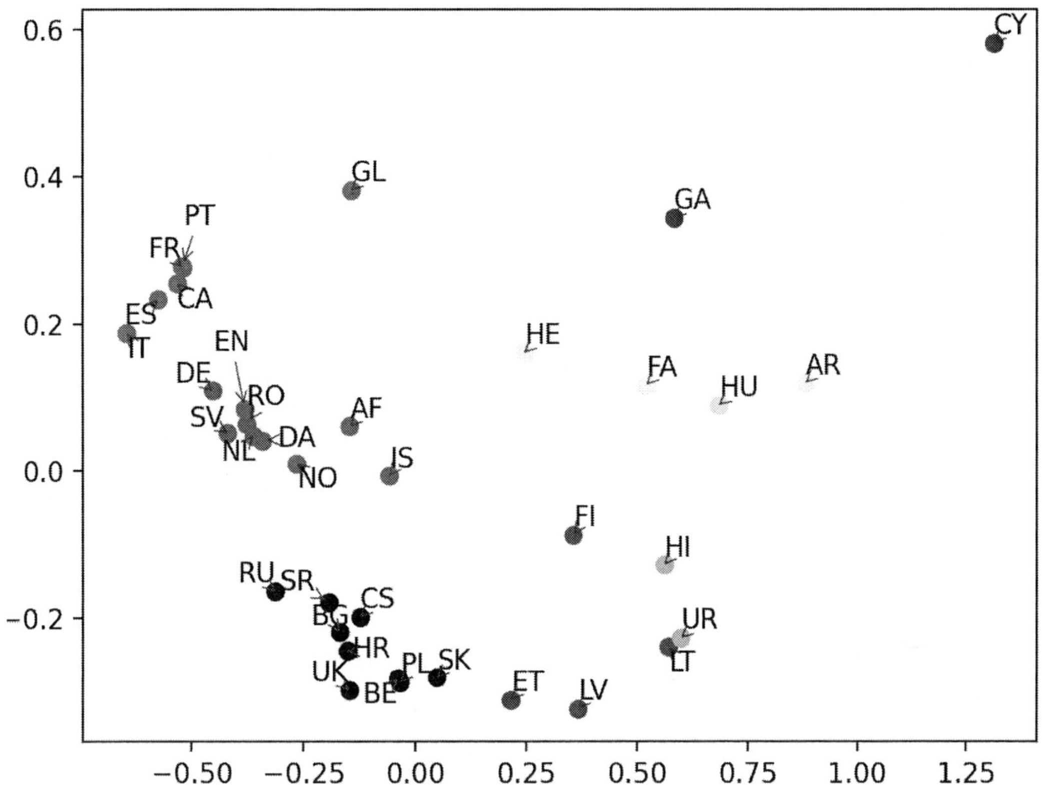

Figure 5: The 9 clusters resulted from k-means. The original 36-dimensional vectors are visualized using their first two principle components.

4 Discussion and Conclusions

In this work we used a cross-lingual model trained on UPOS for measuring the proximity between languages. We showed that our new language-proximity model can reconstruct families of genetically related languages, suggesting that POS information plays a major role in modelling similarity between languages.

We believe that we have demonstrated the potential of a fine-tuned mBERT model to capture some cross-lingual information that is needed for assigning UPOS tags to a text written in an unseen language. On average, models of genetically related languages perform better on each other in this task, even if they are not written in the same script. For example, in Table 1 we show that a Spanish (ES) model performs similarly on English (EN) and Russian (RU), although both Spanish and English are written in the Latin script while Russian is written in the Cyrillic script.

There are a few caveats to this research to note. mBERT was pre-trained on the full collections of Wikipedia articles in the relevant languages. Therefore, the size of those collections varies proportionally to the number of active speakers. To handle that bias, the authors of mBERT had decided to upsample the Wikipedia collections of the less dominant languages, in the main training loop. Wu and Dredze (2020) have recently addressed that problem and showed that mBERT performs better on cross-lingual zero-shot tasks on languages that have large Wikipedia collections. In our work, we handle that bias by designing each individual language vector to have F1 scores from all other languages, including both high-resource and low-resource languages. Therefore, every language is represented by F1 scores achieved by models trained on exactly the same language set.

Another caveat is the size and quality of the treebanks we use for training and testing our models. As noted before, we believe that our approach to represent a language using scores from models trained on all the 36 language included in this research, mitigates this risk.

We make a final practical observation. The results of our study suggest that for UPOS tagging, mBERT may benefit from training on texts written in languages that are genetically similar to the target language, based on the classic tree model. These results are aligned with what have been reported by Wu and Dredze (2020).

References

Ehsaneddin Asgari and Mohammad R.K. Mofrad. 2016. Comparing fifty natural languages and twelve genetic languages using word embedding language divergence (WELD) as a quantitative measure of language distance. In *Proceedings of the Workshop on Multilingual and Cross-lingual Methods in NLP*, pages 65–74, San Diego, California. Association for Computational Linguistics.

Dik Bakker, André Müller, Viveka Velupillai, Søren Wichmann, Cecil H Brown, Pamela Brown, Dmitry Egorov, Robert Mailhammer, Anthony Grant, and Eric W Holman. 2009. Adding typology to lexicostatistics: A combined approach to language classification.

François Barbançon, Steven N Evans, Luay Nakhleh, Don Ringe, and Tandy Warnow. 2013. An experimental study comparing linguistic phylogenetic reconstruction methods. *Diachronica*, 30(2):143–170.

Cecil H Brown, Eric W Holman, Søren Wichmann, and Viveka Velupillai. 2008. Automated classification of the world s languages: a description of the method and preliminary results. *Language Typology and Universals*, 61(4):285–308.

Barry R Chiswick and Paul W Miller. 2005. Linguistic distance: A quantitative measure of the distance between English and other languages. *Journal of Multilingual and Multicultural Development*, 26(1):1–11.

Christos Christodouloupoulos and Mark Steedman. 2015. A massively parallel corpus: The Bible in 100 languages. *Language resources and evaluation*, 49(2):375–395.

Gabor Csardi and Tamas Nepusz. 2006. The igraph software package for complex network research. *InterJournal*, Complex Systems:1695.

Jacob Devlin, Ming-Wei Chang, Kenton Lee, and Kristina Toutanova. 2019. BERT: Pre-training of deep bidirectional transformers for language understanding. In *Proceedings of the 2019 Conference of the North American Chapter of the Association for Computational Linguistics: Human Language Technologies, Volume 1 (Long and Short Papers)*, pages 4171–4186, Minneapolis, Minnesota. Association for Computational Linguistics.

Michael Dobrovolsky, William Delaney O'Grady, and Francis Katamba. 2016. *Contemporary Linguistics*. Longman.

Pablo Gamallo, José Ramom Pichel, and Iñaki Alegria. 2017. From language identification to language distance. *Physica A: Statistical Mechanics and its Applications*, 484:152–162.

Hans Geisler and Johann-Mattis List. 2013. Do languages grow on trees? The tree metaphor in the history of linguistics. *Classification and evolution in biology, linguistics and the history of science. Concepts–methods–visualization*, pages 111–124.

Hila Gonen, Shauli Ravfogel, Yanai Elazar, and Yoav Goldberg. 2020. It's not Greek to mBERT: Inducing word-level translations from multilingual BERT. In *Proceedings of the Third BlackboxNLP Workshop on Analyzing and Interpreting Neural Networks for NLP*, pages 45–56, Online. Association for Computational Linguistics.

Eric W Holman, Søren Wichmann, Cecil H Brown, Viveka Velupillai, André Müller, and Dik Bakker. 2008. Explorations in automated lexicostatistics. *Folia Linguistica*, 42(2):331–354.

Stuart Lloyd. 1982. Least squares quantization in PCM. *IEEE transactions on information theory*, 28(2):129–137.

Giuseppe Longobardi and Cristina Guardiano. 2009. Evidence for syntax as a signal of historical relatedness. *Lingua*, 119(11):1679–1706.

Giuseppe Longobardi, Cristina Guardiano, Giuseppina Silvestri, Alessio Boattini, and Andrea Ceolin. 2013. Toward a syntactic phylogeny of modern Indo-European languages. *Journal of Historical Linguistics*, 3(1):122–152.

André Müller, Søren Wichmann, Viveka Velupillai, Cecil H Brown, Pamela Brown, Sebastian Sauppe, Eric W Holman, Dik Bakker, Johann-Mattis List, Dmitri Egorov, et al. 2010. ASJP world language tree of lexical similarity: Version 3 (July 2010). *Retrieved*, 10(19):2015.

Luay Nakhleh, Don Ringe, and Tandy Warnow. 2005. Perfect phylogenetic networks: A new methodology for reconstructing the evolutionary history of natural languages. *Language*, pages 382–420.

Filippo Petroni and Maurizio Serva. 2008. Language distance and tree reconstruction. *Journal of Statistical Mechanics: Theory and Experiment*, 2008(08):P08012.

Filippo Petroni and Maurizio Serva. 2010. Measures of lexical distance between languages. *Physica A: Statistical Mechanics and its Applications*, 389(11):2280–2283.

August Schleicher. 1853. Die ersten spaltungen des indogermanischen urvolkes. *Allgemeine Monatsschrift für Wissenschaft und Literatur*, 3:786–787.

Maurizio Serva and Filippo Petroni. 2008. Indo-European languages tree by Levenshtein distance. *EPL (Europhysics Letters)*, 81(6):68005.

Kevin Shu, Andrew Ortegaray, Robert C Berwick, and Matilde Marcolli. 2021. Phylogenetics of Indo-European language families via an algebro-geometric analysis of their syntactic structures. *Mathematics in Computer Science*, pages 1–55.

Morris Swadesh. 1950. Salish internal relationships. *International Journal of American Linguistics*, 16(4):157–167.

Thomas Wolf, Lysandre Debut, Victor Sanh, Julien Chaumond, Clement Delangue, Anthony Moi, Pierric Cistac, Tim Rault, Rémi Louf, Morgan Funtowicz, et al. 2019. Huggingface's transformers: State-of-the-art natural language processing. *arXiv preprint arXiv:1910.03771*.

Shijie Wu and Mark Dredze. 2019. Beto, bentz, becas: The surprising cross-lingual effectiveness of BERT. In *Proceedings of the 2019 Conference on Empirical Methods in Natural Language Processing and the 9th International Joint Conference on Natural Language Processing (EMNLP-IJCNLP)*, pages 833–844, Hong Kong, China. Association for Computational Linguistics.

Shijie Wu and Mark Dredze. 2020. Are all languages created equal in multilingual BERT? In *Proceedings of the 5th Workshop on Representation Learning for NLP*, pages 120–130, Online. Association for Computational Linguistics.

Zhibiao Wu and Martha Palmer. 1994. Verb semantics and lexical selection. In *Proceedings of the 32nd Annual meeting of the Associations for Computational Linguistics*, pages 133–138.

A Appendix: F1 Scores

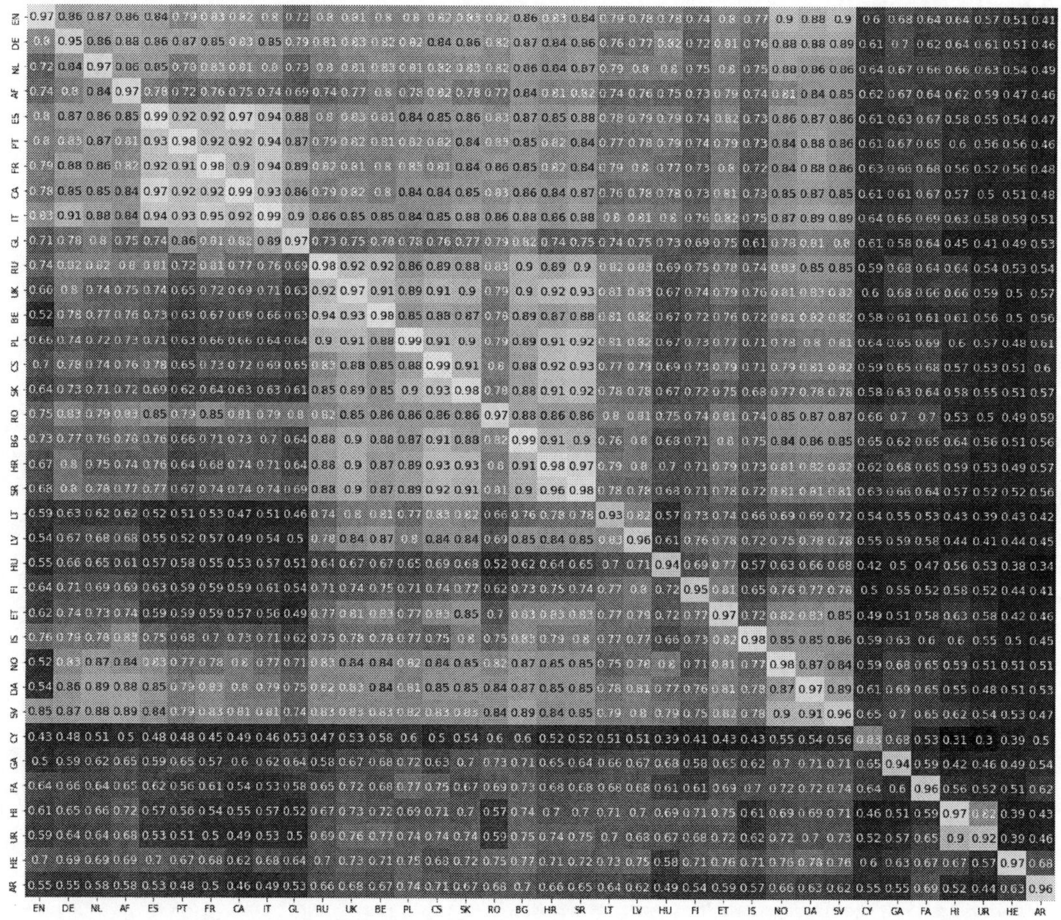

Figure 6: F1 Scores for all language pairs.

A New Framework for Fast Automated Phonological Reconstruction Using Trimmed Alignments and Sound Correspondence Patterns

Johann-Mattis List
DLCE
MPI-EVA
Leipzig
mattis_list@eva.mpg.de

Robert Forkel
DLCE
MPI-EVA
Leipzig
robert_forkel@eva.mpg.de

Nathan W. Hill
Trinity Centre for Asian Studies
University of Dublin
Dublin
nathan.hill@tcd.ie

Abstract

Computational approaches in historical linguistics have been increasingly applied during the past decade and many new methods that implement parts of the traditional comparative method have been proposed. Despite these increased efforts, there are not many easy-to-use and fast approaches for the task of phonological reconstruction. Here we present a new framework that combines state-of-the-art techniques for automated sequence comparison with novel techniques for phonetic alignment analysis and sound correspondence pattern detection to allow for the supervised reconstruction of word forms in ancestral languages. We test the method on a new dataset covering six groups from three different language families. The results show that our method yields promising results while at the same time being not only fast but also easy to apply and expand.

1 Introduction

Phonological reconstruction is a technique by which words in ancestral languages, which may not even be reflected in any sources, are restored through the systematic comparison of descendant words (*cognates*) in descendant languages (Fox, 1995). Traditionally, scholars apply the technique manually, but along with the recent quantitative turn in historical linguistics, scholars have increasingly tried to automate the procedure. Recent automatic approaches for linguistic reconstruction, be they supervised or unsupervised, show two major problems. First, the underlying code is rarely made publicly available, which means that they cannot be further tested by applying them to new datasets. Second, the methods have so far only been tested on a small amount of data from a limited number of language families. Thus, Bouchard-Côté et al. (2013) report remarkable results on the reconstruction of Oceanic languages, but the source code has never been published, and the method was never tested on additional datasets. Meloni et al. (2021) report very promising results for the automated reconstruction of Latin from Romance languages, using a new test set derived from a dataset originally provided by Dinu and Ciobanu (2014), but they could only share part of the data, due to restrictions underlying the data by Dinu and Ciobanu (2014). Bodt and List (2022) experiment with the prediction of so far unelicited words in a small group of Sino-Tibetan languages, which they registered prior to verification (Bodt and List, 2019), but they do not test the suitability of their approach for the reconstruction of ancestral languages. Jäger (2019) presents a complete pipeline by which words are clustered into cognate sets and ancestral word forms are reconstructed, but the method is only tested on a very small dataset of Romance languages.

With increasing efforts to unify and standardize lexical datasets from different sources (Forkel et al., 2018), more and more datasets that could be used to test methods for automated linguistic reconstruction have become available. Additionally, thanks to the huge progress which techniques for automated sequence comparison have made in the past decades (Kondrak, 2000; Steiner et al., 2011; List, 2014), it is much easier today to combine existing methods into new frameworks that tackle individual tasks in computational historical linguistics.

In this study, we present a new framework for automated linguistic reconstruction which combines state-of-the-art methods for automated sequence comparison with fast machine-learning techniques and test it on a newly compiled test set that covers multiple language families.

2 Materials

The number of cross-linguistic datasets amenable for automated processing has been constantly increasing during the past years, as reflected specifically also in the development of standards for data representation that are increasingly used by

Proceedings of the 3rd Workshop on Computational Approaches to Historical Language Change, pages 89 - 96
May 26-27, 2022 ©2022 Association for Computational Linguistics

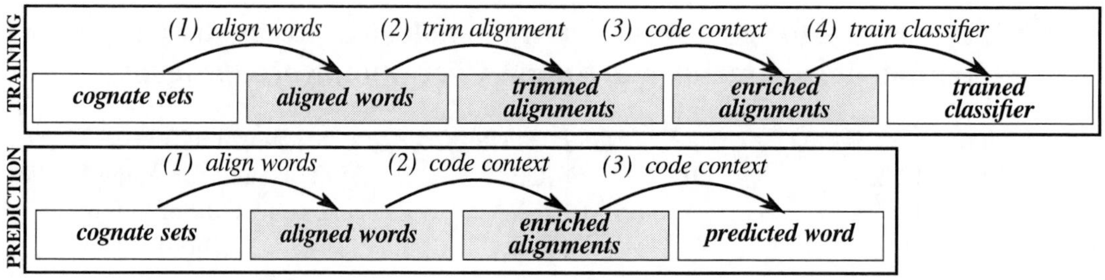

Figure 1: Workflow for the new framework for word prediction and linguistic reconstruction based on gap-free alignments and sound correspondence patterns.

Name	Source	Subgroup	L	C	W
Bai	Wang (2004)	Bai	10	459	3866
*Burmish	Gong and Hill (2020)	Burmish	9	269	1711
*Karen	Luangthongkum (2020)	Karen	11	365	3231
Lalo	Yang (2011)	Lalo (Yi)	8	1251	7815
Purus	Carvalho (2020)	Purus	4	199	693
Romance	Meloni et al. (2021)	Romance	6	4147	18806

Table 1: Datasets used in this study (L=Languages, C=Cognate Sets, W=Word Forms *=new data prepared for this study).

scholars (see Forkel et al. 2018 as well as List et al. 2021b for recent initiatives to make standardized cross-linguistic wordlists available in the form of open repositories). Unfortunately, the number of datasets in which proto-languages are provided along with descendant languages is still rather small. For the experiments reported here, a new cross-linguistic collection of six datasets from three language families (Sino-Tibetan, Purus, and Indo-European) was created. Datasets were all taken from published studies and then converted to Cross-Linguistic Data Formats (CLDF) (Forkel et al., 2018) using the CLDFBench Python package (Forkel and List, 2020) with the `PyLexibank` plugin (Forkel et al., 2021).

CLDF allows for a consistent handling of data when using software like Python or R. In addition, CLDF offers several levels of standardization by allowing to link the data to existing reference catalogs, such as Glottolog (Hammarström et al., 2021) for languages, Concepticon for concepts (List et al., 2021c), or Cross-Linguistic Transcription Systems (Anderson et al., 2018; List et al., 2021a) for speech sounds.

While three of the datasets (Bai, Lalo, and Purus) had been previously included into the Lexibank collection, a repository of lexical datasets in Cross-Linguistic Data Formats (List et al., 2021b), we converted the open part of the Latin dataset by Meloni et al. (2021) to CLDF. Additionally, we converted a selection of a smaller part of the data by Gong and Hill (2020) to CLDF and retro-standardized the data by Luangthongkum (2019). While all datasets provided forms for ancestral languages, not all datasets provided the direct links between these proto-forms and the reflexes in the descendant languages in the form of annotations indicating cognacy. While these were added manually for the Karen data, using the EDICTOR tool for etymological data curation (List, 2017, 2021), we used the automated method for partial cognate detection by List et al. (2016) to cluster proto-forms and reflexes into cognate sets for the data on Bai, Lalo, and Purus.

The datasets, along with their sources and some basic information regarding the number of languages (L), cognate sets (C), and word forms (W) are listed in Table 1. The collection offers a rather diverse selection, in which the amount of data varies both with respect to the number of word forms, cognate sets, and languages.

3 Methods

3.1 Workflow

The new framework can be divided into a training and a prediction stage. The training consists of four steps. In step (1), the cognate sets in the training data are *aligned* with a multiple phonetic alignment algorithm. In step (2), the alignments are *trimmed* by merging sounds in the ancestral language into clusters which would leave no trace in the descendant languages (§ 3.2). In step (3), the alignments of the descendant languages are enriched by *coding for context* that might condition sound changes (§ 3.3). In step (4) the enriched alignment sites are assembled and fed to a *classifier* for training.

The prediction consists of three steps. Given a cognate set as input, the word forms are aligned with the help of the same algorithm for multiple

	1	2	3	4	5	6	7
Latin	k	-	eː	n	aː	r	ɛ
	↑	↑	↑	↑	↑	↑	↑
Romanian	tʃ	-	i	n	a	-	-
Spanish	θ	-	e	n	a	ɾ	-
Portuguese	s	j	-	-	a	ɹ	-

Figure 2: Prediction problems when ancestral segments in multiple alignments do not show reflexes in the descendant languages.

alignment used in the training phase in step (1). In step (2), the alignment is enriched using the same method applied in the training phase and then passed to the classifier to predict the word form in the ancestral language in step (3).

Figure 1 illustrates the workflow, which is flexible with respect to individual methods used for individual steps. For phonetic alignment, we use the Sound-Class-Based Phonetic Alignment (SCA) algorithm (List, 2012), which is the current state-of-the-art method, but any other method that yields multiple alignments could be used. The same holds for the trimming procedure, (see § 3.2), the enrichment procedure, (see § 3.3), or the classifier (see § 3.4).

3.2 Trimming Alignments

Using multiple alignments to predict ancestral or new words is nothing new and has essentially been practised by classical historical linguists for a long time (Grimm, 1822). That multiple alignments can also be used in computational frameworks has been demonstrated by List (2019a), who inferred correspondence patterns from phonetic alignments and later used these correspondence patterns to predict words missing from the data. One problem not considered in this approach, however, is that correspondence patterns can only be inferred for those cases in which descendant languages have a reflex for a given sound in the ancestral language. In those cases where the sound has been lost, a prediction is not possible.

This problem is illustrated in Figure 2, where the Latin ending [ɛ] has no reflex sound in either of the descendant languages in the sample, yielding an alignment column that is completely filled with gap symbols. Our solution to deal with this problem is to post-process the multiple alignments in the training procedure by merging those columns which show only gaps in the descendant languages with the preceding alignment column. This is illustrated in Figure 3, where the Latin ending is now represented as a single sound unit [r.ɛ]. This trimming procedure, which was introduced for by Ciobanu and Dinu (2018) for pairwise alignments and is here extended to multiple alignments, is justified by the fact that correspondence patterns preceding lost sounds usually convey enough information to be distinguished from those patterns in which no sound has been lost.

3.3 Coding Context

Previous alignment-based approaches to automated word prediction have made exclusive use of the information provided by individual correspondence patterns derived from phonetic alignments (List, 2019a). While this has shown to yield already surprisingly good results, we know well that sound change often happens in certain phonetic environments. For example, we know that the initial position of a word is typically much stronger and less prone to change than the final position (Geisler, 1992). Similarly, consonants in the syllable onset position (preceding a vowel) also tend to show different types of sound change compared to consonants in the syllable offset (List, 2014). Last but not least, certain sound changes may be due to "long-range dependencies", or supra-segmental features like tone, which is typically marked in the end of a morpheme in the phonetic transcription of South-East Asian languages. In order to allow a classifier to make use of this information, our framework allows to enrich the phonetic alignments further, by deriving contextual information from individual phonetic alignments and adding it to the correspondence patterns that are then used to train the classifier. An example for this procedure

	1	2	3	4	5	6
Latin	k	-	eː	n	aː	r.ɛ
	↑	↑	↑	↑	↑	↑
Romanian	tʃ	-	i	n	a	-
Spanish	θ	-	e	n	a	ɾ
Portuguese	s	j	-	-	a	ɹ

Figure 3: Trimming alignments by merging sounds in the ancestral languages in those cases where an alignment column does not have sound reflexes in the descendant languages.

	Ro	*Sp*	*Pt*	*P*	*S*	*Ini*		*Lt*
1	tʃ	θ	s	1	C	^	→	k
2	-	-	j	2	C	–	→	-
3	i	e	-	3	V	–	→	eː
4	n	n	-	4	C	–	→	n
5	a	a	a	5	V	–	→	aː
6	-	ɾ	ɹ	6	c	$	→	r.ɛ

Figure 4: Enriching a phonetic alignment by coding various forms of context.

is given in Figure 4, where the phonetic alignment is given in transposed form (switching columns and rows), with each row corresponding to one correspondence pattern. While the information from correspondence patterns alone would only account for the first three columns of the matrix, three additional types of phonetic context have been added. Thus, column *P* indicates the position of a pattern in the form of an index. Column *S* provides information on the syllable structure following List (2014), and column *Ini* indicates, whether a pattern occurs in the beginning (^), the end ($) or the middle (–) of a word form. Enriching alignments should be done in a careful way, in order to avoid over-fitting the classifier. In our experiments, we contrast all eight possible combinations, ranging from the full coding shown in Figure 4, up to a coding of the alignment without additional enrichment.

3.4 Classifiers

Our approach is very flexible with respect to the choice of the classifier. In order to keep the approach *fast*, we decided to restrict our experiments to the use of a Support Vector Machine (SVM) with a linear kernel, since SVMs have been successfully applied in recent approaches in computational historical linguistics dealing with different classification tasks (Jäger et al., 2017; Cristea et al., 2021). We compare this approach with the graph-based method based on correspondence patterns (henceford called CorPaR) presented by List (2019a), which we modified slightly. While the original method uses a greedy algorithm to identify the largest cliques in the network, we now compute all cliques and rank them by counting the number of nodes they cover. An alignment site in an alignment is now compared against the consensus patterns extracted from the cliques in the graph and the prediction for the pattern with the largest number of reflexes is taken as the prediction. When no compatible pattern can be found, a search for the best candidates among patterns that are only partially compatible with the alignment site is invoked. This increases the chances too find a suitable reconstruction in those cases where the correspondence patterns are not fully regular.

3.5 Evaluation

Most scholars tend to report only the edit distance – also called Levenshtein distance (Levenshtein, 1965) – between the predicted and the attested string, both normalized by the length of the longer string and in unnormalized form. However, reporting the edit distance alone has the disadvantage that systematic differences between predicted and attested forms may be penalized too high, which is why we follow List (2019b) in computing the *B-Cubed F-scores* (Amigó et al., 2009) of the alignments of source and target sequences. B-Cubed F-Scores measure the difference between two classifications, ranging from 0 to 1, with 1 indicating complete similarity with respect to the structure of the classifications. Since the prediction of words can be seen as a classification task in which a certain number of sound slots should be classified by rendering them as identical or different from each other, B-Cubed F-Scores do not measure whether automated reconstructions are identical with attested reconstructions in the gold standard, but rather whether automated reconstructions approximate the structure of the reconstructions in the gold standard. As a result, B-Cubed F-Scores can show to which degree an automated reconstruction comes structurally close to the gold standard, even if individual reconstructed sounds differ. Given that B-Cubed F-Scores measure consistency across a set of reconstructed word forms, they should not be applied to individual items.

3.6 Implementation

The new framework is implemented as part of the LingRex Python package (List and Forkel, 2022) and allows the use of classifiers from the Scikit-Learn Python package (Pedregosa et al., 2011).

4 Results

In order to evaluate the framework, we tested two classifiers, a Support Vector Machine, and the Cor-

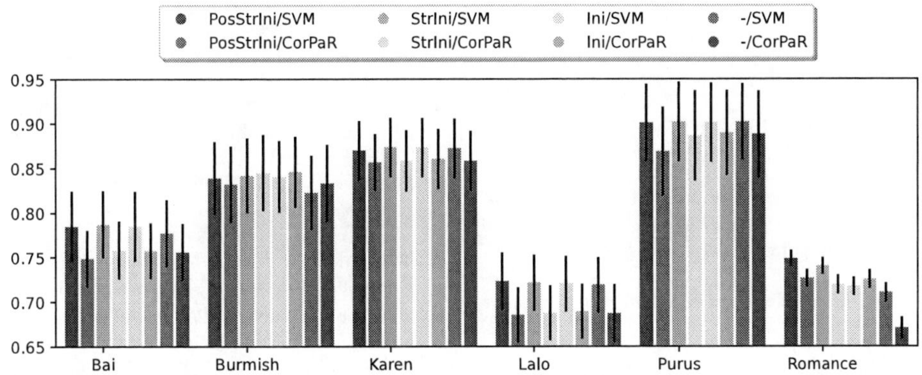

Figure 5: Comparing the results for selected coding techniques and classifiers on individual datasets.

PaR classifier (see § 3.4). Furthermore, we tested three different forms of alignment enrichment by coding individual positions (`Pos`), prosodic structure (`Str`), as well as whether a sound appears in the beginning or the end (`Ini`). For each test, we ran 100 trials in which 90% of the data were used for training and 10% for evaluation.

Classifier	Analysis	ED	NED	BC
SVM	PosStrIni	0.7491	0.1598	0.8110
SVM	PosStr	0.7478	0.1594	0.8115
SVM	PosIni	0.7701	0.1624	0.8077
SVM	StrIni	0.7578	0.1601	0.8110
SVM	Pos	0.7685	0.1618	0.8084
SVM	Str	0.7681	0.1614	0.8086
SVM	Ini	0.7895	0.1641	0.8061
SVM	none	0.8059	0.1673	0.8006
CorPaR	PosStrIni	0.8503	0.1816	0.7862
CorPaR	PosStr	0.8655	0.1826	0.7854
CorPaR	PosIni	0.8425	0.1802	0.7882
CorPaR	StrIni	0.8402	0.1771	0.7924
CorPaR	Pos	0.8836	0.1847	0.7840
CorPaR	Str	0.9048	0.1851	0.7848
CorPaR	Ini	0.8342	0.1763	0.7946
CorPaR	none	0.9379	0.1898	0.7821

Table 2: Results for edit distance, normalized edit distance, and B-Cubed F-Scores on all datasets.

Table 2 shows the results for all eight combinations between the three techniques for alignment enrichment. As can be seen, the SVM classifier outperforms the CorPaR method, although the differences are not very large. While the impact of the alignment enrichment techniques on the results is not very large, we still find that they enhance the results in all SVM trials, while the raw coding of the position (`Pos`) leads to lower scores for the CorPaR classifier in our test set. For the SVM classifier, coding for prosodic structure (`Str`) and information on whether a segment occurs at the beginning, in the middle, or the end of a sequence (`StrIni`) yields the best results with respect to all measures, while `Ini` coding outperforms the other techniques for the CorPaR classifier. From these results, we can see that alignment enrichment is a promising technique that deserves further exploration, but we do not think that the current codings are the last word on the topic.

Figure 5 compares the results for four coding techniques on individual datasets. As can be seem from the figure, the impact of the coding techniques varies quite drastically across datasets. This shows that it would be premature to rule out any of the techniques tested here directly, but rather calls for a careful selection of alignment enrichment techniques dependent on the language family one wants to investigate.

5 Conclusion

In this study, we have presented a new framework for supervised phonological reconstruction, which is implemented in the form of a small Python package. The new framework has the advantage of being easy to use, easy to extend, and fast to apply, while at the same time yielding promising results on a newly compiled collection of datasets from three different languages families. Given that our framework can be easily extended, by varying the individual components of the worfklow, we hope that it will provide a solid basis for future work on phonological reconstruction, as well as the prediction of words from cognate reflexes (Bodt and List, 2022; Dekker and Zuidema, 2021; Beinborn et al., 2013; Fourrier et al., 2021) in computational historical linguistics.

References

Enrique Amigó, Julio Gonzalo, Javier Artiles, and Felisa Verdejo. 2009. A comparison of extrinsic clustering evaluation metrics based on formal constraints. *Information Retrieval*, 12(4):461–486.

Cormac Anderson, Tiago Tresoldi, Thiago Costa Chacon, Anne-Maria Fehn, Mary Walworth, Robert Forkel, and Johann-Mattis List. 2018. A Cross-Linguistic Database of Phonetic Transcription Systems. *Yearbook of the Poznań Linguistic Meeting*, 4(1):21–53.

Lisa Beinborn, Torsten Zesch, and Iryna Gurevych. 2013. Cognate production using character-based machine translation. In *Proceedings of the Sixth International Joint Conference on Natural Language Processing*, pages 883–891.

Timotheus A. Bodt and Johann-Mattis List. 2019. Testing the predictive strength of the comparative method: An ongoing experiment on unattested words in Western Kho-Bwa languages. *Papers in Historical Phonology*, 4(1):22–44.

Timotheus Adrianus Bodt and Johann-Mattis List. 2022. Reflex prediction. A case study of Western Kho-Bwa. *Diachronica*, 39(1):1–38.

Alexandre Bouchard-Côté, David Hall, Thomas L. Griffiths, and Dan Klein. 2013. Automated reconstruction of ancient languages using probabilistic models of sound change. *Proceedings of the National Academy of Sciences of the United States of America*, 110(11):4224–4229.

Alina Maria Ciobanu and Liviu P. Dinu. 2018. Simulating language evolution: A tool for historical linguistics. In *Proceedings of the 27th International Conference on Computational Linguistics: System Demonstrations*, pages 68–72. Association of Computational Linguistics.

Alina Maria Cristea, Liviu P. Dinu, Simona Georgescu, Mihnea-Lucian Mihai, and Ana Sabina Uban. 2021. Automatic discrimination between inherited and borrowed Latin words in Romance languages. In *Findings of the Association for Computational Linguistics: EMNLP 2021*, pages 2845–2855, Punta Cana, Dominican Republic. Association for Computational Linguistics.

Fernando O. de Carvalho. 2021. A comparative reconstruction of proto-purus (arawakan) segmental phonology. *International Journal of American Linguistics*, 87(1):49–108.

Peter Dekker and Willem Zuidema. 2021. Word prediction in computational historical linguistics. *Journal of Language Modelling*, 8(2):295–336.

Liviu Dinu and Alina Maria Ciobanu. 2014. Building a dataset of multilingual cognates for the Romanian lexicon. In *Proceedings of the Ninth International Conference on Language Resources and Evaluation (LREC'14)*, pages 1038–1043, Reykjavik, Iceland. European Language Resources Association (ELRA).

Robert Forkel, Simon J Greenhill, Hans-Jörg Bibiko, Christoph Rzymski, Tiago Tresoldi, and Johann-Mattis List. 2021. *PyLexibank. The python curation library for lexibank [Software Library, Version 2.8.2]*. Zenodo, Geneva.

Robert Forkel and Johann-Mattis List. 2020. Cldfbench. give your cross-linguistic data a lift. In *Proceedings of the Twelfth International Conference on Language Resources and Evaluation*, pages 6997–7004, Luxembourg. European Language Resources Association (ELRA).

Robert Forkel, Johann-Mattis List, Simon J. Greenhill, Christoph Rzymski, Sebastian Bank, Michael Cysouw, Harald Hammarström, Martin Haspelmath, Gereon A. Kaiping, and Russell D. Gray. 2018. Cross-Linguistic Data Formats, advancing data sharing and re-use in comparative linguistics. *Scientific Data*, 5(180205):1–10.

Clémentine Fourrier, Rachel Bawden, and Benoît Sagot. 2021. Can cognate prediction be modelled as a low-resource machine translation task? In *Findings of the Association for Computational Linguistics: ACL-IJCNLP 2021*, pages 847–861, Online. Association for Computational Linguistics.

Anthony Fox. 1995. *Linguistic reconstruction*. Oxford University Press, Oxford.

Hans Geisler. 1992. *Akzent und Lautwandel in der Romania*. Narr, Tübingen.

Xun Gong and Nathan Hill. 2020. *Materials for an Etymological Dictionary of Burmish*. Zenodo, Geneva.

Jacob Grimm. 1822. *Deutsche Grammatik*, 2 edition, volume 1. Dieterichsche Buchhandlung, Göttingen.

Harald Hammarström, Martin Haspelmath, Robert Forkel, and Sebastiaon Bank. 2021. *Glottolog [Dataset, Version 4.5]*. Max Planck Institute for Evolutionary Anthropology, Leipzig.

Gerhard Jäger. 2019. Computational historical linguistics. *Theoretical Linguistics*, 45(3-4):151–182.

Gerhard Jäger, Johann-Mattis List, and Pavel Sofroniev. 2017. Using support vector machines and state-of-the-art algorithms for phonetic alignment to identify cognates in multi-lingual wordlists. In *Proceedings of the 15th Conference of the European Chapter of the Association for Computational Linguistics. Long Papers*, pages 1204–1215, Valencia. Association for Computational Linguistics.

Grzegorz Kondrak. 2000. A new algorithm for the alignment of phonetic sequences. In *Proceedings of the 1st North American chapter of the Association for Computational Linguistics conference*, pages 288–295.

Vladimir. I. Levenshtein. 1965. Dvoičnye kody s ispravleniem vypadenij, vstavok i zameščenij simvolov. *Doklady Akademij Nauk SSSR*, 163(4):845–848.

Johann-Mattis List. 2012. SCA: Phonetic alignment based on sound classes. In Marija Slavkovik and Dan Lassiter, editors, *New directions in logic, language, and computation*, pages 32–51. Springer, Berlin and Heidelberg.

Johann-Mattis List. 2014. *Sequence comparison in historical linguistics*. Düsseldorf University Press, Düsseldorf.

Johann-Mattis List. 2017. A web-based interactive tool for creating, inspecting, editing, and publishing etymological datasets. In *Proceedings of the 15th Conference of the European Chapter of the Association for Computational Linguistics. System Demonstrations*, pages 9–12, Valencia. Association for Computational Linguistics.

Johann-Mattis List. 2019a. Automatic inference of sound correspondence patterns across multiple languages. *Computational Linguistics*, 45(1):137–161.

Johann-Mattis List. 2019b. Beyond Edit Distances: Comparing linguistic reconstruction systems. *Theoretical Linguistics*, 45(3-4):1–10.

Johann-Mattis List. 2021. *EDICTOR. A web-based tool for creating, editing, and publishing etymological datasets [Software Tool, Version 2.0.0]*. Max Planck Institute for Evolutionary Anthropology, Leipzig.

Johann-Mattis List, Cormac Anderson, Tiago Tresoldi, and Robert Forkel. 2021a. *Cross-Linguistic Transcription Systems [Dataset, Version 2.1.0]*. Max Planck Institute for the Science of Human History, Jena.

Johann-Mattis List and Robert Forkel. 2022. *LingRex: Linguistic reconstruction with LingPy*. Max Planck Institute for Evolutionary Anthropology, Leipzig.

Johann-Mattis List, Robert Forkel, Simon J. Greenhill, Christoph Rzymski, Johannes Englisch, and Russell D. Gray. 2021b. Lexibank: A public repository of standardized wordlists with computed phonological and lexical features [Preprint, Version 1]. *Research Square*, pages 1–31.

Johann-Mattis List, Philippe Lopez, and Eric Bapteste. 2016. Using sequence similarity networks to identify partial cognates in multilingual wordlists. In *Proceedings of the Association of Computational Linguistics 2016 (Volume 2: Short Papers)*, pages 599–605, Berlin. Association of Computational Linguistics.

Johann-Mattis List, Christoph Rzymski, Simon J. Greenhill, Nathanael E. Schweikhard, Kristina Pianykh, Annika Tjuka, Carolin Hundt, and Robert Forkel. 2021c. *Concepticon. A resource for the linking of concept lists [Dataset, Version 2.5.0]*. Max Planck Institute for the Science of Human History, Jena.

Theraphan Luangthongkum. 2019. A view on Proto-Karen phonology and lexicon. *Journal of the Southeast Asian Linguistics Society*, 12(1):i–lii.

Carlo Meloni, Shauli Ravfogel, and Yoav Goldberg. 2021. Ab antiquo: Neural proto-language reconstruction. In *Proceedings of the 2021 Conference of the North American Chapter of the Association for Computational Linguistics: Human Language Technologies*, pages 4460–4473, Online. Association for Computational Linguistics.

F. Pedregosa, G. Varoquaux, A. Gramfort, V. Michel, B. Thirion, O. Grisel, M. Blondel, P. Prettenhofer, R. Weiss, V. Dubourg, J. Vanderplas, A. Passos, D. Cournapeau, M. Brucher, M. Perrot, and E. Duchesnay. 2011. Scikit-learn: Machine learning in Python. *Journal of Machine Learning Research*, 12:2825–2830.

Lydia Steiner, Peter F. Stadler, and Michael Cysouw. 2011. A pipeline for computational historical linguistics. *Language Dynamics and Change*, 1(1):89–127.

Feng Wang. 2004. *Language contact and language comparison. The case of Bai*. Phd, City University of Hong Kong, Hong Kong.

Cathryn Yang. 2011. *Lalo regional varieties: Phylogeny, dialectometry and sociolinguistics*. PhD dissertation, La Trobe University, Bundoora.

A Appendix

A.1 Source Code and Data

The new data collection along with the source code and the data needed to replicate the results reported in this study have been curated on GitHub at `https://github.com/lingpy/supervised-reconstruction-paper` (Version 1.0) and archived with Zenodo (DOI: `https://doi.org/10.5281/zenodo.6426074`).

A.2 Table of Results for Individual Datasets

A.2.1 SVM

DATASET	PosStrIni	StrIni	Str	Ini	none
Bai	0.7848	0.7870	0.7832	0.7846	0.7770
Burmish	0.8388	0.8418	0.8420	0.8405	0.8226
Karen	0.8696	0.8736	0.8734	0.8731	0.8723
Lalo	0.7232	0.7214	0.7204	0.7202	0.7191
Purus	0.9011	0.9021	0.9016	0.9013	0.9022
Romance	0.7487	0.7401	0.7310	0.7171	0.7103

A.2.2 CorPaR

DATASET	PosStrIni	StrIni	Str	Ini	none
Bai	0.7485	0.7581	0.7560	0.7572	0.7560
Burmish	0.8319	0.8449	0.8422	0.8458	0.8331
Karen	0.8564	0.8581	0.8614	0.8604	0.8581
Lalo	0.6852	0.6874	0.6890	0.6893	0.6871
Purus	0.8688	0.8865	0.8730	0.8897	0.8880
Romance	0.7262	0.7192	0.6871	0.7253	0.6705

Caveats of Measuring Semantic Change of Cognates and Borrowings using Multilingual Word Embeddings

Clémentine Fourrier **Syrielle Montariol**
Inria
firstname.lastname@inria.fr

Abstract

Cognates and borrowings carry different aspects of etymological evolution. In this work, we study semantic change of such items using multilingual word embeddings, both static and contextualised. We underline caveats identified while building and evaluating these embeddings. We release both said embeddings and a newly-built historical words lexicon, containing typed relations between words of varied Romance languages.

1 Introduction

Languages are in constant evolution over time; words appear, disappear, and their syntactic form and semantic function evolve (Blank and Koch, 1999). However, languages evolutions can be closely inter-related, following phenomena of interactions and inheritance. Cognates and borrowings, which are the targets of our study, are direct consequences of these phenomena. **Cognates** are words which descend from the same ancestor word (their proto-form) belonging to a shared common direct parent language. For example, the French word *chat* 'cat' is cognate with Spanish *gatto* and Romanian *cătușă*, as they all descend from Latin *cattus* 'cat', a direct ancestor of these three languages. When a word is an evolution of a form which does not come from a direct ancestor, it is called a **borrowing**. English *cat* also comes from *cattus*,[1] but as Latin is not a direct ancestor of English, it is therefore a borrowing of English to Latin. We consider the relation between *cat* and *chat* to be of 'borrowing' type by extension. Borrowings mostly occur to designate 'realities that were unknown before the adopting speech community got in contact with the "giving" culture and its language' or to replace already existing meanings by the word of the related dominant culture (Krefeld, 2013). To study semantic variation, we look at our words' **glosses**, which are expressions of their meaning, here as their English translations or definitions. In our previous example, while the French and Spanish cognates both retained the original sense 'cat', the Romanian cognate went through a semantic change and is translated as 'handcuff'.

Semantic change studies historically relied on specific word relations, cognates and 'borrowings' (Durkin, 2015), found through the comparative method (formalised by Osthoff and Brugmann (1878)). The last few years have seen the emergence of new tools such as contextualised embeddings to study semantic variation (Martinc et al., 2020), enabling the comparison of word senses across domains, periods and languages. We join both approaches and expand on the work of Uban et al. (2021), who use 'static' (non-contextualised) embeddings to study semantics of cognates and borrowings in contemporary Romance languages and English. In this work, we use static as well as contextualised embedding to study the semantic evolution of cognates and borrowings, for both contemporary and older Romance languages, as well as English. To this end, we first create a dataset of cognates and borrowings from the widely studied Romance family (contemporary: Spanish, French, Italian, Portuguese, Romanian, old: Latin, Old Spanish, Middle French), to which we add English.[2] Then, we compare several methods to tackle the issue of obtaining, for low-resource historical languages, embeddings spaces aligned with the ones of contemporary languages. Both dataset and embeddings are released with the paper.[3] Lastly, we use these embeddings to study semantic shift for both diachronic (between parent and child) and synchronic (between children) cognates or borrowing

[1]Latin *cattus* is, that we know of, the most plausible origin of the proto-Germanic reconstructed word **kattuz*, ancestor of English *cat*

[2]The language codes are the following: Spanish (ES), French (FR), Italian (IT), Portuguese (PT), Romanian (RO), Latin (LA), Old Spanish (OSP), Middle French (FRM), English (EN).

[3]github.com/clefourrier/historical-semantic-change

Proceedings of the 3rd Workshop on Computational Approaches to Historical Language Change, pages 97 - 112

relations, and find that contextualised embeddings allow us to reach more accurate conclusions. At each step, we highlight the possible pitfalls.

2 Related works

Cognates and borrowings transcribe different aspects of their languages history, and are often studied through the lens of orthographic (Ciobanu and Dinu, 2015, 2019) or phonetic combined with semantic variation (Kondrak, 2001). Uban et al. (2021), which we extend, study semantic variation in modern Romance languages between cognates and borrowings by considering their modern-day embeddings as a 'snapshot in time' of their meaning. As their dataset is not available, we can not use as a benchmark; however, like several public etymological databases, among which CogNet (Batsuren et al., 2019), containing cognates and borrowings without differentiating between both relation types, and EtymDB2 (Fourrier and Sagot, 2020), too small for our needs but which differentiate between both types, we build a dataset using the Wiktionary[4] as etymological source.

Semantic change across languages is actively researched in the linguistic and sociology research communities (Boberg, 2012), as it offers valuable information for sociological and historical analysis. In the NLP domain, many authors apply diachronic embeddings models to more than one language (Hamilton et al., 2016; Schlechtweg et al., 2020), but without considering their interactions. Some work studies variations between languages or dialects, diachronically (Martinc et al., 2020; Montariol and Allauzen, 2021) or synchronically (Hovy and Purschke, 2018; Beinborn and Choenni, 2020). However, although several annotated datasets are available to evaluate diachronic semantic change detection methods (Schlechtweg et al., 2020), cross-lingual semantic change does not have such resource and cognates and borrowings seem like a promising proxy for evaluating these methods.

3 Datasets and Corpora Construction

We create a dataset of cognates and borrowings in all languages under study. To complement it, we need corpora in each language to train or extract word embeddings; such corpora are publicly available for highly studied languages. We use a sample of the OSCAR corpus (Ortiz Suarez et al., 2019; Abadji et al., 2021) for contemporary languages and Latin. For Middle French and Old Spanish, we use less well-known resources.

3.1 Reference dataset construction

From the latest version of the Wiktionary, our goal is to construct a simple relational set of triplets (lang, lexeme, gloss) to other triplets for cognates and borrowings.

Parsing and general information extraction (for lexeme, language, relations) is described in Appendix A.[5] As extracting glosses proved less straightforward, we detail it here. We encountered three types of problem. 1) In the Wiktionary, some words have English translations as glosses, while others have English definitions: for example, the first definition of 'eau' (water) is 'Water, a liquid that is transparent, colorless, odorless and tasteless in its pure form, the primary constituent of lakes, rivers, seas and oceans', while for 'fort' (strong) it is 'strong; powerful' and 'skilled, proficient, successful, ...', a translation. Splitting glosses on punctuation to store the different semantic aspects as words is therefore indispensable in translation cases, but introduces mistakes when definitions are present. These cases were manually checked, but some mistakes might still remain. 2) All English words are defined (which makes sense, as the Wiktionary technically is an English multilingual dictionary). In order to have an homogeneous base, and as we try to keep translations only, we therefore make the choice to use English lexemes as their own 'translation' to English. 3) Some words (especially in Latin) are only defined as inflections or derivations of other words (e.g. capitum, only defined as 'genitive plural of caput'). In those cases, the gloss is not retained. After cleaning (also detailed in App. A), we construct our database, looking only at inheritance relations (App. A.2). Though cognate-typed relations exist in the Wiktionary, we deliberately choose to ignore them, as they can induce noise for our task: to define cognacy, we stood so far on the side of historical linguistics, but the term can sometimes more broadly refer to words with shared form and meaning, regardless of etymology (Frunza and Inkpen, 2009). This underlines the attention to sources which needs to be paid when constructing one's own database.

Statistics by language are detailed in App. A.4,

[4]The Wiktionary is a user-built free multilingual dictionary, found at en.wiktionary.org

[5]github.com/clefourrier/historical-semantic-change

Table 3. The cognate set contains a total of 34,574 word pairs, linking 8,334 unique words from all languages except English, which only has cognates to itself, as it does not descend from Latin and therefore cannot have cognates with any of the Romance languages. The borrowing set contains a total of 5,042 word pairs, linking 2,925 unique words. Here, most relations include English, with less than 100 pairs in relations without English.

3.2 Historical languages datasets

For **Middle French** (FRM, 1340–1610), we collect data from several datasets (see App. C.1): LEM17, a linguistically annotated corpus of modern French; MCVF 1.0/2.0 and PPCHF 1.0, parsed historical French data; OpenMedFr, plain versions of Middle French texts; and BFM2019, annotated Middle French texts. We manually filter these datasets to select all texts in the correct time period and clean them (see App. C.2).

For **Old Spanish** (OSP, 10th to 15th century), we extract data from the Digital Library of Old Spanish Texts[6], then clean it using the transcription norms described on the website.

After preprocessing, we obtain FRM/OSP datasets of 3.1M/4.7M words respectively.

4 Cross-lingual embeddings

We compare the semantic function of words in cognates and borrowings pairs. To this end, we explore various ways of obtaining aligned word embeddings in all languages (multilingual embeddings), using static and contextualised embeddings. The former are trained using FastText (Bojanowski et al., 2016) and aligned a posteriori, while the latter are extracted using the multilingual language model mBERT (Devlin et al., 2019) from corpora in all the languages under study. Trained embeddings and language models can be found for all our contemporary languages. However, historical languages such as Middle French and Old Spanish suffer from a scarcity of resources that we have to address.

4.1 Static embeddings

Available FastText embeddings. They were trained on Wikipedia data and either already cross-lingually aligned for our contemporary languages (Bojanowski et al., 2016), or available unaligned for Latin (Grave et al., 2018).

Training FastText embeddings. OSP and FRM do not have available embeddings: we therefore train some, using default subword tokenisation and an embedding size of 300.[7] However, we expect the quality of these new embeddings to be lower than the pre-trained ones, as 1) the imposed embedding size is likely too big with respect to the training data size, which could affect embedding ability to store relevant information, and 2) we were not able to define an adapted preprocessing.[8]

Aligning all embeddings spaces. Alignment is needed to obtain a coherent representation space between languages, and can be done either in a supervised or unsupervised way (Lample et al., 2017; Conneau et al., 2017). Preliminary experiments of unsupervised alignment (Alaux et al., 2018) led to extremely poor results. Consequently, we use bilingual lexicons[9] to supervise the alignment of Latin embeddings with Spanish, with around 2k bilingual word pairs used for supervision. Having no such dictionary for OSP/FRM, we use transparent words with their closest language (respectively SP/FR) to perform a supervised alignment, extracting for each language a bilingual lexicon of around 8k transparent words.

Extracting embeddings To build word embeddings, we had to manage un-homogeneous data with respect to diacritic: many cognates and borrowings seem absent from the embeddings vocabulary, especially for languages with diacritics (FR, RO, ES) or spelling variations (FRM) not homogenised in the embedding training corpora. We define a set of rules to extract embeddings despite word form variations. To embed word glosses (when made up of several words/sentences), we remove stopwords and compute the mean of all sequence word embeddings.

4.2 Contextualised embeddings

For contemporary languages and Latin, we use a sample of the OSCAR corpus (Ortiz Suarez et al., 2019; Abadji et al., 2021) to build our contextualised embeddings, as, given its very large

[6]http://www.hispanicseminary.org/t&c/nar/index-en.htm

[7]We use the same parameters as the pre-trained embeddings, to be able to align them together.

[8]OSP and FRM are too different from their descendants (e.g strong spelling variations inside FRM) to just use their languages preprocessing as such, and very few resource exist for these languages (e.g lists of stopwords).

[9]github.com/clefourrier/CopperMT/blob/master/inputs/raw_data/romance_bilingual

size (e.g. for Spanish, more than 25 billion tokens), working on the whole corpus would be time-intensive. For the other languages, we use the corpora descibed in Section 3.2.

We use an mBERT [10] model trained on 104 languages, including Latin and all our contemporary languages, from the `transformers` library (Wolf et al., 2020). Its training on Wikipedia data, allows for fairer comparison with FastText embeddings.

Massive multilingual pre-trained language models have been shown to perform well on new languages in a zero-shot fashion (Muller et al., 2021), especially those closely related to already seen high resource languages. Thus, we expect mBERT to perform well on OSP and FRM, but we also compare fine-tuning it on our FRM and OSP corpora using the masked language modelling task. We study cognates and borrowings representations *in context*, by computing the average embedding across all target word occurrences in corpora of their respective languages (Martinc et al., 2020). We compute word embeddings as the sum of the last 4 encoder layers of the model. When a word is divided into sub-words, we take the average of the sub-word embeddings

For word gloss embeddings (that we see as a representation of meaning), as we often have several words or a sentence as definition, we can directly generate their embeddings without contextualisation in a corpus. When the gloss is composed of several words, we try both averaging the representations of all tokens in the gloss, and using the embedding of the CLS representation. To compare them, we compute the cosine similarity between the target word embedding and the embedding of its associated gloss. Taking the CLS embedding leads to a similarity of 0.61 on average, while the average of all token embeddings leads to 0.67; we choose the latter to represent word meanings.

5 Results

Our metric is cosine similarity, commonly used in semantic change detection (Kutuzov et al., 2018). Our results are summarised in Table 1 (full results in App. B). Language pairs are split into parent to child (with LA, FRM, or OSP), and child to child (between contemporary languages) relations. We also differentiate cognates and borrowing pairs whose meaning stayed the same (un-shifted, equal gloss between the two items) or changed between the two languages (shifted, different gloss between the two items).[11]

We display similarity (across all our languages) between cognates / borrowings and their counterparts in an un-shifted (line 1) or shifted (l. 2) pair. We also display the average difference between these two scores (l. 3), this time computed per language pair: we expect it to be a measure of the models ability to capture semantic shift. The last two lines show the average embedding similarity between an item and its meaning,[12] which should be constant on average for a given language pair, since it reflects embedding alignment distance between the languages of interest and English.[13]

Embedding space quality. For **FastText** , the average similarity between item and meaning (l. 4 and 5) varies considerably from one language pair to another, which indicates variation in embedding alignment quality between English and other languages. This score also varies inside a given language pair (between borrowing/cognates or shifted/un-shifted words), which could further indicate embedding space quality problems. Indeed, an item embeddings and the embedding of its English gloss should always be relatively similar when using properly aligned embeddings spaces. We also observe that, contrary to expectations, publicly available pre-aligned embeddings (child-to-child) often have even higher variance and lower item-meaning similarity (therefore a worst alignment to English) than our aligned low-resource historical embeddings (parent-to-child). On the other hand, for **mBERT** embeddings, this similarity score is constant (with a slight variation between cognates and borrowings, likely explained by the fact that language pairs distribution between cognates and borrowings is different), which reflects a high embedding alignment quality. One should therefore be wary of conclusions drawn from the aligned FastText embeddings, even publicly available pre-aligned ones, which might lead to incorrect assumptions by introducing hidden factors into play. We will therefore draw conclusions only us-

[10] `bert-base-multilingual-cased`

[11] Semantic change would normally be seen as more of a continuum than a binary, but this was the more feasible approach with respect to our data.

[12] The item is the word form, where its meaning is the word English gloss.

[13] Note that even though we use definition embeddings, they should be comparable with word embeddings (Bosc and Vincent, 2018).

Relation		FastText				mBERT			
		Parent to child		Child to child		Parent to child		Child to child	
		cog	bor	cog	bor	cog	bor	cog	bor
item(a) ↔ item(b)	un-shifted	50±20	38±18	14±18	1±10	84± 9	86± 9	86±10	82± 9
	shifted	35±20	14±16	21±17	1± 9	79± 9	77± 9	79±10	76± 8
	difference	16± 7	16± 8	3± 6	-1± 3	4± 3	4± 7	2± 2	5± 4
item ↔ gloss	un-shifted	35±17	67±34	22±22	47±49	67± 5	72± 6	69± 6	71± 6
	shifted	29±24	62±40	16±16	49±48	69± 5	72± 6	69± 6	72± 6

Table 1: Aggregated results of cosine similarity (%) and standard deviation, for both FastText and mBERT embeddings. cog stands for cognate, bor for borrowing.

	FR-ES		FR-IT	
	cog	bor	cog	bor
% for un-shifted	84±8	92±4	84±8	87±5
% for shifted	79±9	84±8	80±9	83±8
#items	1884	22	1740	36

Table 2: item(a) ↔ item(b) mBERT similarity (%).

ing mBERT.

We also compared vanilla and fine-tuned OSP and FRM mBERT embeddings (Tables 8 and 9 in App. B); fine-tuning shows no significant improvement, though for some edge cases, it seems to increase semantic shift sensitivity slightly while decreasing similarity with other embedding spaces; consequently, we keep the simplest approach, the vanilla mBERT model. When working on historical data, it is interesting to study whether fine-tuning results justify its cost, or if zero-shot transfer can directly provide good enough results.

Global comparison Using mBERT embeddings, the only difference in similarity scores for items occurs between un-shifted and shifted word embeddings, with un-shifted pairs similarity being on average 4 points higher than shifted pairs (not necessarily statistically significant). Some outliers cases can be found in the per-language tables (see Table 6 in App. B), where shifted cognates have higher intra-pair similarity compared to un-shifted cognates for the same language pair. However, this situation only happens for languages with less than 20 cognates examples of shifted or un-shifted pairs (e.g. OSP-FRM, 12 shifted cognates), and are likely not significant.

There is virtually no difference between cognates or borrowings embeddings similarity. As a side note, FastText embeddings would have shown that cognates are more similar than borrowings, and a word is more similar to its parent than to its siblings: a hasty analysis using bad quality embeddings could have lead us to draw seductive but erroneous conclusions from the FastText embeddings.

Focus In order to investigate differences at the language pair level for the mBERT embeddings, we focus on two language pairs which have at least 20 samples for both shifted and un-shifted pairs of cognates and of borrowings: FR-ES and FR-IT (Table 2).[14] Both present a trend where borrowings are more similar than cognates and un-shifted words more similar than shifted words (as expected).

6 Conclusion

In this work, we create a cognate and borrowing dataset for English and Romance languages from different periods, as well as two aligned embeddings sets for all languages. When assessing embedding quality and alignment, we show that FastText embeddings, even when already pre-trained and aligned, are poorer than the mBERT ones on all respects. We therefore use the latter to study semantic change between cognates and borrowings: as expected, un-shifted word pairs are on average more similar than shifted ones. Furthermore, we observe a trend between cognates and borrowings, the latter being seemingly more similar than the former. Further analysis would be needed to determine whether this difference can be confirmed, by looking at chosen cognate and borrowings of similar histories in more languages. In summary, properly designed embeddings can be used to support historical lexicographic studies, while well-understood phenomena underlying cognates and borrowings can help design and evaluate cross-lingual word embeddings.

[14] There is a difference in data size of two orders of magnitude between small borrowing sets and bigger cognate sets, therefore conclusions must be taken with a pinch of salt.

References

Julien Abadji, Pedro Javier Ortiz Suárez, Laurent Romary, and Benoît Sagot. 2021. Ungoliant: An optimized pipeline for the generation of a very large-scale multilingual web corpus. Proceedings of the Workshop on Challenges in the Management of Large Corpora (CMLC-9) 2021. Limerick, 12 July 2021 (Online-Event), pages 1 – 9, Mannheim. Leibniz-Institut für Deutsche Sprache.

Jean Alaux, Edouard Grave, Marco Cuturi, and Armand Joulin. 2018. Unsupervised hyperalignment for multilingual word embeddings. *CoRR*, abs/1811.01124.

Khuyagbaatar Batsuren, Gabor Bella, and Fausto Giunchiglia. 2019. CogNet: A large-scale cognate database. In *Proceedings of the 57th Annual Meeting of the Association for Computational Linguistics*, pages 3136–3145, Florence, Italy. Association for Computational Linguistics.

Lisa Beinborn and Rochelle Choenni. 2020. Semantic drift in multilingual representations. *Computational Linguistics*, 46(3):571–603.

Andreas Blank and Peter Koch. 1999. Why do new meanings occur? a cognitive typology of the motivations for lexical semantic change. In *Historical Semantics and Cognition*, page 61–89.

Charles Boberg. 2012. English as a minority language in quebec. *World Englishes*, 31.

Piotr Bojanowski, Edouard Grave, Armand Joulin, and Tomas Mikolov. 2016. Enriching word vectors with subword information. *arXiv preprint arXiv:1607.04606*.

Tom Bosc and Pascal Vincent. 2018. Auto-encoding dictionary definitions into consistent word embeddings. In *Proceedings of the 2018 Conference on Empirical Methods in Natural Language Processing*, pages 1522–1532, Brussels, Belgium. Association for Computational Linguistics.

Alina Maria Ciobanu and Liviu P. Dinu. 2015. Automatic discrimination between cognates and borrowings. In *Proceedings of the 53rd Annual Meeting of the Association for Computational Linguistics and the 7th International Joint Conference on Natural Language Processing (Volume 2: Short Papers)*, pages 431–437, Beijing, China. Association for Computational Linguistics.

Alina Maria Ciobanu and Liviu P. Dinu. 2019. Automatic identification and production of related words for historical linguistics. *Computational Linguistics*, 45(4):667–704.

Alexis Conneau, Guillaume Lample, Marc'Aurelio Ranzato, Ludovic Denoyer, and Hervé Jégou. 2017. Word translation without parallel data. *arXiv preprint arXiv:1710.04087*.

Jacob Devlin, Ming-Wei Chang, Kenton Lee, and Kristina Toutanova. 2019. BERT: Pre-training of deep bidirectional transformers for language understanding. In *Proceedings of the 2019 Conference of the North American Chapter of the Association for Computational Linguistics: Human Language Technologies, Volume 1 (Long and Short Papers)*, pages 4171–4186, Minneapolis, Minnesota. Association for Computational Linguistics.

Philip Durkin. 2015. Etymology.

Clémentine Fourrier and Benoît Sagot. 2020. Methodological aspects of developing and managing an etymological lexical resource: Introducing EtymDB-2.0. In *Proceedings of the 12th Language Resources and Evaluation Conference*, pages 3207–3216, Marseille, France. European Language Resources Association.

Oana Frunza and Diana Inkpen. 2009. Identification and disambiguation of cognates, false friends, and partial cognates using machine learning techniques. *International Journal of Linguistics*, 1(1):1–37.

Edouard Grave, Piotr Bojanowski, Prakhar Gupta, Armand Joulin, and Tomas Mikolov. 2018. Learning word vectors for 157 languages. In *Proceedings of the Eleventh International Conference on Language Resources and Evaluation (LREC 2018)*, Miyazaki, Japan. European Language Resources Association (ELRA).

William L. Hamilton, Jure Leskovec, and Dan Jurafsky. 2016. Diachronic word embeddings reveal statistical laws of semantic change. In *Proceedings of the 54th Annual Meeting of the Association for Computational Linguistics (Volume 1: Long Papers)*, pages 1489–1501. Association for Computational Linguistics.

Dirk Hovy and Christoph Purschke. 2018. Capturing regional variation with distributed place representations and geographic retrofitting. In *Proceedings of the 2018 Conference on Empirical Methods in Natural Language Processing*, pages 4383–4394, Brussels, Belgium. Association for Computational Linguistics.

Grzegorz Kondrak. 2001. Identifying cognates by phonetic and semantic similarity. In *Second Meeting of the North American Chapter of the Association for Computational Linguistics*.

Thomas Krefeld. 2013. Cognitive ease and lexical borrowing: the recategorization of body parts in romance. In *Cognitive ease and lexical borrowing: the recategorization of body parts in Romance*, pages 259–278. De Gruyter Mouton.

Andrey Kutuzov, Lilja Øvrelid, Terrence Szymanski, and Erik Velldal. 2018. Diachronic word embeddings and semantic shifts: a survey. In *Proceedings of the 27th International Conference on Computational Linguistics*, pages 1384–1397, Santa Fe, New

Mexico, USA. Association for Computational Linguistics.

Guillaume Lample, Alexis Conneau, Ludovic Denoyer, and Marc'Aurelio Ranzato. 2017. Unsupervised machine translation using monolingual corpora only. *arXiv preprint arXiv:1711.00043*.

Matej Martinc, Petra Kralj Novak, and Senja Pollak. 2020. Leveraging contextual embeddings for detecting diachronic semantic shift. In *Proceedings of the 12th Language Resources and Evaluation Conference*, pages 4811–4819, Marseille, France. European Language Resources Association.

Syrielle Montariol and Alexandre Allauzen. 2021. Measure and evaluation of semantic divergence across two languages. In *Proceedings of the 59th Annual Meeting of the Association for Computational Linguistics and the 11th International Joint Conference on Natural Language Processing (Volume 1: Long Papers)*, pages 1247–1258, Online. Association for Computational Linguistics.

Benjamin Muller, Antonios Anastasopoulos, Benoît Sagot, and Djamé Seddah. 2021. When being unseen from mBERT is just the beginning: Handling new languages with multilingual language models. In *Proceedings of the 2021 Conference of the North American Chapter of the Association for Computational Linguistics: Human Language Technologies*, pages 448–462, Online. Association for Computational Linguistics.

Pedro Javier Ortiz Suarez, Benoit Sagot, and Laurent Romary. 2019. Asynchronous pipelines for processing huge corpora on medium to low resource infrastructures. Proceedings of the Workshop on Challenges in the Management of Large Corpora (CMLC-7) 2019. Cardiff, 22nd July 2019, pages 9 – 16, Mannheim. Leibniz-Institut f"ur Deutsche Sprache.

Hermann Osthoff and Karl Brugmann. 1878. *Morphologische Untersuchungen auf dem Gebiete der indogermanischen Sprachen*. Hirzel, Leipzig, Germany.

Dominik Schlechtweg, Barbara McGillivray, Simon Hengchen, Haim Dubossarsky, and Nina Tahmasebi. 2020. SemEval-2020 task 1: Unsupervised lexical semantic change detection. In *Proceedings of the Fourteenth Workshop on Semantic Evaluation*, pages 1–23, Barcelona (online). International Committee for Computational Linguistics.

Ana Sabina Uban, Alina Maria Cristea, Anca Dinu, Liviu P. Dinu, Simona Georgescu, and Laurentiu Zoicas. 2021. Tracking semantic change in cognate sets for English and Romance languages. In *Proceedings of the 2nd International Workshop on Computational Approaches to Historical Language Change 2021*, pages 64–74, Online. Association for Computational Linguistics.

Thomas Wolf, Lysandre Debut, Victor Sanh, Julien Chaumond, Clement Delangue, Anthony Moi, Pierric Cistac, Tim Rault, Remi Louf, Morgan Funtowicz, Joe Davison, Sam Shleifer, Patrick von Platen, Clara Ma, Yacine Jernite, Julien Plu, Canwen Xu, Teven Le Scao, Sylvain Gugger, Mariama Drame, Quentin Lhoest, and Alexander Rush. 2020. Transformers: State-of-the-art natural language processing. In *Proceedings of the 2020 Conference on Empirical Methods in Natural Language Processing: System Demonstrations*, pages 38–45, Online. Association for Computational Linguistics.

A Extracting cognates and borrowings data

A.1 Extraction

Parsing the Wiktionary The Wiktionary dumps mixes several formatting types, mostly HTML for the page tags and a pseudo-markdown for the internal structure of each article, which is not homogeneous between entries. The first step of processing was 1) to cut the Wiktionary by page, by literally cutting it on page HTML tags, and 2) at the same time, to only keep the title (lexeme) using HTML title tags and the text (core of the page) without the rest of the HTML using HTML text tags. Some pages were automatically discarded, if containing "Wiktionary", "App." or "Thesaurus" in their titles, as they are out of scope for the database.

Storing words and relations Once each page was cut, we cleaned the text, by extracting lexeme (first line), langs (second level pseudo markdown separation), and associated information (third levels pseudo markdown separations). The associated information was then cleaned using regexes, to find meanings (lines starting with an enumeration marker), descendants (using ‘desc’, ‘desctree’, and ‘bor=1’ as markers), ascendants (using ‘inh’ and ‘root’ as markers),[15] and supposed cognates (using ‘cog’ as marker). Lexemes were normalized using unicodedata. This allowed us to construct a list of Word objects, storing lexeme, lang, gloss, parent words, children words, and plausible cognates. (Related words were stored as "word_lang" in order to filter them). For each word, we added to its ancestor the set of its ancestors’ ancestors, and we converted gloss for English lexemes to the English lexeme itself.

A.2 Constructing our cognates and borrowing sets

Lastly, we converted this list to our cognate and borrowing sets. For each word, we first stored indirect parents as borrowing relations (borrowing set) and direct parents as cognate relations (cognate set), for parent languages in our languages of interest. Then, we looked at each direct ancestor’s children (no matter the direct ancestor language): if a given child was direct, both its relation to the parent and to the initial word were stored as cognates (for language pairs of interest). Else, we stored both relations in our ‘borrowings’ set (id.). In other terms, two words are kept if they share a common proto-form. If their ancestor is direct, we save them as cognates, else borrowings. We use an extended version of the notions of cognacy and borrowing defined in the introduction, and consider that the proto-words are also both cognates with their direct descendants, and in a borrowing relationship with their indirect descendants.

A.3 Cleaning

Extraction problems Splitting the document on HTML page limits was sometimes linked to pages not being cut at the right place, and the title tag not being recognised: some lexemes were stored as ‘<tag>’ (they were removed). Some irregularities in meaning definitions appeared, such as #English not being removed, or some reference urls being accidentally added to the English meanings. All these were manually managed.

Special characters Some symbols were not homogeneous in the Wiktionary originally, and appeared under several forms, such as ‘l’ for ‘or’, ‘&lt’ for ‘<’, ‘&gt’ for ‘>’, ‘&amp’ for ‘&’, among others. They were manually removed to ensure consistency.

A.4 Results

Our most doted language pairs usually contain relations between generally higher-resourced contemporary languages (FR-ES, IT-ES, PT-ES, FR-IT, IT-PT, more than 1,000 pairs), as well as, surprisingly, the FR-FRM pair. Pairs with Latin and other contemporary languages follow, with our least doted language pairs being Middle French or Old Spanish to any language other than French or Spanish, and most languages to themselves (word pairs including two different descendants from a common origin word in the same language).

[15]The ‘from’ marker was too noisy and therefore ignored.

Cognates											
Lang	#words	#uniq	Pair								
Total	34574	8334	EN	ES	FR	FRM	IT	LA	OSP	PT	RO
EN	896	498	448	0	0	0	0	0	0	0	0
ES	6156	1403	0	270	1047	225	1222	763	263	1255	841
FR	6062	1377	0	1047	230	1208	958	660	84	952	693
FRM	2253	630	0	225	1208	13	200	202	21	198	173
IT	5363	1058	0	1222	958	200	141	696	101	1080	824
LA	3573	1309	0	763	660	202	696	0	78	668	506
OSP	710	188	0	263	84	21	101	78	2	91	68
PT	5451	1103	0	1255	952	198	1080	668	91	209	789
RO	4110	768	0	841	693	173	824	506	68	789	108

borrowings											
Lang	#words	#uniq	Pair								
Total	5042	2925	EN	ES	FR	FRM	IT	LA	OSP	PT	RO
EN	2456	873	0	418	711	226	399	0	40	405	257
ES	435	354	418	0	12	4	0	1	0	0	0
FR	756	574	711	12	0	0	18	0	1	11	3
FRM	242	177	226	4	0	0	6	0	1	4	1
IT	424	348	399	0	18	6	0	1	0	0	0
LA	4	1	0	1	0	0	1	0	0	1	1
OSP	42	36	40	0	1	1	0	0	0	0	0
PT	421	341	405	0	11	4	0	1	0	0	0
RO	262	221	257	0	3	1	0	1	0	0	0

Table 3: Cognate and borrowings pairs relations

B Full results tables

The tables contain the number of cognate pairs kept for each language pairs, as well as an embedding similarity score between 1) both cognates/borrowings of a given pair, 2) both glosses of a given pair, 3) each cognate/borrowing to its gloss. Results are split by language pair and category (meaning shift or no meaning shift).

Cognates shifted in meaning	EN-EN	ES-EN	ES-ES	ES-FRM	ES-IT	ES-LA	ES-OSP	ES-RO
cognate (a) ↔ cognate (b)	27 ± 18		32 ± 18	4 ± 8	45 ± 21	35 ± 16	38 ± 10	28 ± 16
meaning (a) ↔ meaning (b)	27 ± 18		42 ± 19	52 ± 24	55 ± 24	59 ± 20	69 ± 19	50 ± 23
cognate ↔ meaning	100 ± 0		26 ± 17	13 ± 18	26 ± 16	19 ± 16	22 ± 16	23 ± 16
#items	706	0	474	304	2002	1172	276	1230
Cognates similar in meanings	**EN-EN**	**ES-EN**	**ES-ES**	**ES-FRM**	**ES-IT**	**ES-LA**	**ES-OSP**	**ES-RO**
cognate (a) ↔ cognate (b)			49 ± 26	3 ± 8	62 ± 17	41 ± 15	40 ± 8	43 ± 17
meaning (a) ↔ meaning (b)			100 ± 0	100 ± 0	100 ± 0	100 ± 0	100 ± 0	100 ± 0
cognate ↔ meaning			22 ± 22	24 ± 27	41 ± 16	27 ± 17	29 ± 20	34 ± 18
#items	0	0	14	64	286	86	136	230
Cognates shifted in meaning	**FR-EN**	**FR-ES**	**FR-FR**	**FR-FRM**	**FR-IT**	**FR-LA**	**FR-OSP**	**FR-RO**
cognate (a) ↔ cognate (b)		39 ± 20	32 ± 17	5 ± 7	41 ± 21	26 ± 11	25 ± 11	27 ± 16
meaning (a) ↔ meaning (b)		52 ± 23	33 ± 18	63 ± 24	54 ± 23	56 ± 21	54 ± 25	49 ± 24
cognate ↔ meaning		25 ± 16	25 ± 16	13 ± 17	24 ± 16	18 ± 15	20 ± 14	22 ± 15
#items	0	1690	410	1194	1512	1026	108	1024
Cognates similar in meanings	**FR-EN**	**FR-ES**	**FR-FR**	**FR-FRM**	**FR-IT**	**FR-LA**	**FR-OSP**	**FR-RO**
cognate (a) ↔ cognate (b)		53 ± 20	66 ± 29	3 ± 8	57 ± 16	31 ± 9	32 ± 8	40 ± 16
meaning (a) ↔ meaning (b)		100 ± 0	100 ± 0	100 ± 0	100 ± 0	100 ± 0	100 ± 0	100 ± 0
cognate ↔ meaning		35 ± 17	31 ± 20	19 ± 24	38 ± 15	28 ± 15	27 ± 18	34 ± 16
#items	0	256	10	706	250	74	30	198
Cognates shifted in meaning	**FRM-EN**	**FRM-FRM**	**IT-EN**	**IT-FRM**	**IT-IT**	**IT-LA**	**IT-OSP**	**LA-EN**
cognate (a) ↔ cognate (b)		42 ± 30		5 ± 9	33 ± 17	30 ± 12	33 ± 10	
meaning (a) ↔ meaning (b)		35 ± 12		53 ± 25	41 ± 21	60 ± 21	61 ± 25	
cognate ↔ meaning		-0 ± 6		13 ± 18	24 ± 16	19 ± 15	23 ± 14	
#items	0	14	0	270	236	1088	134	0
Cognates similar in meanings	**FRM-EN**	**FRM-FRM**	**IT-EN**	**IT-FRM**	**IT-IT**	**IT-LA**	**IT-OSP**	**LA-EN**
cognate (a) ↔ cognate (b)		64 ± 21		5 ± 8	47 ± 30	30 ± 12	34 ± 10	
meaning (a) ↔ meaning (b)		100 ± 0		100 ± 0	100 ± 0	100 ± 0	100 ± 0	
cognate ↔ meaning		-8 ± 8		24 ± 25	24 ± 21	25 ± 18	30 ± 17	
#items	0	8	0	68	12	74	42	0
Cognates shifted in meaning	**LA-FRM**	**LA-LA**	**LA-OSP**	**OSP-EN**	**OSP-FRM**	**OSP-OSP**	**RO-EN**	**RO-FRM**
cognate (a) ↔ cognate (b)	3 ± 7		28 ± 9		2 ± 6	76 ± 0		4 ± 8
meaning (a) ↔ meaning (b)	53 ± 22		66 ± 18		70 ± 30	23 ± 0		44 ± 24
cognate ↔ meaning	6 ± 10		13 ± 9		7 ± 12	22 ± 10		11 ± 15
#items	274	0	96	0	12	2	0	170
Cognates similar in meanings	**LA-FRM**	**LA-LA**	**LA-OSP**	**OSP-EN**	**OSP-FRM**	**OSP-OSP**	**RO-EN**	**RO-FRM**
cognate (a) ↔ cognate (b)	-1 ± 7		27 ± 11		2 ± 7			4 ± 7
meaning (a) ↔ meaning (b)	100 ± 0		100 ± 0		100 ± 0			100 ± 0
cognate ↔ meaning	12 ± 14		18 ± 14		13 ± 15			17 ± 19
#items	30	0	20	0	20	0	0	102
Cognates shifted in meaning	**RO-IT**	**RO-LA**	**RO-OSP**	**RO-RO**				
cognate (a) ↔ cognate (b)	30 ± 17	21 ± 10	18 ± 10	29 ± 24				
meaning (a) ↔ meaning (b)	52 ± 23	57 ± 21	54 ± 26	38 ± 16				
cognate ↔ meaning	23 ± 15	15 ± 13	16 ± 14	19 ± 15				
#items	1210	682	64	136				
Cognates similar in meanings	**RO-IT**	**RO-LA**	**RO-OSP**	**RO-RO**				
cognate (a) ↔ cognate (b)	39 ± 17	26 ± 10	26 ± 8	40 ± 18				
meaning (a) ↔ meaning (b)	100 ± 0	100 ± 0	100 ± 0	100 ± 0				
cognate ↔ meaning	32 ± 17	22 ± 14	26 ± 13	20 ± 8				
#items	230	44	38	6				

Table 4: Cognate results for fasttext embeddings

Borrowings shifted in meaning	EN-EN	ES-EN	ES-ES	ES-FRM	ES-IT	ES-LA	ES-OSP	ES-RO
borrowing (a) ↔ borrowing (b)		13 ± 16		-2 ± 4		29 ± 0		
meaning (a) ↔ meaning (b)		38 ± 21		62 ± 4		47 ± 0		
borrowing ↔ meaning		64 ± 38		10 ± 16		14 ± 14		
#items	0	704	0	4	0	2	0	0

Borrowings similar in meanings	EN-EN	ES-EN	ES-ES	ES-FRM	ES-IT	ES-LA	ES-OSP	ES-RO
borrowing (a) ↔ borrowing (b)		37 ± 15		-0 ± 8				
meaning (a) ↔ meaning (b)		100 ± 0		100 ± 0				
borrowing ↔ meaning		69 ± 33		31 ± 30				
#items	0	40	0	4	0	0	0	0

Borrowings shifted in meaning	FR-EN	FR-ES	FR-FR	FR-FRM	FR-IT	FR-LA	FR-OSP	FR-RO
borrowing (a) ↔ borrowing (b)	14 ± 17	46 ± 15			43 ± 13			38 ± 10
meaning (a) ↔ meaning (b)	42 ± 24	51 ± 16			63 ± 22			78 ± 5
borrowing ↔ meaning	61 ± 40	22 ± 15			28 ± 16			38 ± 13
#items	1066	10	0	0	28	0	0	4

Borrowings similar in meanings	FR-EN	FR-ES	FR-FR	FR-FRM	FR-IT	FR-LA	FR-OSP	FR-RO
borrowing (a) ↔ borrowing (b)	39 ± 17	63 ± 11			60 ± 18		43 ± 0	36 ± 0
meaning (a) ↔ meaning (b)	100 ± 0	100 ± 0			100 ± 0		100 ± 0	100 ± 0
borrowing ↔ meaning	69 ± 33	39 ± 19			47 ± 13		39 ± 19	36 ± 15
#items	206	12	0	0	8	0	2	2

Borrowings shifted in meaning	FRM-EN	FRM-FRM	IT-EN	IT-FRM	IT-IT	IT-LA	IT-OSP	LA-EN
borrowing (a) ↔ borrowing (b)	-1 ± 7		15 ± 16	4 ± 11		32 ± 0		
meaning (a) ↔ meaning (b)	34 ± 21		39 ± 21	42 ± 16		60 ± 0		
borrowing ↔ meaning	51 ± 50		63 ± 39	3 ± 16		18 ± 18		
#items	278	0	702	10	0	2	0	0

Borrowings similar in meanings	FRM-EN	FRM-FRM	IT-EN	IT-FRM	IT-IT	IT-LA	IT-OSP	LA-EN
borrowing (a) ↔ borrowing (b)	-1 ± 8		33 ± 19					
meaning (a) ↔ meaning (b)	100 ± 0		100 ± 0					
borrowing ↔ meaning	49 ± 51		67 ± 36					
#items	72	0	36	0	0	0	0	0

Borrowings shifted in meaning	LA-FRM	LA-LA	LA-OSP	OSP-EN	OSP-FRM	OSP-OSP	RO-EN	RO-FRM
borrowing (a) ↔ borrowing (b)				8 ± 10			9 ± 12	
meaning (a) ↔ meaning (b)				36 ± 21			31 ± 17	
borrowing ↔ meaning				58 ± 42			60 ± 42	
#items	0	0	0	56	0	0	384	0

Borrowings similar in meanings	LA-FRM	LA-LA	LA-OSP	OSP-EN	OSP-FRM	OSP-OSP	RO-EN	RO-FRM
borrowing (a) ↔ borrowing (b)				3 ± 7	12 ± 0		22 ± 7	
meaning (a) ↔ meaning (b)				100 ± 0	100 ± 0		100 ± 0	
borrowing ↔ meaning				52 ± 49	7 ± 5		61 ± 39	
#items	0	0	0	6	2	0	14	0

Borrowings shifted in meaning	RO-IT	RO-LA	RO-OSP	RO-RO
borrowing (a) ↔ borrowing (b)		24 ± 0		
meaning (a) ↔ meaning (b)		49 ± 0		
borrowing ↔ meaning		21 ± 20		
#items	0	2	0	0

Borrowings similar in meanings	RO-IT	RO-LA	RO-OSP	RO-RO
borrowing (a) ↔ borrowing (b)				
meaning (a) ↔ meaning (b)				
borrowing ↔ meaning				
#items	0	0	0	0

Table 5: Borrowings results for fasttext embeddings

Cognates shifted in meaning	EN-EN	ES-EN	ES-ES	ES-FRM	ES-IT	ES-LA	ES-OSP	ES-RO
cognate (a) $\leftrightarrow$ cognate (b)	73 ± 8		79 ± 6	77 ± 8	84 ± 10	74 ± 8	87 ± 8	77 ± 8
meaning (a) $\leftrightarrow$ meaning (b)	84 ± 6		81 ± 6	81 ± 6	83 ± 7	83 ± 7	84 ± 5	81 ± 7
cognate $\leftrightarrow$ meaning	73 ± 5		70 ± 5	69 ± 5	70 ± 5	68 ± 6	74 ± 5	69 ± 5
#items	620	0	450	322	1962	906	300	1200

Cognates similar in meanings	EN-EN	ES-EN	ES-ES	ES-FRM	ES-IT	ES-LA	ES-OSP	ES-RO
cognate (a) $\leftrightarrow$ cognate (b)			76 ± 6	81 ± 7	89 ± 8	77 ± 10	86 ± 8	81 ± 9
meaning (a) $\leftrightarrow$ meaning (b)			100 ± 0	100 ± 0	100 ± 0	100 ± 0	100 ± 0	100 ± 0
cognate $\leftrightarrow$ meaning			65 ± 7	67 ± 6	68 ± 5	65 ± 7	72 ± 7	67 ± 5
#items	0	0	10	64	270	46	150	216

Cognates shifted in meaning	FR-EN	FR-ES	FR-FR	FR-FRM	FR-IT	FR-LA	FR-OSP	FR-RO
cognate (a) $\leftrightarrow$ cognate (b)		79 ± 9	77 ± 7	90 ± 8	80 ± 9	72 ± 8	77 ± 7	76 ± 8
meaning (a) $\leftrightarrow$ meaning (b)		83 ± 7	79 ± 6	83 ± 7	82 ± 7	82 ± 7	82 ± 5	81 ± 6
cognate $\leftrightarrow$ meaning		70 ± 5	69 ± 6	69 ± 6	69 ± 5	68 ± 6	74 ± 6	68 ± 6
#items	0	1632	388	1314	1500	824	112	974

Cognates similar in meanings	FR-EN	FR-ES	FR-FR	FR-FRM	FR-IT	FR-LA	FR-OSP	FR-RO
cognate (a) $\leftrightarrow$ cognate (b)		84 ± 8	78 ± 3	91 ± 8	84 ± 8	75 ± 8	79 ± 8	80 ± 7
meaning (a) $\leftrightarrow$ meaning (b)		100 ± 0	100 ± 0	100 ± 0	100 ± 0	100 ± 0	100 ± 0	100 ± 0
cognate $\leftrightarrow$ meaning		68 ± 5	70 ± 5	69 ± 6	68 ± 5	66 ± 6	72 ± 6	66 ± 5
#items	0	252	8	780	240	56	34	198

Cognates shifted in meaning	FRM-EN	FRM-FRM	IT-EN	IT-FRM	IT-IT	IT-LA	IT-OSP	LA-EN
cognate (a) $\leftrightarrow$ cognate (b)		82 ± 5		79 ± 8	78 ± 6	77 ± 8	82 ± 8	
meaning (a) $\leftrightarrow$ meaning (b)		73 ± 8		81 ± 7	81 ± 7	83 ± 7	84 ± 5	
cognate $\leftrightarrow$ meaning		66 ± 8		69 ± 5	69 ± 5	68 ± 6	74 ± 6	
#items	0	10	0	292	236	874	134	0

Cognates similar in meanings	FRM-EN	FRM-FRM	IT-EN	IT-FRM	IT-IT	IT-LA	IT-OSP	LA-EN
cognate (a) $\leftrightarrow$ cognate (b)		84 ± 3		80 ± 8	86 ± 9	81 ± 9	84 ± 6	
meaning (a) $\leftrightarrow$ meaning (b)		100 ± 0		100 ± 0	100 ± 0	100 ± 0	100 ± 0	
cognate $\leftrightarrow$ meaning		64 ± 9		67 ± 5	66 ± 4	66 ± 5	73 ± 5	
#items	0	10	0	76	10	52	42	0

Cognates shifted in meaning	LA-FRM	LA-LA	LA-OSP	OSP-EN	OSP-FRM	OSP-OSP	RO-EN	RO-FRM
cognate (a) $\leftrightarrow$ cognate (b)	74 ± 8		77 ± 7		83 ± 6	84 ± 0		74 ± 7
meaning (a) $\leftrightarrow$ meaning (b)	79 ± 7		82 ± 6		89 ± 3	87 ± 0		80 ± 6
cognate $\leftrightarrow$ meaning	67 ± 6		72 ± 7		74 ± 5	78 ± 4		67 ± 6
#items	272	0	90	0	12	2	0	172

Cognates similar in meanings	LA-FRM	LA-LA	LA-OSP	OSP-EN	OSP-FRM	OSP-OSP	RO-EN	RO-FRM
cognate (a) $\leftrightarrow$ cognate (b)	76 ± 8		78 ± 6		79 ± 5	79 ± 0		78 ± 6
meaning (a) $\leftrightarrow$ meaning (b)	100 ± 0		100 ± 0		100 ± 0	100 ± 0		100 ± 0
cognate $\leftrightarrow$ meaning	66 ± 6		70 ± 6		71 ± 7	72 ± 1		67 ± 5
#items	24	0	22	0	26	2	0	110

Cognates shifted in meaning	RO-IT	RO-LA	RO-OSP	RO-RO
cognate (a) $\leftrightarrow$ cognate (b)	79 ± 8	73 ± 8	76 ± 5	77 ± 7
meaning (a) $\leftrightarrow$ meaning (b)	81 ± 7	81 ± 7	84 ± 4	80 ± 6
cognate $\leftrightarrow$ meaning	68 ± 5	66 ± 6	73 ± 6	69 ± 6
#items	1218	548	66	144

Cognates similar in meanings	RO-IT	RO-LA	RO-OSP	RO-RO
cognate (a) $\leftrightarrow$ cognate (b)	81 ± 9	75 ± 10	79 ± 6	83 ± 13
meaning (a) $\leftrightarrow$ meaning (b)	100 ± 0	100 ± 0	100 ± 0	100 ± 0
cognate $\leftrightarrow$ meaning	66 ± 4	64 ± 5	71 ± 6	62 ± 7
#items	224	34	48	6

Table 6: Cognates results for BERT embeddings, using the last 4 layers

Borrowings shifted in meaning	EN-EN	ES-EN	ES-ES	ES-FRM	ES-IT	ES-LA	ES-OSP	ES-RO
borrowing (a) ↔ borrowing (b)		75 ± 8		83 ± 2				
meaning (a) ↔ meaning (b)		79 ± 6		74 ± 5				
borrowing ↔ meaning		72 ± 5		70 ± 5				
#items	0	636	0	4	0	0	0	0

Borrowings similar in meanings	EN-EN	ES-EN	ES-ES	ES-FRM	ES-IT	ES-LA	ES-OSP	ES-RO
borrowing (a) ↔ borrowing (b)		85 ± 7		92 ± 1				
meaning (a) ↔ meaning (b)		100 ± 0		100 ± 0				
borrowing ↔ meaning		73 ± 5		67 ± 5				
#items	0	40	0	4	0	0	0	0

Borrowings shifted in meaning	FR-EN	FR-ES	FR-FR	FR-FRM	FR-IT	FR-LA	FR-OSP	FR-RO
borrowing (a) ↔ borrowing (b)	78 ± 10	84 ± 8			83 ± 8			83 ± 7
meaning (a) ↔ meaning (b)	80 ± 6	81 ± 10			84 ± 6			83 ± 1
borrowing ↔ meaning	72 ± 6	71 ± 5			71 ± 5			70 ± 2
#items	974	10	0	0	28	0	0	4

Borrowings similar in meanings	FR-EN	FR-ES	FR-FR	FR-FRM	FR-IT	FR-LA	FR-OSP	FR-RO
borrowing (a) ↔ borrowing (b)	87 ± 8	92 ± 4			87 ± 5		92 ± 0	73 ± 0
meaning (a) ↔ meaning (b)	100 ± 0	100 ± 0			100 ± 0		100 ± 0	100 ± 0
borrowing ↔ meaning	72 ± 6	69 ± 5			70 ± 5		79 ± 4	69 ± 1
#items	200	12	0	0	8	0	2	2

Borrowings shifted in meaning	FRM-EN	FRM-FRM	IT-EN	IT-FRM	IT-IT	IT-LA	IT-OSP	LA-EN
borrowing (a) ↔ borrowing (b)	75 ± 8		77 ± 8	81 ± 6				
meaning (a) ↔ meaning (b)	82 ± 6		79 ± 6	82 ± 5				
borrowing ↔ meaning	71 ± 6		72 ± 5	67 ± 5				
#items	274	0	632	10	0	0	0	0

Borrowings similar in meanings	FRM-EN	FRM-FRM	IT-EN	IT-FRM	IT-IT	IT-LA	IT-OSP	LA-EN
borrowing (a) ↔ borrowing (b)	82 ± 8		85 ± 9					
meaning (a) ↔ meaning (b)	100 ± 0		100 ± 0					
borrowing ↔ meaning	71 ± 6		74 ± 5					
#items	82	0	34	0	0	0	0	0

Borrowings shifted in meaning	LA-FRM	LA-LA	LA-OSP	OSP-EN	OSP-FRM	OSP-OSP	RO-EN	RO-FRM
borrowing (a) ↔ borrowing (b)				76 ± 8			74 ± 8	
meaning (a) ↔ meaning (b)				84 ± 4			80 ± 6	
borrowing ↔ meaning				77 ± 3			70 ± 6	
#items	0	0	0	56	0	0	340	0

Borrowings similar in meanings	LA-FRM	LA-LA	LA-OSP	OSP-EN	OSP-FRM	OSP-OSP	RO-EN	RO-FRM
borrowing (a) ↔ borrowing (b)				75 ± 11	82 ± 0		75 ± 10	
meaning (a) ↔ meaning (b)				100 ± 0	100 ± 0		100 ± 0	
borrowing ↔ meaning				74 ± 6	72 ± 2		70 ± 5	
#items	0	0	0	6	2	0	16	0

Borrowings shifted in meaning	RO-IT	RO-LA	RO-OSP	RO-RO
borrowing (a) ↔ borrowing (b)				
meaning (a) ↔ meaning (b)				
borrowing ↔ meaning				
#items	0	0	0	0

Borrowings similar in meanings	RO-IT	RO-LA	RO-OSP	RO-RO
borrowing (a) ↔ borrowing (b)				
meaning (a) ↔ meaning (b)				
borrowing ↔ meaning				
#items	0	0	0	0

Table 7: Borrowings results for BERT embeddings, using the last 4 layers

C Corpora for Embeddings Training

C.1 Data collection sources

All datasets are under open, CC BY, or CC BY-NC-SA licences, and our chosen subset will be released with the paper. LEM17 is found at https://github.com/e-ditiones/LEM17, MCVF 1.0/2.0 and PPCHF 1.0 at https://github.com/beatrice57/mcvf-plus-ppchf, OpenMedFr at https://github.com/OpenMedFr/texts, BFM2019 at http://txm.ish-lyon.cnrs.fr/bfm/?path=/BFM2019, and the Digital Library of Old Spanish Texts at http://hispanicseminary.org/t&c/nar/index-en.htm.

C.2 FRM preprocessing

The LEM files were in csv format for UD, and only the words (first column) were extracted. The BFM2019 and MCVF v1 files were in XML format, and the div containing text were selected. The MCVF v2 and PPCHF files were in text format, parsed, and text was extracted from the correct lines. Lastly, the OpenMedFr were already in raw text format, and we only had to remove the comment lines and page indications. Then, all files were automatically separated on end of sentence punctuation mark (full stop, exclamation mark, question mark), then manually on indicators of dialogue (dashes, quotation marks) to keep one sentence per line. The line creation process could have introduced some noise. One specificity of FRM is the presence of extremely long sentences divided into sub-sentences with commas. Thus, we perform a secondary split around commas when the sentences are too long to ease the model fine-tuning and embeddings extraction steps.

C.3 Fine-tuning experiments

Cognates un-shifted in meanings	OSP-ft	OSP$_{ft}$-FR	OSP-ES	OSP$_{ft}$-ES	OSP-RO	OSP$_{ft}$-RO
cognate (a) ↔ cognate (b)	79 ± 8	75 ± 7	86 ± 8	79 ± 7	79 ± 6	74 ± 8
meaning (a) ↔ meaning (b)	100 ± 0	100 ± 0	100 ± 0	100 ± 0	100 ± 0	100 ± 0
cognate ↔ meaning	72 ± 6	67 ± 5	72 ± 7	68 ± 5	71 ± 6	66 ± 5
Cognates shifted in meaning	**OSP-ft**	**OSP$_{ft}$-FR**	**OSP-ES**	**OSP$_{ft}$-ES**	**OSP-RO**	**OSP$_{ft}$-RO**
cognate (a) ↔ cognate (b)	77 ± 7	72 ± 8	87 ± 8	79 ± 7	76 ± 5	70 ± 6
meaning (a) ↔ meaning (b)	82 ± 5	82 ± 5	84 ± 5	84 ± 5	84 ± 4	84 ± 4
cognate ↔ meaning	74 ± 6	69 ± 5	74 ± 5	69 ± 5	73 ± 6	69 ± 5
Shift measure	1	3	-0	1	3	4
Cognates un-shifted in meanings	**OSP-IT**	**OSP$_{ft}$-IT**	**OSP-LA**	**OSP$_{ft}$-LA**	**OSP-FRM**	**OSP$_{ft}$-FRM**
cognate (a) ↔ cognate (b)	84 ± 6	79 ± 4	78 ± 6	72 ± 7	79 ± 5	71 ± 7
meaning (a) ↔ meaning (b)	100 ± 0	100 ± 0	100 ± 0	100 ± 0	100 ± 0	100 ± 0
cognate ↔ meaning	73 ± 5	69 ± 3	70 ± 6	66 ± 4	71 ± 7	67 ± 5
Cognates shifted in meaning	**OSP-IT**	**OSP$_{ft}$-IT**	**OSP-LA**	**OSP$_{ft}$-LA**	**OSP-FRM**	**OSP$_{ft}$-FRM**
cognate (a) ↔ cognate (b)	82 ± 8	76 ± 8	77 ± 7	69 ± 8	83 ± 6	74 ± 7
meaning (a) ↔ meaning (b)	84 ± 5	84 ± 5	82 ± 6	82 ± 6	89 ± 3	89 ± 3
cognate ↔ meaning	74 ± 6	69 ± 5	72 ± 7	68 ± 5	74 ± 5	70 ± 3
Shift measure	2	3	1	3	-4	-3
Cognates un-shifted in meanings	**FRM-ft**	**FRM$_{ft}$-FR**	**FRM-ES**	**FRM$_{ft}$-ES**	**FRM-RO**	**FRM$_{ft}$-RO**
cognate (a) ↔ cognate (b)	91 ± 8	84 ± 6	81 ± 7	78 ± 7	78 ± 6	75 ± 7
meaning (a) ↔ meaning (b)	100 ± 0	100 ± 0	100 ± 0	100 ± 0	100 ± 0	100 ± 0
cognate ↔ meaning	69 ± 6	68 ± 6	67 ± 6	67 ± 6	67 ± 5	67 ± 5
Cognates shifted in meaning	**FRM-ft**	**FRM$_{ft}$-FR**	**FRM-ES**	**FRM$_{ft}$-ES**	**FRM-RO**	**FRM$_{ft}$-RO**
cognate (a) ↔ cognate (b)	90 ± 8	83 ± 7	77 ± 8	74 ± 7	74 ± 7	70 ± 7
meaning (a) ↔ meaning (b)	83 ± 7	83 ± 7	81 ± 6	81 ± 6	80 ± 6	80 ± 6
cognate ↔ meaning	69 ± 6	68 ± 6	69 ± 5	68 ± 5	67 ± 6	66 ± 6
Shift measure	2	2	4	4	5	5
Cognates un-shifted in meanings	**FRM-IT**	**FRM$_{ft}$-IT**	**FRM-LA**	**FRM$_{ft}$-LA**	**FRM-OSP**	**FRM$_{ft}$-OSP**
cognate (a) ↔ cognate (b)	80 ± 8	77 ± 6	76 ± 8	71 ± 7	79 ± 5	73 ± 6
meaning (a) ↔ meaning (b)	100 ± 0	100 ± 0	100 ± 0	100 ± 0	100 ± 0	100 ± 0
cognate ↔ meaning	67 ± 5	66 ± 5	66 ± 6	65 ± 6	71 ± 7	71 ± 7
Cognates shifted in meaning	**FRM-IT**	**FRM$_{ft}$-IT**	**FRM-LA**	**FRM$_{ft}$-LA**	**FRM-OSP**	**FRM$_{ft}$-OSP**
cognate (a) ↔ cognate (b)	79 ± 8	75 ± 7	74 ± 8	69 ± 8	83 ± 6	77 ± 6
meaning (a) ↔ meaning (b)	81 ± 7	81 ± 7	79 ± 7	79 ± 7	89 ± 3	89 ± 3
cognate ↔ meaning	69 ± 5	68 ± 5	67 ± 6	66 ± 6	74 ± 5	73 ± 5
Shift measure	2	2	2	2	-4	-3

Table 8: Statistics when using mBERT embeddings, with OSP/FRM finetuning ($_{ft}$-) or without, for Old Spanish and Medieval French cognates. The 'shift measure' is the average difference between semantic item similarity, between non-shifted and shifted pairs.
The semantic shift between shifted and un-shifted items is slightly increased for fine-tuned OSP, and not at all for FRM, at the cost of an alignment drift with the meanings (line 3). We consider that this extremely small improvement is not worth the cost, and therefore only use vanilla embeddings. However, it would still be worth investigating how to improve fine-tuning.

Borrowings un-shifted in meanings	OSP-EN	OSP$_{ft}$-EN		
borrowing (a) ↔ borrowing (b)	75 ± 11	70 ± 12		
meaning (a) ↔ meaning (b)	100 ± 0	100 ± 0		
borrowing ↔ meaning	74 ± 6	69 ± 6		
Borrowings shifted in meaning	**OSP-EN**	**OSP$_{ft}$-EN**		
borrowing (a) ↔ borrowing (b)	76 ± 8	71 ± 7		
meaning (a) ↔ meaning (b)	84 ± 4	84 ± 4		
borrowing ↔ meaning	77 ± 3	72 ± 5		
Shift measure	-1	-2		
Borrowings un-shifted in meanings	**FRM-ES**	**FRM$_{ft}$-ES**	**FRM-EN**	**FRM$_{ft}$-EN**
borrowing (a) ↔ borrowing (b)	92 ± 1	86 ± 2	82 ± 8	78 ± 7
meaning (a) ↔ meaning (b)	100 ± 0	100 ± 0	100 ± 0	100 ± 0
borrowing ↔ meaning	67 ± 5	65 ± 6	71 ± 6	71 ± 7
Borrowings shifted in meaning	**FRM-ES**	**FRM$_{ft}$-ES**	**FRM-EN**	**FRM$_{ft}$-EN**
borrowing (a) ↔ borrowing (b)	83 ± 2	82 ± 3	75 ± 8	71 ± 7
meaning (a) ↔ meaning (b)	74 ± 5	74 ± 5	82 ± 6	82 ± 6
borrowing ↔ meaning	70 ± 5	70 ± 4	71 ± 6	70 ± 6
Shift measure	9	5	6	7

Table 9: Statistics when using mBERT embeddings, with OSP/FRM finetuning ($_{ft}$) or without, for Old Spanish and Medieval French borrowings with shifted and unshifted pairs. The 'shift measure' is the average difference between semantic item similarity, between non-shifted and shifted pairs.
We observe that the difference between shifted and non-shifted items decreases this time, when compared to cognates, for OSP-EN and FRM-ES, and increases for FRM-EN. We consider that variations are not consistent enough to draw conclusions.

Lexicon of Changes: Towards the Evaluation of Diachronic Semantic Shift in Chinese

Jing Chen, Emmanuele Chersoni, Chu-Ren Huang
The Hong Kong Polytechnic University
Department of Chinese and Bilingual Studies
Yuk Choi Road 11, Hung Hom, Kowloon, Hong Kong (China)
jing95.chen@connect.polyu.edu.hk, churen.huang@polyu.edu.hk
emmanuele.chersoni@polyu.edu.hk

Abstract

Recent research has brought a wind of using computational approaches to the classic topic of semantic change, aiming to tackle one of the most challenging issues in the evolution of human language. While several methods for detecting semantic change have been proposed, such studies are limited to a few languages, where evaluation datasets are available.

This paper presents the first dataset for evaluating Chinese semantic change in contexts preceding and following the Reform and Opening-up, covering a 50-year period in Modern Chinese. Following the DURel framework, we collected 6,000 human judgments for the dataset. We also reported the performance of alignment-based word embedding models on this evaluation dataset, achieving high and significant correlation scores.

1 Introduction

Lexical semantic change not only satisfies the appetite for linguistic exploration but also reflects the societal and cultural developments (Varian and Choi, 2009; Michel et al., 2011). Recently, this topic has been receiving growing interest from the NLP community, as witnessed a wealth of papers working on this research questions with computational approaches emerged over the past two decades (Kutuzov et al., 2018; Tahmasebi et al., 2019; Schlechtweg et al., 2020). Among these studies, most make use of distributional word representations with temporal information to model diachronic meaning change (Kim et al., 2014; Hamilton et al., 2016a,b; Giulianelli et al., 2020).

Although a variety of computational methods have been proposed for the task of lexical semantic change, evaluation datasets are only available for a limited number of languages, e.g. English, Latin, Italian, Swedish, German, Russian (Schlechtweg et al., 2020; Rodina and Kutuzov, 2020; Basile et al., 2020; Kutuzov and Pivovarova, 2021). Few studies have investigated Chinese in this domain (Tang et al., 2013, 2016) and there is currently no evaluation dataset for detecting Chinese lexical semantic change.

This paper presents the first Chinese evaluation dataset, **ZhShiftEval**, for the detection task. [1] This dataset allows us to evaluate those shifts that occurred to Modern Chinese from 1953 to 2003, over two roughly equal intervals: sub-corpus **C1** (1953-1978) and the sub-corpus **C2** (1979-2003). These two intervals were chosen on the basis of the *Reform and Opening-up*, the most influential milestone in the recent history of China [2]. It is generally assumed that this remarkable social change brought significant changes to the lexicon of Modern Chinese (Diao, 1995).

The remainder of this paper is organized as follows. Section 2 situates our study within previous work. In Section 3, we introduce how the evaluation dataset has been created following the DURel framework. Section 4 qualitatively discusses the dataset itself, and Section 5 presents the preliminary results of static word embeddings on this evaluation dataset.

2 Related Work

Before SemEval 2020, the field lacked shared standard datasets for evaluating lexical semantic change with computational approaches. Most early works were exploratory, testing whether computational models could capture specific established cases of semantic change, but without a quantitative evaluation of the models' performance (Sagi et al., 2009; Kim et al., 2014; Kulkarni et al., 2014).

Some evaluation datasets consisted of a list of target words labeled as 'changed' and 'unchanged'

[1] Researchers interested in the dataset should contact the first author of the study.

[2] Since the decision for the Reform and Opening-up was officially announced by the end of 1978, we set 1979 as the starting point for C2.

Proceedings of the 3rd Workshop on Computational Approaches to Historical Language Change, pages 113 - 118
May 26-27, 2022

with reference to linguistic papers, dictionaries (Tang et al., 2013; Basile et al., 2020), and WordNet (Mitra et al., 2014). However, these datasets are based on a binary judgment on semantic change, ignoring its cumulative nature. In contrast, Gulordava and Baroni (2011) demonstrated a 'gradable' view towards semantic change, asking native speakers to annotate target words with multiple labels for their changing degrees, according to their intuitions.

Schlechtweg et al. (2018) later proposed the **D**iachronic **U**sage **R**elatedness (DURel) framework to construct evaluation datasets for the detection task. They asked annotators to compare and grade the semantic relatedness of target words, from unrelated (1) to identical (4), across the context pairs. The ratings, together with target words, formed a small-scale evaluation dataset for German. Following this framework, Rodina and Kutuzov (2020) and Kutuzov and Pivovarova (2021) created a two-period evaluation dataset, *'RuSemShift'* and a three-period evaluation dataset *'RuShiftEval'* for Russian, assessing those meaning shifts that occurred to Russian words from the pre-Soviet period to the Post-Soviet period.

In SemEval 2020, evaluation datasets for English, German, Swedish, and Latin were released as benchmarks for the shared task (Schlechtweg et al., 2020). The datasets were built under the Diachronic Word Usage Graph (DWUG), an extension of the DURel framework, exploiting usage graphs to represent the gain and loss of senses for target words. The usage graph is weighted and undirected. The nodes represent word usages, and the weights are semantic relatedness scores graded by human annotators (Schlechtweg et al., 2021).

3 Dataset Construction

3.1 Corpora

Detecting lexical semantic change over time requires a diachronic corpus having temporal information about texts. The dataset exploited in this study is derived from *People's Daily*, one of the most popular newspapers. This dataset has texts approximately ranging from the 1950s to the early 2000s, which are stored in MD format and in different folders according to the publication year of every newspaper article. To our knowledge, it is by far the largest diachronic Chinese dataset that is publicly accessible to full texts. [3]

The *Reform and Opening up* is assumed as the most influential and significant milestone in the second half of the last century in China. An exploding number of new lexical usages emerged in the process of this pronounced social development, which further introduced significant changes to Modern Chinese (Diao, 1995). Setting the year of the *Reform and Opening-up* as the borderline, we split the dataset into two subcorpora. Thanks to the temporal information of every single text, we obtained two time-specific subcorpora: texts produced from 1953 to 1978 are used to represent the C1 period, before the Reform and opening-up, and those from 1979 to 2003 are set to represent the C2 period, after the Reform and opening-up. The statistics of subcorpora are listed in Table 1.

Periods	Word tokens (million)	Word types (million)
1953 – 1978	262	1.73
1979 – 2003	331	2.54

Table 1: Overview of subcorpora: *C1 and C2*.

3.2 Word List

The word list for annotation includes 20 words, consisting of 10 words that changed their meaning over time and 10 stable words as counterparts. As for the changed words, we first manually picked them from previous literature, such as dictionaries (Guo and Chen, 1999; Shen, 2009) and linguistic books (Diao, 1995) as candidates. We then only included words satisfying the following conditions: 1) have high frequencies in both two corpora; 2) the changes suggested by the linguistic references are reflected in the corpus, either strongly or weakly. This step is conducted by scrutinizing 20 sampled sentences from each subcorpus.

We sampled stable words for each shifted word as counterparts. The changed word and its counterpart must have the same part of speech and the same frequency percentage in both two periods. The diachronic stability of stable words is checked by making use of dictionaries (Diao, 1995; Department of Chinese Lexicography, 2019), as well as with the intuitions of native speakers with linguistic backgrounds.

[3] A reviewer suggested two other diachronic Chinese datasets for consideration. One is the Google Ngram corpus, which contains a Chinese subset, but the access is limited to 5-grams. Another one is the more recent diachronic Chinese corpus (Zinin and Xu, 2020). However, the small scale of the earlier subcorpus (less than 1 million characters) and the fact that it is written in Classic Chinese would make the training process more problematic. These datasets, however, could be useful for future investigations.

3.3 Sampling

In the DURel framework, two metrics are used for quantifying degrees of semantic change (Schlechtweg et al., 2018; Rodina and Kutuzov, 2020): (1) ΔLATER $= Mean_L - Mean_E$, comparing the average score of mean relatedness across the context pairs consisting of two sentences from the LATER group and the context pairs having two sentences from the EARLIER group ; (2) the COMPARE score was obtained by directly calculating the mean relatedness in the COMPARE group comprised of one context in C1 period and the other from the C2 period. According to the design, ΔLATER is specifically robust to detect those monosemous words in the EARLIER period that acquired new senses in the LATER period. However, if a changed word has already finished the process of semantic replacement in the LATER period, probably this metric would not be informative anymore. The COMPARE metric was thus proposed to directly compare words usages from the two time intervals.

Following this rationale, we formulated 3 groups of use pairs for each target word, named *C1*, *C2* and *C1C2*, and then randomly sampled 20 use pairs from our subcorpora (see Table 1). In total, each target word would have 60 use pairs, and 1,200 use pairs for all 20 target words.

Each usage pair (see Table 2) is comprised of two sentences containing the target word sampled from relative subcorpora. Enough context information for each sentence is guaranteed by manually checking. The average length of context is around 15 words.

Target word	Context 1	Context 2	Score	Comment
火	极苦的生活和残酷的压迫激起了采煤工人的暴动，暴动的工人一把 火点燃了煤窑	鲁菜卖火了— 山东由农业大省向强省迈进		

Table 2: An example of the use pair in COMPARE group: 火 'fire'.

3.4 Annotation

We recruited five native speakers of Mandarin Chinese with linguistics backgrounds as annotators, all of them with a MA degree in Linguistics.

Following Schlechtweg et al. (2018), annotators are asked to give scores to target words by comparing the semantic relatedness across each usage pair (see Table 3). They are also allowed to give a 0 score if they cannot make a decision.

Excluding judgments with 0 grades, 5,968 responses have been collected. The Krippendorff's alpha was calculated based on five annotators' ratings. The inter-annotator correlation score is 0.515, comparable to the scores reported for other datasets constructed under the framework of DURel (Schlechtweg et al., 2018, 2020; Kutuzov and Pivovarova, 2021).

	Description
1	Unrelated
2	Distantly related
3	Closely related
4	Identical

Table 3: Four-point scale of relatedness. Taken from Schlechtweg et al. (2018).

4 Dataset Analysis

As described in previous sections, the ΔLATER metric subtracts the mean relatedness of the EARLIER group from the LATER group. Therefore, a positive ΔLATER value is assigned when usages of the annotated word in the C2 group are more similar, whereas negative ΔLATER is assigned to words with less similar usages in the C2 group. Positive and negative ΔLATER values can be considered as two different sub-types of semantic change: innovative meaning change and reductive meaning change, roughly representing the gain or loss of word senses (Schlechtweg et al., 2018). The absolute ΔLATER value assesses the strength of semantic change.

As shown in Figure 1, most annotated words are predicted as stable words, with ΔLATER values around 0. The two topmost words '推出'*(push out; launch)*, '机制'*(machine-made; mechanism)* and the two bottommost words: '拐'*(crutch, traffic)*, '炒'*(to fry, to speculate(in the stock market))* are predicted as the words with stronger effects of semantic change.

The successful predictions on '推出', '机制', '炒' coincide with documented linguistic publications (Diao, 1995; Shen, 2009), verifying ΔLATER as an effective measure of lexical semantic change. Interestingly, the metric predicted '拐' as a changed word, despite it being originally a stable control word. A closer inspection of all three groups of sampled sentences suggested that '拐' is used more frequently with the 'crutch' meaning in the subcorpus C1, but it shows a high prevalence of the 'trafficking' meaning in the sub-corpus C2. However, the usage fluctuation detected here has to take into account the corpus bias, as 'trafficking' is more likely to occur in a newspaper corpus.

Technically speaking, words such as '机制' and '拐' are homographs with different meanings, i.e. different words with less related or even unrelated meanings. The detected shift actually shows the competition among different meanings with the same surface form, rather than the gain or loss of senses. For example, '机制' in the sampled texts from C1 period dominantly refers to a way of manufacturing as 'machine-made' (against 'handmade'). With the process of industrialization, ' machine-made ' objects became so prevalent in everyday life that the need to mention this feature quickly became obsolete and the usage slipped into obscurity. Meanwhile, the program of Reform and Opening-up was carried out thoroughly, especially concerning the revolution of the Socialist market economy system and mechanism. For this reason, '机制' with the 'mechanism' meaning became dominant in the C2 period.

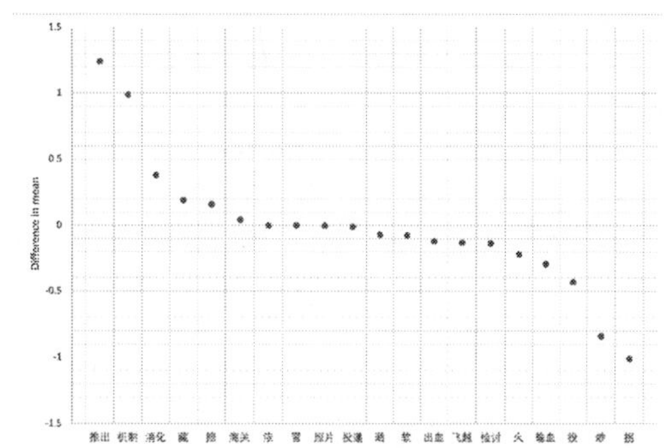

Figure 1: Rank of the target words according to the Δ LATER metric.

The COMPARE metric directly compares the semantic relatedness of a usage pair within the COMPARE group, which consists of sentences from two different periods. Higher COMPARE scores would be assigned to more stable words, like '照片(photo),' '雪(snow)', getting full scores of 4. Lower COMPARE scores are assigned to the shifting ones, e.g. the four changed words predicted by the ΔLATER metric (see Figure 2).

Moreover, this metric captured a shifting word '软(soft)'. A closer checking on sampled sentences suggested that '软' is polysemous in the C1 group, but with a dominant usage meaning 'soft texture of concrete stuff'. In the C2 group, its metaphorical senses even became more diverse, like 'soft science, soft power', meanwhile, the 'soft texture' sense lost its prevalence based on our observation. The multiple changes made the ΔLATER score not salient *per se*, but they were captured by the COMPARE metric, where usages from two different historical periods are directly compared.

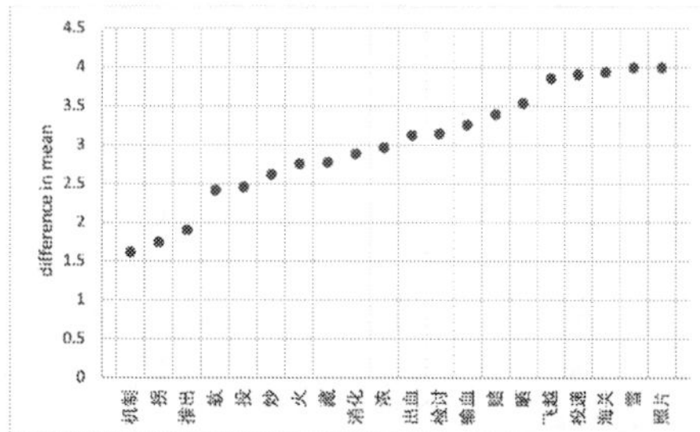

Figure 2: Rank of target words according to the COMPARE metric.

5 Evaluation

The SemEval shared task has indicated that traditional static embeddings may outperform more recent paradigms - e.g., contextualized embeddings (Devlin et al., 2019)- in the task of semantic change detection (Schlechtweg et al., 2020). Therefore, we trained a static word embedding model for this task and evaluated its performance on our newly-created dataset in this study.

We first trained our vectors on each subcorpus using both the Skip-gram model and the Continuous bag of words, which are the two most widely used static word embeddings models (Mikolov et al., 2013a,b). To have an assessment of the quality of the word embeddings trained on our subcorpora, we performed a preliminary evaluation on the Chinese word similarity dataset *COS960*, introduced by Huang et al. (2019).

The results indicated that the quality of the word embedding models was satisfactory (see Table 4). The vectors obtained with the Skip-gram models were better performing, with higher correlation scores for both periods: 0.56 for the C1 period and 0.61 for the C2 period ($p < 0.05$). We thus assumed that Skip-Gram embeddings would provide a better basis for detecting the diachronic semantic change in our study.

We then aligned word representations for the two periods into a shared space with the Orthogonal Procrustes algorithm (Hamilton et al., 2016a,b), projecting word embeddings for the C2 period onto

C1's space and making vectors living in different intervals comparable. The cosine similarity between two vectors for the same word form is calculated as the degree of meaning change. According to the cosine similarity, we ranked those words appearing in both the C1 and C2 periods, where the higher the similarity, the more stable the meaning.

	Skip-gram	CBOW
C1	0.5608	0.4539
C2	0.6144	0.5018

Table 4: Spearman correlation scores between cosine similarities and human ratings for the vectors trained on the subcorpora C1 and C2 (all the correlation scores are significant at $p < 0.05$).

Compared with the scores derived with the COMPARE metric, the Skip-gram model achieved a Spearman correlation score of 0.584. As for the ΔLATER, we took the absolute value indicating the degree of semantic drift for the correlation calculation (the positive and the negative ΔLATER values represent different sub-types of semantic change, but leave this to future investigations). This time, the Skip-gram model achieved a Spearman correlation coefficient of -0.625. Both two correlation scores are statistically significant at $p < 0.05$. As expected, the performance of the Skip-gram model on the detection task is positively correlated with the COMPARE metric and negatively correlated with the ΔLATER metric.

6 Conclusion

This paper presented the first human-annotated evaluation dataset for the task of Chinese lexical semantic change detection. This dataset was built following the DURel framework, which allows us to evaluate the usage drift that occurred in coincidence with the *Reform and Opening-up* in recent Chinese history. Our data further suggested that interpretation of the ΔLATER metric could be extended to the competition among different usages of the same surface form, in order to accommodate historical changes involving homographs. We finally examined the performance of the Skip-gram model on our evaluation dataset and found that it achieves a relatively high correlation coefficient with the two metrics.

This paper served as a first, exploratory study on modeling lexical semantic change in Chinese, on the basis of a limited number of words.

In the near future, our goal is to scale up the dataset and to examine the performance of more models for Chinese, including the more recent contextualized embeddings (Devlin et al., 2019). Moreover, using finer-grained intervals for diachronic meaning change detection and exploring the diatopic variation between different Chinese dialects are also possible directions of our future work (Wang et al., 2022; Zampieri et al., 2019).

References

Pierpaolo Basile, Annalina Caputo, Tommaso Caselli, Pierluigi Cassotti, and Rossella Varvara. 2020. DIACR-Ita @ EVALITA2020: Overview of the EVALITA2020 Diachronic Lexical Semantics (DIACR-Ita) Task. In *Proceedings of EVALITA*.

Chinese Academy of Social Science Department of Chinese Lexicography, Institute of Linguistics. 2019. *Contemporary Chinese Dictionary (Xiandai Hanyu Cidian)*, the 7th edition. Commercial Press, Peking.

Jacob Devlin, Ming-Wei Chang, Kenton Lee, and Kristina Toutanova. 2019. BERT: Pre-training of Deep Bidirectional Transformers for Language Understanding. In *Proceedings of NAACL*.

Yanbin Diao. 1995. *The Development and Reform of Mainland Chinese in the New Era*. Hung Yeh Publishing, Taibei.

Mario Giulianelli, Marco Del Tredici, and Raquel Fernández. 2020. Analysing Lexical Semantic Change with Contextualised Word Representations. In *Proceedings of ACL*.

Kristina Gulordava and Marco Baroni. 2011. A Distributional Similarity Approach to the Detection of Semantic Change in the Google Books Ngram Corpus. In *Proceedings of the GEMS 2011 Workshop on GEometrical Models of Natural Language Semantics*.

Dasong Guo and Haihong Chen. 1999. *Chinese Neologisms for a Fifty-year (1949-1999)*. Shandong Education Press, Jinan.

William L. Hamilton, Jure Leskovec, and Dan Jurafsky. 2016a. Cultural Shift or Linguistic Drift? Comparing Two Computational Measures of Semantic Change. In *Proceedings of EMNLP*.

William L. Hamilton, Jure Leskovec, and Dan Jurafsky. 2016b. Diachronic Word Embeddings Reveal Statistical Laws of Semantic Change. In *Proceedings of ACL*.

Junjie Huang, Fanchao Qi, Chenghao Yang, Zhiyuan Liu, and Maosong Sun. 2019. COS960: A Chinese Word Similarity Dataset of 960 Word Pairs. *arXiv preprint arXiv:1906.00247*.

Yoon Kim, Yi-I Chiu, Kentaro Hanaki, Darshan Hegde, and Slav Petrov. 2014. Temporal Analysis of Language through Neural Language Models. *arXiv preprint arXiv:1405.3515.*

Vivek Kulkarni, Rami Al-Rfou, Bryan Perozzi, and Steven Skiena. 2014. Statistically Significant Detection of Linguistic Change.

Andrey Kutuzov and Lidia Pivovarova. 2021. Three-part Diachronic Semantic Change Dataset for Russian. In *Proceedings of the ACL International Workshop on Computational Approaches to Historical Language Change.*

Andrey Kutuzov, Lilja vrelid, Terrence Szymanski, and Erik Velldal. 2018. Diachronic Word Embeddings and Semantic Shifts: A Survey. In *Proceedings of COLING.*

Jean-Baptiste Michel, Yuan Kui Shen, Aviva Presser Aiden, Adrian Veres, Matthew K Gray, Google Books Team, Joseph P Pickett, Dale Hoiberg, Dan Clancy, and Peter Norvig. 2011. Quantitative Analysis of Culture Using Millions of Digitized Books. *Science*, 331(6014):176–182.

Tomas Mikolov, Kai Chen, Greg Corrado, and Jeffrey Dean. 2013a. Efficient Estimation of Word Representations in Vector Space. *arXiv preprint arXiv:1301.3781.*

Tomas Mikolov, Wen-tau Yih, and Geoffrey Zweig. 2013b. Linguistic Regularities in Continuous Space Word Representations. In *Proceedings of NAACL-HLT.*

Sunny Mitra, Ritwik Mitra, Martin Riedl, Chris Biemann, Animesh Mukherjee, and Pawan Goyal. 2014. That's Sick Dude!: Automatic Identification of Word Sense Change across Different Timescales. In *Proceedings of ACL.*

Julia Rodina and Andrey Kutuzov. 2020. RuSemShift: A Dataset of Historical Lexical Semantic Change in Russian. In *Proceedings of COLING.*

Eyal Sagi, Stefan Kaufmann, and Brady Clark. 2009. Semantic Density Analysis: Comparing Word Meaning across Time and Phonetic Space. *Proceedings of the EACL Workshop on GEMS: Geometrical Models of Natural Language Semantics.*

Dominik Schlechtweg, Barbara McGillivray, Simon Hengchen, Haim Dubossarsky, and Nina Tahmasebi. 2020. SemEval-2020 Task 1: Unsupervised Lexical Semantic Change Detection. In *Proceedings of SemEval.*

Dominik Schlechtweg, Sabine Schulte im Walde, and Stefanie Eckmann. 2018. Diachronic Usage Relatedness (DURel): A Framework for the Annotation of Lexical Semantic Change. In *Proceedings of NAACL-HLT.*

Dominik Schlechtweg, Nina Tahmasebi, Simon Hengchen, Haim Dubossarsky, and Barbara McGillivray. 2021. DWUG: A Large Resource of Diachronic Word Usage Graphs in Four Languages. *arXiv preprint arXiv:2104.08540.*

Mengying Shen. 2009. *New Words and New Expressions in Chinese New Era (1949-299).* Sichuan Lexicographical Press, Chengdu.

Nina Tahmasebi, Lars Borin, and Adam Jatowt. 2019. Survey of Computational Approaches to Lexical Semantic Change. *arXiv preprint arXiv:1811.06278.*

Xuri Tang, Weiguang Qu, and Xiaohe Chen. 2013. Semantic Change Computation: A Successive Approach. In *Behavior and Social Computing*, pages 68–81, Cham. Springer International Publishing.

Xuri Tang, Weiguang Qu, and Xiaohe Chen. 2016. Semantic Change Computation: A Successive Approach. *World Wide Web*, 19.

Hal Varian and Hyunyoung Choi. 2009. Predicting the Present with Google Trends. *Economic Record*, 88.

Shan Wang, Ruhan Liu, and Chu-Ren Huang. 2022. Social Changes through the Lens of Language: A Big Data Study of Chinese Modal Verbs. *PLOS ONE*, 17:1–31.

Marcos Zampieri, Shervin Malmasi, Yves Scherrer, Tanja Samardžić, Francis Tyers, Miikka Silfverberg, Natalia Klyueva, Tung-Le Pan, Chu-Ren Huang, Radu Tudor Ionescu, Andrei M. Butnaru, and Tommi Jauhiainen. 2019. A Report on the Third VarDial Evaluation Campaign. In *Proceedings of the NAACL Workshop on NLP for Similar Languages, Varieties and Dialects.*

Sergey Zinin and Yang Xu. 2020. Corpus of Chinese Dynastic Histories: Gender Analysis over Two Millennia. In *Proceedings of LREC.*

Low Saxon dialect distances at the orthographic and syntactic level

Janine Siewert
University of Helsinki
janine.siewert@helsinki.fi

Yves Scherrer
University of Helsinki
yves.scherrer@helsinki.fi

Martijn Wieling
University of Groningen
m.b.wieling@rug.nl

Abstract

We compare five Low Saxon dialects from the 19th and 21st century from Germany and the Netherlands with each other as well as with modern Standard Dutch and Standard German. Our comparison is based on character n-grams on the one hand and PoS n-grams on the other and we show that these two lead to different distances. Particularly in the PoS-based distances, one can observe all of the 21st century Low Saxon dialects shifting towards the modern majority languages.

1 Introduction

We are investigating dialect similarity in 19th and 21st century Low Saxon based on data from Germany and the Netherlands. Traditionally, Low Saxon dialect classification has mostly been based on phonological and morphological traits, such as the ones presented by Schröder (2004). In this study, however, we focus on the orthographic and the syntactic side and compare how these relate to each other. We compare two levels as we expect the intensity and nature of the majority language influence to differ here. The choice of these two particular levels was motivated by the fact that orthography can be inspected without annotation and for syntax, we could train sufficiently reliable PoS taggers[1], which at this point is not possible for morphology and phonology. Furthermore, we investigate how the dialect closeness on both levels has changed over time.

An interesting area to pay attention to with respect to dialect distance is the Dutch-German border. Like Goossens (2019) observed, the Low Saxon dialects along the border have started to diverge under the influence of the majority languages. According to him, this divergence is most pronounced at the lexical level, but convergence towards the majority language has also been attested in phonology, morphology and syntax. While studies on the divergence of dialects along the border often focus on the occurrence and frequency of particular traits based on interviews, cf. Smits (2011), we address the overall (dis)similarity in prose texts.

Since in the 19th century school education and majority language media played a smaller role in everyday life compared with today, we assume the effect of language contact with Dutch and German to be less visible in the morphology and syntax of 19th century Low Saxon, as such changes to the language system itself take time and gradually add up. On the other hand, the border is probably already clearly discernable at the orthographic level due to reading and writing education in the majority language, which we assume to have had a more immediate influence, particularly in areas where the Low Saxon literary production had ceased (nearly) completely after Middle Low Saxon times. Therefore, from the 19th to the 21st century, we expect a greater change in distance towards the majority languages at the PoS level than at the character level. We thus hypothesize that the Low Saxon dialects will appear closer to each other on the syntactic side with distance to the majority languages decreasing over time, while 19th century dialects might already group together with the respective majority language at the orthographic level.

2 Background

The West Germanic language Low Saxon (also called "Low German") today is primarily spoken in Northern Germany and the North-Eastern Netherlands by around 5 million people and enjoys official recognition in both countries (Moseley, 2010). As a result of the lack of an interregional standard language, Low Saxon speakers tend to use their own dialects in all language use cases. As there is no official common orthography either, one needs to take into consideration two layers of variation: on the one hand spelling variation and on the other ac-

[1] Around 85% accuracy based on a manually annotated test set.

Proceedings of the 3rd Workshop on Computational Approaches to Historical Language Change, pages 119 - 124
May 26-27, 2022 ©2022 Association for Computational Linguistics

tual dialect variation. People may for instance stick to their own dialect but switch writing systems depending on whom they address.[2] This multilayered variation poses challenges to the development of NLP for Low Saxon but at the same time presents an interesting case for historical dialectology of written language.

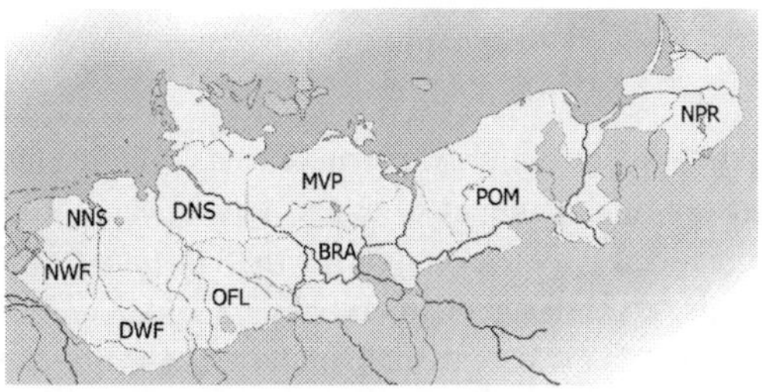

Figure 1: Major Low Saxon dialect groups: Dutch North Saxon (NNS), German North Saxon (DNS), Dutch Westphalian (NWF), German Westphalian (DWF), Eastphalian (OFL), Mecklenburgish-West-Pomeranian (MVP), Brandenburgish-South-Marchian (BRA), East Pomeranian (POM) and Low Prussian (NPR).

Figure 1 shows the major dialect groups of modern Low Saxon. The eastern dialects East Pomeranian (POM) and Lower Prussian (NPR) were spoken in these areas prior to WWII.

3 Data

The majority of our dataset is taken from the LSDC dataset (Siewert et al., 2020) since, as far as we are aware, this is the only dataset for modern Low Saxon annotated for dialect and century. Especially in regard to the 19th century data, we supplemented it with relevant prose texts from Leopold and Leopold (1882)[3] and the Twentse Taalbank (van der Vliet, 2021).

The overall size of the dataset is 120,720 sentences and 2,410,261 tokens and it covers eight dialect regions: Dutch North Saxon, German North Saxon, Dutch Westphalian, German Westphalian, Eastphalian, Mecklenburgish-West-Pomeranian, Brandenburgish-South-Marchian and Low Prussian. In this rough division, Dutch Westphalian includes all Dutch Low Saxon dialects except for Gronings, which consequently is identical with Dutch North Saxon here. The first five of these dialects are included in our current experiments. As we currently lack annotated data from Mecklenburgish-West-Pomeranian (MVP), Brandenburgish-South-Marchian (BRA) and Lower Prussian (NPR) for the 20th and 21st century, we cannot yet perform diachronic comparisons and thus exclude these dialects from our experiments as well. Furthermore, we do not use the 20th century data in our comparisons as it still consists mostly of data from only two dialects.

In our experiments, we thus used data from the five dialects presented in Table 1. We distinguish dialects from the 19th and 21st century and treat these as separate data points.

	19th	21st
German North Saxon (DNS)	3,869	475
Dutch North Saxon (NNS)	1,774	16,964
German Westphalian (DWF)	2,557	10,225
Dutch Westphalian (NWF)	4,925	9,150
Eastphalian (OFL)	278	7,896

Table 1: Sentences per dialect and century in our dataset.

For comparison, we also used UD data in Standard German (Borges Völker et al., 2019) and Standard Dutch (Bouma and van Noord, 2017) containing 153,035 and 18,078 sentences, respectively. These datasets seem to consist mostly of data from the late 20th and 21st century.

The Low Saxon data was converted to CoNLL-U format and automatically PoS tagged with the help of the Stanza tagger (Qi et al., 2020)[4] trained on UD data in Danish (Johannsen et al., 2015), Dutch (Bouma and van Noord, 2017), German (McDonald et al., 2013), and Swedish (Borin et al., 2008) in addition to manually annotated Low Saxon data.

In connection with the publication of the paper, our dataset, as well as the n-gram counts that form the basis for our experiments, will be added to LSDC-morph repository[5] on the Helsinki-NLP GitHub page.

4 Methods

Dialect similarity at the orthographic level based on character n-grams[6] will be compared to dialect

[2] Personal observation from conversations on social media.

[3] Digitised by dbnl: `https://dbnl.nl/tekst/leop008sche00_01/`

[4] We use the stand-alone version of the tagger available at `https://github.com/yvesscherrer/stanzatagger`.

[5] `https://github.com/Helsinki-NLP/LSDC-morph`

[6] Character n-grams, of course, do not purely represent the orthography as they will also capture actual dialect characteristics such as inflectional suffixes, but this is the closest one can get without adding a phonological or phonetic layer.

similarity based on PoS tag sequences to investigate if these lead to different dialect groupings.

Malmasi and Zampieri (2017) observed in their experiments for identifying Swiss German dialects that approaches based on character n-grams outperform word-based ones and, in their study on British dialects, Wolk and Szmrecsanyi (2016) have employed part-of-speech n-grams for corpus-based dialectometry, concluding that this approach can achieve results comparable to manually selected features.

4.1 N-grams

We extract character bigrams and trigrams from tokenised and lower-cased text. Trigrams consisting of the last letter of the previous word, a space sign and the first letter of the following word are included. As for PoS bigrams and trigrams, we exclude n-grams containing the tags 'SYM', 'X' and '_'. We remove PoS and character n-grams with an overall frequency of 5 or below and the counts of the remaining n-grams are normalised with tf-idf.

4.2 Distance measures

For dialect distance measuring, we make use of scikit-learn (Pedregosa et al., 2011) PCA with k-means clustering with cluster sizes ranging from 2 to 5.[7] The input for our experiments are matrices with raw n-gram counts which we first normalise using tf-idf and subsequently reduce to two dimensions with PCA for visualisation purposes. The results to be seen in Figure 2 and 3 are based on this PCA-reduced data. We ran the models several times and observed marginal changes only for a larger number of clusters, when cluster borders divided very close dialects. Consequently, the random initialisation did not have a substantial effect on the results. Additionally, we compared these results to k-means clustering without PCA reduction and to hierarchical clustering and obtained similar results, cf. appendix A.

5 Results

As expected, the PCA-based closeness and the clustering at the character-based level differ clearly from the PoS-based results, but not all of the divergences correspond to our expectations.

[7] Inspired by this example: https://scikit-learn.org/stable/auto_examples/cluster/plot_kmeans_digits.html

5.1 Character n-grams

As can be seen from Figure 2, in a two-cluster case based on character n-grams, the varieties group according to country borders, with German Low Saxon clustering in the lower left corner and Dutch Low Saxon and Dutch (NDL) in the lower right corner. German (DEU) at the top is grouped into the same cluster with German Low Saxon, but at a substantial distance from the dialects. When using three clusters, German is the first to be separated into its own cluster (cf. appendix A). In case of Dutch Low Saxon, the greater closeness to standard Dutch in 21st century Low Saxon compared with 19th century Low Saxon suggests that the Low Saxon dialects in the Netherlands increasingly conform to the principles of the Dutch orthography. Such a general tendency, however, cannot be observed for German Low Saxon.

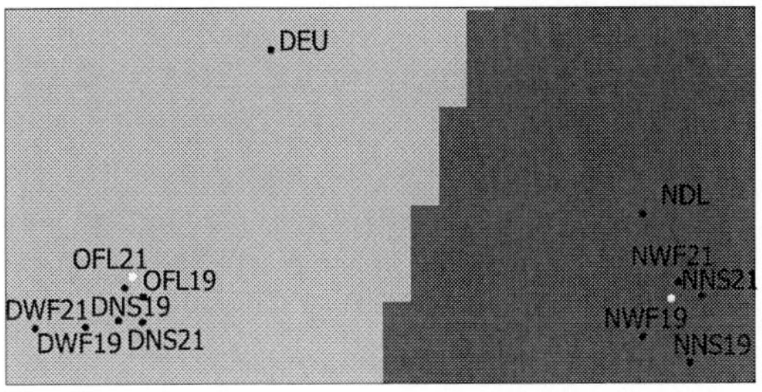

Figure 2: Dialect distances based on character n-grams

5.2 PoS n-grams

Compared to character n-grams, the PoS n-grams as presented in Figure 3 show a greater closeness of the Low Saxon dialects from both sides of the border. Specifically, when clustering into three groups, 19th century Low Saxon forms the left cluster, 21st century Low Saxon the middle one, and standard Dutch and German cluster on the right hand side.

When restricting the number of clusters to two, Dutch and German form one cluster and the Low Saxon dialects from both centuries form another.

For the PoS n-gram case, the century seems to play a greater role than the state border, since the clustering suggests that Low Saxon has become closer to the majority languages in terms of syntax.

It is remarkable that the overall distance between Dutch Low Saxon and German Low Saxon does not seem to have changed drastically over time. Dutch North Saxon and Dutch Westphalian seem to have approached each other and the same appears to be true for German North Saxon and Eastphalian.

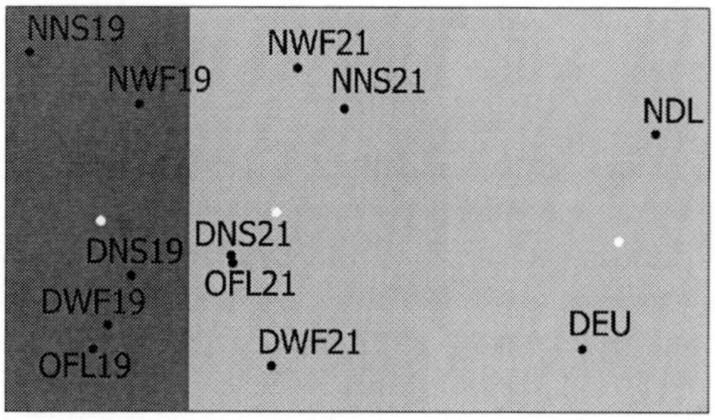

Figure 3: Dialect distances based on PoS n-grams

6 Discussion

Based on our knowledge of and about Low Saxon dialects, the overall results appear meaningful despite the comparatively low tagging accuracy of 85%.

In the PoS-based experiments, the fact that a noticeable distance between neighbouring dialect regions divided by a country border can already be observed in the 19th century data raises the question of how representative the written dialect is of the actual Low Saxon spoken by the average population. Given that written Low Saxon is commonly produced by people who have received their education in the majority language, this may have an influence on the kind of written language produced. On the other hand, one needs to keep in mind the size of the dialect regions. Both the German Westphalian group (DWF) and particularly the German North Saxon (DNS) group stretching from the Dutch border to Schleswig-Holstein are on their own larger than the whole Dutch Low Saxon area and not all of the texts included are written in varieties particularly close to the border. A more fine-grained dialect subdivision, where e.g., the Groningen dialect could be compared with East Frisian, would therefore be desirable for the future as well. However, this does not seem feasible in our research project at this point due to the lack of sufficient data sources for many of these dialects.

The noticeable distance between German Low Saxon and German in the character-based experiments compared with the closeness of Dutch and Dutch Low Saxon might partly be explained by the greater phonological differences between German and Low Saxon, but in addition to that, one might also consider that local writing systems for German Low Saxon tend to adhere to certain orthographic principles not found in the German orthography. One of these is that even the umlauted vowels *ä*, *ö* and *ü* may occur as digraphs, especially in closed syllables, e.g., in the words *däänsch/däänsk* 'Danish', *sööt* 'sweet' and *düüster* 'dark', according to both the Sass[8] spelling (Kahl and Thies, 2009) and the Münsterland spelling (Kahl, 2009).

The overall PoS-based distance of Dutch Low Saxon and Standard Dutch appears to be comparable to the overall distance between German Low Saxon and Standard German. This is interesting as, due to the greater phonological similarity (e.g. no High German consonant shift) on the one hand and the character n-gram results on the other, one might expect the distance between Dutch Low Saxon and Dutch to be relatively smaller on the syntactic level as well.

The relatively greater distance of 21st century German Westphalian to the other two German Low Saxon dialects deserves some attention, too. One possible explanation could be the Westphalian dialects' more conservative morphology. Whereas several dialects of German Westphalian still inflect nouns in three cases and have preserved subjunctive forms of verbs (Lindow et al., 1998)[9], it might be the case that Dutch Low Saxon, German North Saxon and Eastphalian more commonly resort to prepositions and auxiliary verbs.

The relative closeness of German and Dutch in the PoS-based results came as a surprise as well, but the genre might play a role here: Whereas Dutch and German data largely represents more formal language from non-fiction texts such as news texts, much of the Low Saxon data sources belong to various forms of literature. While the possibility of an influence of genre differences on the distance between 19th and 21st century Low Saxon dialects cannot be completely ruled out either, it seems less likely as the majority of the data from both centuries consists of fiction texts and stories.

Due to the relatively modern data in Dutch and German, the conclusions to be drawn from our comparison are restricted. For a more meaningful comparison, one should include 19th century Dutch and German as – even though gradual assimilation to the majority language is what one would expect – it might still be the case that the distance between 19th century Low Saxon and the Dutch and German

[8]Named after the creator Johannes Saß.

[9]While, according to Lindow et al. (1998, 152), the treefold case distinction is still in use in parts of Southern Eastphalian as well, our dataset does not include texts from this region as far as we are aware.

of that time was not as significant as the distance presented here would suggest.

7 Future research

In our future research, we will include more Low Saxon dialects, especially Mecklenburgish-West-Pomeranian, and add the 20th century as well as Dutch and German data from relevant time periods. The eastern dialects like Mecklenburgish-West-Pomeranian would constitute a meaningful addition since we could then examine the extent to which the common division into West Low Saxon and East Low Saxon / East Low German is apparent at the levels of language under scrutiny.

Morphological tagging would be a valuable addition as well, which we plan to include in the future. At this point, the accuracy is still too low, at around 60-70%, which is why more annotation work is required. In the future, we will create more training data for both PoS and morphological tagging through manual correction of the automaticcally tagged data.

Regarding dimensionality reduction, we intend to more closely inspect which features are considered most central by the model to investigate whether the dialect distances are based on actual dialect characteristics or if the results have been influenced by artifacts of the dataset.

We hope that the datasets gathered and annotated by us will facilitate the development of NLP tools for and research into Low Saxon.

Acknowledgements

This work has been supported by the Academy of Finland through project No. 342859 "CorCoDial – Corpus-based computational dialectology".

References

Emanuel Borges Völker, Maximilian Wendt, Felix Hennig, and Arne Köhn. 2019. HDT-UD: A very large Universal Dependencies treebank for German. In *Proceedings of the Third Workshop on Universal Dependencies (UDW, SyntaxFest 2019)*, pages 46–57, Paris, France. Association for Computational Linguistics.

Lars Borin, Markus Forsberg, and Lennart Lönngren. 2008. Saldo 1.0 (svenskt associationslexikon version 2). *Språkbanken, University of Gothenburg*.

Gosse Bouma and Gertjan van Noord. 2017. Increasing return on annotation investment: The automatic construction of a Universal Dependency treebank for Dutch. In *Proceedings of the NoDaLiDa 2017 Workshop on Universal Dependencies (UDW 2017)*, pages 19–26, Gothenburg, Sweden. Association for Computational Linguistics.

Jan Goossens. 2019. „Dialektverfall" und „Mundartrenaissance" in Westniederdeutschland und im Osten der Niederlande. In Gerhard Stickel, editor, *Varietäten des Deutschen: Regional- und Umgangssprachen*, pages 399–404. De Gruyter.

Anders Johannsen, Héctor Martínez Alonso, and Barbara Plank. 2015. Universal dependencies for danish. In *International Workshop on Treebanks and Linguistic Theories (TLT14)*, pages 157–167.

Heinrich Kahl and Heinrich Thies. 2009. *der neue Sass - Plattdeutsches Wörterbuch*. Wachholtz Verlag, Neumünster.

Klaus-Werner Kahl. 2009. *Wörterbuch des Münsterländer Platt*. Aschendorff Verlag, Münster.

Joh. A. Leopold and L. Leopold. 1882. *Van de Schelde tot de Weichsel*. J.B. Wolters, Groningen.

Wolfgang Lindow, Dieter Möhn, D Stellmacher, H Taubken, and J Wirrer. 1998. Niederdeutsche grammatik.

Shervin Malmasi and Marcos Zampieri. 2017. German dialect identification in interview transcriptions. In *Proceedings of the Fourth Workshop on NLP for Similar Languages, Varieties and Dialects (VarDial)*, pages 164–169.

Ryan McDonald, Joakim Nivre, Yvonne Quirmbach-Brundage, Yoav Goldberg, Dipanjan Das, Kuzman Ganchev, Keith Hall, Slav Petrov, Hao Zhang, Oscar Täckström, et al. 2013. Universal dependency annotation for multilingual parsing. In *Proceedings of the 51st Annual Meeting of the Association for Computational Linguistics (Volume 2: Short Papers)*, pages 92–97.

Christopher Moseley, editor. 2010. *Atlas of the World's Languages in Danger*, 3 edition. UNESCO Publishing, Paris. Online version: `http://www.unesco.org/culture/en/endangeredlanguages/atlas`.

F. Pedregosa, G. Varoquaux, A. Gramfort, V. Michel, B. Thirion, O. Grisel, M. Blondel, P. Prettenhofer, R. Weiss, V. Dubourg, J. Vanderplas, A. Passos, D. Cournapeau, M. Brucher, M. Perrot, and E. Duchesnay. 2011. Scikit-learn: Machine learning in Python. *Journal of Machine Learning Research*, 12:2825–2830.

Peng Qi, Yuhao Zhang, Yuhui Zhang, Jason Bolton, and Christopher D. Manning. 2020. Stanza: A Python natural language processing toolkit for many human languages. In *Proceedings of the 58th Annual Meeting of the Association for Computational Linguistics: System Demonstrations*.

Ingrid Schröder. 2004. Niederdeutsch in der Gegenwart: Sprachgebiet – Grammatisches – Binnendifferenzierung. In Dieter Stellmacher, editor, *Niederdeutsche Sprache und Literatur der Gegenwart*, pages 35–97. Georg Olms Verlag, Hildesheim, Zürich and New York.

Janine Siewert, Yves Scherrer, Martijn Wieling, and Jörg Tiedemann. 2020. LSDC - a comprehensive dataset for low Saxon dialect classification. In *Proceedings of the 7th Workshop on NLP for Similar Languages, Varieties and Dialects*, page 25–35, Barcelona, Spain (Online). International Committee on Computational Linguistics (ICCL).

Tom Smits. 2011. Dialectverlies en dialectnivellering in nederlands-duitse grensdialecten. *Taal en Tongval*, 63(1):175–196.

Goaitsen van der Vliet. 2021. Twentse taalbank. `http://www.twentsetaalbank.nl/`. Accessed: 2021-12-15.

Christoph Wolk and Benedikt Szmrecsanyi. 2016. Top-down and bottom-up advances in corpus-based dialectometry. *The future of dialects: Selected papers from Methods in Dialectology XV*, 1:225.

A Results of other clustering approaches

In this appendix, we list the outcomes of other clustering approaches.

A.1 K-means clustering

Dialect	Clusters				
	2P	2C	3P 1st	3P 2nd	3C
19th DNS	1	0	0	2	1
19th DWF	1	0	0	2	1
19th OFL	1	0	0	2	1
19th NNS	1	1	0	0	0
19th NWF	1	1	0	0	0
21st DNS	1	0	2	2	1
21st DWF	1	0	2	2	1
21st OFL	1	0	2	2	1
21st NNS	1	1	2	0	0
21st NWF	1	1	2	0	0
Dutch	0	1	1	1	0
German	0	0	1	1	2

Figure 4: Results of k-means clustering based on data without PCA-based dimensionality reduction. The overall results are similar, only in the case of three PoS-based clusters, there was variation between runs as to whether the Low Saxon dialects cluster according to century or according to state. P = PoS, C = character.

A.2 Hierarchical clustering

The hierarchical clustering[10] uses the following dialect numbering: 0 = 19th DWF, 1 = 19th DNS, 2 = 19th OFL, 3 = 19th NWF, 4 = 19th NNS, 5 = 21st NWF, 6 = 21st DWF, 7 = 21st NNS, 8 = 21st OFL, 9 = 21st DNS, 10 = DEU, 11 = NDL.

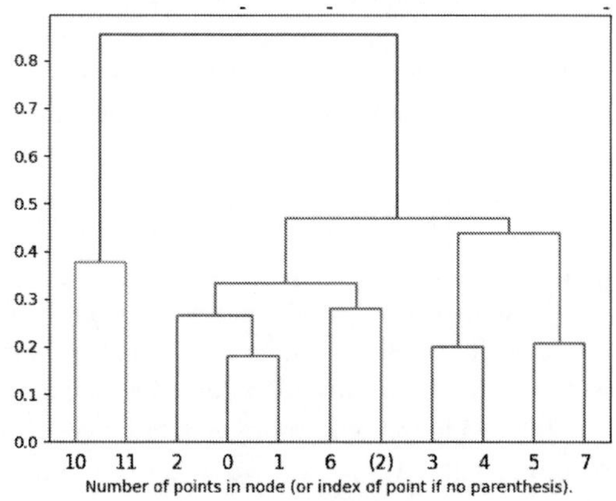

Figure 5: PoS-based hierarchical clustering using Euclidean metric and ward linkage.

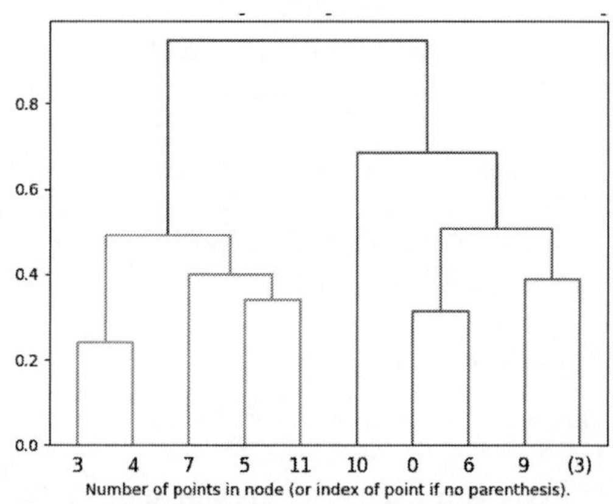

Figure 6: Character-based hierarchical clustering using Euclidean metric and ward linkage.

[10]Partly based on this example: `https://scikit-learn.org/stable/auto_examples/cluster/plot_agglomerative_dendrogram.html`

"Vaderland", "Volk" and "Natie": Semantic Change Related to Nationalism in Dutch Literature Between 1700 and 1880 Captured with Dynamic Bernoulli Word Embeddings

Marije Timmermans*
GBBO, De Bilt,
The Netherlands
marije.r.t@gmail.com

Eva Vanmassenhove
Department of CSAI
Tilburg University
The Netherlands
e.o.j.vanmassenhove@uvt.nl

Dimitar Shterionov
Department of CSAI
Tilburg University
The Netherlands
d.shterionov@uvt.nl

Abstract

Languages can respond to external events in various ways - the creation of new words or named entities, additional senses might develop for already existing words or the valence of words can change. In this work, we explore the semantic shift of the Dutch words "natie" ("nation"), "volk" ("people") and "vaderland" ("fatherland") over a period that is known for the rise of nationalism in Europe: 1700-1880 (Jensen, 2016). The semantic change is measured by means of Dynamic Bernoulli Word Embeddings (Rudolph and Blei, 2018) which allow for comparison between word embeddings over different time slices. The word embeddings were generated based on Dutch fiction literature divided over different decades. From the analysis of the absolute drifts, it appears that the word "natie" underwent a relatively small drift. However, the drifts of "vaderland" and "volk" show multiple peaks, culminating around the turn of the nineteenth century. To verify whether this semantic change can indeed be attributed to nationalistic movements, a detailed analysis of the nearest neighbours of the target words is provided. From the analysis, it appears that "natie", "volk" and "vaderland" became more nationalistically-loaded over time.

1 Introduction

The nineteenth century is often characterized as the era of modernity and nationalism (Leerssen, 2006; Hobsbawm, 2012; Jensen, 2016; Gellner, 1983). However, the development of the modernist mindset did not happen overnight. Brunner et al. (1972) call this cultural transition period from the early modern period to the modern period the *Sattelzeit* or saddle period. In this period, from roughly 1750 to 1850, the reading public expanded, people became used to thinking about the past and the future, ideologies such as nationalism arose, and abstract concepts became more politically applicable.

This paper aims to contribute to the study of the development of the cultural thought of nationalism during the *Sattelzeit* in Dutch society by researching fiction literature from 1700 to 1880. By employing a dynamic word embedding model we examine whether the (literary) contexts of three target words "natie" ("nation"), "volk" ("people") and "vaderland" ("fatherland") have changed over the course of the eighteenth century and nineteenth century. The dynamic word embedding model allows us to measure to what extent the contexts might have changed by quantifying the semantic drift leveraging the target words' embeddings. By doing so we aim to establish whether there is indeed a measurable semantic change or drift that coincides with the upcoming cultural and political thoughts of the era.

2 Related Work

In history, studying how concepts have changed over time is called *Begriffsgeschichte* or conceptual history. Influential in conceptual history are the works from Kosselleck (2002), Foucault (1970) and Skinner (2002). Van Sas (1999) studied different representations of the Dutch nation by looking at words expressing concepts related to nationalism over the centuries, using political texts and literature from the fifteenth century to 1940.

In the field of digital humanities, dynamic word embeddings can be employed to measure how words change over time. Word embeddings are distributional representations of words constructed based on their distribution in texts, i.e. these embeddings quantify how often words co-occur with other words in (preferably large) corpora. This idea is based on the distributional hypothesis, which presumes that the meaning of a word can be derived from its linguistic context (Firth, 1957). Semantic representations can be learned using Natural Language Processing techniques, such as `Word2Vec` (Mikolov et al., 2013), that automat-

Proceedings of the 3rd Workshop on Computational Approaches to Historical Language Change, pages 125 - 130
May 26-27, 2022

ically learn associations by leveraging information from large corpora. These distributional methods have been proven suitable to capture (broad) semantic changes in large generic corpora (Hamilton et al., 2016; Kutuzov et al., 2018; Tahmasebi et al., 2021). More recently, word embeddings have also been used to investigate semantic shifts in historical contexts, e.g. shifts in gender bias in historical newspapers (Wevers, 2019), changes in gender and ethnic stereotypes (Garg et al., 2018), evolution of concepts (Orlikowski et al., 2018), study of parliamentary debates (Van Lange and Futselaar, 2018) and others.

A practical difficulty with dynamic word embeddings arises when attempting to compare the embeddings over different time periods. This problem is referred to as the alignment problem and different solutions have been proposed (Di Carlo et al., 2019; Hamilton et al., 2016). A second challenge, especially when dealing with historical data, is the fact that large corpora are required to train word embeddings (e.g. the model of Hamilton et al. (2016) required a dataset of 100,000,000 words per time slice). Kim et al. (2014), Bamler and Mandt (2017), Yao et al. (2018) and Rudolph and Blei (2018) proposed a dynamic word embedding model for handling such sparse data.

For the current research we employ the Dynamic Bernoulli Embedding model of (Rudolph and Blei, 2018). Rudolph and Blei (2018) demonstrated that Dynamic Bernoulli Embeddings give good predictive performance for time windows with sparse data. Moreover, their method is able to capture changes of rare words. Both Dynamic Filtering of Skip-Gram and Dynamic Bernoulli Embedding are able to detect drifts within very sparse datasets. However, the Dynamic Bernoulli Embedding has been shown to keep words that do not change over time more stable (Montariol and Allauzen, 2019). In our experiments, we apply the Dynamic Bernoulli Embedding model to Dutch literature to study the semantic shift of words related to nationalism, with the goal to contribute to the analysis of the historical discourse on nationalism.

3 Experimental Setup

3.1 Dataset

The data is retrieved from the Digital Library of Dutch Language (DBNL)[1] which contains thousands of literary texts as well as secondary literature and additional information (e.g. biographies and portrayals) from The Netherlands and Belgium. We limited the data collected to fiction, since these works are more widespread than non-fiction and given that the content of popular genres in the nineteenth century had nationalistic tendencies. The historical novel romantically celebrated the nation's past, while the rustic novel and the realistic novel showed their readers the social and moral representation of the nation (Rigney, 2020; Leerssen, 2020). While rhyme and other stylistic specifics can have an effect of the position and context of the target words, poetry is also included since it is makes up a large percentage of literary works in the DBNL. This is in particular true for the earlier decades of the time period of interest.

The final dataset compiled from DBNL consists of 414 fiction books, such as prose, plays and youth literature from the time period between 1700 and 1880. To capture change over time, the data is sliced into bins per decade, based on their publication dates. The data is divided in a training (80%) and a validation (20%) set.

3.2 Preprocessing Steps

We applied spelling normalization based on the work by Braun (2002). Stop words were removed using the NLTK package (Bird et al., 2009) and the word frequency in texts from the target time period (1700-1880). Additionally, words that are less than two characters/numbers were pruned as well as words occurring less than ten times in the documents. These steps ensure a compacter dictionary for the model.

3.3 Dynamic Bernoulli Embeddings

We employ the Dynamic Bernoulli Embedding model (Rudolph and Blei, 2018). Rudolph and Blei (2018). This model is a type of exponential family embeddings that captures sequential changes in the data representations. It extends Bernoulli embeddings for text which provide a conditional model for individual text entries to text data over time. This model has a good predictive performance for time windows with sparse data. It has been proven that this model captures changes of (rare) words while keeping words that do not change relatively stable (Montariol and Allauzen, 2019). The number of passes over the data is ten, with an additional first pass, or zeroth pass, where the embedding vector is trained on all the time slices, for initialization. The dimension of the embeddings are set to 100,

[1] https://www.dbnl.org/

and the number of negative samples is set to 20. These settings are based on the settings of Rudolph and Blei (2018). After 100 mini batches, the positive likelihood (L_{pos}) is calculated on the validation set and saved. The context size employed is six.

Model	**values**
context size	*6*
passes over data	*10 + 0th*
dim. of embeddings	*100*
Hyperparameters	**values**
minibatch	*100, 300, 500*
learning rate	*0.2, 0.02, 0.002, 0.0002*
drift	*1, 5 and 10*

Table 1: Model and hyperparameter settings that were explored for the experiments (based on the optimal hyperparameters identified by Rudolph and Blei (2018))

The hyperparameters that need to be determined are the batch size, the learning rate and the precision of the random drift. We limited the search for optimal hyperparameters based on the experiments described in Rudolph and Blei (2018). The model is expensive to run, so for efficiency reasons, instead of testing a combination of all the settings, we first determine the optimal batch size, while keeping the other hyperparameters on their default setting. We keep the batch size setting that gives the highest L_{pos} on the validation set, for comparing different learning rates. This is repeated for the last setting, the precision of the random drift. Then, the model with the one with the highest L_{pos} is chosen as the final model.

4 Results

The Dynamic Bernoulli Embedding models are evaluated with the Bernoulli positive likelihood on the validation set, or L_{pos}. This metric is used to select the hyperparameter settings. The results of the experiments are represented in Table 2.

In Table 3 the absolute drift of the target words are given. The absolute drift is the metric used to measure how much the context, or the usage of a word changes over time. According to the final model, the target word that has the largest absolute drift and thus changed the most over time is "volk" (0.1800), followed by "vaderland" (0.1128). The target word "natie" shows the smallest absolute drift (0.0644). As a reference frame, the word with the largest absolute drift in our dataset is the word "we" (informal form of the Dutch 1st person plural pronoun "wij", "we" in English), with an absolute drift of 0.3864. Looking at the position of the words with the largest absolute drift, the words "volk", "vaderland","natie" are in the 157st, 882nd and 3711th place of a total of 61114 terms. We ought to note that many of the words with large drifts are either words with old spelling forms or names. First, words with old spelling have a hight absolute drift since they go out of use in later decades - their position in the word embedding does only rely on the drifting prior mechanism. Although we implemented a spelling normalization step as a pre-processing step, not all spelling inconsistencies were successfully corrected. Second, names used in fictional literature are also among the words with the largest drifts due to the fact that they only appear in some books (and in some decades).

Minibatches	Learning rate	Drift	Lpos val
100	0.002	1	-6854684
300	0.2	1	-11756400
	0.02	1	-6560637
	0.002	1	-6281450
	0.002	5	-7143437
	0.002	**10**	**-6064922**
	0.0002	1	-7961574
500	0.002	1	-6287337

Table 2: Overview of hyperparameter settings that were explored together with the L_{pos} on the validations set for every setting.

Target Word	Embedding
Mean absolute drift	0.0253
"natie" ("nation")	0.0644
"volk" ("folk")	0.1800
"vaderland" ("fatherland")	0.1128

Table 3: Absolute drifts for the target words and the mean absolute drift of all words

Figure 1 illustrates the drift of the target words over the different time slices. This graph shows that while "natie" has a small absolute drift, the drift becomes a bit larger over time, but it stays below the average drift of words.

The word "vaderland"shows three peaks in their drift over time. The first peak coincides roughly with the emergence of the word "vaderland" in Dutch book titles (Kloek, 1999). The second peak is around 1780, which is the decade of the politi-

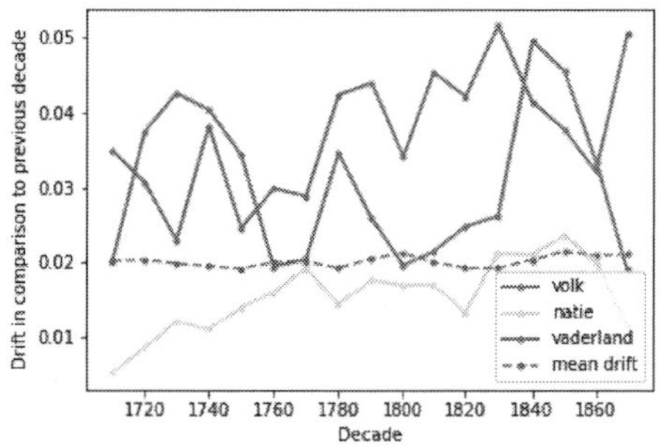

Figure 1: The drift of target words and neutral words, in comparison to their position in the previous decade

cization of the Dutch enlightenment (Kloek, 1999). The third peak of drift happens in the decade of the Dutch constitutional reform of 1848 and the revolutions in Europe of the same year.

Aside from the absolute drift and the drift over time, the nearest neighbours of the target words in the embedding of a specific time slice were analyzed. The nearest neighbors can be understood as the word most often used in a similar context of the target words, and are thus considered semantically close according to the distributional hypothesis. Due to the page-limit, we restrict ourselves to a brief illustration of the nearest neighbors of the word "vaderland". We allude at some of the findings we observed for the word "volk" and "natie".

The word "volk" changes fast from the last quarter of the eighteenth century onwards. The nearest neighbors of "volk" in the earlier decades of the eighteenth century are mainly related to biblical themes. De Kruif (2001) explains that biblical literature was popular in the eighteenth century. The interpretation of the word "volk" changes from "people of Israel" towards the meaning of "people as a mob" in later decades, which explains the larger drift from the 1780s onwards.

For "vaderland", the nearest neighbors are "geboorteland" ("country of birth") and "geboortegrond" ("place of birth"). Among the neighbors are also some more affectionate words such as "dierbare" ("dear") and "dierbaarst" ("dearest") and "vrijgevochten" ("free-spirited"). Aside from that, among the top 10 nearest neighbours, we can find terms alluding at a fatherland's past: "wapenroem" ("fame of arms"), "onafhankelijkheid" ("independence"), and, specific to the Dutch past, "bataven" ("batavian(s)"). From 1780 onwards, the words "nederland" ("The Netherlands") and "vlaanderland" ("Flanders") are present in the top 10. We give an example of the top 10 nearest neighbours of the word "vaderland" in Table 4.

For "volk", the word "oproerig" ("rebellious") is the nearest neighbor for every decade except the last one. Other words like "oproer" ("rebellion"), "muitziek" and "muitzucht" ("mutinious") emphasize the dangerous/negative connotation of "people" ("people as a mob"). These words furthermore appear more frequently and get a higher position in the top 10 nearest neighbors in the later decades. "Natie" showed almost no variation over time, as was expected by the low absolute drift. For "natie", many of its nearest neighbours across the different time slices were words referring to institutions

While "natie" didn't undergo a traceable semantic shift according to the final mode, we nevertheless looked into the nearest neighbours over the decades. "Handeldrijvende" ("trading") is the nearest neighbor in all decades, followed by "naäpen" ("copying", as in what a copycat does) and "Nationaliteit" ("nationality"). Further down the neighbouring words we encounter institutions (universities ("universiteiten"), courts ("gerechtshoven", "rechtbanken"), governments ("gouvernments"), people's government ("volksregering"), and republic ("republiek").

5 Conclusions and Future Work

In this study the emergence and development of nationalism in Dutch culture is studied by looking at the semantic change of the target words "natie", "volk" and "vaderland". This is done by applying the Dynamic Bernoulli Model, proposed by Rudolph and Blei (2018), to Dutch fiction literature between 1700-1880, during the emergence and development of nation building and nationalism (Gellner, 1983). Furthermore, through the analysis of the nearest neighbours we show how the contextual meaning of the target words changed. To the best of our knowledge, this is the first research that uses Dynamic Bernoulli Embeddings to contribute to an analysis of historical discourse, which in this case is the debate on the origins and spread of nationalism in the Netherlands. The results of this study show that there are measurable changes in the dynamic word embeddings of words related to nationalism over the course of the eighteenth and nineteenth century during a period that is known as the *Sattelzeit*.

We want to acknowledge certain limitations of

1760	1770	1780	1790	1800	1810
geboorteland	geboorteland	geboorteland	geboorteland	geboorteland	geboorteland
geboortegrond	volksbestaan	volksbestaan	volksbestaan	geboortegrond	geboortegrond
volksbestaan	geboortegrond	geboortegrond	geboortegrond	volksbestaan	volksbestaan
dierbaarst	dierbaarst	dierbaarst	dierbaarst	dierbaarst	dierbaar
eendrachtsband	eendrachtsband	eendrachtsband	eendrachtsband	dierbaar	dierbaarst
vrijgevochten	onafhanklijkheid	vrijgevochten	dierbaar	eendrachtsband	eendrachtsband
onafhanklijkheid	vrijgevochten	dierbaar	onafhanklijkheid	onafhanklijkheid	onafhanklijkheid
wapenroem	wapenroem	bataven	vrijgevochten	vaderlande	vaderlande
vaderlande	bataven	onafhanklijkheid	bataven	bataven	vrijgevochten
roemvol	dierbaar	**vlaanderland**	**vlaanderland**	**vlaanderland**	**nederland**

Table 4: Top 10 nearest neighbors for the target word "vaderland" for the time slice 1760 – 1810. The words "vlaanderland" and "nederland" (marked in bold) start showing among the 10 nearest neighbors from 1780.

our study. The method we employed in our study is sense-agnostic (e.g. homonyms) and works on a vocabulary common to all the investigated time slices, meaning that only words appearing in the entire corpus can contribute to the analysis of the target words. Additionally, historical sources often employ a non-standardized spelling. Despite our preprocessing to standardize the spelling using general rules, it is possible that some variations have been missed.

A more in-depth analysis of how semantic shifts of words can reflect the development of nation building, nationalism (or in general the arrival of certain ideologies) is a research direction we aim to further explore in future work. Future work could also benefit from a more in-depth exploration of the hyperparameter settings and their combinations.

References

Robert Bamler and Stephan Mandt. 2017. Dynamic word embeddings. In *Proceedings of the 34th International Conference on Machine Learning, volume 70 of Proceedings of Machine Learning Research*, pages 380–389, Sydney, Australia. PMLR.

Steven Bird, Edward Loper, and Ewan Klein. 2009. *Natural Language Processing with Python*. O'Reilly Media, Beijing.

Loes Braun. 2002. Information Retrieval from Dutch Historical Corpora. Master's thesis, Maastricht University.

Otto Brunner, Werner Conze, Reinhart Koselleck, and Arbeitskreis für Moderne Sozialgeschichte, editors. 1972. *Geschichtliche Grundbegriffe*, 4. aufl edition. Number historisches Lexikon zur politisch-sozialen Sprache in Deutschland / hrsg. von Otto Brunner; Werner Conze; Reinhart Koselleck. [Hrsg. im Auftrag des Arbeitskreises für Moderne Sozialgeschichte e.V.] ; Bd. 2 in Geschichtliche Grundbegriffe. Klett-Cotta, Stuttgart. OCLC: 246138897.

José De Kruif. 2001. Classes of readers: Owners of books in 18th-century The Hague. *Poetics*, 28(5-6):423–453.

Valerio Di Carlo, Federico Bianchi, and Matteo Palmonari. 2019. Training Temporal Word Embeddings with a Compass. In *Proceedings of the AAAI Conference on Artificial Intelligence*, volume 33, pages 6326–6334.

J.R. Firth. 1957. A synopsis of linguistic theory 1930-1955. In Frank Palmer, editor, *Selected Papers of J.R. Firth 1952-1959*. Longman.

Michel Foucault. 1970. The archaeology of knowledge. *Social Science Information*, 9(1):175–185.

Nikhil Garg, Londa Schiebinger, Dan Jurafsky, and James Zou. 2018. Word embeddings quantify 100 years of gender and ethnic stereotypes. *Proceedings of the National Academy of Sciences*, 115(16):E3635–E3644.

Ernest Gellner. 1983. *Nations and nationalism*. New perspectives on the past. Blackwell, Oxford.

William L. Hamilton, Jure Leskovec, and Dan Jurafsky. 2016. Diachronic Word Embeddings Reveal Statistical Laws of Semantic Change. In *Proceedings of the 54th Annual Meeting of the Association for Computational Linguistics (Volume 1: Long Papers)*, pages 1489–1501. Association for Computational Linguistics.

E.J. Hobsbawm. 2012. *Nations and nationalism since 1780*. Cambridge University Press.

Lotte Jensen. 2016. *The Roots of Nationalism: National Identity Formation in Early Modern Europe, 1600-1815*. Amsterdam University Press.

Yoon Kim, Yi-I Chiu, Kentaro Hanaki, Darshan Hegde, and Slav Petrov. 2014. Temporal Analysis of Language through Neural Language Models. In *Proceedings of the ACL 2014 Workshop on Language Technologies and Computational Social Science*, pages 61–65, Baltimore, MD, USA. Association for Computational Linguistics.

J.J. Kloek. 1999. Vaderland en letterkunde. In Niek van Sas, editor, *Vaderland*, number I in Nederlandse Begripsgeschiedenis. Amsterdam University Press, Amsterdam.

R. Koselleck. 2002. *The practice of conceptual history: Timing history, spacing concepts.* Stanford University Press.

Andrey Kutuzov, Lilja Øvrelid, Terrence Szymanski, and Erik Velldal. 2018. Diachronic word embeddings and semantic shifts: a survey. In *Proceedings of the 27th International Conference on Computational Linguistics*, pages 1384–1397.

J.T. Leerssen. 2006. *National thought in Europe: A cultural history*. Amsterdam University Press.

J.T. Leerssen. 2020. Literary realism and the nation. In J.T. Leerssen, editor, *Encyclopedia of Romantic Nationalism in Europe*. Amsterdam University Press.

Tomas Mikolov, Ilya Sutskever, Kai Chen, Greg S Corrado, and Jeff Dean. 2013. Distributed Representations of Words and Phrases and their Compositionality. In *Advances in neural information processing systems*, volume 26, pages 3111–3119. Curran Associates, Inc.

Syrielle Montariol and Alexandre Allauzen. 2019. Empirical Study of Diachronic Word Embeddings for Scarce Data. In *Proceedings of Recent Advances in Natural Language Processing*, pages 795–803, Varna, Bulgaria.

Matthias Orlikowski, Matthias Hartung, and Phillipp Cimiano. 2018. Learning Diachronic Analogies to Analyze Concept Change. In *Conference: 2nd Joint SIGHUM Workshop on Computational Linguistics for Cultural Heritage, Social Sciences, Humanities and Literature*, pages 1–11, Santa Fe, New Mexico, United States of America.

Ann Rigney. 2020. The historical novel. In J.T. Leerssen, editor, *Encyclopedia of Romantic Nationalism in Europe*. Amsterdam University Press.

Maja Rudolph and David Blei. 2018. Dynamic Embeddings for Language Evolution. In *WWW*, pages 1003–1011.

Quentin Skinner. 2002. *Visions of politics*. Cambridge University Press.

Nina Tahmasebi, Lars Borin, and Adam Jatowt. 2021. Survey of computational approaches to lexical semantic change detection.

M. Van Lange and R. Futselaar. 2018. Debating evil: Using word embeddings to analyze parliamentary debates on war criminals in The Netherlands. In *Proceedings of the Conference on Language Technologies & Digital Humanities*, pages 147–153. Znanstvena založba Filozofske fakultete v Ljubljani.

Niek Van Sas, editor. 1999. *Vaderland. Een geschiedenis vanaf de vijftiende eeuw tot 1940.* Amsterdam University Press.

M. Wevers. 2019. Using word embeddings to examine gender bias in Dutch newspapers, 1950-1990. pages 92–97.

Zijun Yao, Yifan Sun, Weicong Ding, Nikhil Rao, and Hui Xiong. 2018. Dynamic Word Embeddings for Evolving Semantic Discovery. In *Proceedings of the Eleventh ACM International Conference on Web Search and Data Mining*, WSDM '18, pages 673–681, New York, NY, USA. Association for Computing Machinery.

Using neural topic models to track context shifts of words: a case study of COVID-related terms before and after the lockdown in April 2020

Olga Kellert and **Md Mahmud Uz Zaman**
University of Göttingen, Germany
`olga.kellert@phil.uni-goettingen.de` and
`mail.mahmuduzzaman@gmail.com`

Abstract

This paper explores lexical meaning changes in a new dataset, which includes tweets from before and after the COVID-related lockdown in April 2020. We use this dataset to evaluate traditional and more recent unsupervised approaches to lexical semantic change that make use of contextualized word representations based on the BERT neural language model to obtain representations of word usages. We argue that previous models that encode local representations of words cannot capture global context shifts such as the context shift of *face masks* since the pandemic outbreak. We experiment with neural topic models to track context shifts of words. We show that this approach can reveal textual associations of words that go beyond their lexical meaning representation. We discuss future work and how to proceed capturing the pragmatic aspect of meaning change as opposed to lexical semantic change.

1 Introduction

Various approaches have been suggested in previous research to analyze semantic change such as semantic narrowing or broadening or the appearance of new words. Traditional quantitative approaches to semantic change identify meaning change by relative-frequency-based methods (Gulordava and Baroni, 2011). Another traditional method is the n-gram approach, that identifies the change in likelihood of words co-occurrence across time (Gulordava and Baroni, 2011; Butler and Simon-Vandenbergen, 2021; Luo, 2021). While these approaches can detect and track lexical changes that rely on local lexical and syntactic differences of words in time, they cannot capture lexical changes that rely on more distant relations between words (Giulianelli et al., 2020).

More recent computational approaches to semantic change, have exploited a pre-trained neural language model BERT (Devlin et al., 2019) to obtain contextualized representations for every occurrence of a word of interest and measure changes of semantic clusters in time (Giulianelli et al., 2020). Contextualized embeddings can help to detect lexical changes in case linguistic differences are encoded in non-local word relations such as in the whole construction like in *here comes your coach, Cinderella* or in *you can always go, coach* (Giulianelli et al., 2020). These constructions capture lexical changes by being associated with different uses of the word *coach*, which linguistically represent notions like (in)animacy.

Our goal in this paper is to capture more global relations between words than word relations in constructions. We want to capture context shifts by global representations of words that share the same paragraph or document. We use neural contextualized embeddings (Devlin et al., 2019) to generate better topics, which we consider as proxies for various word contexts, similar to constructions as proxies for word senses in previous approaches (Giulianelli et al., 2020). By studying thematic relations between words in time, we find out changes in these relations. This approach is not new and has been already applied by (Sagi et al., 2013). The authors used classical topic modeling to find out new associations of words. Words associations have been described in cognitive linguistics by the notion of semantic frames (Lakoff, 2008; Fillmore et al., 2002). According to (Lakoff, 2008), every word evokes a certain frame, i.e. a conceptual structure used in human communication. Words evoke certain images, feelings and (personal) experiences that can be expressed by other words used in the same context. In order to capture new associations of words in time, Sagi et al. (2013) used topic models to track new thematic relations of words like *war* after September 11, 2001. The underlined assumption of their approach is that context shifts or shifts of semantic frames are closely related to topic shifts (Sagi et al., 2013).

We apply this idea to our dataset to track changes

Proceedings of the 3rd Workshop on Computational Approaches to Historical Language Change, pages 131 - 139
May 26-27, 2022 ©2022 Association for Computational Linguistics

of word associations by topic modeling. Our new contribution is the use of an improved version of topic models, namely neural topic models (Bianchi et al., 2021; Grootendorst, 2022). Neural topic models exploit the advantages of transformer based pre-trained language models and considerably improve the coherence of topics(Bianchi et al., 2021; Grootendorst, 2022). A set representing the topic about fruits is considered more coherent if it contains words that represent fruits such as "apple, pear, lemon, banana, kiwi", not if it contains elements that represent other objects as well such as "apple, knife, lemon, banana, spoon." (Bianchi et al., 2021). Previous work has shown that adding contextual information to neural topic models provides a significant increase in topic coherence, which is missing in Bag-of-Words representations (Bianchi et al., 2021; Grootendorst, 2022). Incorporation of contextualized representations can thus improve a topic model's performance. By using improved topic models, we hope to improve analyses of context shifts of words uses.

In this work, we exploit a particular version of neural topic models, namely BERTopic (Grootendorst, 2022), which includes three ingredients: (1) a specific version of pre-trained neural language model BERT (Devlin et al. (2019)) to obtain contextualised representations, (2) additional semantic clustering of these representations, and (3) calculation of topic words on the basis of c-TF-IDF, which we define in §2.5 and in the Appendix B. Despite other existent neural Topic Models such as combined TM and Top2Vec(Bianchi et al., 2021; Angelov, 2020), we have chosen BERTopic, because it is an appropriate method for modeling changes in a corpus containing short messages as it contains c-TF-IDF method (Ghosh et al., 2017; Wang and Deng, 2017). This method is particularly useful for analyzing corpora comprised of short documents such as tweets.

We make the following contributions:

1. We present an approach of using neural topic models to measure context shifts of words that make use of state-of-the-art contextualised word representations.

2. We use this approach on short documents, namely tweets, from before and after COVID-19 related lockdown in April 2020.

3. We provide a quantitative and a qualitative analysis of context shifts by comparing the use of COVID-related words per topic.

Overall, our study demonstrates the potential of using neural topic models for analysing context shifts of words that have preserved their lexical meaning and are thus difficult to capture by a local analysis.

The paper is organized as follows. We first start with the traditional frequency and n-gram approaches that show which words have increased in relative frequency and which words have obtained new linguistic neighbors. We then apply unsupervised approaches to lexical semantic change that make use of Word Embeddings. Finally, we apply unsupervised topic analysis to capture thematic relations between words and context shifts. The paper finishes with a discussion and evaluation of these approaches.

2 Methodology

2.1 Data collection

We have used English tweets from the Social Media platform Twitter divided into two periods: before and after the lockdown in April 2020. The four countries with the highest number of tweets in our data set are: 1. United States, 2.Canada, 3. UK and 4. Australia. We have a similar number of tweets per country in the two periods. Before the lockdown, data is distributed in 3 years: from 2017 Oct we have around 9k, from 2018 January around 12k and the rest 59 k from 2019 June. The data after the lockdown was collected from just after lockdown 2020 April, which includes around 76k. The number of tweets covered in both datasets were around 80K. After doing all the necessary pre-processing steps, the number of unique words were around 90k in both datasets (94k before lockdown and 87k after lockdown).

2.2 Relative frequency analysis

We filtered out the most frequent words (Top words) that appeared before and after lockdown and calculated the relative frequency as well as the difference in relative frequency of these words. The details of this approach can be found in the table A. The theoretical prediction of the frequency method is that if a word gets an additional meaning over time, its relative frequency will also rise.

The list in table 1 contains most frequent words from the two periods and their relative frequency. We highlighted the words that do not appear before the lockdown.

	Word	rf before	rf after	rf diff
0	home	0.012	0.03	0.025
1	**quarantine**	0.0	0.02	0.0196
2	easter	0.00004	0.02	0.0193
3	**covid**	0.0	0.03	0.015
.	.	.	.	.
8	stay	0.0024	0.0126	0.010
.	.	.	.	.
15	**coronavirus**	0.0	0.008	0.008
.	.	.	.	.
18	safe	0.0009	0.0075	0.0066
19	**stayhome**	0.0	0.0065	0.0065
.	.	.	.	.
24	social	0.0015	0.0075	0.006
.	.	.	.	.
33	**lockdown**	0.0	0.0054	0.0054
.	.	.	.	.
42	**distancing**	0.0	0.0049	0.0049
.	.	.	.	.

Table 1: Top 50 partial list of words with relative frequency differences. Words that do not appear before the lockdown are in bold

In table 1, we see that the increase in relative frequency of words before and after lockdown is in many cases pandemic related as in lines 1,3,15,33 and 42. However, contextual information is missing to evaluate the increase of relative frequency of other words and to detect a potential lexical change.

2.3 N-gram analysis

The n-gram analysis can capture lexical meaning changes by differences in collocation neighbors and differences in the likelihood of the bigram and trigram (Manning and Schutze, 1999). We demonstrate this point by using Bigram and Trigram Collocation finder packages from nltk library (Bird et al., 2009). We merged all the documents as a list of words (around 1 Million words both in before and after lockdown datasets) and reported the top 5 collocations of the words *distance* and *mask* based on likelihood ratio. We see a change in collocations and likelihood ratio in Table 2 in two periods of these words (Butler and Simon-Vandenbergen, 2021; Luo, 2021). However, a collocation analysis does not capture the global context of word meanings. Take the word *mask*, for instance. Table 2 shows that this word was more often used as 'face mask' after the lockdown. However, what also changed after the lockdown is that the word *mask* is now used in a different pragmatic context than before the lockdown, namely in the everyday life practices around the world including western countries, where wearing masks was not part of everyday life practice before the lockdown. To capture this effect, a different approach is needed that includes a more global contextual information of word senses.

2.4 Word Embeddings

The representation of word meanings by Embeddings is nowadays a very standard approach (Giulianelli et al., 2020; Devlin et al., 2019; Mikolov et al., 2013). We follow this line of approach to use word meaning representations by Word Embeddings to capture semantic changes in times on our dataset. For creating Word Embeddings, we have used Gensim word2vec package[1]. We also used Google's Word Embeddings built before the lockdown as a second model for testing.

The analysis in table 3 shows that Word Embeddings for the word *distance* change over time as the top words associated with this word are not the same before and after the lockdown. Compare *hiking* and *film* before the lockdown in column left with *distancing* and *practicing* after the lockdown in column right. The meaning of the textually related words after the lockdown are clearly more pandemic related as evidenced by the word *practicing* (e.g. *practicing social distancing*). Note that the size of the dataset as evidenced by Google's dataset from before the lockdown in the Middle Column does not change the fact that the word *distance* has different word representations from before and after the lockdown. However, Word Embeddings do not capture the global context of word meanings either, if we think about *face masks* and their use in various contexts of our everyday life. To capture contextual meaning shift, we use Topic Modeling as an approximation to track pragmatic meanings or semantic frames of new word senses (Sagi et al., 2013).

2.5 Topic modeling approach

We applied BERTopic (Grootendorst, 2022) for creating topics from the set of sentences. We used our dataset without stop-words for this purpose. BERTopic is a topic modeling technique that leverages transformers and c-TF-IDF to create dense clusters allowing for easily interpretable topics

[1] https://radimrehurek.com/gensim/auto_examples/tutorials/run_word2vec.html

Word	Before (top 5)	After (top 5)
distance	**(walking, distance), 36.75**	**(social, distance), 752.43**
	(distance, summerofyes), 22.08	(safe, distance), 71.17
	(mincing, distance), 22.08	(distance, learning), 69.44
	(twxn__, distance, 22.08)	(distance, runner), 22.64
	(long, distance), 18.45	(distance, cruise), 21.41
mask	**(eye,mask), 26.53**	**(face, mask), 496.4**
	(blackface, mask), 22.19	(yashicamm, mask), 244.43
	(firespitter, mask), 22.19	(mask, covid), 107.83
	(mask, colorsofbeauty, 22.19)	(a, mask), 99.56
	(mask, mermay), 22.19	(covid, mask), 35.02

Table 2: N-gram analysis of 2 words: *distance and mask*

Before lockdown	Google	After lockdown
hiking, 0.92	distances, 0.75	distancing, 0.94
film, 0.91	Distance, 0.55	practicing, 0.91
race, 0.91	withing_striking, 0.541	holi, 0.84
competition, 0.91	SMA##_remained_##.##, 0.53	self, 0.81
views, 0.91	Distances, 0.51	practice, 0.81
sweat, 0.91	visiting_http:www.newswire.cawebcast, 0.51	distancin, 0.80
riding, 0.91	Chainsaws_hummed, 0.51	donation, 0.80

Table 3: Top most 7 word embedding comparison of word *distance* between before and after lockdown and Google Word Embedding

whilst keeping important words in the topic descriptions (Appendix B). The inverse document part of classic TF-IDF measures how much information a term provides to a document. However in c-TF-IDF, the whole cluster is considered as a document and hence the top 10 terms or topic words become representative of the cluster. The c-TF-IDF method can be used to scale better and works even when topic reductions are used (Grootendorst, 2022). The model produced 202 topics from before lockdown dataset and 220 topics after the lockdown dataset. A topic is represented by a list of 10 Topic words. We define pragmatic contexts or semantic frames as topics and investigate word distributions per topic to track word contexts. We suggest two analyses of word distributions per topic. The first analysis represents distributions of words as topic words and the second analysis represents distributions of words as tokens. By looking at distributions of words as topic words in the first analysis, we capture only frequent words and their contexts or topics. The latter analysis allows us also to capture contexts of less frequent words. The differences in distributions in time will inform us about context shifts of words.

2.5.1 Distribution of words as topic words per topic

Table 4 represents words that are used as topic words after the lockdown, but not before the lockdown. We have already seen in the frequency Table 1, which words appear only in the dataset after the lockdown. However, looking at new words as topic words provides us much more information. Table 4 not only informs us about which words became much more frequent, but also in which contexts or topics these words occur. For instance, the most frequent topic of the word *lockdown* is related to the pandemic situation as evidenced by words such as *coronavirus, covid, virus* (Topic 24) and thus gives us insights about the cause of the lockdown. Other less frequent topics with the word *lockdown* inform us about where the lockdown occurred (Topic 70) and what the consequences of the lockdown are (Topic 135). The most frequent topic with the word *virus* as a topic word is connected to the lockdown (Topic 24). Less frequent topics are associated with locations where the virus occurred and their effects on social practices.The words *quarantine* and *stay* both appear in Topic 5, which is a topic about suggestions to *stay home*, to *cook* and *chill* during the *quarantine*. The word

Word	Number of Topics		Topic IDs
	Before	After	After
mask	0	1(465)	18
quarantine	0	1(1427)	5
stay	0	4(954)	5,24,33,145
distance	0	1(353)	13
lockdown	0	3(262)	24,70,135
corona	0	3(560)	24,34,90
virus	0	3(85)	24,34,90

Table 4: Distribution of words as topic words per topic before and after lockdown dataset. The number of tweets is given in the brackets. Topic IDs refer to topics from table 7

distance appears in Topic 13 about *practicing social distancing* in *parks* and by *hiking*. The word *mask* appears in Topic 18, which represents preventive measures against virus infection such as *facemask, hand gloves*. The word *stay* appears in four different topics as a topic word, that are related to suggestions to *stay home, stay safe* and *stay healthy*.

Note that some terms in Table 4 appear in the same topics such as the word *corona, virus* and some terms share common topics such as the words *stay, distance, corona, virus* (Topic 24). This observation emphasizes the thematic relatedness of these words with the COVID-outbreak. However, the frequency of the words as topic words is not equally distributed per topic as table 4 shows. The word *mask* is more prominent in Topic 18, whereas *quarantine* and the word *stay* are more prominent in Topic 5. This observation emphasizes the specific contexts of use of these words and their specific meanings.

2.5.2 Distribution of words as tokens per topic

The second analysis represents the distribution of words as tokens and not as topic words per topic (Table 5). It shows that words like *mask, stay, distance* changed their context in time by appearing in a much wider range of topics after the lockdown than before and that these topics cover many topics of our everyday life experience. This means that these words are used in conversations about drinking beer with friends, music events, eating pizza, having a haircut and other mundane topics. For instance, the word *mask* appears in only 3 topics as a token before the lockdown, namely in topics about casino in Las Vegas, homosexual activism (LGBTQ) and commercial discount (Topics 20,23 and 59 in Table 6). Since the lockdown, the word *mask* appears in many more topics, namely in 33 different topics. The most salient topic, i.e. the topic with the highest number of tweets, is the topic about preventive measures against virus infection (Topic 18) as already shown in Table 4. In addition to this salient topic, *mask* appears in topics about everyday life activities and events such as tweets about Easter (bunny, eggs) in Topic 3, tweets about food in Topic 4, tweets about photography and selfies in Topic 22, Topic 41 about reposts of tweets (Table 7). The number of tweets containing the word *mask* in these topics representing everyday life activities is much lower than in the salient Topic 18 about preventive measures against virus infection. However, it is considerably higher than the number of tweets with the word *mask* before the lockdown. The wider range of topics of the word *mask* after the lockdown can be therefore considered as an indicator for a contextual change of this word.

The most frequent collocations in (Table 5) show that in both periods *mask* is used as *face mask* in the most salient topics. Just by looking at collocations, we do not know how *face mask* is used before and after the lockdown. This emphasizes our criticism of local analyses in §2.3. The topic descriptions of the word *mask* adds contextual information about this word, which is why a topic analysis is a better analysis. However, collocations can also change with a topic change as (Table 5) shows. For instance, the word *stay* is not only used in different topics, but also in different collocations before and after the lockdown. This said, context shifts or topic shifts of words can correlate with collocation shifts, but they do not need to. It is this important observation that motivates the use of our method.

To sum up, we have shown that a topic analysis provides information about context shifts of word uses and the change of thematic word relations in time.

3 Conclusion

We have introduced a novel dataset that contains lexical change triggered by the COVID-related outbreak. We have used this dataset to discuss different analyses capable of capturing linguistic change, namely the relative frequency analysis, the n-gram analysis and lexical change captured by Word Embeddings. We have shown that these analyses miss

Word	Number of Topics		3 Top collocations of tweets in Topics	
	Before	After	Before	After
mask	3	33	'face','mask', 16.67 'mask','look', 12.56	'face','mask', 379.94 'wear','mask',118.00 'wearing', 'mask', 98.31
quarantine	0	42		'quarantine','day', 105.40 'quarantine','quarantinelife',73 'quarantine','stayhome', 58.57
stay	56	121	'stay', 'tuned', 256.21 'stay', 'hydrated',32.65 'stay','focused', 22.22	'stay','home', 1085.74 'stay', 'safe', 1019.46 'stay', 'tuned', 371.55
distance	6	49	'walking','distance', 41.62 'mincing','distance',19.78 'twxn__', 'distance', 19.78	'social','distance', 386.603 'distance','learning',49.22 'keeping', 'distance', 47.11

Table 5: Distribution of words as tokens before and after lockdown dataset. Top 3 collocations are calculated only considering the tweets of the topics.

an important aspect of meaning change, namely the pragmatic aspect. This meaning change represents a change of cultural or everyday practices associated with words such as *mask*. We suggested tracking the pragmatic change via Topic Modeling by looking at the distribution of words per topic in two different periods. We discovered that topics capture the contextual meaning of a word by the textual association with other words. Changes of word distributions in topics can give us insights about pragmatic meaning change of words.

Exploring context shift by neural topic models falls into the family of neural models used to track and measure language change by contextualized word representations (Giulianelli et al., 2020; Del Tredici et al., 2019). In this sense, our contribution is very much related to this work as all these models have a similar architecture and capture the meaning of words. However, we use neural contextualized embedding for an improved version of topic modeling and use then topics as proxies for word contexts. This method allows us to explore more global relations between words by looking at their relations to other words in the same document or text. We admit that this is a very approximate approach of capturing the pragmatic aspect of words with an unsupervised method. One important issue of this approach is that it is very much dependent on the data size and the size of each document or tweet, which influence the quantity of topics and the topic specification. Another important point is that it does not capture the very many implicit discourse relations between Topic words such as causal relations between the lockdown and the virus in Topic 24 in Table 7. One way to approach this issue is to use unsupervised approaches of capturing discourse relations between Topic words of the same topic (Liu and Lapata, 2018), which we reserve for future work.

4 Acknowledgments

This project has received funding from the German Research Foundation (DFG) 2021 (No. KE 2048/1-1). We would like to thank Dr. Nicholas Matlis, the Language Technology Group of the university of Hamburg for providing us useful feedback as well as the anonymous ACL reviewers for their helpful comments.

References

Dimo Angelov. 2020. Top2vec: Distributed representations of topics. *arXiv preprint arXiv:2008.09470*.

Federico Bianchi, Silvia Terragni, and Dirk Hovy. 2021. Pre-training is a hot topic: contextualized document embeddings improve topic coherence. In *59th Annual Meeting of the Association for Computational Linguistics and the 11th International Joint Conference on Natural Language Processing*. Association for Computational Linguistics.

Steven Bird, Ewan Klein, and Edward Loper. 2009. *Natural language processing with Python: analyzing text with the natural language toolkit.* " O'Reilly Media, Inc.".

David M Blei, Andrew Y Ng, and Michael I Jordan. 2003. Latent dirichlet allocation. *Journal of machine Learning research*, 3(Jan):993–1022.

Christopher S Butler and Anne-Marie Simon-Vandenbergen. 2021. Social and physical distance/distancing: A corpus-based analysis of recent changes in usage. *Corpus Pragmatics*, 5(4):427–462.

Marco Del Tredici, Raquel Fernández, and Gemma Boleda. 2019. Short-term meaning shift: A distributional exploration. In *Proceedings of NAACL-HLT*, pages 2069–2075.

Jacob Devlin, Ming-Wei Chang, Kenton Lee, and Kristina Toutanova. 2019. Bert: Pre-training of deep bidirectional transformers for language understanding. In *Proceedings of the 2019 Conference of the North American Chapter of the Association for Computational Linguistics: Human Language Technologies, Volume 1 (Long and Short Papers)*, pages 4171–4186.

Charles J Fillmore, Collin F Baker, and Hiroaki Sato. 2002. The framenet database and software tools. In *LREC*.

Samujjwal Ghosh, PK Srijith, and Maunendra Sankar Desarkar. 2017. Using social media for classifying actionable insights in disaster scenario. *International Journal of Advances in Engineering Sciences and Applied Mathematics*, 9(4):224–237.

Mario Giulianelli, Marco Del Tredici, and Raquel Fernández. 2020. Analysing lexical semantic change with contextualised word representations. In *Proceedings of the 58th Annual Meeting of the Association for Computational Linguistics*, pages 3960–3973.

Maarten Grootendorst. 2022. Bertopic: Neural topic modeling with a class-based tf-idf procedure. *arXiv preprint arXiv:2203.05794*.

Kristina Gulordava and Marco Baroni. 2011. A distributional similarity approach to the detection of semantic change in the Google Books ngram corpus. In *Proceedings of the GEMS 2011 Workshop on GEometrical Models of Natural Language Semantics*, pages 67–71, Edinburgh, UK. Association for Computational Linguistics.

George Lakoff. 2008. *Women, fire, and dangerous things: What categories reveal about the mind*. University of Chicago press.

Yang Liu and Mirella Lapata. 2018. Learning structured text representations. *Transactions of the Association for Computational Linguistics*, 6:63–75.

Huan Luo. 2021. How has the coronavirus pandemic affected our use of language? a corpus-based study of neologisms and semantic shifts in english and chinese web texts.

Christopher Manning and Hinrich Schutze. 1999. *Foundations of statistical natural language processing*. MIT press.

Leland McInnes, John Healy, and Steve Astels. 2017. hdbscan: Hierarchical density based clustering. *J. Open Source Softw.*, 2(11):205.

Leland McInnes, John Healy, Nathaniel Saul, and Lukas Grossberger. 2018. Umap: Uniform manifold approximation and projection. *The Journal of Open Source Software*, 3(29):861.

Tomas Mikolov, Kai Chen, Greg Corrado, and Jeffrey Dean. 2013. Efficient estimation of word representations in vector space.

Eyal Sagi, Daniel Diermeier, and Stefan Kaufmann. 2013. Identifying issue frames in text. *PloS one*, 8(7):e69185.

Hao Wang and Sanhong Deng. 2017. A paper-text perspective: studies on the influence of feature granularity for chinese short-text-classification in the big data era. *The Electronic Library*.

A Creation of Top words

After some standard pre-processing, we created Top words from the datasets, by the following steps:

1. Took the list of sentences and removed stop-words

2. Create a two dimensional vector for each words and documents. For example if we have 100 sentences and 100 unique words in the whole set, the resulting dimension will be (100*100). The package was used from sklearn: CountVectorizer.

3. Extracted and saved the following parameters for each word in the dataset.

   (a) Total found (total_occur): The number of times in total the word appeared in the whole dataset.

   (b) Number of documents (number_docs): The number how many documents the word appeared.

   (c) Relative frequency (rf):
   rf = Total_found / Total Documents.

   (d) Cumulative score (cs): A scoring system to give emphasis on number of documents the word occurred by multiplying it with relative frequency.
   Cs = rf * number_docs

4. Sorted the words in the dataset based on cs scores and reported Top 100

B Topic Modeling

BERTopic (Grootendorst, 2022) is a topic modeling technique that leverages transformers and c-TF-IDF to create dense clusters allowing for easily interpretable topics whilst keeping important words in the topic descriptions.

B.1 Our implementation procedure:

We have used BERTopic for creating topics from the set of sentences. We have used our dataset without stop-words for this purpose.

The process is as below

1. Created topics using the model
2. Created dictionary of topic words.
3. Filtered out the topics which matches any of the covid related words

B.2 Topic modeling Theory

Topic modeling technique LDA (Blei et al., 2003) is well known but has some limitations like bag of words, Fixed K (the number of topics is fixed and must be known ahead), non hierarchical, etc. BERTopic on the other hand does not pose these problems.

The procedure how BERTopic works can be divided in 3 steps:

1. Converting sentences into embeddings : The first step is to convert the documents into embeddings. BERT is used to create the embeddings.
2. Clustering the embeddings based HDBScan (McInnes et al., 2017) (a density based Unsupervised clustering technique). This stage comprises two parts: Dimensionality reduction and Clustering. UMAP (McInnes et al., 2018) is used for Dimensionality reduction and Hierarchical Density based clustering is used for Clustering the embeddings.
3. cTF-IDF : Finally, class based TF-IDF (cTF-IDF) is used to extract words that represent a clustering.

   $W_{t,c} = tf_{t,c} \cdot log(1 + \frac{A}{tf_t})$.

   Where the term frequency models the frequency of term t in a class c or in this instance. Here,the class c is the collection of documents concatenated into a single document for each cluster. Then, the inverse document frequency is replaced by the inverse class frequency to measure how much information a term provides to a class. It is calculated by taking the logarithm of the average number of words per class A divided by the frequency of term t across all classes. To output only positive values, we add one to the division within the logarithm (Grootendorst, 2022).

Topic ID	Topic words	Number of tweets
20	vegas, las, casino, lasvegas, vegastraffic, nv, nevada, hotel, clark, accident	280
23	pride, gay, lgbtq, pridemonth, month, lgbt, happy, gaypride, rainbow, loveislove	262
59	code, discount, discountcode, fwcom, bestprice, fyi, orders, extra, get, sexy	118

Table 6: Topics related to COVID words which appeared as a token from before lockdown dataset

Topic IDs	Topic words	Number of tweets
3	easter, birthday, happy, bunny, family, happyeaster, everyone, eggs, sunday, hope	2147
4	pizza, dinner, chicken, cake, garlic, cookies, sauce, pork, rice, fried	1394
5	quarantine, quarantinelife, quarantined, day, stayhome, life, quarantinecooking, cooking, best, quarantineandchill	1241
13	distancing, social, park, hike, walk, trail, socialdistancing, distance, practicing, hiking	718
18	mask, masks, face, skin, wear, facemask, dermatology, wearing, hand, gloves	628
22	photography, camera, photographer, selfie, portrait, photos, streetphotography, pictures, model, photooftheday	581
24	coronavirus, covid, virus, pandemic, corona, lockdown, stayhome, update, tests, outbreak	543
33	amp, safe, call, stay, got, back, keep, need, many, things	393
34	francisco, san, california, angeles, los, thoughts, coronavirus, diego, photo, posted	373
41	repost, getrepost, reposted, makerepost, talkkellyzola, makeyourselfhappy, onlinetradefair, makeyourselfproud, iamyourlovestory, thanks	285
47	run, miles, running, mile, ran, runner, marathon, ismoothrun, race, runners	206
70	lockdown, isolation, locked, portelizabeth, self, christchurch, lock, cuenca, zealand, europa	149
90	stigma, fighting, ireland, stigmabase, hong, kong, china, coronavirus, northern, health	106
135	notes, unreliable, lockeddown, testing, data, proverty, lockdown, rate, heavily, adequate	59
145	staysafe, weloveourhealthcareworkers, stayhome, stayhealthy, greenwich, stay, gratitude, village, staystrong, healthy	45

Table 7: Topic words related to COVID found in the dataset after the lockdown.

Roadblocks in Gender Bias Measurement for Diachronic Corpora

Saied Alshahrani Esma Wali Abdullah R Alshamsan Yan Chen Jeanna Matthews
Department of Computer Science
Clarkson University, Potsdam, NY, USA
alshahsf,walie,alshamar,cheny3,jnm@clarkson.edu

Abstract

The use of word embeddings is an important NLP technique for extracting meaningful conclusions from corpora of human text. One important question that has been raised about word embeddings is the degree of gender bias learned from corpora. Bolukbasi et al. (2016) proposed an important technique for quantifying gender bias in word embeddings that, at its heart, is lexically based and relies on sets of highly gendered word pairs (e.g., mother/father and madam/sir) and a list of professions words (e.g., doctor and nurse). In this paper, we document problems that arise with this method to quantify gender bias in diachronic corpora. Focusing on Arabic and Chinese corpora, in particular, we document clear changes in profession words used over time and, somewhat surprisingly, even changes in the simpler gendered defining set word pairs. We further document complications in languages such as Arabic, where many words are highly polysemous/homonymous, especially female professions words.

Keywords

word embedding, gender bias, NLP, Arabic, Chinese, profession words, diachronic

TLR

We document hurdles in applying a popular gender bias measurement technique using word embeddings of profession words and highly gendered word pairs for diachronic corpora in Arabic and Chinese.

1 Introduction

Natural Language Processing (NLP) plays a significant role in many powerful applications such as speech recognition, text translation, and autocomplete and is at the heart of many critical automated decision systems making crucial recommendations about our future world. Word embedding systems are widely used to represent text data as vectors and enable NLP computation. Systems such as Word2Vec (Mikolov et al., 2013), GloVe (Pennington et al., 2014), and BERT (Devlin et al., 2018) ingest large corpora of human text and can be used to learn semantic and syntactic relationships between words.

At the same time, it has been demonstrated that these systems learn a wide variety of societal biases embedded in human text including racial bias, gender bias, and religious bias (Caliskan et al., 2017; Abid et al., 2021). In a widely cited paper, Bolukbasi et al. (2016) demonstrated that a system trained with a corpora of Google News would complete the word comparison "man is to computer programmer as woman is to what?" with the response "homemaker" suggesting an alarming level of gender bias when used in tasks such as sorting resumes for computer programming jobs. Chen et al. (2021) extended these techniques beyond English to eight other languages (Chinese, Spanish, Arabic, German, French, Farsi, Urdu, and Wolof) and applied them to Wikipedia corpora in each of these languages. They documented persistent gender bias and lack of representation in the modern NLP pipeline.

NLP research often uses large, modern datasets like Google News and Wikipedia. Developers of a wide variety of NLP-based applications begin with large pre-trained models that are also based on large corpora of human text (Bender et al., 2021). These pre-trained models also largely reflect the speech/writing of modern English speakers producing digital text. The speech/writing of speakers of the more than 7,000 languages spoken worldwide is often under-represented (Wali et al., 2020). Similarly, historical speech/writing is often under-represented despite the fact that historical speech/writing is often considered foundational to cultural identity. Investments in multilingual NLP

Proceedings of the 3rd Workshop on Computational Approaches to Historical Language Change, pages 140 - 148
May 26-27, 2022 ©2022 Association for Computational Linguistics

and processing of diachronic corpora are essential if we want our NLP-based automated decision making systems to more widely reflect foundational cultural norms and identity from around the world.

The inspiration for this paper was to re-examine Bolukbasi et al.'s popular NLP-technique for quantifying gender bias from the perspective of applying it to diachronic corpora in Arabic and Chinese. Specifically, Bolukbasi et al.'s method begins with identifying a set of profession words and a set of highly gendered word pairs (defining set). In this paper, we explore the degree to which these words might change over time. We document ways in which this method is fundamentally fragile for diachronic corpora because of the way these sets of words would change over time.

In Section 2, for background, we elaborate on Bolukbasi et al. and Chen et al.'s multilingual extensions and some other relevant related work. Section 3 describes our experience with two different diachronic Arabic corpora, especially the impact on changes in profession set words over time. In Section 4, we discuss changes in some defining set words in Chinese using the Google Ngram Viewer. We conclude and discuss future work in Section 5.

2 Background and Related Work

Bolukbasi et al. (2016) pioneered a method for quantifying the amount of gender bias learned in by word embedding systems and many researchers have built on their techniques including Chen et al. (2021) who observed substantial hurdles in extending the techniques beyond English. In this paper, we build on both Bolukbasi et al. and Chen et al.'s work to examine additional hurdles that would arise when attempting to apply these techniques to diachronic corpora.

Bolukbasi et al.'s original method is based on two sets of words. The first set (the defining set) consists of 10 highly gendered word pairs (she-he, daughter-son, her-his, mother-father, woman-man, gal-guy, Mary-John, girl-boy, herself-himself, and female-male) and the second (profession set) consists of 327 profession words such as nurse, teacher, writer, engineer, scientist, manager, driver, banker, musician, artist, and chef. They used the difference between the defining set word pairs to define a gendered vector space and then evaluated the relationship of the profession words relative to this gendered vector space. Ideally, profession words would not reflect a strong gender bias. However, in practice, they often do. According to such a metric, the word doctor might be male biased or the word nurse female biased based on how these words are used in the corpora from which the word embedding model was produced.

Bolukbasi et al. (2016) uses these two sets of words to compute a gender bias metric for each word and from there to express the gender bias of a corpora. Specifically, each word is expressed as a vector by Word2Vec and then the center of the vectors for each defining set pair is calculated. For example, to calculate the center of the definitional pair woman/man, they average the vector for "woman" with the vector for "man". Then, they calculate the distance of each word in the definitional pair from the center by subtracting the center from each word in the pair (e.g., "woman" - center). They then apply Principal Component Analysis (PCA) to the matrix of these distances. PCA is an approach that compresses multiple dimensions into fewer dimensions, ideally in a way that the information within the original data is not lost. Usually, the number of reduced dimensions is 1-3 as it allows for easier visualization of a dataset. Bolukbasi et al. (2016) used the first eigenvalue from the PCA matrix (i.e. the one that is larger than the rest). Because the defining set pairs were chosen to be highly gendered, they expected this dimension to be related primarily to gender and therefore called it the gender direction or the g direction. Finally, the g direction is a vector, and there is a vector representing each word. Therefore, they used cosine similarity between the vector for each word, w, and the g direction vector as the measure of gender bias for that word. For a corpora or other collection of words, one can average the gender bias of words contained in the corpora as a measure of gender bias in the corpora using the equation of Bolukbasi et al. (2016) for the direct gender bias of an embedding:

$$\text{DirectBias}_c = \frac{1}{|N|} \sum_{w \in N} |\cos(\vec{w}, g)|^c$$

where N is the given gender neutral words, and c is a parameter that determines the strictness in measuring gender bias.

Chen et al. (2021) extended the Bolukbasi et al.' method to eight languages besides English - Chinese, Spanish, Arabic, German, French, Farsi, Urdu, and Wolof. In order to do so, they first made modifications to the defining set to make it more translatable across the 9 languages. For example, they dropped pairs like she-he, her-his, gal-guy, Mary-John, herself-himself, and female-male because of problems in translation for some languages and adding pairs like queen-king, wife-husband, and madam-sir. Second, they observed that the Bolukbasi et al.'s method cannot be applied directly to languages such as Spanish, Arabic, German, French, and Urdu that primarily use grammatically gendered nouns (e.g., escritor/escritora in Spanish vs. writer in English). They solved this problem using a weighted average of the number of occurrences of each variant of the professional word (male, female, or neutral) multiplied by the gender bias score for that variant.

In this work, we build on both (Bolukbasi et al., 2016; Chen et al., 2021) and focus on the unique challenges that arise when applying these techniques to diachronic corpora. Specifically, we examined changes in both the profession set and defining set over time in Arabic and Chinese. Certainly, professions have changed drastically over that amount of time and so a method based on profession set words like Bolukbasi et al.'s method will have substantial challenges. We explored this using corpora including a database of Arabic poems spanning 11 eras from the Pre-Islamic period (before 610) to modern day. While we saw less change over time in the usage of the simpler defining set words than in the profession set words, we did observe some interesting changes in even the defining set words over time, especially in Chinese. In the process of this work, we also documented further complications in languages such as Arabic, where many words are highly polysemous/homonymous, especially female professions words.

Wevers (2019) also used word embeddings to examine gender bias over time. They used a collection of Dutch Newspaper articles spanning over four eras (1950-1990), training four embedding models per newspaper, one per era, using the Gensim implementation of Word2Vec to demonstrate how word embeddings can be used to examine historical language change. They observed clear differences in gender bias and changes within and between newspapers over time. Slight shifting of bias was observed in some themes like shifting towards female bias in themes related to sexuality and leisure (mostly seen in newspapers with religious background). Shifting towards male bias in themes related 'money', 'grooming', and negative emotions, especially in newspapers with a liberal background, was also observed.

Rudolph and Blei (2018) developed dynamic embeddings building on exponential family embeddings to capture the language evolution or how the meanings of words change over time. They used three datasets of the U.S. Senate speeches from 1858 to 2009, the history of computer science ACM abstracts from 1951 to 2014, and machine learning papers on the ArXiv from 2007 to 2015. They demonstrated how words like Intelligence, Iraq, computer, Bush, data change their meaning over time. They observed that the dynamic embeddings provided a better fit than classical embeddings and captured interesting patterns about how language changes. For example, a word's meaning can change (e.g., computer); its dominant meaning can change (e.g., values); or its related subject matter can change (e.g., Iraq).

Xu et al. (2019) demonstrated the characterization of the semantic weights of subword units in the composition of word meanings. They used a subword-incorporated or a word embedding model variant for the evaluation and revealed interesting patterns change in multiple languages. Their training datasets consist of Wikimedia dumps for 6 Languages (up until July 2017) consisting of Chinese and other Indo-European languages like English, French, German, and Italian. The results revealed major differences in the long-term temporal patterns of semantic weights between Chinese and five Indo-European languages. For example, in Chinese, the weights on subword units (characters) show a decreasing trend, i.e., individual characters play less semantic roles in newer words than older ones whereas the opposite trend was observed in other languages. Therefore, Chinese words are treated more as a whole semantic unit "synthetically", while words in Indo-European languages require more attention into the subword units "analytically". These results provide evidence towards word formations to the linguistic theories. For example, the notion of "word" in Chinese is always changing: Modern Chinese has multiple characters as a whole semantic unit opposite to its older counterpart. The semantic weight carried by a single character is decreasing over time. This is strong evidence in support of the claim that Chinese has been evolving towards more detailed multisyllabic words from concise and monosyllabic words.

Time Periods	Number of Books	Vocab Size	Token Size
Books Before Islam	3	16,460	39,255
Books Before 1900	2,820	2,075,505	566,366,883
Books After 1900	773	1,335,027	136,870,579
Duplicate Books	11	-	-
Unknown Books	2,931	-	-
All Shamela's Books	6,527	2,520,372	703,276,717

Table 1: Measurements of Shamela Library dataset in terms of the number of books, vocabulary size (unique words), and token size (all words) for each time period. We did not train a GloVe model on the unknown books alone or the duplicate books and therefore are not reporting vocab size and token size.

3 Changes in Arabic Over Time

Building on both Bolukbasi et al. (2016) and Chen et al. (2021), we consider how the sets of profession words required by the Bolukbasi et al.'s method would need to change over time in Arabic. We begin by describing two diachronic datasets that we used and how we processed these datasets, then we describe the changes in the profession word usage over time.

3.1 Datasets and Methodology

In this paper, we use two Arabic datasets: Shamela Library (المكتبة الشاملة) that is released by Shamela Library Foundation (2012), and Arabic Poem Comprehensive Dataset (APCD) by (Yousef et al., 2018). Shamela Library is a free project that collects thousands of Islamic religious and other related sciences books. APCD is a collection of Arabic poems spanning 11 eras, from the Pre-Islamic (before 610) to the Modern age (1924 - Now). Arabic NLP researchers commonly use these two datasets to study Arabic classics.

We processed the Shamela Library dataset version of 6,538 Arabic books (6,527 unique books after removing duplicates) in Microsoft Word format (1997-2004).[1] The books in this corpora were not labeled according to the publication dates. Thus, to study the language change over time in the Arabic language, we further classified Shamela's Arabic books into three different time periods based either on their publication date or the authors' date of death when publication date was not available. We identified books written before Islam or before 610 (only three books), books written before 1900 (2,820 books), and books written on or after 1900 (773 books). We were not able to identify publication dates or the authors' dates of death of the remaining 2,931 books due to not having any; Table 1 summarizes some key attributes of this dataset.

We also processed the APCD, an Arabic poetry dataset that is collected mainly from the Poetry Encyclopedia (الموسوعة الشعرية) that is released by Abu Dhabi Department of Culture and Tourism (2016) and Diwan (الديوان) (Diwan, 2013). Unlike Shamela, this dataset was already labeled by era, making it a good choice for studying language change over time. It has, before preprocessing, approximately 1,831,770 poetic verses labeled by their meter, the poet's name, and the era they were written in. One drawback of this corpora is that it is relatively small. Table 2 summarizes some key attributes of this dataset.

We then produced a total of 16 GloVe models (Pennington et al., 2014) from the three time periods of Shamela, the 11 eras of APCD, all Shamela, and all APCD.[2] Each GloVe model is a context-independent model that produces a one-word vector (word embedding) for each word even if that word appears in the context a few times unlike BERT and ELMo (Devlin et al., 2018; Peters et al., 2018). Each GloVe model provides vocabulary size, token size, and word vectors. It is important to note that before training GloVe models, it was necessary to preprocess the two datasets using Linux/Unix command-line utilities like `tr` (for translating or

[1]We contribute the scripts we wrote to process these corpora and overcome several challenges with the data. For example, one challenge we faced was correctly converting back and forth between the Arabic Windows-1256 to the Unicode (UTF-8) encoding schemes. The Arabic books were written in an old version of Microsoft Word (1997-2004), which caused encoding scheme conversion errors, resulting in unreadable characters by native Arabic speakers or even NLP tools. Scripts can be found here: `https://github.com/Clarkson-Accountability-Transparency/gBiasRoadblocks`

[2]Bolukbasi et al. (2016) used Word2Vec to generate word embeddings, and in this paper, we chose GloVe instead because GloVe performs better than Word2Vec in the Arabic language (Naili et al., 2017)

Eras	Poetic Verses	Vocab Size	Token Size
Pre-Islamic (before 610)	21,907	60,082	204,450
Islamic (610-661)	2,942	12,388	24,461
Umayyad (661–750)	63,776	119,533	610,563
Between Umayyad and Abbasid	24,077	65,220	221,058
Abbasid (750–1258)	234,494	252,339	2,156,195
Andalusian (756–1269)	111,011	151,503	1,024,653
Fatimid (909–1171)	124,129	172,460	1,171,842
Ayyubid (1174–1252)	112,350	152,165	1,061,503
Mamluk (1250–1517)	164,780	198,748	1,550,669
Ottoman (1517–1924)	159,576	186,795	1,492,132
Modern (1924 - Now)	778,723	462,478	7,146,135
All APCD's eras	1,797,765	736,576	16,663,658

Table 2: Measurements of Arabic Poem Comprehensive Dataset in terms of number of poetic verses, vocabulary size (unique words), and token size (all words) for each era.

deleting characters), `sed` (for filtering and transforming text), `iconv` (for converting between encoding schemes), and `awk` (for pattern scanning and language processing), along with CAMeL tools (Obeid et al., 2020), an open-source python toolkit for Arabic NLP, to dediacritize the Arabic diacritical marks and remove unnecessary characters.

3.2 Modern and Historical Professions

We began with a consideration of how the profession sets used in Bolukbasi et al. (2016) and Chen et al. (2021) would need to change over time. First, we identified 50 modern profession words that we expect would simply not exist in the older time periods/eras in Shamela and APCD datasets.[3] For example, the profession of electrician would not have existed before the advent of electricity. Second, we identified 50 historical profession words that we think exist in older time periods/eras in Shamela and APCD datasets but which are much less common in modern times.

As in Chen et al. (2021), we further categorized each word based on gender. In Arabic, most profession words have a male variant and a female variant in which the spelling is changed slightly based on gender, for example female pilot (طيَّارة) and male pilot (طيَّار). Linguistically, many professions that would be extremely uncommon for men or women do have a male or female version of the word (e.g., it is rare for a woman to have the profession chamberlain/head of staff (حَاجِب), but there is a female word for that profession). However, in some cases, either the male or female version does not even exist linguistically (e.g., there is no male word of midwife (قَابِلة) profession). There are also more rare neutral words, like musician (موسِيقَار), that is used for both genders with no spelling changes.

In the APCD dataset, we found, as expected, that there are some modern professions that occur noticeably only in the modern era of the Arabic poems, but do not appear at all in the previous historical eras, such as the male engineer (مُهَندِس) that occurs 17 times, and the neutral profession of an electrician (كَهرَبائِي) that occurs only four times in the modern age, indicating that those modern professions are increasingly appearing in the modern age of the Arabic poems and confirming that Arabic native speakers (i.e., Arabs) still use the poems as an effective way to document the Arabic language changes over time.

On the other side of history, in the Shamela dataset, we found that a few historical professions frequently occur in the time periods before 1900 but not significantly after 1900. Some professions reflect essential shifts in legality. For example, one profession that is fortunately no longer legal or acceptable is male slaver (نَخَّاس). Fortunately, the male slaver profession appears much less often (only 12 times) in the time period after 1900, while it appears unpleasantly 118 times before the 1900 time periods. As another example, male chamberlain/head of staff (حَاجِب) appears 9,518 before the 1900 time periods, but only appears 914 times in

[3] We point to an expanded technical report with the full list of used modern and historical profession words. The report can be accessed here: `https://lin-web.clarkson.edu/~jmatthew/LChange2022/`

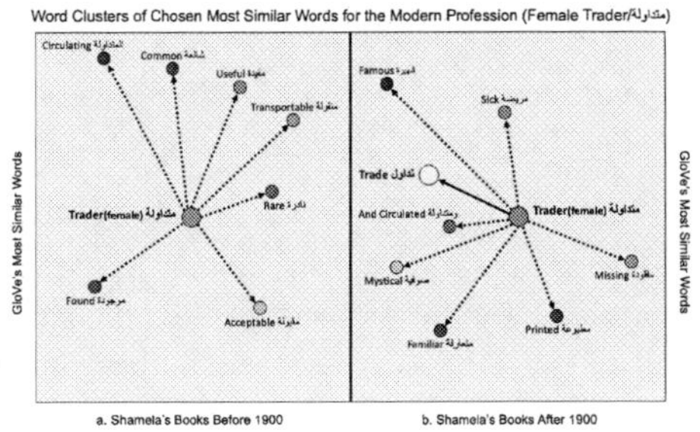

Figure 1: a. A word cluster of chosen GloVe's most similar words of the female profession trader (مُتَدَاوِلَة) in Shamela Library dataset in the time period before 1900, demonstrating that its word cluster is including different words with different meanings due to its homonymy. b. A word cluster of chosen GloVe's most similar words of the female profession trader (مُتَدَاوِلَة) in Shamela Library dataset in the time period after 1900, illustrating that a new related-trading activity word joining the profession word cluster, (trade/تَدَاوُل)[4]

the time period after 1900, showing that this male profession/position is on its way to extinction.

3.3 Polysemous/Homonymous Professions

The Arabic language is one of the most morphologically rich languages, with a high level of orthographic ambiguity, causing native speakers to use the optional diacritical marks to differentiate between two words (Grosvald et al., 2019).[5]

We noticed in the Shamela Library dataset that a few modern profession words change their connotations over time, and many profession words have alternate meanings due to the Arabic's orthographical ambiguity. We also found that this was especially true of female profession words. For example, the word (مُدَرِّسَة) for female teacher also means a school building (مَدْرَسَة), another word (طَيَّارَة) for a female pilot also means an airplane (طَيَّارَة). In all these cases, this complicates the use of both word counts and word embeddings in tracking the relative uses of profession words over time.

One homonymous example is the female trader (مُتَدَاوِلَة) profession. The same word (مُتَدَاوِلَة) also means common, famous, familiar, or circulating to describe a current news event. We see this alternate meaning dominate the usage of the word, complicating any attempt to study the prevalence of females engaged in this profession. Interestingly, we see evidence of change over time in the usage of this word. To investigate the semantic meaning of related words to the trading activity, we studied GloVe's most similar words (calculated based on the cosine similarity between two word vectors) for this profession word in two time periods of the Shamela Library dataset: before 1900 and after 1900. As shown in Figure 1a, before 1900, none of most similar words reflect the trading profession word (مُتَدَاوِلَة). However, in Figure 1b, after 1900, we see a word related to trading activity (trade/تَدَاوُل) appear in the most similar words of GloVe model. Thus, the connotation of the female trader (مُتَدَاوِلَة) profession is changing over time to more often reflect the actual profession of female trader (مُتَدَاوِلَة) and not just the alternate meaning of current news events.

3.4 Illegal Professions

In the religion of Islam, some professions are forbidden, for example, all types of usury, and serving, selling, or drinking alcohol. We examined a set of illegal/religiously forbidden profession words in Islam across the 11 ages of the Arabic poems, such as male usurer (مُرَابِي), female usurer (مُرَابِية), male bartender (سَاقِي), and female bartender (سَاقِيَة). Specifically, we closely focused on the diachronic semantic meaning change of the bartending profession words in the parallel eras of the APCD dataset. Interestingly, we found that bartending profession words in the early ages of the Arabic poems like Pre-Islamic, Islamic, and Umayyad only point to providing water to people but not serving wine even though the wine does exist. Those bartending profession words are polysemous and could carry other meanings like the male bartender (سَاقِي) could have a meaning of the phrase 'my leg' (سَاقِي), while the female bartender (سَاقِيَة) could have as well the

[4]English translations of the word clusters are automatically generated using Google Translator API that is included in the deep-translator Python model (`https://deep-translator.readthedocs.io`).

[5]In our preprocessing, we removed the optional diacritical marks as is generally recommended for Arabic NLP as a first step to reducing some data sparsity (Obeid et al., 2020). Unfortunately, removing diacritical marks increases the orthographic ambiguity, but retaining them would lead to a high degree of variance for the same word because the placement of diacritical marks varies with the grammatical placement of the word in a sentence. It is a difficult tradeoff for Arabic NLP that other researchers are attempting to tackle with advanced techniques, such as stemming and lemmatization (Kadri and Nie, 2006; Mubarak, 2017).

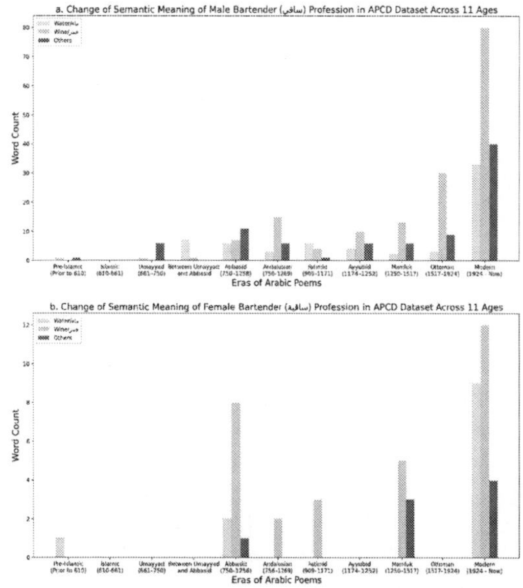

Figure 2: a. A word count of the occurrence of the male bartender (سَاقِي) across the 11 ages of the Arabic poems in the APCD dataset, showing the related meanings of the profession word like serving water, wine, or could be entirely meaning something that entirely unrelated to the profession word's meaning of serving drinks. b. A word count of the occurrence of the female bartender (سَاقِيَة) across the 11 ages of the Arabic poems in the APCD dataset, showing the related meanings like serving water, wine, or could be entirely meaning something that entirely unrelated to the profession word's meaning of serving drinks.

meaning of 'a water creek or an aqueduct' (سَاقِيَة).

To thoroughly investigate the occurrence of those profession words regarding their correlation with water – the allowed/halal drink, and the wine — the forbidden/haram drink in Islam, we manually analyzed the Arabic poems of each age and decided whether that word occurrence is a water-related meaning, wine-related meaning, or other unrelated meanings to both of the drinks. Figure 2a shows that the male bartender (سَاقِي) profession word started to appear in the Arabic poems as a profession of serving alcohol generally, wine exclusively, as a symbol of love, passion, and adoration for women from the age of between Umayyad and Abbasid until the Modern age.

One example of that is when the Abbasid Arabic poet, Abu Bakr Al-Sanobi (أبو بكر الصنوبري), said in his famous poem, the Pole of Pleasure in the Descriptions of Wines (قطب السرور في أوصاف الخمور): "O bartender of wine, do not forget us, O Goddess of Oud, spur singing (أيَا سَاقِيَ الخَمرِ لا تَنسنا – ويا ربّة العُودِ حُثّي الغِنَا)." Another example of that in another age, the Ottoman age, is for the Arabic poet, Abdul Ghani Al-Nabulsi (عبد الغني النابلسي), said in this romantic poem, Bartender O Bartender (ساقي يا ساقي): "Bartender O bartender, Give me some of his remaining wine (سَاقِي يَا سَاقِي – اسقِينِي مِن خَمرِهِ البَاقِي)

Similarly, in Figure 2b, the female bartender (سَاقِيَة) started to appear as a profession of serving wine from the age of between Umayyad and Abbasid until the Modern age as same as the male bartender (سَاقِي) profession word, except they did not appear in the two ages of Ayyubid and Ottoman. While the female and male bartender (سَاقِي و سَاقِيَة) surprisingly appeared in correlation with wine in the Arabic poems despite its religious forbiddance, both of the two profession words also refer to water-related words. For example, the female bartender (سَاقِيَة) refers to the 'water creek or aqueduct.' One example to show that is when the Modern Arabic poet, Rashid Ayoub (رشيد أيوب), said in his poem: "I sat in the meadow alone at the water creek, in which the water echoed the sound of my melodies",

جَلَستُ فِي الرَّوضِ وَحدِي عِندَ سَاقِيَةٍ

يُرَدِّدُ المَاء فِيهَا صَوت أَلحَانِي

4 Changes in Chinese Over Time

Although our primary focus in this study has been on Arabic, we found interesting evidence of change over time in Chinese as well. Classical Chinese (before 1900) uses a vocabulary and grammar that differs significantly from modern Chinese. We were surprised to find evidence not just of changes in professions over time, but also changes in defining set words. As we found in the diachronic corpora in Arabic, we expected changes in profession words over hundreds of years, but thought that the more fundamental defining set words like woman/man, girl/boy and madam/sir would not change substantially.

In Chinese, the word 'woman' can be translated in many ways, including "女子", "女人", and "妇女". The word "女子" was popularly used in an-

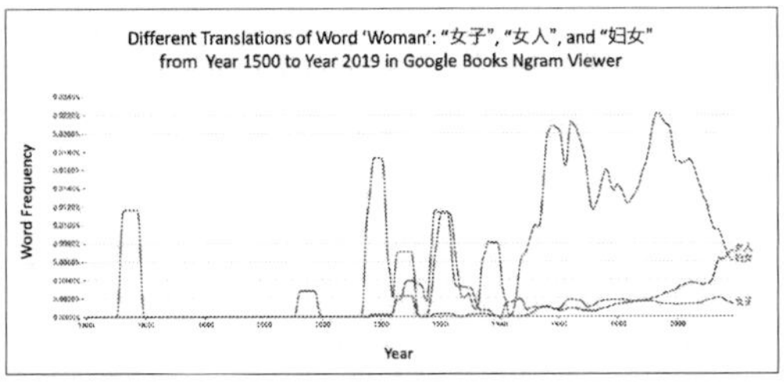

Figure 3: A timeline of word frequencies of different translations of word 'woman': "女子", "女人", and "妇女" that were found in multi-sources printed between 1500 and 2019 using Google Books Ngram Viewer.

cient times, but its usage has decreased in modern writing. In Figure 3, we used Google Books Ngram Viewer to chart the word frequencies of the different translations of the word 'woman': "女子", "女人", and "妇女" found in sources printed between 1500 and 2019 in Google's Books corpora in English, Chinese, French, German, Hebrew, Italian, Russian, or Spanish (Karch, 2021). This shows us that as languages evolve over time, defining sets, like profession sets, may also have to evolve to measure gender bias using methods like the Bolukbasi et al. (2016)'s method.

Besides using Google Books Ngram Viewer, we also assembled a small collection of works that might be considered "classics" in Chinese spanning the period 475 BC - 1992, for example 司马迁 (Records of the Grand Historian) by Qian Sima, 萧红 (Tales of Hulan River) by Hong Xiao, and 论语 (The Analects). We found that roughly half of the profession words used by Chen et al. (2021) did not appear, and that also two of the defining set words "boy" and "madam" used did not appear. Interestingly, Google Books Ngram Viewer showed that the word 'madam' was used very frequently between 1905 and 1910, but our small classics corpora did not include texts written in that time period. Again, these results indicate that as languages evolve over time, profession sets and even defining set words would have to evolve to measure gender bias.

5 Conclusion and Future Work

In order for NLP to reflect the rich multilingual, multicultural, and historical heritage of human text, it is essential that NLP techniques be extended beyond modern digital English text to multilingual and diachronic corpora. In this paper, we have explored the challenges of applying an important technique for measuring the gender bias learned by word embedding systems to diachronic corpora. We also have shown how techniques like those pioneered by Bolukbasi et al. (2016) and extended by Chen et al. (2021) have fundamental limitations when analyzing corpora spanning large periods of time. We showed that their technique based on analyzing the gender bias of profession words would have difficulty because professions change drastically over hundreds of years. Interestingly, we also documented changes in defining and profession set words over time and also challenges with polysemous/homonymous profession words especially female profession words in Arabic.

In this paper, we have focused mostly on identifying the problems with techniques applied successfully to measure gender bias in modern corpora like Google News or Wikipedia. In the future work, we plan to focus more on modifying profession sets and defining sets over time to overcome these problems. Our results indicate that as languages evolve over time, defining sets and profession sets would have to evolve to measure gender bias.

In this study, we focused on Arabic and Chinese, but we would like to extend our work to more languages. Adding an English corpora may be our next step. Although we like to actively focus on languages besides English, English can serve as an important comparison point because so much of the modern NLP tool chain has been optimized for English. We may be able to study the impact of changes in profession sets and defining sets over time with fewer complicating factors. We would also like to experiment with different advanced Arabic NLP techniques like stemming and lemmatization (Kadri and Nie, 2006; Mubarak, 2017) and see how applying such techniques could improve the results and reduce Arabic's orthographical ambiguity or even other Arabic NLP-related current issues like correcting spelling errors, especially in Arabic dialects, where there are no official orthography rules (Habash et al., 2018).

6 Acknowledgments

We'd like to thank the Clarkson Open Source Institute for their help and support with infrastructure and hosting of our experiments. We'd like to thank Abigail Matthews and Thomas Middleton for their help and support in writing and reviewing the manuscript.

References

Abubakar Abid, Maheen Farooqi, and James Zou. 2021. Persistent anti-muslim bias in large language models. In *Proceedings of the 2021 AAAI/ACM Conference on AI, Ethics, and Society*, pages 298–306.

Emily M. Bender, Timnit Gebru, Angelina McMillan-Major, and Shmargaret Shmitchell. 2021. On the dangers of stochastic parrots: Can language models be too big? New York, NY, USA. Association for Computing Machinery.

Tolga Bolukbasi, Kai-Wei Chang, James Y Zou, Venkatesh Saligrama, and Adam T Kalai. 2016. Man is to computer programmer as woman is to homemaker? debiasing word embeddings. *Advances in neural information processing systems*, 29.

Aylin Caliskan, Joanna J Bryson, and Arvind Narayanan. 2017. Semantics derived automatically from language corpora contain human-like biases. *Science*, 356(6334):183–186.

Yan Chen, Christopher Mahoney, Isabella Grasso, Esma Wali, Abigail Matthews, Thomas Middleton, Mariama Njie, and Jeanna Matthews. 2021. Gender bias and under-representation in natural language processing across human languages. In *Proceedings of the 2021 AAAI/ACM Conference on AI, Ethics, and Society*, pages 24–34.

Jacob Devlin, Ming-Wei Chang, Kenton Lee, and Kristina Toutanova. 2018. Bert: Pre-training of deep bidirectional transformers for language understanding. *arXiv preprint arXiv:1810.04805*.

Diwan. 2013. Poetry dataset. *https://www.aldiwan.net/*.

Shamela Library Foundation. 2012. Shamila library dataset. *https://shamela.ws/page/download*.

Michael Grosvald, Sarah Al-Alami, and Ali Idrissi. 2019. Word reading in arabic: Influences of diacritics and ambiguity. In *36th West Coast Conference on Formal Linguistics*, pages 176–181. Cascadilla Proceedings Project.

Nizar Habash, Fadhl Eryani, Salam Khalifa, Owen Rambow, Dana Abdulrahim, Alexander Erdmann, Reem Faraj, Wajdi Zaghouani, Houda Bouamor, Nasser Zalmout, et al. 2018. Unified guidelines and resources for arabic dialect orthography. In *Proceedings of the Eleventh International Conference on Language Resources and Evaluation (LREC 2018)*.

Youssef Kadri and Jian-Yun Nie. 2006. Effective stemming for arabic information retrieval. In *Proceedings of the International Conference on the Challenge of Arabic for NLP/MT*.

Marzieh Karch. 2021. How to use the ngram viewer tool in google books. In *https://www.lifewire.com/google-books-ngram-viewer-1616701*.

Tomas Mikolov, Kai Chen, Greg Corrado, and Jeffrey Dean. 2013. Efficient estimation of word representations in vector space. *arXiv preprint arXiv:1301.3781*.

Hamdy Mubarak. 2017. Build fast and accurate lemmatization for arabic. *arXiv preprint arXiv:1710.06700*.

Marwa Naili, Anja Habacha Chaibi, and Henda Hajjami Ben Ghezala. 2017. Comparative study of word embedding methods in topic segmentation. *Procedia Computer Science*, 112:340–349. Knowledge-Based and Intelligent Information Engineering Systems: Proceedings of the 21st International Conference, KES-20176-8 September 2017, Marseille, France.

Ossama Obeid, Nasser Zalmout, Salam Khalifa, Dima Taji, Mai Oudah, Bashar Alhafni, Go Inoue, Fadhl Eryani, Alexander Erdmann, and Nizar Habash. 2020. Camel tools: An open source python toolkit for arabic natural language processing. In *Proceedings of the 12th language resources and evaluation conference*, pages 7022–7032.

Abu Dhabi Department of Culture and Tourism. 2016. Poetry encyclopedia. *https://poetry.dctabudhabi.ae*.

Jeffrey Pennington, Richard Socher, and Christopher D Manning. 2014. Glove: Global vectors for word representation. In *Proceedings of the 2014 conference on empirical methods in natural language processing (EMNLP)*, pages 1532–1543.

Matthew E Peters, Mark Neumann, Mohit Iyyer, Matt Gardner, Christopher Clark, Kenton Lee, and Luke Zettlemoyer. 2018. Deep contextualized word representations." arxiv preprint. *arXiv preprint arXiv:1802.05365*.

Maja Rudolph and David Blei. 2018. Dynamic embeddings for language evolution. In *Proceedings of the 2018 World Wide Web Conference*, pages 1003–1011.

Esma Wali, Yan Chen, Christopher Mahoney, Thomas Middleton, Marzieh Babaeianjelodar, Mariama Njie, and Jeanna Neefe Matthews. 2020. Is machine learning speaking my language? a critical look at the nlp-pipeline across 8 human languages. *arXiv preprint arXiv:2007.05872*.

Melvin Wevers. 2019. Using word embeddings to examine gender bias in dutch newspapers, 1950-1990. *arXiv preprint arXiv:1907.08922*.

Yang Xu, Jiasheng Zhang, and David Reitter. 2019. Treat the word as a whole or look inside? subword embeddings model language change and typology. In *Proceedings of the 1st International Workshop on Computational Approaches to Historical Language Change*, pages 136–145.

Waleed A. Yousef, Omar M. Ibrahime, Taha M. Madbouly, Moustafa A. Mahmoud, Ali H. El-Kassas, Ali O. Hassan, and Abdallah R. Albohy. 2018. Arabic poem comprehensive dataset. *https://hci-lab.github.io/ArabicPoetry-1-Private/PCD*.

LSCDiscovery: A shared task on semantic change discovery and detection in Spanish

Frank D. Zamora-Reina[1], **Felipe Bravo-Marquez**[1], **Dominik Schlechtweg**[2]
[1]Department of Computer Science, University of Chile, IMFD & CENIA
[2]Institute for Natural Language Processing, University of Stuttgart
fzamora@dcc.uchile.cl, fbravo@dcc.uchile.cl,
schlecdk@ims.uni-stuttgart.de

Abstract

We present the first shared task on semantic change discovery and detection in Spanish and create the first dataset of Spanish words manually annotated for semantic change using the DURel framework (Schlechtweg et al., 2018). The task is divided in two phases: 1) Graded Change Discovery, and 2) Binary Change Detection. In addition to introducing a new language the main novelty with respect to the previous tasks consists in predicting and evaluating changes for all vocabulary words in the corpus. Six teams participated in phase 1 and seven teams in phase 2 of the shared task, and the best system obtained a Spearman rank correlation of 0.735 for phase 1 and an F1 score of 0.716 for phase 2. We describe the systems developed by the competing teams, highlighting the techniques that were particularly useful and discuss the limits of these approaches.

1 Introduction

Lexical Semantic Change Detection (LSCD) is the task of detecting words which have changed their meaning over time in a diachronic corpus of text (Schlechtweg et al., 2020), usually an unsupervised task. In recent years, several LSCD shared tasks have been organized (Schlechtweg et al., 2020; Basile et al., 2020; Kutuzov and Pivovarova, 2021). These tasks have contributed to a better understanding of LSCD, but have also had their shortcomings: (i) they have used mainly small pre-selected sets of target words creating an unrealistic evaluation scenario for the application of computational models in historical semantics and lexicography where researchers typically aim to cover the full vocabulary of a language (Kurtyigit et al., 2021), (ii) different formalizations of the LSCD task have been proposed including binary classification and ranking tasks (Schlechtweg et al., 2018; Schlechtweg and Schulte im Walde, 2020; Schlechtweg, 2022) and these have been employed inconsistently, and (iii) none of them have focused on Spanish, despite the fact that there are more than 450 million native speakers of this language.

We tackle these shortcomings by organizing a shared task on Spanish diachronic data with a more realistic evaluation scenario requiring participants to provide Lexical Semantic Change (LSC) predictions for the full corpus vocabulary (Discovery). Additionally, we cover previous scenarios by asking participants to predict LSC only in the limited sample of annotated target words (Detection). By offering a range of additional optional tasks (defined on the same annotated data) participants are able to evaluate and compare models on various formalizations of the LSCD task. In order to derive gold LSC labels for target words, we annotate and publish the largest existing data set of semantic proximity judgments covering 100 words with approximately 62k judgments from 12 human native speakers.[1]

2 Related Work

The detection of lexical semantic changes is of great interest in research areas such as historical semantics, lexicography, linguistics and NLP. For a comprehensive review of the literature on the area we refer the reader to the recent surveys (Tahmasebi et al., 2021; Kutuzov et al., 2018; Hengchen et al., 2021). In previous years several shared tasks have been organized: SemEval-2020 Task 1 (Schlechtweg et al., 2020) for English, German, Latin, and Swedish, DIACR-Ita for Italian (Basile et al., 2020), and RuShiftEval for Russian (Kutuzov and Pivovarova, 2021).[2] All shared tasks applied an evaluation setup where LSC was measured between pairs of time periods.

SemEval used a total of 156 target words for all languages with no development/test split. Ap-

[1]The data set is available at https://zenodo.org/record/6300104.

[2]There was also a student shared task on German data (Ahmad et al., 2020).

Proceedings of the 3rd Workshop on Computational Approaches to Historical Language Change, pages 149 - 164
May 26-27, 2022 ©2022 Association for Computational Linguistics

proximately half of these were drawn from etymological dictionaries or research literature, while the other half was drawn from the corpus vocabularies by selecting lemmas with similar POS and frequency as the first half of target words. Target word occurrences in sentences (usages) were combined into pairs and these were annotated for their semantic proximity (Schlechtweg et al., 2021). Target words were excluded if they had a high number of undecidable use pairs or were annotated too sparsely. Sense clusters were inferred from the annotation. From the clusters a binary (sense loss/gain vs. none) and a graded (Jensen-Shannon distance between cluster distributions) change score were derived and used to evaluate participants on a corresponding binary classification and ranking task.

DIACR-Ita used a total of 18 target words with no development/test split. All of these were drawn from an etymological dictionary. Target word usages were annotated with word sense definitions. Words with a high number of OCR errors and annotator disagreements were excluded. From the annotation Binary Change scores similar to SemEval were derived and used to evaluate participants on a binary classification task.

RuShiftEval used a total of 111 target words (all nouns) split into 12 for development and 99 for testing. These were selected in a similar procedure to SemEval: approximately half of these were drawn from etymological dictionaries, research literature or "invented" by the authors, while the other half was drawn from the corpus vocabularies by selecting lemmas with similar POS and frequency as the first half of target words. Target word usages from different time periods were combined into usage pairs and annotated for semantic proximity. From these the DURel COMPARE score (see Subsection 3.3 for more details) (Schlechtweg et al., 2018) was derived, which can be seen as an approximation of SemEval's Graded Change score (Schlechtweg, 2022). Participants were evaluated in a ranking task on the COMPARE scores.

As we can see, target words in previous shared tasks have been strongly preselected and systems have been evaluated on different tasks. They have also yielded (seemingly) contradictory results: while type-based model architectures have dominated in SemEval and DIACR-Ita, token-based architectures have dominated in RuShiftEval. In all tasks clustering-based models have shown rather low performance.

3 Task description

Our task was designed in two phases:

1. Graded Change Discovery, and
2. Binary Change Detection.

Note that *discovery* introduces additional difficulties for models as compared to the more simple semantic change *detection*, e.g. because a large number of predictions is required and the target words are not preselected, balanced or cleaned (cf. Kurtyigit et al., 2021). Yet, discovery is an important task, with applications such as lexicography where dictionary makers aim to cover the full vocabulary of a language.

3.1 Phase 1: Graded Change Discovery

Similar to Kurtyigit et al. (2021), we define the task of **Graded Change Discovery** as follows:

> Given a diachronic corpus pair C_1 and C_2, rank the intersection of their (content-word) vocabularies according to their degree of change between C_1 and C_2.

The participants were asked to rank the set of content words in the lemma vocabulary intersection of C_1 and C_2 according to their degree of semantic change between C_1 and C_2 where a higher rank means stronger change. The true degree of semantic change of a target word w was given by the Jensen-Shannon distance (Lin, 1991; Donoso and Sanchez, 2017) between w's word sense frequency distributions in C_1 and C_2 (cf. Schlechtweg et al., 2020). The two word sense frequency distributions were estimated via human annotation of word usage samples for w from C_1 and C_2 (see Subsection 4.4). Participants' predictions were *not* evaluated on the full set of target words, as this would be unfeasible to annotate, but on an (unpublished) random sample of words from the full set of target words. The predictions were scored against the ground truth via Spearman's rank-order correlation coefficient (Bolboaca and Jäntschi, 2006).

3.2 Phase 2: Binary Change Detection

Similar to Schlechtweg et al. (2020), we define the task of **Binary Change Detection** as follows:

Given a target word w and two sets of its usages U_1 and U_2, decide whether w lost or gained senses from U_1 to U_2, or not.

The participants were asked to classify a preselected set of content words into two classes, 0 for no change and 1 for change. The true binary labels of word *w* were inferred from *w*'s word sense frequency distributions in $C1$ and $C2$ (see Subsection 3.1). Participants' predictions were scored against the ground truth with the following metrics: F1 (main metric), Precision, and Recall. A crucial difference compared to Graded Change Discovery was that the public target words corresponded exactly to the hidden words on which we evaluated. Also, we published the usages sampled for annotation. Hence, participants could work with the exact annotated data, which was not possible in the first phase where participants could only work with the full corpora (from which the usages for annotation were sampled).

3.3 Optional tasks

Participants could submit predictions for several optional tasks:

Graded Change Detection was defined similar to Graded Discovery. The only difference was that the public target words corresponded exactly to the hidden words on which we evaluated. Participants were scored with Spearman correlation.

Sense Gain Detection was similar to Binary Change Detection. However, only words which gained (not lost) senses receive label 1. Participants were scored with F1, Precision and Recall.

Sense Loss Detection was similar to Binary Change Detection. However, only words which lost (not gained) senses received label 1. Participants were scored with F1, Precision and Recall.

COMPARE asked participants to predict the negated DURel COMPARE metric (Schlechtweg et al., 2018). This metric is defined as the average of human semantic proximity judgments of usage pairs for *w* between $C1$ and $C2$.[3] It can be seen as an approximation of JSD (Graded Change) (Schlechtweg, 2022). Participants were scored with Spearman correlation.

Corpus	Time period	Tokens
Old corpus (C_1)	1810–1906	$\sim 13M$
Modern corpus (C_2)	1994–2020	$\sim 22M$

Table 1: Sizes of both corpora.

Participants' submission files only needed to include predictions corresponding to the obligatory tasks in order to get a valid submission. They did not see the leaderboard while the evaluation phases were running. Furthermore, participants only had three valid submissions for each evaluation phase.[4]

4 Data

In this section, we describe the corpora, the selection process of target words, the sampling of usages and their annotation. Moreover, we explain how the target words were presented to the participants considering the two phases of the shared task.

4.1 Corpora

We created two corpora covering disjoint time periods: 1810 to 1906 (old corpus, $C1$) and 1994 to 2020 (modern corpus, $C2$) (see Table 1). The former was created using different sources freely available from Project Gutenberg[5] and the latter using different sources available from the OPUS project[6] (Tiedemann, 2012). For the old corpus, all the sources collected were concatenated. As for the modern corpus, four datasets were used: Spanish portion of TED2013, Spanish portion of News-Commentary v16, Spanish portion of MultiUN and Spanish version of Europarl corpus. TED2013 was used in its entirety, while 50 snippets with 5000 lines each were extracted from the other datasets by cutting the corpora into snippets of the mentioned size and randomly choosing 50 of them.

Both corpora were parsed using spaCy (Honnibal et al., 2020).[7] Each corpus contains four

[3]Contrary to the original metric we first take the median of all annotator judgments for each usage pair and then average these values. For details see: `https://github.com/Garrafao/WUGs`.

[4]We decided not to include the binary subtasks in phase 1, as the usage samples were not published which meant that participants needed to work with the full corpora instead of the samples on which the gold scores were inferred. We assumed that the sampling error between usages in the full corpora and our samples is much larger for Binary Change than for Graded Change (cf. Schlechtweg, 2022).

[5]`https://www.gutenberg.org/browse/languages/es`

[6]`https://opus.nlpl.eu/`

[7]Find details issues in Appendix A.

versions of the original dataset (raw, tokenized, lemmatized and POS-tagged).

4.2 Target words

4.2.1 Phase 1 (Graded Discovery)

Public target words was a list of 4385 words created in the following way: we first took the corpus vocabulary intersection from the lemmatized versions of both corpora. Then we removed words below a minimum frequency threshold of 40 for the old corpus and 73 for the modern corpus.[8] Then we removed all non-content words, i.e., we left only nouns, verbs, adjectives and adverbs. The final list of target words was published and participants were required to submit results for all 4385 words in the development and evaluation phase 1.

Hidden target words The large number of public target words was crucial to our task. However, it was not feasible to annotate all of them. Hence, we only annotated a subset of the public target words for semantic change. Participants' predictions for development and evaluation phase 1 were evaluated only on this subset of target words, which remained hidden from the participants. We selected the hidden target words in the following way: Initially, a list of 15 changing words was selected by scanning etymological dictionaries and consulting with a linguistic specialist to obtain words for changes from $C1$ to $C2$. Likewise, it was verified that these words were in both corpora. Additionally, a list of 85 words were randomly sampled from the public target words. The $85 + 15 = 100$ words were annotated as described in Section 4.4. Then, 20 words were excluded based on inter-annotator agreement.[9] The remaining set of 80 target words were split randomly into two groups, 20 words for the development set and 60 for the evaluation set (see Table 3). Uploaded submissions were scored against these 20/60 annotated words during development/evaluation phases.

4.2.2 Phase 2 (Binary Detection)

The target words corresponded to the 20/60 hidden words from Phase 1 for development/evaluation.

[8]40 was chosen by us for the old corpus and then we calculated 73 for the new corpus to reflect the same proportion of the frequency threshold to corpus size.

[9]We removed target words with agreements of less than 0.3 Krippendorf's α and less than 0.3 on a version of Krippendorf's α where expected disagreements were calculated from the full annotated data (instead of for each word separately). The latter measure is less sensitive to skewed judgment distributions for individual words.

↑	4: Identical
	3: Closely Related
	2: Distantly Related
	1: Unrelated

Table 2: DURel relatedness scale (Schlechtweg et al., 2018).

There it was no distinction here between public and hidden target words. Participants also got access to the annotated usages (20+20 from each corpus). Uploaded submissions were scored against the 20/60 public annotated words.

4.3 Word usages

All occurrences of the target words per corpus were extracted according to the lemma. Then, 20 usages were randomly sampled per target word from each corpus.

4.4 Annotation

We applied the SemEval procedure to annotate target word usages, as described in Schlechtweg et al. (2020, 2021). Annotators were asked to judge the semantic relatedness of pairs of word usages, such as the two usages of *servidor* in (1) and (2), on the scale in Table 2.

(1) Todo esto lo hago con mi iPhone; se va derecho al **servidor**, allí se hace el trabajo de archivo, clasificación y ensamble.
*'I do all this with my iPhone; it goes straight to the **server**, there the work of archiving, sorting and assembling is done.'*

(2) Llamó a grandes voces a sus **servidores**, y únicamente le contestó el eco en aquellas inmensas soledades, y se arrancó los cabellos y se mesó las barbas, presa de la más espantosa desesperación.
*'He called out to his **servants**, and only the echo in those immense solitudes answered him, and he pulled out his hair and ruffled his beard, prey to the most frightening desperation.'*

The annotated data of a word was represented in a Word Usage Graph (WUG), where vertices represented word usages, and weights on edges represented the (median) semantic relatedness judgment of a pair of usages such as (1) and (2). The final

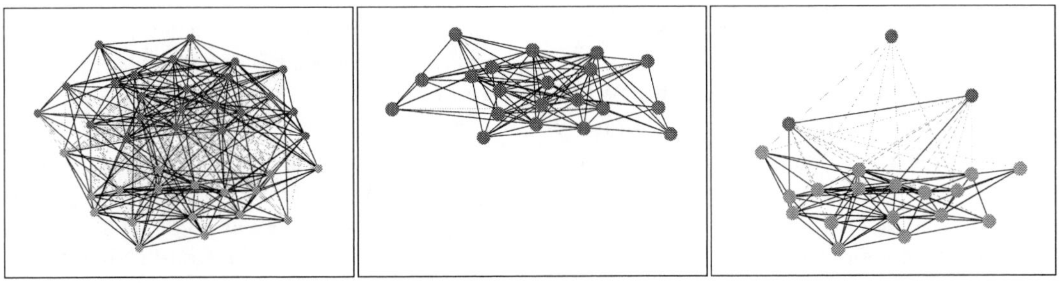

$G, D = (23, 17)$ $G_1, D_1 = (20, 0)$ $G_2, D_1 = (3, 17)$

Figure 1: Word Usage Graph *servidor* (left), subgraphs for old corpus G_1 (middle) and for modern corpus G_2 (right). The colors correspond to the clusters. **black**/gray lines indicate **high**/low edge weights.

WUGs were clustered with correlation clustering (Bansal et al., 2004; Schlechtweg et al., 2020, 2021) (see Figure 1, left) and split into two subgraphs G_1 and G_2 representing nodes from subcorpora C_1 and C_2 respectively (middle and right). Clusters were then interpreted as word senses and changes in clusters over time as lexical semantic change.[10]

In contrast to Schlechtweg et al., we used the openly available DURel interface for annotation and visualization.[11] This also implied a change in sampling procedure, as the system implemented only random sampling of usage pairs (without SemEval-style optimization, i.e., sampling in rounds with connection of clusters). For each target word we sampled $|U_1| = |U_2| = 20$ usages (sentences) per subcorpus (C_1, C_2) and uploaded these to the DURel system, which presented usage pairs to annotators in randomized order. We recruited twelve Spanish native speakers (4 Chileans, 4 Colombians, 2 Cubans, 1 Spaniard and 1 Venezuelan). All had university level education, while seven had a background in linguistics of which two had one in historical linguistics. We monitored agreement between annotators during the annotation process and discussed some strong annotation disagreements with certain annotators. This led to the exclusion of one annotator early in the process who often completely inverted the annotation scale (e.g. judged 1 while agreeing that the two usages have identical meanings).

Similar to Schlechtweg et al. (2020), we ensured the robustness of the obtained clusterings by continuing the annotation of a target word until all clusters in its WUG were connected by at least one judgment.[12] For 16 words the annotation had to be stopped before this condition was met. We manually inspected the unconnected clusters of some words and concluded that missing connections did not lead to clustering errors.

We finally labeled a target word as Binary Change if it gained or lost a cluster over time. For instance, *servidor* in Figure 1 was labeled as change as it gained the orange cluster from C_1 to C_2. Consequently, *servidor* was also labeled as gaining a sense; but not as losing a sense, since the blue cluster persists. Graded Change was defined as the Jensen-Shannon distance between the normalized cluster frequency distributions D_1 and D_2 yielding a high value of 0.82 (ranges between 0.0 and 1.0) for *servidor*, as sense probabilities changed drastically. The negated COMPARE score was derived by averaging over all graph edges with nodes from different time periods and negating this value, yielding a high score of -1.97 (ranges between -4.0 and -1.0) for *servidor*.[13] Following Schlechtweg et al. (2020) we used k and n as lower frequency thresholds for the binary notions to avoid that small random fluctuations in sense frequencies caused by sampling variability or annotation error were misclassified as change. As proposed in Schlechtweg and Schulte im Walde (submitted) for comparability across sample sizes we set $k = 1 \leq 0.01 * |U_i| \leq 3$ and $n = 3 \leq 0.1 * |U_i| \leq 5$, where $|U_i|$ was the number of usages from the respective time period.[14]

[10]We used Schlechtweg et al. (2020, 2021)'s code provided at `https://www.ims.uni-stuttgart.de/data/wugs`.

[11]`https://www.ims.uni-stuttgart.de/data/durel-tool`.

[12]Note that this condition was more strict than Schlechtweg et al. (2020)'s where only connection of multi-clusters (clusters with more than one usage) was guaranteed. Their condition was always met in our data.

[13]Find a more detailed discussion of different change scores in Schlechtweg et al. (2020) and Schlechtweg (2022).

[14]That is, k was always between 1 and 3. There are three possible cases: $k = 1$ if $0.01 * |U_i| \leq 1$, $k = 0.01 * |U_i|$ if $1 < 0.01 * |U_i| < 3$, $k = 3$ if $0.01 * |U_i| \geq 3$. Similarly for

This resulted in $k = 1$ and $n = 3$ for all target words.

Find an overview over the final set of WUGs in Table 3. We reached an inter-annotator agreement of Krippendorff's $\alpha = .53$ and Spearman's $\rho = .57$ which was comparable to previous studies (e.g. Schlechtweg et al., 2018; Rodina and Kutuzov, 2020; Kurtyigit et al., 2021; Baldissin et al., 2022).[15]

5 Systems

We now summarize the baseline systems as well as the systems and resources used by the participating teams.

5.1 Baselines

For both phases we use five baselines:

baseline1 *Skip-Gram with Negative Sampling + Orthogonal Procrustes + Cosine Distance (SGNS+OP+CD)* This approach learned vector representations for each word (type-based) in two input corpora with a shallow neural language model (Mikolov et al., 2013a,b).[16] These were then aligned using Orthogonal Procrustes (Hamilton et al., 2016). For phase 1, the method computed Graded Change as the cosine distance between old and modern vectors for all words in the vocabulary. This same value was used in the COMPARE subtask. In phase 2, binary predictions were computed by setting a threshold to the cosine distances, which was calculated as the sum between the mean and the standard deviation (std) of all these distances (Kaiser et al., 2020b). All words with values above the threshold were classified as *change*, and values below were classified as *no change*. This approach has shown high performance in several previous studies and shared tasks (Schlechtweg et al., 2019; Pömsl and Lyapin, 2020; Kaiser et al., 2020b; Pražák et al., 2020).

baseline2 *Normalized Log-Transformed Frequency Difference (FD)* For phase 1, this method calculated the frequency of each target word in each of the two corpora, normalized it by the logarithm of the total corpus frequency and then calculated absolute differences between these values as a measure of change. We submitted these values for the change graded and COMPARE subtasks. For phase 2, the method applied the same thresholding approach used in baseline1. For the sense loss subtask, it first verified that the target word presents change using the value of the change binary subtask. Then, if the differences were negative, the words were classified as loss $= 1$ and as loss $= 0$ otherwise. For sense gain the labeling is reversed.

baseline3 *Grammatical profiles* were generated from tagged and parsed corpora (Kutuzov et al., 2021). These profiles were essentially frequency vectors of various morphological and syntactic features (for example, *case = Nominative*, or *syntax role = subject*) for a given word in a given historical corpus. The cosine distance between the profile vectors of the same word for the two periods was used as an estimate of graded semantic change and COMPARE. Binary predictions were generated from ordered lists of graded scores for all target words by applying an offline change-point detection algorithm based on dynamic programming. The algorithm finds a point (a word) in an ordered list of scores, where the scores become significantly higher. This word and all words with score values above it were assigned the class "changed". This baseline did not produce predictions for the sense loss and sense gain subtasks.[17]

baseline4 *Minority class* This baseline produced predictions by labeling each word with the minority class label of the respective Binary Change score (change binary, loss, gain). This is label 1 (change) in all cases. It only applied to phase 2.

baseline5 *Random baseline* This baselines produced random predictions for all subtasks in both phases. For phase 1, we generated random values between 0 and 1 from a uniform distribution for all hidden target words and computed Spearman correlation with the gold scores. This process was repeated 100 times and we reported the average performance over all repetitions. For phase 2, we used a parallel procedure generating random labels $\in \{0, 1\}$ from a uniform distribution.[18]

n.

[15]We provide WUGs as Python NetworkX graphs, descriptive statistics, inferred clusterings, change values and interactive visualizations for all target words and the respective code at `https://www.ims.uni-stuttgart.de/data/wugs` (DWUG ES).

[16]As parameters we chose dim=100, window size=10, epochs=5, number of negative samples=5, subsampling threshold=0.001 (cf. Kaiser et al., 2020a).

[17]All results for baseline3 were computed and submitted by Andrey Kutuzov using the code at `https://github.com/glnmario/semchange-profiling`.

[18]Baseline3, baseline4 and baseline5 were added after the shared task finished.

Data set	n	N/V/A	|U|	AN	JUD	AV	KRI	SPR	UNC	LOSS	LSC$_B$	LSC$_G$
development	20	13/4/3	40	10	12k	40	.53	.59	0	.53	.55	.39
evaluation	60	30/14/16	40	12	38k	40	.58	.60	0	.45	.47	.37
discarded	20	8/6/6	40	12	12k	40	.27	.33	0	.52	.30	.18
full	100	51/24/25	40	12	62k	40	.53	.57	0	.48	.45	.34

Table 3: Overview target words. n = no. of target words, N/V/A = no. of nouns/verbs/adjectives+adverbs, $|U|$ = avg. no. of usages per word, AN = no. of annotators, JUD = total no. of judged usage pairs, AV = avg. no. of judgments per usage pair, KRI = Krippendorff's α, SPR = weighted mean of pairwise Spearman, UNC = avg. no. of uncompared multi-cluster combinations, LOSS = avg. of normalized clustering loss * 10, LSC$_{B/G}$ = mean binary/Graded Change score.

5.2 Participating systems

Below we present a summary of the methods developed by the participants:[19]

HSE *(Kashleva et al., 2022)* This team participated with two different methods. The first consisted of fine-tuning BERT (Devlin et al., 2019) on the lemmatized versions of the corpora in order to extract embeddings of the target words separately for each period, which are then clustered using K-means. Graded Change was estimated as the average cosine distance between all pairs of cluster centroids in the first and second periods. In order to estimate Binary Change, the Graded Change scores were thresholded by clustering them into two clusters.

The second method was based on grammatical profiles (Kutuzov et al., 2021). The frequency of morphological and syntactic categories for each target word in both corpora (parsed with UdPipe, Straka and Straková, 2017) were counted and used as features in two time-specific vectors. Graded Change was measured by the cosine distance between these vectors, while Binary Change was measured by thresholding the graded scores.

GlossReader *(Rachinskiy and Arefyev, 2022)* This system fine-tuned the XLM-R multilingual language model (Conneau et al., 2019) as part of a gloss-based Word Sense Disambiguation (WSD) system on a large English WSD dataset. It employed zero-shot cross-lingual transferability to build contextualized embeddings for Spanish data. The Graded Change score for each word was calculated as the Average Pairwise (Manhattan) Distance (APD) between the embeddings for (non-preprocessed) word usages in the old and new corpus. Binary changes were estimated by thresholding these scores. For the sense gain and sense loss subtasks the same predictions were reused.

UAlberta *(Teodorescu et al., 2022)* This team applied different methods to the two subtasks. For Graded Change Discovery, they followed the design of CIRCE (Pömsl and Lyapin, 2020) and computed distances based on both static (type-based) and contextual (token-based) embeddings, with their relative weights tuned on the development set. For static embeddings, they used SGNS+OP+Euclidean Distance on the lemmatized versions of the corpora. For contextual embeddings, the XLM-R model was trained on the combined corpus (tokenized) to predict masked instances of the target words and Graded Change was measured using Euclidean APD. For Binary Change Detection, they framed the task as a WSD problem, creating sense frequency distributions for target words in the old and modern corpus with an end-to-end WSD system (Orlando et al., 2021). It was assumed that the word semantics has changed if: (1) a sense is observed in the modern corpus but not in the old corpus (or vice versa), or (2) the relative change for any sense exceeds a tuned threshold.

CoToHiLi *(Sabina Uban et al., 2022)* This team proposed a type-based embedding model combined with hand-crafted linguistic features. The system computed several features for every target word based on embedding distances between time periods and linguistic hand-crafted features, which were then weighted into an ensemble model to predict the final score. First, the system obtained word embeddings separately on the two corpora (tokenized) with the Continuos Bag-of-Words (CBOW) model (Mikolov et al., 2013a,b), which were then

[19]The descriptions are based on the system description papers submitted by the participating teams, with the exception of Rombek who did not provide a paper but gave us a brief description by e-mail.

aligned to obtain a common embedding space. The alignment algorithms used were: supervised alignment using a seed word dictionary and a linear mapping method, a semi-supervised algorithm and unsupervised alignment based on adversarial training (Artetxe et al., 2016, 2017, 2018a,b). Finally, cosine distance between embeddings of the same word in different corpora was used as an indicator of graded semantic change. For the binary task, the system used thresholding the graded scores.

DeepMistake *(Homskiy and Arefyev, 2022)* This team employed a Word-in-Context (WiC) model, i.e., a model designed to determine if a particular word has the same meaning in two given contexts. In essence, they attempted to directly apply a model trained on a related task to our problem. The WiC model was initially trained by fine-tuning the XLM-R language model on the Multilingual and Cross-lingual Word-in-Context (MLC-WiC) dataset (Martelli et al., 2021). Subsequently, it was further fine-tuned on the provided annotations for the development set in this shared task and on the Spanish portion of the multi-language XL-WSD dataset (Pasini et al., 2021). Graded Change was measured similarly to APD by averaging same-sense probabilities between embeddings for usages (no preprocessing) from different time periods. For the change binary subtask, the authors applied thresholding to the Graded Change scores, for the sense gain and sense loss subtasks the same predictions were reused.

They also experimented with clustering by representing word usages and their same-sense probabilities in a weighted undirected graph, which was then clustered with Correlation Clustering. Graded Change was measured with JSD, while Binary Change was measured with the Binary Change score definition from Section 4.4.

BOS *(Kudisov and Arefyev, 2022)* The system described by this team was based on generating lexical substitutes that describe old and new senses of a given word. These were generated using the XLM-R masked language model. For polysemous words, lexical substitutes depended on the meaning expressed in a particular context. For each target word, usages were sampled from both corpora, lemmatized and used to generate lexical substitutes. Next, two sets of vectors were built for old and new usages where each usage is represented by a vector of the probabilities of its substitutes. For Graded Change the Cosine APD between old and new vectors was computed, while for Binary Change a threshold was applied to this score. The authors also proposed three different approaches based on pairwise distances for the sense gain and loss subtasks.

Rombek This system adapted ideas from the Word Sense Induction (WSI) task. Lexical substitutes were generated in the same way as with the BOS system (see above) and arranged in a matrix. Agglomerative clustering was then applied to each target word to obtain clusters with candidate senses. JSD was applied between clusters to obtain Graded Change estimates. Thresholding was applied to produce binary predictions.[20]

5.3 Summary

Most systems were based on three main components: (i) a semantic representation of words or word usages as vectors, (ii) an aggregation method over vectors, and (iii) a change measure. Type-based systems usually employed an additional alignment step over semantic representations. Also, the preprocessing of data was crucial for the performance of contextualized embeddings (Laicher et al., 2021).

Preprocessing Some teams only used the tokenized version of the shared task dataset (CoToHiLi, UAlberta), while other teams only used the lemmatized version (UAlberta, BOS, HSE). One team varied the preprocessings with systems (UAlberta): lemmatization for type-based embeddings and tokenization, lemmatization and POS-tagging for the WSD system. Two teams did not use any sort of preprocessing (GlossReader, DeepMistake), while two teams used substitution with dynamic patterns (e.g. *<mask> (y [target]), [target] (por ejemplo <mask>))* for their lexical substitution models (BOS, Rombek).

Semantic representations Most systems used token-based contextualized embeddings such as BERT (HSE) and XLM-R (DeepMistake, GlossReader, Rombek, UAlberta, BOS). Some teams further fine-tuned these embeddings on Language Modeling, WSD or WSI/WiC tasks. One team (DeepMistake) fine-tuned on the semantic proximity judgments from the published development data. Only three teams used type-based semantic rep-

[20]This team did not submit a paper to the shared task.

resentations including SGNS (UAlberta), CBOW (CoToHiLi) and Grammatical Profiling (HSE).

Vector aggregation Participating teams used different approaches to aggregate vectors into more abstract semantic representations. A common strategy was to model the COMPARE score by computing Average Pairwise Distances (APD) between vectors from different time periods (DeepMistake, GlossReader, UAlberta, BOS). This strategy has shown to perform well in various previous studies and shared tasks (Kutuzov and Giulianelli, 2020; Laicher et al., 2021; Kurtyigit et al., 2021; Arefyev et al., 2021). Another strategy was to cluster the vectors (HSE, Rombek, DeepMistake). Clustering algorithms used are: Agglomerative Clustering (Rombek), K-means (HSE) and Correlation Clustering (DeepMistake). One system used a WSD system to assign cluster labels (UAlberta).

Change Measure For Graded Change most teams using contextualized embeddings directly relied on APD scores as described above. They used different distance measures such as: Cosine (BOS), Euclidean (UAlberta) and Manhattan (GlossReader) distances. One team averaged same-sense probabilities (DeepMistake). The teams relying on clustering mostly used the JSD to measure Graded Change (Rombek, DeepMistake). One team instead used cosine distance between cluster centroids (HSE). The teams relying on type-based representations used either Cosine (CoToHiLi, HSE) or Euclidean distance (UAlberta). For Binary Change most teams relied on thresholding the graded predictions (DeepMistake, GlossReader, Rombek, HSE, CoToHiLi, BOS). This strategy has shown high performance in several previous studies and shared tasks (Schlechtweg et al., 2020; Kaiser et al., 2020b; Kurtyigit et al., 2021). Two teams using a clustering approach measured Binary Change by applying exactly the definition from the annotation process (DeepMistake) or a similar definition (UAlberta).

6 Results

The results shown in Tables 4, 5 and 6 correspond to the best submissions per subtask.[21]

Graded Change Discovery As shown in Table 4, **GlossReader** and **DeepMistake** obtained first and second place in the main task of evaluation phase 1, while **HSE** came third.[22] These were the only teams that managed to outperform baseline1 (SGNS+OP+CD) and baseline3 (Grammatical Profiles). The three winning systems were based on fine-tuned versions of contextualized embeddings with average vector aggregation (GlossReader, DeepMistake) or clustering (HSE). Interestingly, the top two systems did not model the JSD between cluster distributions (as done on the annotation to derive gold scores), but instead model the COMPARE score (with APD). We discuss this observation further in Subsection 6.1.

COMPARE Discovery GlossReader and DeepMistake also reached the first and second place on the COMPARE task in evaluation phase 1. This is not surprising, because they actually modeled the COMPARE score with APD. Consequently, also the correlation was considerably higher than with Graded Change (e.g. $\rho = 0.842$ vs. 0.735). Baseline1 took the third place.

Binary Change Detection For Phase 2 (Tables 5 and 6), again **GlossReader** performed best, this time followed by **UAlberta** and **Rombek**. Interestingly, with the exception of GlossReader the systems used in Phase 1 did not obtain a good performance in Phase 2. However, participants managed to outperform all baselines with the exception of HSE not outperforming baseline4 (minority class). Two out of the winning systems used thresholding (GlossReader, Rombek), i.e., they modeled the COMPARE score or the JSD and then thresholded these scores to obtain Binary Change predictions. From these teams only UAlberta inferred sense clusters. Hence, here we saw again what we saw for phase 1: the top-performing teams were often not modeling the annotation procedure.

Sense Gain/Loss Detection The top performance for sense gain (F1 $= 0.591$) was clearly lower than for Binary Change, while for loss the top performance (F1 $= 0.688$) approaches the one for Binary Change. The best results for sense gain were obtained by **DeepMistake**, followed by **BOS** and **GlossReader**. In the sense loss subtask, **GlossReader** obtained the best performance, followed by **Rombek** and **BOS**. GlossReader and DeepMistake submitted the same results to both subtasks as for Binary Change Detection implicitly assuming

[21] In the case of HSE who used two different systems, the displayed results correspond to the token-based system.

[22] Since not not all users reported a team name on Codalab, some leaderboard entries are filled with usernames.

Task		Change graded	COMPARE
#	Team name	SPR	SPR
1	GlossReader	**0.735 (1)**	0.842 (1)
2	DeepMistake	**0.702 (2)**	0.829 (2)
3	HSE	**0.553 (3)**	0.558 (4)
4	baseline1	0.543 (4)	0.561 (3)
5	baseline3	0.508 (5)	0.459 (5)
6	Rombek	0.497 (6)	0.456 (6)
7	CoToHiLi	0.282 (7)	–
8	baseline2	0.092 (8)	0.088 (7)
9	baseline5	0.064 (9)	-0.072 (8)
10	BOS	-0.125 (10)	-0.129 (9)

Table 4: Summary of system performance in phase 1. Teams are ranked according to SPR score for the Graded Change subtask in decreasing order. The values corresponding to the three best systems are highlighted in bold type.

Task		Change binary			Change graded	COMPARE
#	Team name	F1	P	R	SPR	SPR
1	GlossReader	**0.716 (1)**	0.615 (3)	0.857 (3)	0.735 (1)	0.842 (1)
2	UAlberta	**0.709 (2)**	0.549 (7)	1.000 (1)	–	–
3	Rombek	**0.687 (3)**	0.590 (4)	0.821 (4)	0.535 (5)	0.546 (5)
4	BOS	0.658 (4)	0.510 (8)	0.929 (2)	0.209 (8)	0.163 (7)
5	DeepMistake	0.655 (5)	0.633 (2)	0.679 (6)	0.676 (2)	0.821 (2)
6	CoToHiLi	0.636 (6)	0.553 (6)	0.750 (5)	0.282 (7)	–
7	baseline4	0.636 (6)	0.467 (11)	1.0 (1)	–	–
8	HSE	0.586 (7)	0.567 (5)	0.607 (7)	0.553 (3)	0.558 (4)
9	baseline3	0.548 (8)	0.500 (9)	0.607 (7)	0.373 (6)	0.423 (6)
10	baseline1	0.537 (9)	0.846 (1)	0.393 (9)	0.543 (4)	0.561 (3)
11	baseline5	0.508 (10)	0.484 (10)	0.536 (8)	0.064 (10)	-0.072 (9)
12	baseline2	0.222 (11)	0.500 (9)	0.143 (10)	0.092 (9)	0.088 (8)

Table 5: Summary of the results of Phase 2 for substasks Graded Change, COMPARE and Binary Change. Teams are ranked according to F1 score for subtask Change binary in decreasing order. The values corresponding to the three best systems are highlighted in bold type.

that gain and loss always occur together. In this way, they mostly outperformed Rombek and BOS who tried a more principled approach.

Graded Change/COMPARE Detection The top performance for these tasks was the same in evaluation phase 1 and 2 ($\rho = 0.735$ and 0.842). Some teams had the same results in both phases (GlossReader, HSE, CoToHiLi) and thus likely submitted the same predictions. Two teams improved their results (Rombek, BOS), while one team had lower results (DeepMistake). We are unsure about the impact of the published target words and their usages on these results, as teams did not consistently report whether they used this information in phase 2.

6.1 Discussion

The Graded Change Discovery subtask was solved with a rather high performance by the winning team ($\rho = 0.735$). This is comparable to the top performance in SemEval ($\rho = 0.725$ for DE) obtained with type-based embeddings. The COMPARE Discovery subtask was solved with even higher performance ($\rho = 0.842$). This is comparable to the top performance in RuShiftEval ($\rho = 0.822$). However, the results in our shared task were obtained under harder conditions, i.e., for a large number of uncleaned target words (Discovery).[23] This suggests that, as far as Graded Change is concerned, LSCD

[23] We assume that the performance of participating systems obtained on the hidden target words generalizes roughly to the full set of public target words as the sample was taken largely random.

	Task	Sense gain			Sense loss		
#	Team name	F1	P	R	F1	P	R
1	GlossReader	**0.511 (3)**	0.333 (5)	0.929 (2)	**0.688 (1)**	0.564 (2)	0.880 (2)
2	DeepMistake	**0.591 (1)**	0.433 (1)	0.929 (2)	0.582 (5)	0.533 (3)	0.640 (4)
3	HSE	0.250 (8)	0.192 (9)	0.357 (5)	0.364 (7)	0.421 (5)	0.320 (5)
4	baseline1	–	–	–	–	–	–
5	Rombek	0.50 (4)	0.409 (2)	0.643 (4)	**0.681 (2)**	0.727 (1)	0.640 (4)
6	baseline3	–	–	–	–	–	–
7	BOS	**0.520 (2)**	0.361 (4)	0.929 (2)	**0.610 (3)**	0.529 (4)	0.720 (3)
8	baseline2	0.211 (9)	0.400 (3)	0.143 (6)	0 (8)	0 (8)	0 (7)
9	UAlberta	0 (10)	0 (10)	0 (7)	0 (8)	0 (8)	0 (7)
10	CoToHiLi	0.462 (5)	0.316 (6)	0.857 (3)	0 (8)	0 (8)	0 (7)
11	baseline4	0.378 (6)	0.23 (8)	1.0 (1)	0.588 (4)	0.416 (6)	1.0 (1)
12	baseline5	0.333 (7)	0.313 (7)	0.357 (5)	0.367 (6)	0.375 (7)	0.36 (6)

Table 6: Summary of the results of Phase 2 for subtasks Sense loss and Sense gain. The values corresponding to the three best systems are highlighted in bold type.

systems are applicable to solve real-world problems and may be useful in historical semantics or lexicography. However, the more relevant task for these fields is Binary Change Detection/Discovery (Schlechtweg and Schulte im Walde, 2020). The results for Binary Change Detection were lower ($F1 = 0.716$), but still clearly higher than the best baseline (0.636). Results in SemEval were mixed, but mostly not higher than $F1 = 0.7$ (DE), while results in DIACR-Ita were high with an accuracy of 0.94, which was, however, obtained with a different metric and on a very small and strongly preselected set of target words. A future challenge will thus be to improve performance on the binary task.

Our shared task was clearly dominated by token-based systems. Out of seven participants only two used a (standalone) type-based system which also performed much worse than the winning teams (CoToHiLi, HSE).[24] Also, our type-based baseline1 was clearly outperformed by a number of token-based systems (three in phase 1 and six in phase 2). This confirms the tendency observed in RuShiftEval where token-based systems outperformed type-based ones on LSCD. Before that, in SemEval and DIACR-Ita the type-based systems had dominated. Potential reasons for this switch are the understanding of biases in contextualized embeddings (Laicher et al., 2021), their optimization through fine-tuning (Arefyev et al., 2021; Arefyev and Bykov, 2021) and the optimization of vector aggregation methods (Kutuzov and Giulianelli, 2020; Laicher et al., 2021; Arefyev et al., 2021).

In our task, we saw clustering methods amongst the best-performing systems (HSE, UAlberta) for the first time. This is an important development, because the current top-performing system (GlossReader), as well as many other systems not relying on clustering, did not model the target word annotation procedure (cf. Subsection 4.4). Instead, it exploited correlations between the COMPARE score and JSD as well as Binary Change. These scores are known to correlate strongly in current LSCD datasets (Schlechtweg, 2022), including ours. The correlation between gold (negated) COMPARE and JSD scores in our dataset is 0.92, while it is 0.69 for gold (negated) COMPARE and Binary Change. This means that modeling the COMPARE score is a good predictor for Graded as well as Binary Change. However, this also means that, the current best-performing systems have a clear upper bound on their potential to solve LSCD tasks (where this upper bound is higher for Graded than for Binary Change). Hence, if we want to break through this upper bound in the future, we need to develop or improve other system types possibly relying on clustering to model the annotation procedure.[25]

In order to see how far the current approach of thresholding COMPARE/JSD/graded scores carries, we compared performance of the top three systems in evaluation phase 1 across binarization thresholds in Figure 2. As we can see, the three

[24]The result reported by the HSE team in the leaderboard corresponds to the first method described in Section 5.2.

[25]Homskiy and Arefyev (2022) had promising results with applying the clustering framework used in the annotated data and semantic proximity graphs derived from fine-tuned contextualized embeddings.

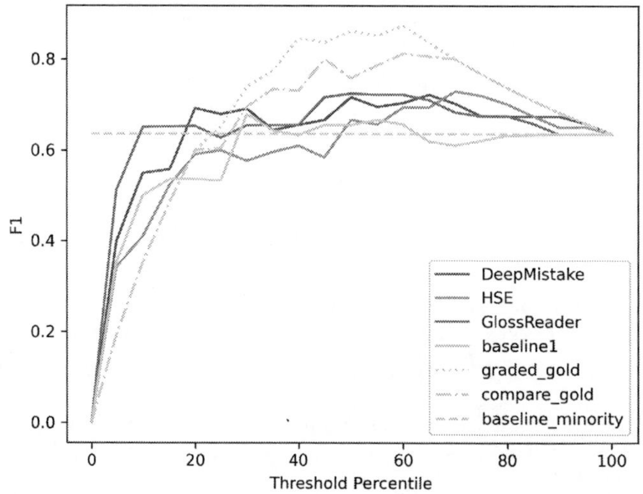

Figure 2: F1 scores over binarization thresholds based on percentiles on submitted Graded Change predictions for top four teams in evaluation phase 1.

systems had a similar maximum performance of roughly F1 $= 0.72$ around a binarization threshold of $50 - 70$ %.[26] At 100 % they all converged to the minority class baseline (all target words labeled as 1). The upper bound on this approach was given by the maximum performance of the gold JSD (graded_gold) and the gold COMPARE score (compare_gold). These upper bounds were 0.88 and 0.81 respectively. This means that perfectly modeling the COMPARE or even the JSD score can reach high but never perfect performance on Binary Change.

7 Conclusion

We conducted the first shared task on semantic change discovery and detection in Spanish. We manually annotated 100 Spanish words for semantic change between two corpora, an old one covering the period between 1810 and 1906, and a modern one covering the years between 1994 and 2020. The discovery part of our task imposed several computational challenges for participants, as it required calculating semantic change scores for all words in the vocabulary.

We received predictions from six teams in phase 1 and seven teams in phase 2. Participants applied systems using static and contextualized word embeddings in combination with various fine-tuning procedures, vector aggregation methods and change measures. Graded Change Discovery was solved with high performance while Binary Change Detection still remains far from being solved. The most successful method winning both main tasks is a system fine-tuning contextualized multilingual XML-R embeddings on WSD data, aggregating vectors into cross-corpus pairs and measuring change as the average of their distances, or a binarization of these values. However, we showed that this approach has a clear upper bound which will not allow to solve the tasks completely reliably in the future. Another interesting result from our task was that clustering approaches are amongst the winning teams for the first time.

We hope that this shared task will help pave the way for future research in the discovery and detection of semantic lexical changes for the Spanish language, and that our data can be used in the future for the proposal of novel ideas and techniques.

8 Acknowledgements

This work was supported by ANID FONDECYT grant 11200290, U-Inicia VID Project UI-004/20, ANID -Millennium Science Initiative Program - Code ICN17_002, the National Center for Artifi-

[26]Interestingly, HSE here obtained maximum performance amongst all systems (0.73), much higher than their submission in evaluation phase 2. A similar observation holds for our baseline1. This shows how crucial threshold selection is in this approach.

cial Intelligence CENIA FB210017, Basal ANID, and SemRel Group (DFG Grants SCHU 2580/1 and SCHU 2580/2). Dominik Schlechtweg has been funded by the project 'Towards Computational Lexical Semantic Change Detection' supported by the Swedish Research Council (2019–2022; contract 2018-01184) and by the research program 'Change is Key!' supported by Riksbankens Jubileumsfond (under reference number M21-0021).

References

Adnan Ahmad, Kiflom Desta, Fabian Lang, and Dominik Schlechtweg. 2020. Shared task: Lexical semantic change detection in german. *CoRR*, abs/2001.07786.

Nikolay Arefyev and Dmitrii Bykov. 2021. An interpretable approach to lexical semantic change detection with lexical substitution. volume 2021-June, pages 31–46. ABBYY PRODUCTION LLC.

Nikolay Arefyev, Maksim Fedoseev, Vitaly Protasov, Daniil Homskiy, Adis Davletov, and Alexander Panchenko. 2021. Deepmistake: Which senses are hard to distinguish for a word-in-context model. volume 2021-June, pages 16–30.

Mikel Artetxe, Gorka Labaka, and Eneko Agirre. 2016. Learning principled bilingual mappings of word embeddings while preserving monolingual invariance. In *Proceedings of the 2016 Conference on Empirical Methods in Natural Language Processing*, pages 2289–2294, Austin, Texas. Association for Computational Linguistics.

Mikel Artetxe, Gorka Labaka, and Eneko Agirre. 2017. Learning bilingual word embeddings with (almost) no bilingual data. In *Proceedings of the 55th Annual Meeting of the Association for Computational Linguistics*, pages 451–462.

Mikel Artetxe, Gorka Labaka, and Eneko Agirre. 2018a. Generalizing and improving bilingual word embedding mappings with a multi-step framework of linear transformations. In *Proceedings of the Thirty-Second AAAI Conference on Artificial Intelligence*, pages 5012–5019.

Mikel Artetxe, Gorka Labaka, Iñigo Lopez-Gazpio, and Eneko Agirre. 2018b. Uncovering divergent linguistic information in word embeddings with lessons for intrinsic and extrinsic evaluation. In *Proceedings of the 22nd Conference on Computational Natural Language Learning*, pages 282–291, Brussels, Belgium. Association for Computational Linguistics.

Gioia Baldissin, Dominik Schlechtweg, and Sabine Schulte im Walde. 2022. DiaWUG: A Dataset for Diatopic Lexical Semantic Variation in Spanish. In *Proceedings of the 13th Language Resources and Evaluation Conference*, Marseille, France. European Language Resources Association.

Nikhil Bansal, Avrim Blum, and Shuchi Chawla. 2004. Correlation clustering. *Machine Learning*, 56(1-3):89–113.

Pierpaolo Basile, Annalina Caputo, Tommaso Caselli, Pierluigi Cassotti, and Rossella Varvara. 2020. Overview of the EVALITA 2020 Diachronic Lexical Semantics (DIACR-Ita) Task. In *Proceedings of the 7th evaluation campaign of Natural Language Processing and Speech tools for Italian (EVALITA 2020)*, Online. CEUR.org.

Sorana-Daniela Bolboaca and Lorentz Jäntschi. 2006. Pearson versus spearman, kendall's tau correlation analysis on structure-activity relationships of biologic active compounds. *Leonardo Journal of Sciences*, 5(9):179–200.

Alexis Conneau, Kartikay Khandelwal, Naman Goyal, Vishrav Chaudhary, Guillaume Wenzek, Francisco Guzmán, Edouard Grave, Myle Ott, Luke Zettlemoyer, and Veselin Stoyanov. 2019. Unsupervised cross-lingual representation learning at scale. *arXiv preprint arXiv:1911.02116*.

Jacob Devlin, Ming-Wei Chang, Kenton Lee, and Kristina Toutanova. 2019. BERT: Pre-training of deep bidirectional transformers for language understanding. In *Proceedings of the 2019 Conference of the North American Chapter of the Association for Computational Linguistics: Human Language Technologies, Volume 1 (Long and Short Papers)*, pages 4171–4186, Minneapolis, Minnesota. Association for Computational Linguistics.

Gonzalo Donoso and David Sanchez. 2017. Dialectometric analysis of language variation in twitter. In *Proceedings of the Fourth Workshop on NLP for Similar Languages, Varieties and Dialects*, pages 16–25, Valencia, Spain.

W. L. Hamilton, J. Leskovec, and D. Jurafsky. 2016. Cultural shift or linguistic drift? Comparing two computational measures of semantic change. In *Proceedings of the 2016 Conference on Empirical Methods in Natural Language Processing*, pages 2116–2121, Austin, Texas.

Simon Hengchen, Nina Tahmasebi, Dominik Schlechtweg, and Haim Dubossarsky. 2021. Challenges for Computational Lexical Semantic Change. In Nina Tahmasebi, Lars Borin, Adam Jatowt, Yang Xu, and Simon Hengchen, editors, *Computational Approaches to Semantic Change*, volume Language Variation, chapter 11. Language Science Press, Berlin.

Daniil Homskiy and Nikolay Arefyev. 2022. Deepmistake at lscdiscovery: Can a multilingual word-in-context model replace human annotators? In *Proceedings of the 3rd International Workshop on Computational Approaches to Historical Language Change*, Dublin, Ireland. Association for Computational Linguistics.

Matthew Honnibal, Ines Montani, Sofie Van Landeghem, and Adriane Boyd. 2020. spaCy: Industrial-strength Natural Language Processing in Python.

Jens Kaiser, Dominik Schlechtweg, Sean Papay, and Sabine Schulte im Walde. 2020a. IMS at SemEval-2020 Task 1: How low can you go? Dimensionality in Lexical Semantic Change Detection. In *Proceedings of the 14th International Workshop on Semantic Evaluation*, Barcelona, Spain. Association for Computational Linguistics.

Jens Kaiser, Dominik Schlechtweg, and Sabine Schulte im Walde. 2020b. OP-IMS @ DIACR-Ita: Back to the Roots: SGNS+OP+CD still rocks Semantic Change Detection. In *Proceedings of the 7th evaluation campaign of Natural Language Processing and Speech tools for Italian (EVALITA 2020)*, Online. CEUR.org. Winning Submission!

Kseniia Kashleva, Alexander Shein, Elizaveta Tukhtina, and Svetlana Vydrina. 2022. Hse at lscdiscovery in spanish: Clustering and profiling for lexical semantic change discovery. In *Proceedings of the 3rd International Workshop on Computational Approaches to Historical Language Change*, Dublin, Ireland. Association for Computational Linguistics.

Artem Kudisov and Nikolay Arefyev. 2022. Bos at lscdiscovery: Lexical substitution for interpretable lexical semantic change detection. In *Proceedings of the 3rd International Workshop on Computational Approaches to Historical Language Change*, Dublin, Ireland. Association for Computational Linguistics.

Sinan Kurtyigit, Maike Park, Dominik Schlechtweg, Jonas Kuhn, and Sabine Schulte im Walde. 2021. Lexical semantic change discovery. In *Proceedings of the 59th Annual Meeting of the Association for Computational Linguistics and the 11th International Joint Conference on Natural Language Processing (Volume 1: Long Papers)*, Online. Association for Computational Linguistics.

Andrey Kutuzov and Mario Giulianelli. 2020. UiO-UvA at SemEval-2020 Task 1: Contextualised Embeddings for Lexical Semantic Change Detection. In *Proceedings of the 14th International Workshop on Semantic Evaluation*, Barcelona, Spain. Association for Computational Linguistics.

Andrey Kutuzov, Lilja Øvrelid, Terrence Szymanski, and Erik Velldal. 2018. Diachronic word embeddings and semantic shifts: a survey. In *Proceedings of the 27th International Conference on Computational Linguistics*, pages 1384–1397, Santa Fe, New Mexico, USA. Association for Computational Linguistics.

Andrey Kutuzov and Lidia Pivovarova. 2021. Rushifteval: a shared task on semantic shift detection for russian. *Komp'yuternaya Lingvistika i Intellektual'nye Tekhnologii: Dialog conference*.

Andrey Kutuzov, Lidia Pivovarova, and Mario Giulianelli. 2021. Grammatical profiling for semantic change detection. In *Proceedings of the 25th Conference on Computational Natural Language Learning*, pages 423–434, Online. Association for Computational Linguistics.

Severin Laicher, Sinan Kurtyigit, Dominik Schlechtweg, Jonas Kuhn, and Sabine Schulte im Walde. 2021. Explaining and improving BERT performance on lexical semantic change detection. In *Proceedings of the 16th Conference of the European Chapter of the Association for Computational Linguistics: Student Research Workshop*, pages 192–202, Online. Association for Computational Linguistics.

Jianhua Lin. 1991. Divergence measures based on the shannon entropy. *IEEE Transactions on Information theory*, 37:145–151.

Federico Martelli, Najla Kalach, Gabriele Tola, and Roberto Navigli. 2021. SemEval-2021 task 2: Multilingual and cross-lingual word-in-context disambiguation (MCL-WiC). In *Proceedings of the 15th International Workshop on Semantic Evaluation (SemEval-2021)*, pages 24–36, Online. Association for Computational Linguistics.

Tomas Mikolov, Kai Chen, Greg Corrado, and Jeffrey Dean. 2013a. Efficient estimation of word representations in vector space. In *1st International Conference on Learning Representations, ICLR 2013, Scottsdale, Arizona, USA, May 2-4, 2013, Workshop Track Proceedings*.

Tomas Mikolov, Ilya Sutskever, Kai Chen, Greg Corrado, and Jeffrey Dean. 2013b. Distributed representations of words and phrases and their compositionality. In *Proceedings of NIPS*.

Riccardo Orlando, Simone Conia, Fabrizio Brignone, Francesco Cecconi, and Roberto Navigli. 2021. AMuSE-WSD: An all-in-one multilingual system for easy Word Sense Disambiguation. In *Proceedings of the 2021 Conference on Empirical Methods in Natural Language Processing: System Demonstrations*, pages 298–307, Online and Punta Cana, Dominican Republic. Association for Computational Linguistics.

Tommaso Pasini, Alessandro Raganato, Roberto Navigli, et al. 2021. Xl-wsd: An extra-large and cross-lingual evaluation framework for word sense disambiguation. In *Proceedings of the AAAI Conference on Artificial Intelligence*. AAAI Press.

Martin Pömsl and Roman Lyapin. 2020. CIRCE at SemEval-2020 Task 1: Ensembling Context-Free and Context-Dependent Word Representations. In *Proceedings of the 14th International Workshop on Semantic Evaluation*, Barcelona, Spain. Association for Computational Linguistics.

Ondřej Pražák, Pavel Přibákň, Stephen Taylor, and Jakub Sido. 2020. UWB at SemEval-2020 Task 1: Lexical Semantic Change Detection. In *Proceedings of the 14th International Workshop on Semantic Evaluation*, Barcelona, Spain. Association for Computational Linguistics.

Maxim Rachinskiy and Nikolay Arefyev. 2022. Glossreader at lscdiscovery: Train to select a proper gloss in english – discover lexical semantic change in spanish. In *Proceedings of the 3rd International Workshop on Computational Approaches to Historical Language Change*, Dublin, Ireland. Association for Computational Linguistics.

Julia Rodina and Andrey Kutuzov. 2020. RuSemShift: a dataset of historical lexical semantic change in Russian. In *Proceedings of the 28th International Conference on Computational Linguistics (COLING 2020)*. Association for Computational Linguistics.

Ana Sabina Uban, Alina Maria Cristea, Anca Daniela Dinu, Simona Georgescu, and Laurentiu Zoicas. 2022. Cotohili at lscdiscovery: the role of linguistic features in predicting semantic change. In *Proceedings of the 3rd International Workshop on Computational Approaches to Historical Language Change*, Dublin, Ireland. Association for Computational Linguistics.

Dominik Schlechtweg. 2022. *Human and Computational Measurement of Lexical Semantic Change*. Ph.D. thesis, University of Stuttgart, Stuttgart, Germany.

Dominik Schlechtweg, Anna Hätty, Marco del Tredici, and Sabine Schulte im Walde. 2019. A Wind of Change: Detecting and Evaluating Lexical Semantic Change across Times and Domains. In *Proceedings of the 57th Annual Meeting of the Association for Computational Linguistics*, pages 732–746, Florence, Italy. Association for Computational Linguistics.

Dominik Schlechtweg, Barbara McGillivray, Simon Hengchen, Haim Dubossarsky, and Nina Tahmasebi. 2020. SemEval-2020 Task 1: Unsupervised Lexical Semantic Change Detection. In *Proceedings of the 14th International Workshop on Semantic Evaluation*, Barcelona, Spain. Association for Computational Linguistics.

Dominik Schlechtweg and Sabine Schulte im Walde. 2020. Simulating Lexical Semantic Change from Sense-Annotated Data. In *The Evolution of Language: Proceedings of the 13th International Conference (EvoLang13)*.

Dominik Schlechtweg and Sabine Schulte im Walde. submitted. Clustering Word Usage Graphs: A Flexible Framework to Measure Changes in Contextual Word Meaning.

Dominik Schlechtweg, Sabine Schulte im Walde, and Stefanie Eckmann. 2018. Diachronic Usage Relatedness (DURel): A framework for the annotation of lexical semantic change. In *Proceedings of the 2018 Conference of the North American Chapter of the Association for Computational Linguistics: Human Language Technologies*, pages 169–174, New Orleans, Louisiana.

Dominik Schlechtweg, Nina Tahmasebi, Simon Hengchen, Haim Dubossarsky, and Barbara McGillivray. 2021. DWUG: A large resource of diachronic word usage graphs in four languages. In *Proceedings of the 2021 Conference on Empirical Methods in Natural Language Processing*, pages 7079–7091, Online and Punta Cana, Dominican Republic. Association for Computational Linguistics.

Milan Straka and Jana Straková. 2017. Tokenizing, POS tagging, lemmatizing and parsing UD 2.0 with UDPipe. In *Proceedings of the CoNLL 2017 Shared Task: Multilingual Parsing from Raw Text to Universal Dependencies*, pages 88–99, Vancouver, Canada. Association for Computational Linguistics.

Nina Tahmasebi, Lars Borin, and Adam Jatowt. 2021. Survey of computational approaches to lexical semantic change detection.

Daniela Teodorescu, Spencer McIntosh von der Ohe, and Grzegorz Kondrak. 2022. Ualberta at lscdiscovery: Lexical semantic change detection via word sense disambiguation. In *Proceedings of the 3rd International Workshop on Computational Approaches to Historical Language Change*, Dublin, Ireland. Association for Computational Linguistics.

Jörg Tiedemann. 2012. Parallel data, tools and interfaces in opus. In *Proceedings of the Eight International Conference on Language Resources and Evaluation (LREC'12)*, Istanbul, Turkey. European Language Resources Association (ELRA).

Appendix

A Lemmatization

Manual inspection showed that spaCy sometimes yielded erroneous lemmatization. This happened more frequently for sentences in the old corpus and for tokens at the beginning of sentences as shown in the example below:

Example:
"Decidióse ésta por Teresa la expósita, y así se vio a la vagamunda tomar bajo su amparo a la pobre desheredada como ella."
Lemmatization:
Decidióse este por Teresa el expósita , y así él ver a el vagamunda tomar bajo su amparo a el pobre desheredado como él .

As can be seen, the lemma of the word *Decidióse* was not found, nor was the word converted to lowercase. SpaCy version 3.1.1 with es_core_news_md (3.1.0) was used.

B Target indices of annotated usages

In the first version of the extracted word usages which were uploaded to the DURel interface for annotation there were frequent errors for the target word indices. As a result, the wrong target words were marked in these usages. However, annotators were instructed to search for the correct target words and to judge these instead. We corrected the indices for the data provided to participants during the shared task. However, we later noticed that some indices included punctuation immediately following the target word as shown below:

Example
lemma: sexo
context: 136. Los apellidos de familia no varían de terminación para los diferentes **sexos;** y así se dice «don Pablo Herrera», «doña Juana Hurtado», «doña Isabel Donoso». 137 (b).
indexes_target_token: 75:81

After the shared task we uploaded a data version with corrected indices.

BOS at LSCDiscovery: Lexical Substitution for Interpretable Lexical Semantic Change Detection

Artem Kudisov[▽] **Nikolay Arefyev**[◇,▽,△]

[▽]Lomonosov Moscow State University / Moscow, Russia
[△]National Research University Higher School of Economics / Moscow, Russia
[◇]Samsung Research Center Russia / Moscow, Russia
dark.artbeam@gmail.com, nick.arefyev@gmail.com

Abstract

We propose a solution for the LSCDiscovery shared task on Lexical Semantic Change Detection in Spanish. Our approach is based on generating lexical substitutes that describe old and new senses of a given word. This approach achieves the second best result in sense loss and sense gain detection subtasks. By observing those substitutes that are specific for only one time period, one can understand which senses were obtained or lost. This allows providing more detailed information about semantic change to the user and makes our method interpretable.

1 Introduction

LSCDiscovery is a shared task on Lexical Semantic Change Detection (LSCD) in Spanish (D. Zamora-Reina et al., 2022). The participants were provided with two corpora in Spanish, corresponding to 1810-1906 and 1994-2020 respectively, and were asked to solve two subtasks. In the first subtask the participants were asked to rank the given list of about 4K words according to the degree of their semantic change. The second subtask required to determine for each given word if its senses occurring in two corpora are different (and optionally, if it has acquired some new senses, and if it has lost any old ones).

2 Background

Our approach is based on the bag-of-substitutes (BOS) representation of word meaning in context (Başkaya et al., 2013; Arefyev and Zhikov, 2020). Lexical substitutes are those words that can replace a given target word in a given text fragment without making this fragment ungrammatical or substantially changing the meaning of the target word. For ambiguous words, lexical substitutes depend on their meaning expressed in a particular context. For instance, some reasonable substitutes for the word *fly* in the sentence *A noisy fly sat on my shoulder* are *bug*, *beetle*, *butterfly*, *firefly*, *insect*, etc. But in the sentence *We will fly to London* they are different: *walk*, *run*, *bike*, etc.

In order to generate lexical substitutes, we employ the XLM-R[1] masked language model (Conneau et al., 2020). This model was pre-trained on 2.5T of data in 100 languages as a masked language model, i.e. it received text fragments with some tokens hidden (replaced with the special `<mask>` token) and was trained to guess those hidden tokens by their context. This kind of pre-training is partially aligned with the lexical substitution task because the model can predict words compatible with the given context. However, there are no guarantees that these words are similar or related by meaning to the target word. Suitable types of lexical substitutes (e.g., synonyms, hypernyms, co-hyponyms) and suitable degree of their similarity to the target word depend on the target task and can be controlled with various techniques explored in (Arefyev et al., 2020). In our solution, we employ the dynamic patterns proposed by Amrami and Goldberg (2018) and explained in 3.2.

Unlike the traditional bag-of-words representation, which contains those words that occur in a text fragment, the BOS representation is built from lexical substitutes. Thus, it better represents the meaning of some specific target word in a given text fragment rather than the whole fragment in general. Clustering of the BOS vectors is a successful approach to solve the Word Sense Induction (WSI) task, i.e. to discover senses of ambiguous words. This approach was explored in many papers, including (Başkaya et al., 2013; Amrami and Goldberg, 2018, 2019; Arefyev et al., 2019, 2020) among others. Also, a substitution-based WSI model was employed to solve the LSCD task in (Arefyev and Zhikov, 2020; Arefyev and Bykov, 2021). However, in our solution we avoid solving the more

[1]The pre-trained xlmr.large from fairseq library is used without any fine-tuning.

Proceedings of the 3rd Workshop on Computational Approaches to Historical Language Change, pages 165 - 172

<mask>-(y-T)		<mask><mask>-(y-T)		<mask>-(incluso-T)	
Substitute	Prob.	Substitute	Prob.	Substitute	Prob.
documentos (documents)	0.367	archivos (records)	0.016	documentos (documents)	0.391
libros (books)	0.160	escritos (letters)	0.012	libros (books)	0.082
datos (data)	0.052	informes (reports)	0.010	datos (data)	0.039
actos (acts)	0.036	dos documentos (two documents)	0.010	textos (texts)	0.037
textos (texts)	0.032	expedientes (records)	0.008	contratos (contracts)	0.014

Table 1: For the word *actas* (*reports*) in *ayer recibimos dos actas literales* (*yesterday we received two verbatim reports*), 5 most probable substitutes with 1 or 2 subwords are shown. The patterns with *y* (*and*) and *incluso* (*including*).

general and probably more difficult WSI task that requires clustering. Instead, we propose methods to directly obtain LSCD predictions from the BOS vectors.

3 Model description

For each target word we sample some examples of its usage from both corpora and generate lexical substitutes for them. Then we build two sets of BOS vectors for old and new examples, describing old and new senses of the word respectively. Finally, the distances from old to new examples are calculated, and their average is returned as the predicted score of graded change. Following previous works on LSCD (Giulianelli et al., 2020; Laicher et al., 2021), we will denote this average as the Average Pairwise Distance (APD). Notice that our vector representation is very different from those works.

For the second subtask, if APD is greater than a certain threshold, we predict that this word has changed its meaning. To determine whether it has acquired new senses and whether any old senses were lost, we propose three different methods based on pairwise distances.

3.1 Collected data

For each target word w_i, we lemmatize[2] both corpora and retrieve all examples with w_i in different grammatical forms. Then we take the same number N_i of examples from the old and the modern set of examples.[3]

3.2 Substitute generation

For each example we generate several types of substitutes with different dynamic patterns, post-

[2]We used the Spanish lemmatizer from Spacy proposed by the organizers.

[3]If possible, $N_i = 100$ examples are sampled without replacement from each set. Otherwise, we take all $N_i < 100$ examples from the smaller set and sample the same number of examples from another set.

Pattern	weight
<mask>	0.25
<mask>-(y-T)	0.25
T-(y-<mask>)	0.25
<mask>-(incluso-T)	0.0625
T-(incluso-<mask>)	0.0625
<mask>-(por-ejemplo-T)	0.0625
T-(por-ejemplo-<mask>)	0.0625

Table 2: In LS_m1_7, we employ 7 single-subword patterns with *y* (*and*), *incluso* (*including*) and *por ejemplo* (*for example*) with the specified weights.

LS_m1_2 patterns	LS_m2_2 patterns	weight
<mask>-(y-T)	<mask><mask>-(y-T)	0.5
T-(y-<mask>)	<mask><mask>-(y-T)	0.5

Table 3: In LS_m1_2 and LS_m2_2 we employ 2 single-subword and 2 two-subword patterns respectively.

process them and combine together to get a single vector representation. Dynamic patterns are similar to the Hearst patterns by nature (Hearst, 1992). They were proposed in (Amrami and Goldberg, 2018) to obtain from masked language models those substitutes that do not only fit the given context, but also are similar or related to the target word by meaning. For instance, using patterns with the Spanish conjunction *y* (English: *and*) we hope to obtain mostly co-hyponyms of the target word, while patterns with the adverb *incluso* (English: *including*) shall bias the model towards generating hypernyms or hyponyms, depending on the position of the target word. Table 1 shows some examples.

Table 2 lists all dynamic patterns we use. All patterns contain the special token <mask> that XLM-R is asked to recover, and some of them contain the variable T representing the target word. Given a pattern and an example for some target word, first we replace the target word with this pattern, and then replace the variable T (if any) back with the target word. For simplicity, let us consider an example in English. Given the sentence

We can fly to London and using the pattern *<mask> (and T)*, we first obtain *We can <mask> (and T) to London*, and finally have *We can <mask> (and fly) to London*.

The vocabulary of XLM-R consists of 250K subwords in 100 different languages, which are sometimes whole frequent words, but most often pieces of words. To better describe word meaning, we generate substitutes consisting of different number of subwords. To achieve this, we apply patterns with several <mask> tokens, for instance,*<mask><mask> (y T)*.

To find probable sequences of subwords that could fill the <mask> tokens, we apply a slightly modified greedy decoding strategy. For the leftmost <mask> token, $topK = 150$ most probable subwords are predicted first. Then for each of those subwords we generate one continuation using greedy decoding. Below we will say that a substitute is not generated for a particular pattern in a particular example if it was not among $topK$ substitutes generated this way. For computational reasons, we generated only substitutes with one or two subwords and did not apply beam search for decoding. Examples of two-subword substitutes are in table 1.

3.3 Substitute post-processing and combination

Next, we post-process all substitutes for each example: convert them to lower case, remove all words except for the last one from multi-word substitutes, apply stemming.[4] After post-processing, we sum the probabilities of duplicated substitutes.

For each example, we combine substitutes generated for different patterns by calculating the weighted average of the corresponding probability distributions. In **LS_m1** and **LS_m2** (Lexical Substitution with one-subword substitutes and two-subword substitutes respectively), for combination we use patterns and weights presented in Tables 2 and 3. The weights were selected based on a few experiments on the development set consisting of 20 words, so these weights are likely suboptimal. It is possible that one of the substitutes is not generated by XLM-R for a certain pattern. In this case, during combination we assume that the corresponding probability is equal to the minimal probability among all substitutes generated for this pattern.

[4]The Spanish stemming from nltk.stem.snowball was used.

Model/Team	JSD,SPR	COMPARE,SPR
baselines		
baseline1	**0.543** (4)	**0.561** (3)
baseline2	0.092 (8)	0.088 (6)
best results of other teams		
myrachins	**0.735** (1)	**0.842** (1)
UsrD7	0.702 (2)	0.829 (2)
aishein	0.553 (3)	0.558 (4)
our results		
#LS_m1_7+APD	-0.125 (9)	-0.129 (8)
our post-evaluation results		
LS_m1_7+APD	**0.584** (3*)	0.598 (3*)
LS_m1_2+APD	0.562 (3*)	0.562 (3*)
LS_m2_2+APD	0.576 (3*)	**0.637** (3*)

Table 4: Graded Change Discovery results. # denotes the buggy implementation. * denotes possible ranks of the corresponding results in the leaderboard.

3.4 BOS vectors

For each target word w_i we build $2N_i$ BOS vectors for old and new examples. These vectors are basically bag-of-word vectors built for $topK$ most probable substitutes for each example. Only substitutes that were generated for more than 3% and less than 90% of examples of the target word are taken into account[5].

3.5 Graded Change Discovery

APD (Average Pairwise Distance). After building the BOS vectors, we calculate the cosine distance from each old to each new example, resulting in a matrix of size $N_i \times N_i$. The APD is calculated by averaging all cells in this matrix. Finally, we sort test words according to their APDs and submit their ranks as the predicted change scores.[6]

3.6 Binary Change Detection

For the main Binary Change Detection subtask, if the calculated APD is greater than the certain $threshold$[7], then we predict that this word has changed its meaning. In this case we also try to determine if it has acquired new senses and if it has lost some old ones (sense loss and sense gain detection subtasks). We try three methods to determine that.

[5]We used CountVectorizer from scikit-learn, where $min\_df = 0.03$ was selected in range from 0 to 0.05 with 0.01 step and $max\_df = 0.9$ was selected in range from 0.85 to 1 with 0.01 step.

[6]There was a mistake in the original implementation of the ranking procedure. After the competition we fixed it, which significantly improved the results of this method (see table 4 for comparison).

[7]$threshold = 0.8$ was selected on the development set in the range from 0.7 to 0.9 with 0.05 step.

Model/Team	CH, F1	GAIN, F1	LOSS, F1
baselines			
baseline1	0.537 (9)	NaN (8)	NaN (6)
baseline2	0.222 (10)	0.211 (7)	0.000 (6)
best results of other teams			
myrachins	**0.716** (1)	**0.491** (3)	**0.688** (1)
dteodore	0.709 (2)	0.000 (8)	0.000 (6)
rombek	0.687 (3)	0.490 (4)	0.593 (3)
our results			
LS_m1_7+AID	**0.658** (4*)	0.393 (6*)	0.137 (6*)
LS_m2_2+min	0.636 (6*)	0.418 (6*)	**0.610** (2*)
LS_m1_7+perc.	**0.658** (4)	**0.520** (2)	0.600 (2)
our post-evaluation results			
LS_m1_2+AID	0.628 (7*)	0.4 (6*)	0.076 (6*)
LS_m1_2+min	0.628 (7*)	**0.583** (2*)	0.387 (5*)
LS_m1_2+perc.	0.628 (7*)	0.486 (5*)	**0.608** (2*)
LS_m2_2+AID	0.636 (6*)	0.382 (6*)	0.193 (6*)
LS_m2_2+perc.	0.636 (6*)	0.376 (6*)	0.600 (2*)
LS_m1_7+min	**0.658** (4*)	0.533 (2*)	0.564 (5*)

Table 5: Binary Change Detection results. * denotes possible ranks of the corresponding results in the leaderboard.

AID (Average Inner Distance). We calculate APDs between only new examples AID_1 and between only old examples AID_2. If $AID_1 > (AID_2 - b_1)$, we predict that a new sense appeared. If $AID_2 > (AID_1 - b_2)$, we predict that an old sense is lost.[8] Thus, we assume that a difference in average inner distances for two sets of examples indicates that there is a difference in underlying sets of senses.

min. We calculate an $N_i \times N_i$ matrix of pairwise distances from old to new examples and assume that if some new sense appeared, then a new example exists that is far from all old examples. Thus, if there is at least one new example whose minimal distance to the old examples is greater than some $threshold$ [9], we predict that a new sense appeared. Sense loss is determined symmetrically.

perc. (percentile). This is similar to the previous method, but we calculate the 5th percentile instead of the minimum, i.e. we allow at most 5% of examples from the old corpus to be closer to an example of the new sense from the new corpus than the specified threshold. We assume that this should make the model less sensitive to noisy examples and more stable.

[8] $b_1 = 0.03$, $b_2 = 0$. These values were selected on the development set in the range from -0.1 to 0.1 with 0.01 step.

[9] $threshold = 0.8$ was selected on the development set in the range from 0.7 to 0.9 with 0.05 step.

Model	GAIN,F1	LOSS,F1
LS_m1_2+AID	0.4 (6*)	0.076 (6*)
LS_m1_2+min	**0.583** (2*)	0.387 (5*)
LS_m1_2+perc.	0.486 (5*)	0.608 (2*)
LS_m2_2+AID	0.382 (6*)	0.193 (6*)
LS_m2_2+min	0.418 (6*)	**0.610** (2*)
LS_m2_2+perc.	0.376 (6*)	0.600 (2*)
LS_m1_7+AID	0.393 (6*)	0.137 (6*)
LS_m1_7+min	0.533 (2*)	0.564 (5*)
LS_m1_7+perc.	0.520 (2)	0.600 (2)

Table 6: Comparison of aggregation methods. * denotes possible ranks of the corresponding results in the leaderboard.

4 Experiments and Results

4.1 Phase 1: Graded Change Discovery

In this subtask, it was required to rank about 4K target words according to their degree of semantic change (the higher rank, the stronger change). The final quality of ranking was evaluated for 60 hidden words only by the Spearman's correlation with the gold ranks (Bolboaca and Jäntschi, 2006).

Table 4 provides the results for the first phase. Our original implementation of the ranking procedure had mistakes in the ranking procedure, so the results are poor. After the competition, we fixed the mistake and obtained the correct results, which are comparable to the 3rd best participant in the leaderboard.

LS_m1_2 and **LS_m2_2** differ only in the number of masks in the used patterns. So comparing their scores, we can say that using two-subword substitutes is more preferable than one-subword substitutes. In **LS_m2_7** seven patterns are combined compared to two patters in **LS_m1_2**, this gives a significant improvement despite somewhat arbitrarily selected weights. Developing some principled ways of finding promising dynamic patterns and weights for their combination is a reasonable direction for future work. **LS_m1_7** has a slightly higher JSD,SPR score, but its COMPARE,SPR score is lower and it uses a more complex pattern combination than **LS_m2_2**. A more detailed investigation is presented in Appendix A.

4.2 Phase 2: Binary Change Detection

In this subtask the participants were asked to determine if target words have changed their meanings. And if so, how exactly (have acquired and/or have lost senses). Three F1-scores are calculated: Binary Change Detection (CH), Sense Gain Detection (GAIN), Sense Loss Detection (LOSS). Results are presented in Table 5 where we have the 2nd best submission for GAIN and LOSS optional subtasks.

LS_m1_2 + APD and **LS_m2_m2 + APD** have 0.628 and 0.636 CH,F1 scores respectively, which means that using two-subword substitutes is slightly better than one-subword. But in the case of **LS_m1_7 + APD** we already get 0.658 CH,F1 resulting in the 4th rank.

Using **AID** method does result in good GAIN,F1 and LOSS,F1 scores (Table 6). At the same time **min** and **percentile** show a better results but they highly depend on used LS patterns, i.e., in the some cases these methods improves only GAIN,F1 or LOSS,F1 scores, but not both of them.

5 Discriminative substitutes

The main advantage of LS-based models is their interpretability. We can roughly understand word meanings looking at the discriminative substitutes, i.e. the substitutes specific for a particular subset of examples.

Table 7 provides some examples for *disco* (*disc*) and *satélite* (*satellite*). We take old examples O and those new examples M, that were determined by LS_m1+percentile model as being far away from O. Then we find substitutes with the largest ratio $\frac{P(w|M)}{P(w|O)}$[10], i.e. those substitutes that are rarely generated for old examples but frequently generated for new examples that are not similar to any old examples.

Disco (disc)		Satélite (satellite)	
LP	0.72/0.00	CD	1.00/0.00
EP	0.55/0.00	video	1.00/0.00
documentos	0.55/0.00	internet	1.00/0.00
videos	0.50/0.00	televisión	0.88/0.00
mp	0.50/0.00	FM	0.88/0.00
anime	0.44/0.00	señal	0.88/0.00
memoria	0.44/0.00	Internet	0.88/0.00
PC	0.44/0.00	canal	0.88/0.00
USB	0.44/0.00	TV	0.88/0.00
b	0.44/0.00	web	0.88/0.00
MP	0.44/0.00	vídeo	0.77/0.00

Table 7: Discriminative substitutes generated for the `<mask>` *(y T)* pattern. The probabilities $P(w|M)$ and $P(w|O)$ are shown for each substitute. Documentos is 'documents', señal is 'signal', memoria is 'memory' and canal is 'channel'.

From the Table 7 we can see that *disco* (*disc*) and *satélite* (*satellite*) have acquired new senses as *a data storage device* and *satellite television* respectively.

[10] If the word denominator is 0, we demand $P(w|M)$ to be greater 0.2, otherwise we don't consider such word.

6 Efficiency

The set of the target words proposed in Phase 1 was supposed to be a challenge for participants due to its size. For 4385 words given we have collected about 777K examples. Generation of substitutes for all examples took 13 GPU-hours and 310 GPU-hours for each one-mask and two-mask pattern respectively on V100 GPUs. All other steps took incomparably less time.

7 Conclusion

We have proposed an interpretable approach to lexical semantic change detection. This approach shows the 2nd best result for sense loss and sense gain detection subtasks. It provides techniques to understand which senses were obtained or lost by a word.

Acknowledgements

We are grateful to our anonymous reviewers. This research was partially supported by the Basic Research Program at the HSE University and through computational resources of HPC facilities at HSE University (Kostenetskiy et al., 2021).

References

Asaf Amrami and Yoav Goldberg. 2018. Word sense induction with neural bilm and symmetric patterns. In *Proceedings of the 2018 Conference on Empirical Methods in Natural Language Processing*, pages 4860–4867.

Asaf Amrami and Yoav Goldberg. 2019. Towards better substitution-based word sense induction. arXiv.

Nikolay Arefyev and Bykov. 2021. An interpretable approach to lexical semantic change detection with lexical substitution. In *Computational linguistics and intellectual technologies: Papers from the annual conference Dialogue*, 20.

Nikolay Arefyev, Boris Sheludko, and Tatiana Aleksashina. 2019. Combining Neural Language Models for Word Sense Induction. In *Analysis of Images, Social Networks and Texts*, page 105–121. Springer International Publishing.

Nikolay Arefyev, Boris Sheludko, Alexander Podolskiy, and Alexander Panchenko. 2020. Always keep your target in mind: Studying semantics and improving performance of neural lexical substitution. In *Proceedings of the 28th International Conference on Computational Linguistics*, pages 1242–1255, Barcelona, Spain.

Nikolay Arefyev and Vasily Zhikov. 2020. BOS at SemEval-2020 task 1: Word sense induction via lexical substitution for lexical semantic change detection. In *Proceedings of the Fourteenth Workshop on Semantic Evaluation*, pages 171–179, Barcelona (online). International Committee for Computational Linguistics.

Osman Başkaya, Enis Sert, Volkan Cirik, and Deniz Yuret. 2013. AI-KU: Using substitute vectors and co-occurrence modeling for word sense induction and disambiguation. In *Second Joint Conference on Lexical and Computational Semantics (*SEM), Volume 2: Proceedings of the Seventh International Workshop on Semantic Evaluation (SemEval 2013)*, pages 300–306, Atlanta, Georgia, USA. Association for Computational Linguistics.

Sorana-Daniela Bolboaca and Lorentz Jäntschi. 2006. Pearson versus spearman, kendall's tau correlation analysis on structure-activity relationships of biologic active compounds. *Leonardo Journal of Sciences*, 5(9):179–200.

Alexis Conneau, Kartikay Khandelwal, Naman Goyal, Vishrav Chaudhary, Guillaume Wenzek, Francisco Guzmán, Edouard Grave, Myle Ott, Luke Zettlemoyer, and Veselin Stoyanov. 2020. Unsupervised cross-lingual representation learning at scale. In *Proceedings of the 58th Annual Meeting of the Association for Computational Linguistics*, pages 8440–8451, Online. Association for Computational Linguistics.

Frank D. Zamora-Reina, Felipe Bravo-Marquez, and Dominik Schlechtweg. 2022. Lscdiscovery: A shared task on semantic change discovery and detection in spanish. In *Proceedings of the 3rd International Workshop on Computational Approaches to Historical Language Change*, Dublin, Ireland. Association for Computational Linguistics.

Mario Giulianelli, Marco Del Tredici, and Raquel Fernández. 2020. Analysing lexical semantic change with contextualised word representations. In *Proceedings of the 58th Annual Meeting of the Association for Computational Linguistics*, pages 3960–3973, Online. Association for Computational Linguistics.

Marti A Hearst. 1992. Automatic acquisition of hyponyms from large text corpora. In *Proceedings of the 14th conference on Computational linguistics-Volume 2*, pages 539–545. Association for Computational Linguistics.

P. S. Kostenetskiy, R. A. Chulkevich, and V. I. Kozyrev. 2021. HPC resources of the higher school of economics. *Journal of Physics: Conference Series*, 1740:012050.

Severin Laicher, Sinan Kurtyigit, Dominik Schlechtweg, Jonas Kuhn, and Sabine Schulte im Walde. 2021. Explaining and improving BERT performance on lexical semantic change detection. In *Proceedings of the 16th Conference of the European Chapter of the Association for Computational Linguistics: Student Research Workshop*, pages 192–202, Online. Association for Computational Linguistics.

A Substitute analysis

Our models mostly depend on the used LS patterns and ways of their combination. So it is important to make some investigations about them. In this section we study the following questions.

- Which single-subword pattern gives the best results and how these results depend on the number of substitutes generate (topk)?
- Is it better to use single-subword or multi-subword substitutes?
- Do brackets and dashes affect the results?

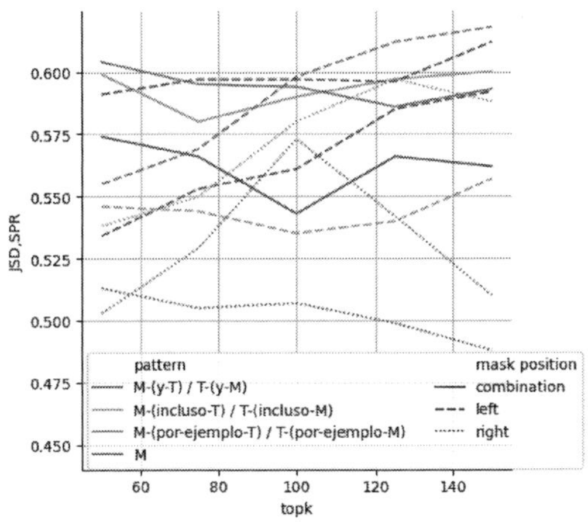

Figure 1: Dependence of the JSD,SPR score on the pattern and topk.

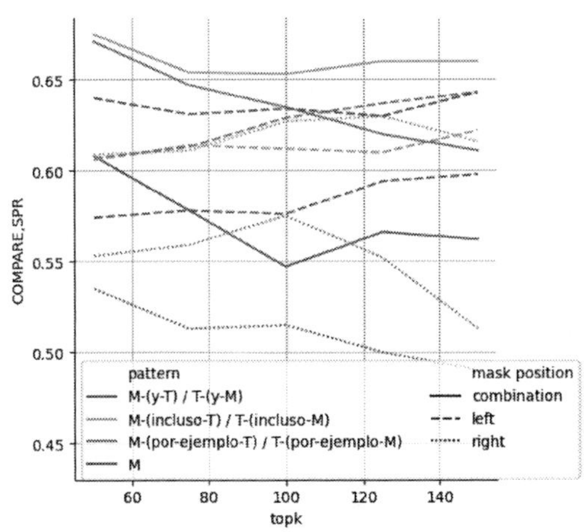

Figure 2: Dependence of the COMPARE,SPR score on the pattern and topk.

For brevity, we will use `M` instead of `<mask>` in the pattern descriptions. In the following figures `mask position` describes the position of the `<mask>` token. For example, if the pattern is *M (y T) / T (y M)*, `mask position=left` refers to the pattern *M (y T)*, and `mask position=right` refers to *T (y M)*. Finally, `mask position=combination` denotes the combination of these patterns with equal weights.

A.1 One-subword subword

In **LS_m1_7** we use 7 patterns with different weights, which were selected after only a few experiments on the development set. In this section we study how the results depend on the patterns and try to find simpler and more intuitive ways of the substitute combination. Figures 1 and 2 show JSD,SPR and COMPARE,SPR for different patterns.

It is interesting that in all cases the `left` patterns give better results than the `right` ones, except for the incluso-based patterns. Also in all cases the combination averages the results of both patterns, again except for the combination of incluso-based patterns which on the contrary improves the results.

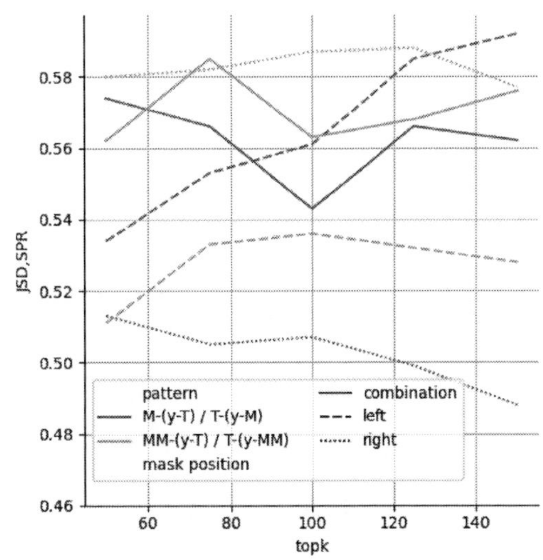

Figure 3: Comparison of one-subword and two-subword substitutes.

A.2 One-subword substitutes vs. two-subword substitutes

We assume that using more masks should improves results because this allows to generate more diverse substitutes. Figure 3 provides comparison of patterns with different number of masks. As we suspect, using *T (y MM)* pattern gives a much better results than *T (y M)*. However combination of two-mask patterns results in just slightly higher score and one-mask pattern *M (y T)* even outperforms *MM (y T)*.

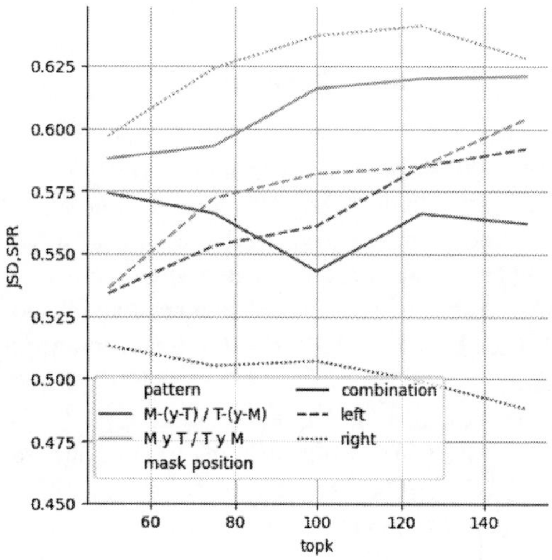

Figure 4: Comparison patterns with and without brackets.

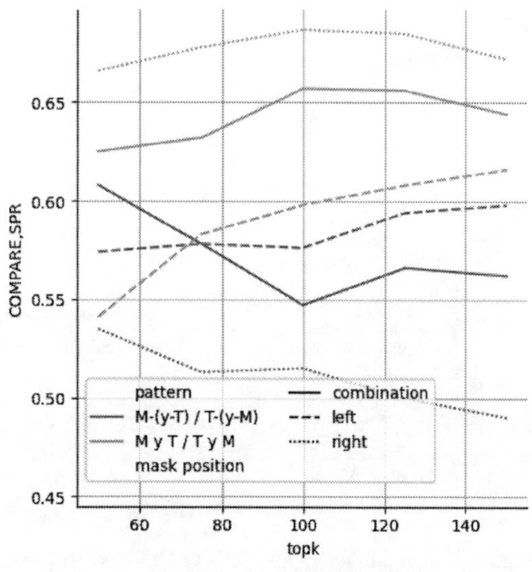

Figure 5: Comparison patterns with and without brackets.

A.3 Patterns without brackets and dashes

In the patterns discussed above we have extra dashes which were added by mistake and potentially could affect the results, so firstly we remove them from patterns. Also we have assumption that using brackets is not common thing in Spanish so such patterns could spoil generated substitutes and final results. To prove it we decide to compare `y`-based patterns with and without brackets and dashes.

In the Figures 4 and 5 we can see that in all cases refusal to use brackets and dashes improves our results quite well, especially the `right` pattern get around 0.1 growth in JSD,SPR and COMPARE,SPR scores.

DeepMistake at LSCDiscovery: Can a Multilingual Word-in-Context Model Replace Human Annotators?

Daniil Homskiy[▽] **Nikolay Arefyev**[◇,▽,△]

[▽]Lomonosov Moscow State University / Moscow, Russia
[△]National Research University Higher School of Economics / Moscow, Russia
[◇]Samsung Research Center Russia / Moscow, Russia
homdanil123@gmail.com, nick.arefyev@gmail.com

Abstract

In this paper we describe our solution of the LSCDiscovery shared task on Lexical Semantic Change Discovery (LSCD) in Spanish (D. Zamora-Reina et al., 2022). Our solution employs a Word-in-Context (WiC) model, which is trained to determine if a particular word has the same meaning in two given contexts. We basically try to replicate the annotation of the dataset for the shared task, but replacing human annotators with a neural network. In the graded change discovery subtask, our solution has achieved the 2nd best result. In the main binary change detection subtask, our F1-score is 0.655 compared to 0.716 of the best submission, corresponding to the 5th place. However, in the optional sense gain detection subtask we have outperformed all other participants.[1]

During the post-evaluation experiments we compared different ways to prepare WiC data in Spanish and fine-tune our model. We have found that it helps leaving only examples annotated as 1 (unrelated senses) and 4 (identical senses) rather than using 2x more examples including intermediate annotations. Generating additional examples from a WSD dataset also significantly improves the results.

1 Introduction

Given a list of words, a Lexical Semantic Change Detection (LSCD) system applied to diachronic corpora shall determine how these words change their meaning over time. The LSCDiscovery (D. Zamora-Reina et al., 2022) shared task on LSCD in Spanish consists of two main subtasks and a few optional ones. In the graded change discovery subtask, the participants were asked to rank 4385 words according to the degree of their change. In the binary change detection subtask, it was necessary to develop a binary classifier that finds among 60 given words those that have either lost some old senses, or obtained some new ones. Two optional binary subtasks required separately finding words with lost senses and words with new senses.

In order to annotate the test set for the shared task, for each word from the test set some examples were sampled from the old and the new corpus. Then human annotators were asked to annotate pairs of examples with scores from 1 to 4 according to the similarity of two occurrences of the same word by meaning. This kind of annotation is very similar to the Word-in-Context (WiC) task, which asks a model to determine if two occurrences of the same word have the same or different meaning.

2 Background

2.1 The Word-in-Context model

In order to solve the LSCD task, we address the Words-in-Context (WiC) task first. The WiC task is a simplified version of the Word Sense Disambiguation (WSD) task that can be reduced to binary classification. Each example in WiC consists of two occurrences of the same usually polysemous target word **w** (probably, in different grammatical forms) in two different contexts. The task is to determine if the target word has the same or different senses in two contexts. In our work we employ the Multilingual and Cross-Lingual Word-in-Context (MCL-WiC) dataset from SemEval-2021 Task2 (Martelli et al., 2021). Table 1 shows some statistics for this dataset.

We employ the WiC model proposed in (Davletov et al., 2021). In this model, the encoder from XLM-R (Conneau et al., 2020) is used to vectorize input examples. XLM-R is a Transformer-based neural network pre-trained as a masked language model (MLM) on about 2TB of texts in 100 languages. This not only makes our WiC model multilingual, but also enables zero-shot cross-lingual

[1]The code is available: https://github.com/Daniil153/DM-in-Spanish-LSCDiscovery

Proceedings of the 3rd Workshop on Computational Approaches to Historical Language Change, pages 173 - 179
May 26-27, 2022 ©2022 Association for Computational Linguistics

trasferability, i.e. after training on the MCL-WiC dataset it can be applied even to those languages that are not present in this dataset (for instance, Spanish).

The architecture of the WiC model is the following. Two input sentences are concatenated and fed into XLM-R in the following format:

`<s>sentence1</s>sentence2</s>`

For each sentence, the outputs of XLM-R on all subwords of the target word are averaged (mean pooling). This results in two embeddings for two occurrences of the target word. Then these two embeddings are combined and fed into the binary classification head (see details below).

2.2 The RuShiftEval-2021 shared task

Our solution for the graded change discovery subtask was initially developed during the RuShiftEval-2021 shared task on LSCD for the Russian language (Kutuzov and Pivovarova, 2021), where it was the second best system during the competition and outperformed the best system in the post-competition experiments (Arefyev et al., 2021). However, in this shared task Spearman's correlation with the gold COMPARE scores (Schlechtweg et al., 2018) was the only metric for evaluation unlike the LSCDiscovery shared task, which offers more diverse metrics and several subtasks.

The best results in RuShiftEval-2021 were achieved with the following hyperparameters and design choices. To combine the embeddings of two occurrences of the target word, the L1-distance between the normalized embeddings and the dot product between the normalized embeddings are concatenated ($(\|\bar{x}-\bar{y}\|_1, \langle\bar{x},\bar{y}\rangle)$). After batch normalization, this representation is fed into a linear classification head. All the weights of the network are fine-tuned with the cross-entropy loss. Two-step fine-tuning procedure consists of fine-tuning on examples in 6 languages from the training and the development sets of the MCL-WiC dataset, and then fine-tuning on examples in Russian from the RuSemShift (Rodina and Kutuzov, 2020) dataset, which served as the training and the development set in RuShiftEval-2021.

3 WiC-based LSCD

3.1 WiC training

To solve the Spanish LSCD task we used the WiC model with the architecture and hyperparameters

Subset/language	size	#words	Avg. len.
MCL-WiC			
en-en	8008	3728	48
ru-ru	708	352	41
fr-fr	708	352	46
ar-ar	708	354	45
zh-zh	708	342	-
en-nen*	32	16	51
RuSemShift			
ru-ru	3898	70	51
DWUG_es			
es-es$^{bin1}_{COMP}$	4831	15	167
es-es$^{bin2}_{COMP}$	2638	15	165
es-es$^{bin1}_{ALL}$	9465	15	168
es-es$^{bin2}_{ALL}$	5443	15	167
es-es$^{bin1}_{COMP}$ (valid)	1376	5	155
Spanish XL-WSD			
es-es	8260	310	98

Table 1: Training and development data for our WiC model. L1-L2 means that the first sentence in each pair is in language L1, while the second sentence is in L2. en-nen* are en-ru, en-ar, en-fr, en-zh cross-lingual examples.

described in 2.2 that have previously shown the best results. Additionally, we fine-tuned the model on the following data in Spanish (see table 1 for statistics).

DWUG_es is the development set from the shared task. In the previous experiments binarizing human annotations and training the WiC model as a binary classifier has shown better results than training it as a regression model. Thus, we try two binarization methods. In the first method (**bin1**), the examples with annotations of 3 or 4 are treated as positive examples, and those with annotations of 1 or 2 as negative. In the second method (**bin2**), the examples with annotations of 2 or 3 were filtered out first, and the rest were treated as before.

Also, we have created the **COMP** version of the training set containing only COMPARE pairs (with the first sentence from the old corpus and the second from the new corpus), and the **ALL** version containing all pairs of sentences. We have separated all COMPARE pairs for 5 out of 20 words and used them as a validation set for early stopping during fine-tuning of the WiC model.

XL-WSD (Pasini et al., 2021) is a WSD dataset in 18 languages. We used only the development and the test subsets in Spanish to create additional training data for the WiC model. After generating all pairs of word occurrences with the same word lemma, the pairs of word occurrences having the same sense label were labeled as positive pairs, while the pairs of occurrences with different sense labels were labeled as negative ones.

The WiC model was initialized with the standard XLM-R weights from MLM pre-training. Then we fine-tuned the model for the WiC task in one, two or three steps.

MCL→RSS. This is the best performing model from (Arefyev et al., 2021), which outperformed the winning solution of the RuShiftEval-2021 shared task in the post-evaluation period. This model was fine-tuned on multilingual MCL-WiC data, and then on RuSemShift data in Russian.

MCL→RSS→DWUG_es. The previous model was additionally fine-tuned on Spanish DWUG to improve the quality for Spanish.

MCL→DWUG_es. We hypothesised that fine-tuning on examples in Russian may hurt the performance for Spanish, thus, excluded this intermediate fine-tuning step from the previous fine-tuning scheme.

MCL→DWUG_es+XL-WSD. Finally, we decided to add the examples from XL-WSD in Spanish to the examples from DWUG_es to fine-tune on as many examples in Spanish as possible.

MCL→RSS→DWUG_es+XL-WSD. Our best model from RuShiftEval-2021 fine-tuned on all examples in Spanish we had.

MCL+RSS+DWUG_es+XL-WSD. We hypothesised that fine-tuning the model in many steps may result in forgetting information from the earlier steps. Thus, we try fine-tuning on all WiC data together in a single step.

3.2 Average Pairwise Distance (APD)

3.2.1 Graded change subtasks

For each target word, we retrieved 100 examples (or all examples, if there were fewer than 100) from the old and the modern corpora provided by the organizers. To find the positions of the target words, we used the lemmatizer from Spacy version 3.1.1 with the Spanish model es_core_news_md[2]. Next we created 100 (or fewer) COMPARE pairs of sentences. In Appendix A we study how the results depend on this number of pairs.

The pairs of sentences are scored by the WiC model. For each pair, the predicted probability of the negative class, i.e. the probability of two occurrences having different senses, is taken from the model. To estimate the graded change, for each target word we average these probabilities for the pairs of sentences containing this target word. The predicted probabilities may violate some metric axioms, hence, they are not distances in the mathematical sense. Nevertheless, we will use the traditional term Average Pairwise Distance (**APD**) (Giulianelli et al., 2020) to denote our final word scores. For the optional COMPARE subtask we used the same scores.

3.2.2 Binary subtasks

To solve the binary subtasks, we use only the examples provided by the organizers for 60 words from the test set. There are 20 old and 20 new examples for each word, let us call them the gold examples. Some pairs consisting of these examples were annotated by humans, and based on these annotations the gold labels were calculated while creating the test set. Thus, using these examples instead of the randomly sampled ones shall improve the chances to correctly predict the gold labels. However, it is likely that some rare new or lost senses are not among those 40 examples provided by the organizers. In real applications sampling more examples will likely be beneficial.

We generate all possible COMPARE pairs of the gold examples and calculate APDs for them. To produce binary predictions, we apply APD thresholding (**APD-t**). The threshold was selected to maximize the F1-score on the development set. The same predictions are used for the binary change, sense loss and sense gain detection subtasks.

3.3 Correlation Clustering (CC)

Since the gold COMPARE score for each word is calculated by averaging human judgements about the similarity of word occurrences taken from different time periods, our APD scores shall correlate well with the negated gold COMPARE scores if our WiC model approximates human judgements reasonably well. However, it is not obvious if they also correlate well with the Jensen-Shannon Distance (JSD) between the inferred sense distributions, which is the main metric in the graded change discovery subtask. Also if a word obtains or loses a rare sense while preserving the most frequent sense, the average distance between old and new examples shall be small and the APD-t method will fail do detect the change.

To address these issues, we try to cluster word uses the same way they were clustered by the organizers while creating the test set, but employing

[2]https://github.com/explosion/spacy-models/releases/tag/es_core_news_md-3.2.0

Method/Team	JSD, SPR	COMP, SPR
Baselines		
baseline1	**0.543** (4)	**0.561**
baseline2	0.092 (8)	0.088
Best results of other teams		
myrachins	**<u>0.735</u>** (1)	**<u>0.842</u>**
aishein	0.553 (3)	0.558
Our submissions: team *DeepMistake*, APD		
MCL→RSS	0.701 (2*)	**0.829**
MCL→RSS→ DWUG_es$^{bin1}_{ALL}$	**0.702** (2)	**0.829**
#MCL→DWUG_es$^{bin1}_{ALL}$	0.650 (2*)	0.787

Table 2: The results of the graded change discovery models. The best result within each block is in **bold**, the best result overall is also **<u>underlined</u>**. * indicates the potential ranks of the corresponding results in the leaderboard if they would have been submitted instead of our best submission. # indicates buggy submissions (incorrect indices of the target words).

Method/Team	JSD, SPR	COMP, SPR
DWUG_es convertion comparison, APD		
MCL→DWUG_es$^{bin1}_{ALL}$	0.660 (2*)	0.800
MCL→DWUG_es$^{bin2}_{ALL}$	**0.672** (2*)	**0.820**
MCL→DWUG_es$^{bin1}_{COMP}$	0.650 (2*)	0.800
MCL→DWUG_es$^{bin2}_{COMP}$	0.669 (2*)	0.815
WiC fine-tuning schemes, APD		
MCL	0.648 (2*)	0.791
MCL→ DWUG_es$^{bin2}_{ALL}$+XL-WSD	0.712 (2*)	0.854
MCL→RSS→ DWUG_es$^{bin2}_{ALL}$+XL-WSD	0.711 (2*)	**<u>0.855</u>**
MCL+RSS+ DWUG_es$^{bin2}_{ALL}$+XL-WSD	**<u>0.719</u>** (2*)	0.838
CC		
MCL→ DWUG_es$^{bin2}_{ALL}$+XL-WSD	0.650 (2*)	0.748
Gold scores		
COMPARE scores	0.920	1.0
JSD scores	1.0	0.920

Table 3: Post-evaluation experiments with the graded change detection models on the gold examples for 60 test words. * indicates the potential ranks of the corresponding results.

annotations from our WiC model instead of human annotations. We generate all possible pairs of the gold examples and score them with the WiC model. Unlike the APD method which relies on the distances between examples from different corpora only, clustering-based methods can benefit from the distances between examples from the same corpus as well.

We use the implementation of Correlation Clustering (**CC**) by Schlechtweg et al. (2021), which presumably was also used to create the test set.[3] This time we employ the binary predictions of the WiC model instead of the predicted probabilities, and treat positive predictions (same sense) as positive edges and negative predictions as negative edges.[4] After clustering, the aforementioned code calculates both the JSD and the COMPARE scores, and also all predictions for the binary subtasks.

3.4 Computational complexity

In order to solve the graded change discovery subtask, it was necessary to calculate scores for 4385 words. The WiC model processed about 388K pairs of sentences in total, or 89 pairs per word on average. This took about 3 hours on one V100 GPU. Additionally, about 7 hours of CPU time was spent to lemmatize both corpora. The calculation of APDs took insignificantly small time.

For the graded change subtasks, we experimented with correlation clustering only after the competition and processed only 60 words from the test set. This took about 18 hours of CPU time.

4 Results

4.1 Graded subtask

Table 2 shows the results for the graded change discovery subtask. Our best submission has shown 2nd best result according to both metrics. The model from RuShiftEval-2021 further fine-tuned on the Spanish development set has shown the best result among our submissions. However, further fine-tuning has brought very small benefits. This is likely due to suboptimal binarization of the Spanish data.

During the post-evaluation experiments, we have studied how the results depend on the training data. The results in table 3 clearly indicate that leaving only annotations of 1 and 4 (bin2) consistently improve performance despite almost 2x reduction in the number of training examples in Spanish. Using ALL pairs gives 2x increase in the number of examples, but only marginal improvement in the performance. This is probably because we use the model to score COMPARE pairs only. Adding examples generated from the Spanish part of XL-WSD gives significant boost. This may be due to training on

[3] https://github.com/Garrafao/WUGs

[4] The negative and positive predictions were converted to the annotations of 1 and 2 respectively. We changed only the arguments specifying the annotation range (min=1, max=2) and the binarization threshold=1.5. The default values for other hyperparameters were used: lowerrangemin=1, lowerrangemax=3, upperrangemin=3, upperrangemax=5, lowerprob=0.01, upperprob=0.1

	Binary change			Sense gain			Sense loss		
Method/Team	**F1**	**P**	**R**	**F1**	**P**	**R**	**F1**	**P**	**R**
				Baselines					
baseline1	**0.537** (9)	**0.846**	**0.393**	-	-	-	-	-	-
baseline2	0.222 (10)	0.500	0.143	0.211 (7)	0.400	0.143	0.0 (6)	0.0	0.0
				Best results of other teams					
myrachins	**0.716** (1)	**0.615**	0.857	**0.491** (3)	0.333	0.927	**0.688** (1)	**0.564**	**0.880**
dteodore	0.709 (2)	0.549	**1.0**	0.0 (8)	0.0	0.0	0.0 (6)	0.0	0.0
rombek	0.687 (3)	0.590	0.821	0.490 (4)	0.343	0.857	0.593 (3)	0.552	0.640
kudisov	0.658 (4)	0.510	0.929	0.520 (2)	**0.361**	**0.929**	0.600 (2)	0.514	0.720
				Our submissions: team *DeepMistake*					
#MCL→ DWUG_es$^{bin1}_{ALL}$ + XL-WSD (CC)	0.420 (10*)	**0.800**	0.290	0.417 (6*)	**0.500**	0.360	0.280 (6*)	**1.0**	0.160
MCL→ DWUG_es$^{bin1}_{ALL}$ + XL-WSD (APD-t)	**0.655** (5)	0.633	**0.679**	**0.591** (1)	0.433	**0.929**	**0.582** (4)	0.533	**0.640**
				Post-evaluation results for APD-t					
MCL→DWUG_es$^{bin1}_{ALL}$	0.706 (3*)	0.600	0.860	0.520 (1*)	0.350	**1.0**	0.650 (2*)	**0.530**	0.840
MCL→DWUG_es$^{bin2}_{ALL}$	0.680 (4*)	0.560	0.860	0.490 (3*)	0.330	**1.0**	0.620 (2*)	0.490	0.840
MCL→DWUG_es$^{bin1}_{COMP}$	0.640 (6*)	**0.610**	0.680	**0.580** (1*)	**0.420**	0.930	0.570 (4*)	0.520	0.640
MCL→DWUG_es$^{bin2}_{COMP}$	0.695 (3*)	0.590	0.860	0.510 (2*)	0.340	**1.0**	0.640 (2*)	0.510	0.840
MCL→ DWUG_es$^{bin2}_{ALL}$ + XL-WSD	**0.712** (2*)	0.580	**0.930**	0.480 (4*)	0.310	**1.0**	**0.660** (2*)	0.510	**0.920**
				Post-evaluation results for CC					
MCL→ DWUG_es$^{bin2}_{ALL}$ + XL-WSD	0.693 (3*)	0.553	0.929	0.462 (4*)	0.316	0.857	0.528 (4*)	0.500	0.560

Table 4: The results for the binary subtasks. * indicates the potential ranks of the corresponding results in the leaderboard if they would have been submitted instead of our best submission. # indicates buggy submissions (CC incorrectly executed).

2.5x more examples, but also 22x more different target words. Fine-tuning on all datasets in one step improves Spearman's correlation with the JSD scores a bit, but not with the COMPARE scores. Comparing multi-step and single-step fine-tuning is an interesting direction for the future work.

The CC method works worse than APD, a thorough analysis is required to understand the reasons. Also we notice that the gold COMPARE scores have Spearman's correlation with the gold JSD scores of 0.92. This means that the limits of the APD method are not achieved yet, and further improvement of the WiC model for better reproduction of human annotations is a reasonable way to improve the results.

4.2 Binary subtask

Table 4 shows the results for the binary subtasks. Our model has outperformed all other participants in the optional sense gain detection subtask. However, the F1-score for the main binary change detection subtask is 6% below the best result. During the post-evaluation experiments we have changed the binarization to bin2, and also set the natural threshold of 0.5, which improved the results for binary change and sense loss detection to the level comparable with 2nd best result in the leaderboard. The APD-t method works better than CC, even though it reuses the same predictions for all binary subtasks.

5 Conclusion

This paper makes the first step towards answering the question in its title: can a multilingual word-in-context model replace human annotators for solving the LSCD task? For now, it seems that our word-in-context model is not good enough to do that. However, we have shown that experimenting with the training data is a promising direction to achieve this goal.

Acknowledgements

We are grateful to our anonymous reviewers. This research was partially supported by the Basic Research Program at the HSE University and through computational resources of HPC facilities at HSE University (Kostenetskiy et al., 2021).

References

N. Arefyev, M. Fedoseev, V. Protasov, D. Homskiy, A. Davletov, and A. Panchenko. 2021. Deepmistake: Which senses are hard to distinguish for a word-in-context model. In *Computational linguistics and intellectual technologies*, 20, page 16 – 30, Russian Federation.

Alexis Conneau, Kartikay Khandelwal, Naman Goyal, Vishrav Chaudhary, Guillaume Wenzek, Francisco Guzmán, Edouard Grave, Myle Ott, Luke Zettlemoyer, and Veselin Stoyanov. 2020. Unsupervised cross-lingual representation learning at scale. In *Proceedings of the 58th Annual Meeting of the Association for Computational Linguistics*, pages 8440–8451, Online. Association for Computational Linguistics.

Frank D. Zamora-Reina, Felipe Bravo-Marquez, and Dominik Schlechtweg. 2022. Lscdiscovery: A shared task on semantic change discovery and detection in spanish. In *Proceedings of the 3rd International Workshop on Computational Approaches to Historical Language Change*, Dublin, Ireland. Association for Computational Linguistics.

Adis Davletov, Denis Gordeev, Nikolay Arefyev, and Emil Davletov. 2021. LIORI at SemEval-2021 task 8: Ask transformer for measurements. In *Proceedings of the 15th International Workshop on Semantic Evaluation (SemEval-2021)*, pages 1249–1254, Online. Association for Computational Linguistics.

Mario Giulianelli, Marco Del Tredici, and Raquel Fernández. 2020. Analysing lexical semantic change with contextualised word representations. In *Proceedings of the 58th Annual Meeting of the Association for Computational Linguistics*, pages 3960–3973, Online. Association for Computational Linguistics.

P. S. Kostenetskiy, R. A. Chulkevich, and V. I. Kozyrev. 2021. HPC resources of the higher school of economics. *Journal of Physics: Conference Series*, 1740:012050.

Andrey Kutuzov and Lidia Pivovarova. 2021. Rushifteval: A shared task on semantic shift detection for russian. In *Computational linguistics and intellectual technologies*, 20, Russian Federation.

Federico Martelli, Najla Kalach, Gabriele Tola, and Roberto Navigli. 2021. Semeval-2021 task 2: Multilingual and cross-lingual word-in-context disambiguation (mcl-wic). In *SEMEVAL*.

Tommaso Pasini, Alessandro Raganato, and Roberto Navigli. 2021. XL-WSD: An extra-large and cross-lingual evaluation framework for word sense disambiguation. In *Proc. of AAAI*.

Julia Rodina and Andrey Kutuzov. 2020. RuSemShift: a dataset of historical lexical semantic change in Russian. In *Proceedings of the 28th International Conference on Computational Linguistics*, pages 1037–1047, Barcelona, Spain (Online). International Committee on Computational Linguistics.

Dominik Schlechtweg, Sabine Schulte im Walde, and S. Eckmann. 2018. Diachronic usage relatedness (durel): A framework for the annotation of lexical semantic change. *ArXiv*, abs/1804.06517.

Dominik Schlechtweg, Nina Tahmasebi, Simon Hengchen, Haim Dubossarsky, and Barbara McGillivray. 2021. DWUG: A large Resource of Diachronic Word Usage Graphs in Four Languages. *CoRR*, abs/2104.08540.

A Graded change detection results depending on the number of pairs sampled

In the post-evaluation phase, we measured the performance of the model in the graded change detection subtask depending on how many pairs of sentences are sampled. For this experiment, we sampled 1000 sentences with replacement from each corpora, built 1000 COMPARE pairs and annotated them with the WiC model. Then for each number of pairs we sampled this number of pairs 100 times, and calculated the APD scores and the target metrics. Finally, we calculated the mean and the standard deviation of the target metrics for each number of pairs.

We compare these results to the results on the gold COMPARE pairs, i.e. annotating with our WiC model the same pairs that were annotated by humans. There are 278 unique pairs per word on average. Also we compare to using all COMPARE pairs consisting of gold examples only. There are 400 such pairs per word consisting of 20 old and 20 new examples.

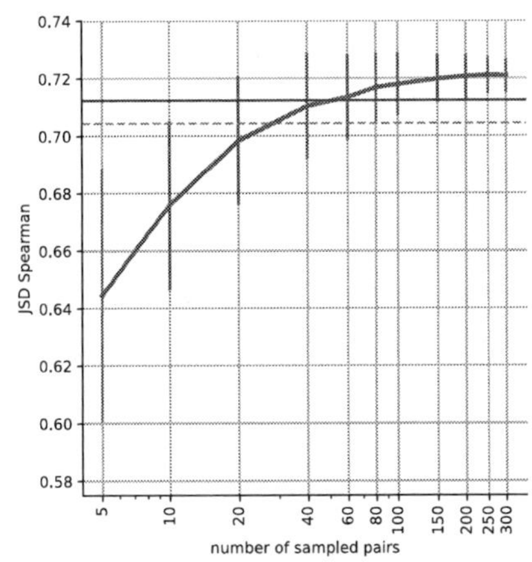

Figure 1: Spearman's correlation of our APD scores with the gold JSD scores depending on the number of COMPARE pairs sampled per word. Model: MCL→DWUG_es$^{bin2}_{ALL}$+XL-WSD. The solid blue horizontal line corresponds to all COMPARE pairs of the gold examples. The dashed purple horizontal line corresponds to the gold COMPARE pairs. Error bars show one standard deviation.

From figures 1, 2 we can conclude that after 100-150 pairs of sentences sampled per word the average quality stops increasing, only the standard deviation decreases slowly.

Interestingly, when the number of pairs is large

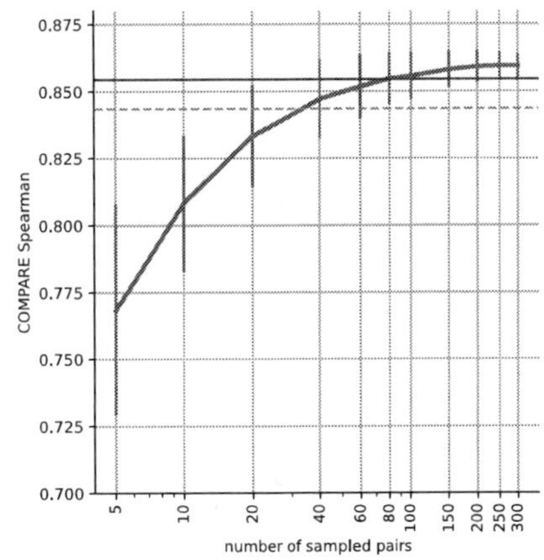

Figure 2: Spearman's correlation of our APD scores with the gold COMPARE scores depending on the number of COMPARE pairs sampled per word. Model: MCL→DWUG_es$^{bin2}_{ALL}$+XL-WSD. The solid blue horizontal line corresponds to all COMPARE pairs of the gold examples. The dashed purple horizontal line corresponds to the gold COMPARE pairs. Error bars show one standard deviation.

enough the results on the retrieved examples are a little bit higher on average than on the gold examples and significantly higher than on the gold COMPARE pairs. This is despite the fact that the gold scores were calculated based on human annotations of the gold pairs, and may be related to the imperfect approximation of human annotations by our WiC model.

UAlberta at LSCDiscovery: Lexical Semantic Change Detection via Word Sense Disambiguation

Daniela Teodorescu, Spencer von der Ohe, Grzegorz Kondrak
Alberta Machine Intelligence Institute, Department of Computing Science
University of Alberta, Edmonton, Canada
{dteodore,vonderoh,gkondrak@ualberta.ca

Abstract

We describe our two systems for the shared task on Lexical Semantic Change Discovery in Spanish. For binary change detection, we frame the task as a word sense disambiguation (WSD) problem. We derive sense frequency distributions for target words in both old and modern corpora. We assume that the word semantics have changed if a sense is observed in only one of the two corpora, or the relative change for any sense exceeds a tuned threshold. For graded change discovery, we follow the design of CIRCE (Pömsl and Lyapin, 2020) by combining both static and contextual embeddings. For contextual embeddings, we use XLM-RoBERTa instead of BERT, and train the model to predict a masked token instead of the time period. Our language-independent methods achieve results that are close to the best-performing systems in the shared task.

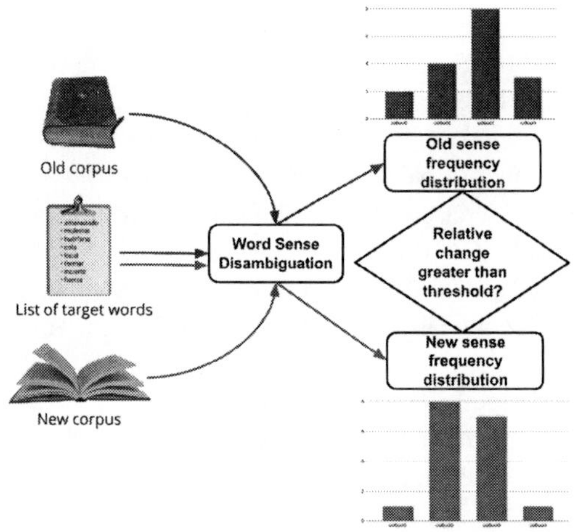

Figure 1: Lexical semantic change detection via WSD.

1 Introduction

Lexical semantic change discovery is a task with growing interest and applications in various areas, such as natural language processing and lexicography (Schlechtweg et al., 2020). The shared task on semantic change discovery and detection in Spanish (LSCDiscovery) consists of two phases: 1) graded change discovery, and 2) binary change detection (Zamora-Reina et al., 2022). We adopt different approaches for both phases.

The two sub-tasks consider different aspects of lexical semantic change (LSC). The definition for graded change discovery follows Kurtyigit et al. (2021): *given a diachronic corpus pair C1 and C2, rank the intersection of their (content-word) vocabularies according to their degree of change between C1 and C2.* For binary LSC detection, the definition is the same as used in the SemEval-2020 Task 1: Unsupervised Lexical Semantic Change Detection (Schlechtweg et al., 2020): *given a target word *w* and two sets of its usages U1 and U2, decide whether *w* lost or gained senses from U1 to U2, or not.* The direction of change is not important in either task. The inputs to the tasks consist of a list of target words and a pair of corpora from different time periods, annotated for the semantic relationship between word usages. The gold labels on a set of target words are inferred from sense frequency distributions derived by clustering the manual annotations (Zamora-Reina et al., 2022). The output in phase 1 is a list of the target words ranked by the amount of change. The output in phase 2 is a list of binary change detection labels per word.

For graded change discovery, our approach is similar to CIRCE (Pömsl and Lyapin, 2020), the top performing system in the SemEval 2020 task for graded change. We use embeddings and Euclidean distance to obtain rankings. However, we obtain contextual embeddings from token prediction instead of time period prediction. In addition, we use XLM-RoBERTa instead of BERT, because it performs well across a variety of tasks in Spanish (Conneau et al., 2020), and models based on this architecture produce effective contextual embeddings (Ethayarajh, 2019).

Proceedings of the 3rd Workshop on Computational Approaches to Historical Language Change, pages 180 - 186
May 26-27, 2022 ©2022 Association for Computational Linguistics

For binary change detection, we propose a novel approach based on framing LSC discovery as word sense disambiguation (WSD) problem, which is the task of determining the meaning of words in context given a sense inventory (Navigli, 2009). Using a recently-proposed WSD system, AMuSE (Orlando et al., 2021), we identify the sense of each target word in context to determine if senses were lost or gained over time. Following the theory of Hauer and Kondrak (2020), we posit that wordnet-type sense inventories match the intuitions of the annotators of the shared task data. Our approach has the advantage of being interpretable, providing interesting insights into the nature of lexical semantic change by identifying specific senses that appear or disappear in texts over time.

Our systems are highly competitive. For phase 1, our system achieves 0.5731 correlation between the ranked words and ground truth on the test set, which would put it in third place, based on our own evaluation performed after the submission deadline. For phase 2, our system obtains F-score of 88% on the development set, and 71% on the evaluation set, which ranks it as second according to the main metric.

2 Related Work

In the SemEval 2020 task for graded change discovery, the CIRCE system performed the best (Schlechtweg et al., 2020). The system ensembles static and contextual embeddings. Static embeddings with Skip-Gram with Negative Sampling (Mikolov et al., 2013) are obtained for each corpus. These embeddings are then aligned using Orthogonal Procrustes analysis (Schönemann, 1966), and the Euclidean distance is found between aligned embeddings. Contextual embeddings from the masked language model BERT (Devlin et al., 2019) are used to classify the time period of sentences, as time specific features are useful to learn. Then, embeddings are extracted from the last hidden layer for each target word. To obtain a distance, the Euclidean distance is computed pairwise between the embeddings from the two corpora and the distances are averaged. The target words are then ranked for both types of embeddings. Finally, the rankings are combined by a weighted average to obtain the final ranking.

We modify the CIRCE approach for our graded change discovery system by using XLM-RoBERTa (Conneau et al., 2020) to obtain contextual embeddings. XLM-RoBERTa is a multilingual masked language model. It uses the same bidirectional transformer architecture as BERT (Devlin et al., 2019) and RoBERTa (Liu et al., 2019), and has the same number of layers and size of layers as RoBERTa. However, compared to BERT and RoBERTa it has a larger vocabulary of 250,000 tokens, and employs the SentencePiece tokenizer (Kudo and Richardson, 2018). Additionally, it is trained on 100 languages, instead of just English (Conneau et al., 2020).

Systems for binary change detection commonly use embeddings for semantic representations, with type embeddings often outperforming token embeddings (Schlechtweg et al., 2020). Some approaches ensemble models (Martinc et al., 2020; Pömsl and Lyapin, 2020) or use a topic model (Sarsfield and Tayyar Madabushi, 2020). Nulty and Lillis (2020) detect change by considering the relationship between nodes in a semantic network graph. Orthogonal Procrustes analysis (Schönemann, 1966) and vector initialization (Kim et al., 2014) are techniques that can be used to align the semantic representations. As a distance metric between embeddings, cosine and Euclidean distance are commonly used.

Our approach based on applying WSD for binary change detection is novel. A previous work has performed word epoch disambiguation for determining changes in word usages overtime, but this task predicts the time period (epoch) for instances (Mihalcea and Nastase, 2012). Some previous work considers changes of senses overtime; however, rather than WSD, they apply sense induction (Mitra et al., 2014; Tahmasebi and Risse, 2017), topic modelling (Lau et al., 2012), or Bayesian models (Frermann and Lapata, 2016).

3 Methods

In this section, we describe our methods separately for each of the two phases. Our code is available for public use.[1]

3.1 Phase 1: Graded Change

We follow the approach implemented in CIRCE (Pömsl and Lyapin, 2020), which has been shown to perform well across a number of languages. We use both static and contextual embeddings because a combination of rankings from both embeddings

[1] https://github.com/sazzy4o/ualberta-lscdiscovery

outperforms the ranking from either. We rank target words based on the distance between embeddings of both corpora.

To obtain static embedding rankings, we use the same methods as CIRCE for the following 3 steps. First, we train static embeddings using Skip-Gram with Negative Sampling (Mikolov et al., 2013) for the lemmatized version of each corpus, and align embeddings from both corpora. Second, we obtain the Euclidean distance between the aligned embeddings. Finally, we rank the target words by the Euclidean distance.

The contextual embeddings used in CIRCE perform poorly compared to the static embeddings. We posit that this is because the time period prediction task is not well aligned with predicting the meaning of words. To address this, we first train a XLM-RoBERTa (Conneau et al., 2020) model to predict randomly masked words in the combined corpus from both time periods. Second, we mask out each instance of a target word, and use our trained model to predict the masked word. From this prediction, we extract the embedding from the features corresponding to the masked token in the last hidden layer outputs of the model. Third, we compute the pairwise Euclidean distance between each pair of target word instances from different time periods. Finally, we rank the target words by the mean distance for each target word.

We follow a similar procedure to CIRCE to obtain the final ranking by ordering the target words by a weighted combination of the static and contextual rankings. However, instead of calculating the weighting based on the accuracy of our contextual model, we tune the weighting to maximize Spearman's rank-order correlation on the development set.

This approach is quite computationally expensive since it requires training the XLM-RoBERTa model. The model takes approximately 3-4 hours using an NVIDIA GeForce RTX 3090 to train. Additionally, it takes approximately 45 minutes to obtain the embeddings for the 60 target words in the test set. The static embeddings are significantly faster to obtain, taking only 3 minutes with an Intel Xeon W-2255 CPU.

3.2 Phase 2: Binary Change

We approach binary semantic change detection as WSD. We implement our approach using AMuSE, a user-friendly end-to-end neural WSD system of Orlando et al. (2021), which incorporates the preprocessing steps of tokenization, lemmatization, and parts of speech (POS) tagging. AMuSE is trained on manual annotations involving English WordNet senses, but thanks to its use of the multilingual XLM-RoBERTa embeddings, it is also applicable to other languages that are represented in BabelNet. According to the Universality Principle of Hauer and Kondrak (2020), there is a one-to-one correspondence between concepts in different languages. We apply AMuSE via the REST API[2] to all sentences that contain the target words.

We depict our process in Figure 1. For each word, we compute its sense frequency distributions in both the old and modern corpora based on the output of the WSD system. If a sense is found in the modern corpus but is missing in the old corpus (or vice versa), a change is deemed to have occurred (label 1). Otherwise, a word has the same set of senses identified in both the old and modern corpus. For each sense, we compute the relative probability change (p_r) as the ratio between the absolute probability difference, and the larger of the two probabilities (Formula 1). The probability of a sense for a target word from the new and old corpora is denoted as p_1 and p_2, respectively.

$$p_r = \frac{|p_1 - p_2|}{\max(p_1, p_2)} \tag{1}$$

The resulting value is compared to a threshold, which we tune on the development data by maximizing F-score. A relative change greater than the threshold (set at 0.65) for any of the word senses indicates that a change occurred for the given word (label 1). Otherwise, we conclude that there is no change (label 0).

The definition of binary change detection suggests that it may be sufficient to determine if the set of senses for a target word remains the same from the old to the modern corpus. We implemented this approach after the submission deadline, and obtained 78% F-score on the development set, which is below the F-score of 88% obtained with our principal method described above.

Additionally, we computed two other metrics for phase 2 after the submission deadline: sense gain and sense loss detection. First, the same methodology is applied for detecting change, as sense gain/loss is only applicable when there is change.

[2]https://nlp.uniroma1.it/amuse-wsd/api-documentation

If change is due to the threshold, we compare if the old or modern probability is greater for sense loss/gain. In scenarios where a sense was missing in either the old sense set or the new sense set, we use the direction of change to detect sense gain/loss. Otherwise, if none of the above scenarios apply, we conclude that there is no sense gain/loss. A lemma can be labelled as having both sense gain and loss. Our approach allows for this by calculating the labels separately, and searching through the senses for a word until gain/loss is detected before assigning the no change label.

We consider our approach for phase 2 as lightweight. Although AMuSE uses XLM-RoBERTa embeddings, we did not have to train them. Approaches that rely on contextual embeddings, such as BERT, may be computationally too expensive to run on all instances (Kurtyigit et al., 2021). Given a few hundred sentences per target word in either corpus, we can run AMuSE on all instances, rather than just a sample. We did not use GPU, and simply ran the script on an Intel Xeon CPU E5-2650 v4. The run time for WSD was approximately a few hours for the development set (20 words) and close to a day for the evaluation set (60 words). WSD results were only computed once and then stored.

Further, we highlight how our approaches for both phases are multilingual. Static embeddings can be trained on the given corpora, and XLM-RoBERTa is multilingual by nature. In phase 2, the AMuSE WSD system allows for state-of-the-art neural WSD in 40 languages. This demonstrates that challenges described by Tahmasebi et al. (2021), such as having a translated corpus to train WSD systems, may not always be the case.

4 Evaluation

We test our methods on the development set, and report the results on the evaluation set. Some results were obtained after the submission deadline.

4.1 Phase 1: Graded Change

We use the tokenized and lemmatized versions of the corpora provided in the competition to obtain contextual and static embeddings, respectively. We use CIRCE's implementation[3] for static embeddings, as well as for combining the predictions between models. We use the implementation of XLM-RoBERTa from the Hugging Face transformers library (Wolf et al., 2020)[4] for contextual embeddings. We initialize the weights of the model to the *xlm-roberta-large* available with the transformers library.[5]

For evaluation, we use Spearman's rank-order correlation coefficient (Bolboaca and Jäntschi, 2006) between our ranking and the provided gold ranking. After tuning weights on the development set, the results of our system are 0.8375 and 0.5731 on the development and evaluation set, respectively. Our results are much better than CIRCE, which achieves a correlation of only 0.1894 averaged over three runs on the evaluation set. Only two submissions to the shared task achieved a higher correlation on the evaluation set.

After analysing the rankings in the development set, we find that *aguantar* and *descendiente* are incorrectly ranked by 7 and 8 positions respectively. Both of these words have a relatively low frequency in the modern corpus. In addition, *descendiente* occurs in the old corpus both as a noun and as a verb. All of the other words are within 6 positions of their correct rank with the majority being 2 or fewer positions from their correct rankings.

	Dev			Eval		
	P	R	F1	P	R	F1
Change	79	100	88	55	100	71
Sense Gain	71	100	83	33	93	49
Sense Loss	30	100	46	50	92	65

Table 1: Results for the binary change tasks (in %) on the development and evaluation sets.

4.2 Phase 2: Binary Change

The results of our method are shown in Table 1. According to the official results, the F-score of 71% on the evaluation set, which is the main metric for binary change detection, ranks our system as second in the competition. It is interesting to note that our approach obtains 100% recall, whereas the baseline provided by the organizers obtains 100% precision on the development set, so whenever the two models agree, their classification is correct. For the optional tasks of sense gain/loss detection, we calculated our results after the official submission deadline. At the time of writing, our results for

[3]https://github.com/mpoemsl/circe

[4]https://huggingface.co/docs/transformers/model_doc/xlm-roberta

[5]https://huggingface.co/xlm-roberta-large

sense gain and loss detection would place third and second, respectively.

According to our error analysis on the development set, our system disagrees with the gold annotation by identifying semantic change in the following three words: *descendiente*, *músculo*, and *reforma*. In each of these cases, new senses were found by AMuSE in the modern corpus; in addition, two senses appear to have been lost for *reforma*. Some instances could be interpreted as genuine lost senses. For example, one of the senses of the noun *reforma*, defined in WordNet 3.0 (Miller, 1995) as "rescuing from error and returning to a rightful course" occurs in the old corpus in the following context: *no puedo enseñar a las niñas más que dos cosas: la* **reforma** *de letra y la fábula mitológica*. This suggests that WSD could be an effective approach for identifying changes in sense inventories.

Further inspection reveals that some instances of a spurious new sense identification may have been caused by incorrect POS tags assigned by AMuSE. The gold annotations seem to consistently assign a single POS tag to each target word. We experimented with a modified approach to binary change detection, which only considers the occurrences in which the assigned POS tag matches the most likely tag for a given lemma in BabelNet (Navigli and Ponzetto, 2010), but the results were slightly lower than for our main method.

5 Conclusion

We presented systems for both graded and binary change discovery in the context of the shared task on Lexical Semantic Change Discovery in Spanish. For the former, we proposed a system based on CIRCE, with the modification of tuning the weights between the static and contextual embeddings, and training the model to predict a masked token rather than the time period. For the latter, we demonstrated that a WSD system can be effective in detecting word meaning changes. Future work could include combining rankings from more than two different models for graded LSC discovery. We would also like to investigate if either of our two methods could be applied to the other of the two subtasks.

Acknowledgements

This research was supported by the Alberta Machine Intelligence Institute (Amii), the Natural Sciences and Engineering Research Council of Canada (NSERC), the Social Sciences and Humanities Research Council (SSHRC), and Alberta Innovates.

References

Sorana-Daniela Bolboaca and Lorentz Jäntschi. 2006. Pearson versus Spearman, Kendall's Tau Correlation Analysis on Structure-Activity Relationships of Biologic Active Compounds. *Leonardo Journal of Sciences*, 5(9):179–200.

Alexis Conneau, Kartikay Khandelwal, Naman Goyal, Vishrav Chaudhary, Guillaume Wenzek, Francisco Guzmán, Edouard Grave, Myle Ott, Luke Zettlemoyer, and Veselin Stoyanov. 2020. Unsupervised Cross-lingual Representation Learning at Scale. In *Proceedings of the 58th Annual Meeting of the Association for Computational Linguistics*, pages 8440–8451, Online. Association for Computational Linguistics.

Jacob Devlin, Ming-Wei Chang, Kenton Lee, and Kristina Toutanova. 2019. BERT: Pre-training of Deep Bidirectional Transformers for Language Understanding. In *Proceedings of the 2019 Conference of the North American Chapter of the Association for Computational Linguistics: Human Language Technologies, Volume 1 (Long and Short Papers)*, pages 4171–4186, Minneapolis, Minnesota. Association for Computational Linguistics.

Kawin Ethayarajh. 2019. How contextual are contextualized word representations? Comparing the geometry of BERT, ELMo, and GPT-2 embeddings. In *Proceedings of the 2019 Conference on Empirical Methods in Natural Language Processing and the 9th International Joint Conference on Natural Language Processing (EMNLP-IJCNLP)*, pages 55–65, Hong Kong, China. Association for Computational Linguistics.

Lea Frermann and Mirella Lapata. 2016. A Bayesian Model of Diachronic Meaning Change. *Transactions of the Association for Computational Linguistics*, 4:31–45.

Bradley Hauer and Grzegorz Kondrak. 2020. Synonymy = translational equivalence. *CoRR*, abs/2004.13886.

Yoon Kim, Yi-I Chiu, Kentaro Hanaki, Darshan Hegde, and Slav Petrov. 2014. Temporal Analysis of Language through Neural Language Models. In *Proceedings of the ACL 2014 Workshop on Language Technologies and Computational Social Science*, pages 61–65, Baltimore, MD, USA. Association for Computational Linguistics.

Taku Kudo and John Richardson. 2018. SentencePiece: A simple and language independent subword tokenizer and detokenizer for neural text processing. In *Proceedings of the 2018 Conference on Empirical Methods in Natural Language Processing: System Demonstrations*, pages 66–71, Brussels, Belgium. Association for Computational Linguistics.

Sinan Kurtyigit, Maike Park, Dominik Schlechtweg, Jonas Kuhn, and Sabine Schulte im Walde. 2021. Lexical Semantic Change Discovery. In *Proceedings of the 59th Annual Meeting of the Association for Computational Linguistics and the 11th International Joint Conference on Natural Language Processing (Volume 1: Long Papers)*, pages 6985–6998, Online. Association for Computational Linguistics.

Jey Han Lau, Paul Cook, Diana McCarthy, David Newman, and Timothy Baldwin. 2012. Word Sense Induction for Novel Sense Detection. In *Proceedings of the 13th Conference of the European Chapter of the Association for Computational Linguistics*, pages 591–601, Avignon, France. Association for Computational Linguistics.

Yinhan Liu, Myle Ott, Naman Goyal, Jingfei Du, Mandar Joshi, Danqi Chen, Omer Levy, Mike Lewis, Luke Zettlemoyer, and Veselin Stoyanov. 2019. Roberta: A robustly optimized BERT pretraining approach. *CoRR*, abs/1907.11692.

Matej Martinc, Syrielle Montariol, Elaine Zosa, and Lidia Pivovarova. 2020. Discovery Team at SemEval-2020 Task 1: Context-sensitive Embeddings Not Always Better than Static for Semantic Change Detection. In *Proceedings of the Fourteenth Workshop on Semantic Evaluation*, pages 67–73, Barcelona (online). International Committee for Computational Linguistics.

Rada Mihalcea and Vivi Nastase. 2012. Word epoch disambiguation: Finding how words change over time. In *Proceedings of the 50th Annual Meeting of the Association for Computational Linguistics (Volume 2: Short Papers)*, pages 259–263, Jeju Island, Korea. Association for Computational Linguistics.

Tomas Mikolov, Ilya Sutskever, Kai Chen, Greg S Corrado, and Jeff Dean. 2013. Distributed Representations of Words and Phrases and their Compositionality. In *Advances in Neural Information Processing Systems*, volume 26. Curran Associates, Inc.

George A. Miller. 1995. WordNet: A Lexical Database for English. *Commun. ACM*, 38(11):39–41.

Sunny Mitra, Ritwik Mitra, Martin Riedl, Chris Biemann, Animesh Mukherjee, and Pawan Goyal. 2014. That's sick dude!: Automatic identification of word sense change across different timescales. In *Proceedings of the 52nd Annual Meeting of the Association for Computational Linguistics (Volume 1: Long Papers)*, pages 1020–1029, Baltimore, Maryland. Association for Computational Linguistics.

Roberto Navigli. 2009. Word Sense Disambiguation: A Survey. *ACM Comput. Surv.*, 41(2).

Roberto Navigli and Simone Paolo Ponzetto. 2010. BabelNet: Building a very large multilingual semantic network. In *Proceedings of the 48th Annual Meeting of the Association for Computational Linguistics*, pages 216–225, Uppsala, Sweden. Association for Computational Linguistics.

Paul Nulty and David Lillis. 2020. The UCD-Net System at SemEval-2020 Task 1: Temporal Referencing with Semantic Network Distances. In *Proceedings of the Fourteenth Workshop on Semantic Evaluation*, pages 119–125, Barcelona (online). International Committee for Computational Linguistics.

Riccardo Orlando, Simone Conia, Fabrizio Brignone, Francesco Cecconi, and Roberto Navigli. 2021. AMuSE-WSD: An All-in-one Multilingual System for Easy Word Sense Disambiguation. In *Proceedings of the 2021 Conference on Empirical Methods in Natural Language Processing: System Demonstrations*, pages 298–307, Online and Punta Cana, Dominican Republic. Association for Computational Linguistics.

Martin Pömsl and Roman Lyapin. 2020. CIRCE at SemEval-2020 Task 1: Ensembling Context-Free and Context-Dependent Word Representations. In *Proceedings of the Fourteenth Workshop on Semantic Evaluation*, pages 180–186, Barcelona (online). International Committee for Computational Linguistics.

Eleri Sarsfield and Harish Tayyar Madabushi. 2020. UoB at SemEval-2020 Task 1: Automatic Identification of Novel Word Senses. In *Proceedings of the Fourteenth Workshop on Semantic Evaluation*, pages 239–245, Barcelona (online). International Committee for Computational Linguistics.

Dominik Schlechtweg, Barbara McGillivray, Simon Hengchen, Haim Dubossarsky, and Nina Tahmasebi. 2020. SemEval-2020 Task 1: Unsupervised Lexical Semantic Change Detection. In *Proceedings of the Fourteenth Workshop on Semantic Evaluation*, pages 1–23, Barcelona (online). International Committee for Computational Linguistics.

Peter H Schönemann. 1966. A generalized solution of the orthogonal procrustes problem. *Psychometrika*, 31(1):1–10.

Nina Tahmasebi, Lars Borin, Adam Jatowt, Yang Xu, and Simon Hengchen, editors. 2021. *Computational approaches to semantic change*. Number 6 in Language Variation. Language Science Press, Berlin.

Nina Tahmasebi and Thomas Risse. 2017. Finding Individual Word Sense Changes and their Delay in Appearance. In *Proceedings of the International Conference Recent Advances in Natural Language Processing, RANLP 2017*, pages 741–749, Varna, Bulgaria. INCOMA Ltd.

Thomas Wolf, Lysandre Debut, Victor Sanh, Julien Chaumond, Clement Delangue, Anthony Moi, Pierric Cistac, Tim Rault, Remi Louf, Morgan Funtowicz, Joe Davison, Sam Shleifer, Patrick von Platen, Clara Ma, Yacine Jernite, Julien Plu, Canwen Xu, Teven Le Scao, Sylvain Gugger, Mariama Drame, Quentin Lhoest, and Alexander Rush. 2020. Transformers: State-of-the-Art Natural Language Processing. In *Proceedings of the 2020 Conference on Empirical Methods in Natural Language Processing: System*

Demonstrations, pages 38–45, Online. Association for Computational Linguistics.

Frank D. Zamora-Reina, Felipe Bravo-Marquez, and Dominik Schlechtweg. 2022. Lscdiscovery: A shared task on semantic change discovery and detection in spanish. In *Proceedings of the 3rd International Workshop on Computational Approaches to Historical Language Change*, Dublin, Ireland. Association for Computational Linguistics.

CoToHiLi at LSCDiscovery: the Role of Linguistic Features in Predicting Semantic Change

Ana Sabina Uban[♠,♡] **Alina Maria Cristea**[♡] **Anca Dinu**[♣,♡]
Liviu P. Dinu[♠,♡] **Simona Georgescu**[♣,♡] **Laurențiu Zoicaș** [♣,♡]

[♡]Human Languages Technologies Research Center, University of Bucharest
[♠] Faculty of Mathematics and Computer Science, University of Bucharest
[♣]Faculty of Foreign Languages and Literatures, University of Bucharest

auban@fmi.unibuc.ro, alina.cristea@fmi.unibuc.ro, anca.dinu@lls.unibuc.ro
ldinu@fmi.unibuc.ro, simona.georgescu@lls.unibuc.ro, laurentiu.zoicas@lls.unibuc.ro

Abstract

This paper presents the contributions of the CoToHiLi team for the LSCDiscovery shared task on semantic change in the Spanish language. We participated in both tasks (graded discovery and binary change, including sense gain and sense loss) and proposed models based on word embedding distances combined with hand-crafted linguistic features, including polysemy, number of neological synonyms, and relation to cognates in English. We find that using linguistically informed features combined using weights assigned manually by experts leads to promising results.

1 Introduction

In recent years, more and more studies in computational linguistics have focused on the issue of lexical semantic change, tracking the shift in the meaning of words by looking at their usage across time in corpora dating from different time periods (Hamilton et al., 2016; Schlechtweg et al., 2020). Vector spaces and word embeddings have widely been used for tracking semantic shifts of words across different time periods.

Previous studies on the computational analysis of lexical semantic change have found that different word properties such as word frequency and polysemy have a role in influencing the potential semantic shift of the word, proposing statistical laws of semantic change such as the law of innovation and the law of differentiation (Hamilton et al., 2016; Xu and Kemp, 2015; Uban et al., 2021b, 2019). Uban et al. (2021a, 2019) have proposed that semantic change can be studied cross-lingually, by comparing present meanings of cognate words, which by definition share a common etymon from which the current meanings have diverged. The resulting implication is that analyzing cognates of the target word in other languages can also potentially provide clues regarding the word's prior semantic change. We provide more details on the linguistic motivation for regarding these features as relevant for the task of analyzing semantic change in the following sections.

2 Background

The LSCDiscovery shared task (D. Zamora-Reina et al., 2022) on predicting semantic change for the Spanish language consisted of two sub-tasks. For the first task - graded discovery - the participants were asked to rank the set of content words (N, V, A) in the lemma vocabulary intersection of C1 and C2 according to their degree of semantic change between C1 to C2. The predictions were scored against the ground truth via Spearman's rank-order correlation coefficient.

For the second sub-task - binary change - participants were be asked to classify a pre-selected set of content words (N, V, A) into two classes, 0 for no change and 1 for change. The second sub-task also included two optional sub-tasks on predicting whether the target word undergoing semantic change has gained or lost senses, also formulated as a binary classification problem. Submissions were graded using precision, recall and F1-score.

The data consisted of two corpora of texts in the Spanish language: *old corpus*, created using different sources freely available from Project Gutenberg (containing texts published between 1810 - 1906), and *modern corpus*, created using different sources available from the OPUS project (with texts published between 1994 - 2020).

We participated in the LSCDiscovery shared task on semantic change in the Spanish language with submissions in both main sub-tasks: graded discovery and binary change, as well as the optional tasks on sense gain and sense loss. For all tasks we experimented with approaches based on distances in word embedding spaces combined with hand-crafted linguistic features.

Proceedings of the 3rd Workshop on Computational Approaches to Historical Language Change, pages 187 - 192
May 26-27, 2022 ©2022 Association for Computational Linguistics

3 System Overview

In this section we describe the features and models used to make automatic predictions on the semantic change of target words, for both sub-tasks. We release all the code used for implementing our submissions.[1]

The general method for our submissions in all tasks has consisted of computing, for every given target word, several metrics including embedding distances and linguistic hand-crafted features, and subsequently weighing them as features in a model used to predict the final score. The list of features used consists of the following:

- word embedding cosine similarity scores - 3 different scores according to the different alignment methods (see following section for details)
- word polysemy degree
- number of neological synonyms of the word
- Levenshtein distance to closest English word

In the following subsections we describe in detail both the features and the models used to achieve predictions.

3.1 Word Embedding Distances

The first type of features we used is based on word embedding distances. Following already standard approaches in the study of semantic change based on diachronic corpora, we trained word embeddings separately on the two provided corpora, subsequently used an alignment algorithm to obtain a common embedding space, and finally measured the cosine-distance between each target word's representation in the two embedding spaces, as a proxy for the degree of its semantic shift between the two periods represented in the corpora.

The embedding algorithm we used is word2vec (Mikolov et al., 2013), trained with default parameters in the gensim library. We trained two separate models using the same settings on the tokenized versions of the corpora (non-lemmatized). We then aligned the obtained embedding spaces using three different approaches based on (Artetxe et al., 2016, 2017, 2018a,b), using the open-source code provided by the authors[2]: supervised alignment using a seed word dictionary and a linear mapping method, semi-supervised alignment, optimized for using a small seed word dictionary, and unsupervised alignment based on adversarial training.

We chose to include the semi-supervised and unsupervised approach because of the small list of seed words used (which we assumed could not guarantee a high-quality aligned embedding space using the supervised method). As seed words for the supervised and semi-supervised settings we used the same list of function words in Spanish derived from the NLTK[3] library, considering the ones that also occur in the given corpora.

For all sub-tasks and systems submitted, we used the aligned embedding spaces produced with the method above. From a computational performance perspective, the most costly process was alignment, with the other steps completing in negligible time on a GPU machine (using the default GPUs made available on the Google Colaboratory[4] platform): from seconds for training the supervised models to minutes for training the embedding spaces. For the alignment stage, we ran the algorithms on a CPU machine with an 8-core i7 processor. The supervised alignment completed in approximately 5 minutes, while the semi-supervised and unsupervised methods completed in 5 to 7 hours each. The training phase for building and aligning the embeddings models was the most costly from this perspective, while the actual inference computed for the sample of 4,000 target words was negligible in comparison (consisting only of retrieving cosine distance scores from the embeddings spaces and combining it with linguistic features scores).

Model	Correlation
LinReg with cosine-dist and ling. feat.	0.282
Manual weighting cosine-dist and ling. feat.	(-)0.325
Baseline1	0.092
Baseline2	0.543

Table 1: Results for graded discovery task

3.2 Linguistic Features

Word Polysemy For each word, we computed its polysemy degree by counting the number of synsets it occurs in in WordNet(Miller, 1995), specifically in Open Multilingual WordNet(Bond and Foster, 2013). The degree of polysemy is measured simply

[1] https://github.com/ananana/LSCDiscovery-cotohili

[2] https://github.com/artetxem/vecmap

[3] http://nltk.org/book/

[4] https://colab.research.google.com/

Model	F1	Precision	Recall
Manual weighting of cosine-dist and ling. feat.	0.636	0.353	0.750
DecisionTree with cosine-dist and ling. feat.	0.4	0.143	0.211
Baseline1	0.537	0.846	0.393
Baseline2	0.222	0.500	0.143

Table 2: Results for binary change detection

Model	F1	Precision	Recall
Manual weighing of cosine-dist and ling. feat.	0.462	0.316	0.857
DecisionTree with cosine-dist and ling. feat.	0.111	0.071	0.087
Baseline1	-	-	-
Baseline2	0.211	0.400	0.143

Table 3: Results for optional task on sense gain

as the number of synsets obtained (without distinguishing between polysemy and homonymy).

We assume that polysemy (i.e., the coexistence of several possible meanings for one word) is a relevant feature since it has been shown to be statistically correlated with the rate of semantic change in various previous studies (Bréal, 1897; Ullmann, 1963; Magué, 2005). Bréal (1897) and Ullmann (1963) labelled polysemy as the core of meaning change, considering that change occurs when a secondary or connotative meaning replaces the main or denotative one. Ullmann (1963) underlines the role of discontinuity as a "natural diachronic consequence of the polysemic principle", explained in terms of using a word outside of its initial context, until its original meaning is either forgotten by the speakers, or becomes secondary. Magué (2005) defines polysemy as the synchronic manifestation of semantic change. A possible difficulty in the present task is that WordNet cannot make the difference between polysemic words and homonyms (i.e., words that share the same form, but have different origins and, hence, meanings). Nonetheless, the Spanish language has tended, throughout its history, to avoid the homonymic clashes, either by introducing a graphic distinction (e.g. Sp. *gravar* "to charge" < Lat. *gravare*, vs Sp. *grabar* "to record" < Fr. *graver*), either by simply replacing one of the homonyms by an unambiguous lexeme. Therefore, the cases of possible confusion between polysemy and homonymy are found in a small percentage.

Number of Neological Synonyms As a second feature, we considered the number of synonyms the target word has, in particular neologisms. We extract synonyms for a target word using WordNet (considering all possible senses of the word). In order to select only neological synonyms, we assume a synonym is a neologism (literally, a new word) if it does not occur in the old corpus provided in the shared task.

Our hypothesis is that a word with new synonyms may have diverged from its original semantic pattern, as its new lexical rival could have been increasingly regarded as more suitable for the position of the target word. Obeying the tendency of economy of language, it is counterproductive to have two or more words occupying the same position in the structure of the lexicon, therefore one either migrates to a different semantic field, either undergoes, most often, a semantic specialization (e.g. Lat. *vivenda* "living necessities" > Sp. *vivienda* "living place"), a generalization (Lat. *denarius* "an ancient Roman silver coin, worth ten asses" > Sp. *dinero* "money" in general) or a cohyponymic transfer (i.e. a word designating a certain element of a class shifts as a denomination for another element belonging to the same class, e.g. Lat. *pavus* "peacock" > Sp. *pavo* "turkey"). This shift generally affects the former holder of a position in the lexical system, giving way to new candidates.

Levenstein distance to English Words English has exerted, in recent decades, a strong influence on the Romance languages, materialized both in lexical borrowings, and especially in semantic borrowings or calques (Dworkin, 2012).

We assume that the existence of a virtual cognate in English (we understand by "virtual cognates" two or more descendants of the same etymon in different languages, without being inherited in each language; in this investigation, we considered as "virtual cognates" any pair consisting of a Romance borrowing from a Latin word and the English loanword originated from the same Latin word, e.g. Sp. *directo* and Eng. *direct*) with a similar pronunciation (whether sharing the same meaning or not) may be an indicator that the target word could have been influenced by its English correspondent(Uban et al., 2021a). As an example, we could mention the case of Sp. *servidor*, whose significant divergence from its original meaning could also be due to the new acceptation it gained, in computer science, through a calque of Eng. *server* "a computer that provides client stations with access to files and printers as shared resources to a computer network". We retrieve candidate cognate words in English by using the Levenshtein distances from the target word to any English word in the vocabulary, and choosing the closest English word as a potential cognate. We use the Levenshtein distance to this word as a feature in our model. Here are just a few examples of Spanish - English word pairs identified by using the Levenshtein distances, where the influence of the English meaning on the current use of the word in Spanish is significant: Sp. *administración*, originally "act of administering", influenced by Eng. *administration* came to mean as well "Government (of a country)"; Sp. *contemplar*, originally "to see", also received the meaning "to consider" under the influence of Eng. *contemplate*; Sp. *vegetales* "plants" is also used in the acceptation of Eng. *vegetables* "plant or part of the plant used as food"; Sp. *nominar* "to give a name" acquired as well the meaning of Eng. *nominate* "propose as a candidate for elections or for an award", etc.

3.3 Linguistically-Informed Weighting of Features

For one of our solutions submitted to the second sub-task we attempt to combine the selected features by manually assigning weights to each feature, using expert judgements from linguists specialized in Romance languages and in historical semantics.

Table 4 shows the weights we assigned to each feature. We chose the highest weights to the word embeddings feature, giving more importance to the ones obtained with the supervised alignment approach. For the linguistic features, we considered word polysemy and number of neological synonyms. The range of possible values for these features contains higher numbers than the embedding cosine distances, with comparable ranges between the two linguistic features (natural numbers with no upper limit in theory), which is why we assign lower weights for the linguistic features. We consider polysemy as more important than number of synonyms (considering the theoretical justifications presented above). Since the third linguistic feature, designed to measure the closeness to an English cognate (approximated with Levenshtein distance to the closest English word) is less precise than the other features in the way it is measured, and since its effect on language change can be more complex, it was difficult to decide on a specific relative weight in this case that could be reliable, so we left this feature out of this solution.

Feature	Weight
embeddings-cosine-unsupervised	0.1
embeddings-cosine-supervised	0.4
embeddings-cosine-semi-supervised	0.1
nr-neo-synonyms	0.02
wordnet-polysemy	0.05

Table 4: Weights for the different features used, manually assigned with the assistance of linguistic experts

While we did not submit results using manual weighting for the first sub-task on graded discovery, we did incorporate them in our submission for the second sub-task which included an optional task on graded discovery. Due to an error when computing the results, we reported the opposite score to the one generated by the model (with a negative sign), leading to a negative rank correlation with the ground truth. We suggest that, disregarding this error, the results can be considered with an opposite sign, leading to a positive correlation.

For binarizing the results, we used a threshold equal to the median score on the full set of target words.

3.4 Supervised Learning of Feature Weights

As a second solution, we learn the relative weights of each of the features considered using a supervised approach by training a simple model on a very small number of annotated examples. As training data, we used the examples and scores provided by the organizers[5] containing a list of 20 target words along with semantic shift scores.

For sub-task 1 (graded discovery) we used a linear regression model, trained to predict the semantic shift degree on the small set of annotated examples.

For sub-task 2 along with the optional subtasks on binary change, we trained a decision tree model to predict binary labels. We binarized the continuous labels in the annotated examples by setting a threshold equal to the median value of semantic shift on the dataset: any score below this threshold was considered a negative label, and any score above it a positive label.

We additionally analyzed the weights learned by the models in order to gain some insights into the importance awarded automatically to each feature. The linear regression model learned the fol-

[5]https://zenodo.org/record/6300105#.YlK2AXVBxhE

lowing weights for the embedding-based cosine scores: 0.35 for the unsupervised alignment space, 0.91 for the supervised space, and 0.34 for the semi-supervised aligned space. For the linguistic features, the model learned a weight of 1 for the neological synonyms feature, 7 for polysemy degree, and 0.27 for the Levenshtein score to English words. We notice that all weights are positive, and interestingly, that their relative importance matches the one considered for setting weights manually based on linguistic motivations.

For predicting decisions on the optional subtasks of sense gain and sense loss, we combined the predictions for binary change with the values of some of the linguistic features considered which could serve as indicators for sense gains or losses, according to the reasons stated before: we consider a word to have lost a sense if it was predicted to have changed its meaning, and it has any neological synonyms, while polysemy is low (less than 2 senses). Any word which was predicted to have changed its meaning and not lost senses was considered to have gained senses.

4 Results

4.1 Task 1: Graded Discovery

We show our results for sub-task 1 in Table 1. We additionally report here the results obtained with the manual weighting system not submitted to the first sub-task, but submitted to the optional graded change task in the second phase. The baselines consisted of: a skip-gram embeddings model with negative sampling, and orthogonal Procrustes for embedding space alignment (baseline 2), and normalized frequency difference.

4.2 Task 2: Binary Change

Results for sub-task 2 are shown in Table 2. We also submitted predictions for the optional task of sense gain, shown in Table 3. We obtained the second place in terms of recall for sense gain. For sense loss, we do not report detailed results since neither of our systems were able to generate correct predictions (obtaining scores of 0.0).

We notice that, in general, the unsupervised approach using manual weighting of features outperformed the supervised approach. This might be due to the very small size of the annotated data, but is also an encouraging result showing the success of incorporating linguistically informed and expert curated measures for predicting semantic change.

5 Conclusions

We have presented our methods and results in participating in the Spanish semantic change shared task. We proposed a system based in part on word embedding distances, which are already the norm in SOTA models for predicting semantic shift (Schlechtweg et al., 2020), and in part on handcrafted linguistic features, chosen based on theoretical linguistic motivation and on empirical evidence of their relevance to semantic change. While we have done minimal experimentation with the parameters and settings used in training word embeddings, and used supervised models trained on very little data, we obtain encouraging results. For the future, we suggest that combining embedding models trained with more fine-tuned parameters optimized for the given task along with features such as the ones described could lead to improved results. We conclude that incorporating linguistically informed features (aside from word frequency) in computational models for predicting semantic change is a valuable and currently under-explored avenue.

Acknowledgements

This research is supported by a grant of the Ministry of Research, Innovation and Digitization, CNCS/CCCDI—UEFISCDI, CoToHiLi project, project number 108, within PNCDI III.

References

Mikel Artetxe, Gorka Labaka, and Eneko Agirre. 2016. Learning principled bilingual mappings of word embeddings while preserving monolingual invariance. In *Proceedings of the 2016 Conference on Empirical Methods in Natural Language Processing*, pages 2289–2294.

Mikel Artetxe, Gorka Labaka, and Eneko Agirre. 2017. Learning bilingual word embeddings with (almost) no bilingual data. In *Proceedings of the 55th Annual Meeting of the Association for Computational Linguistics (Volume 1: Long Papers)*, pages 451–462.

Mikel Artetxe, Gorka Labaka, and Eneko Agirre. 2018a. Generalizing and improving bilingual word embedding mappings with a multi-step framework of linear transformations. In *Proceedings of the Thirty-Second AAAI Conference on Artificial Intelligence*, pages 5012–5019.

Mikel Artetxe, Gorka Labaka, and Eneko Agirre. 2018b. A robust self-learning method for fully unsupervised cross-lingual mappings of word embeddings. In *Proceedings of the 56th Annual Meeting of the Association for Computational Linguistics (Volume 1: Long Papers)*, pages 789–798.

Francis Bond and Ryan Foster. 2013. Linking and extending an open multilingual wordnet. In *Proceedings of the 51st Annual Meeting of the Association for Computational Linguistics (Volume 1: Long Papers)*, pages 1352–1362.

Michel Bréal. 1897. *Essai de sémantique (science des significations)*. Slatkine Reprints, Genéve.

Frank D. Zamora-Reina, Felipe Bravo-Marquez, and Dominik Schlechtweg. 2022. Lscdiscovery: A shared task on semantic change discovery and detection in spanish. In *Proceedings of the 3rd International Workshop on Computational Approaches to Historical Language Change*, Dublin, Ireland. Association for Computational Linguistics.

Steven N Dworkin. 2012. *A history of the Spanish lexicon: A linguistic perspective*. Oxford University Press on Demand.

William L Hamilton, Jure Leskovec, and Dan Jurafsky. 2016. Diachronic word embeddings reveal statistical laws of semantic change. In *Proceedings of the 54th Annual Meeting of the Association for Computational Linguistics (Volume 1: Long Papers)*, pages 1489–1501.

Jean-Philippe Magué. 2005. *Changements sémantiques et cognition: différentes méthodes pour différentes échelles temporelles*. Ph.D. thesis, Université Lumière-Lyon II.

Tomas Mikolov, Kai Chen, Greg Corrado, and Jeffrey Dean. 2013. Efficient estimation of word representations in vector space. *arXiv preprint arXiv:1301.3781*.

George A Miller. 1995. Wordnet: a lexical database for english. *Communications of the ACM*, 38(11):39–41.

Dominik Schlechtweg, Barbara McGillivray, Simon Hengchen, Haim Dubossarsky, and Nina Tahmasebi. 2020. Semeval-2020 task 1: Unsupervised lexical semantic change detection. In *Proceedings of the Fourteenth Workshop on Semantic Evaluation*, pages 1–23.

Ana Uban, Alina Maria Ciobanu, and Liviu P Dinu. 2019. Studying laws of semantic divergence across languages using cognate sets. In *Proceedings of the 1st International Workshop on Computational Approaches to Historical Language Change*, pages 161–166.

Ana-Sabina Uban, Alina Maria Ciobanu, and Liviu P Dinu. 2021a. Cross-lingual laws of semantic change. *Computational approaches to semantic change*, 6:219.

Ana Sabina Uban, Alina Maria Cristea, Anca Dinu, Liviu P Dinu, Simona Georgescu, and Laurentiu Zoicas. 2021b. Tracking semantic change in cognate sets for english and romance languages. In *Proceedings of the 2nd International Workshop on Computational Approaches to Historical Language Change 2021*, pages 64–74.

Stephen Ullmann. 1963. *The principles of semantics*. Oxford, Glasgow.

Yang Xu and Charles Kemp. 2015. A computational evaluation of two laws of semantic change. In *CogSci*.

HSE at LSCDiscovery in Spanish: Clustering and Profiling for Lexical Semantic Change Discovery

Kseniia Kashleva Alexander Shein Elizaveta Tukhtina Svetlana Vydrina*

HSE University

Abstract

This paper describes the methods used for lexical semantic change discovery in Spanish. We tried the method based on BERT embeddings with clustering, the method based on grammatical profiles and the grammatical profiles method enhanced with permutation tests. BERT embeddings with clustering turned out to show the best results for both graded and binary semantic change detection outperforming the baseline.

1 Introduction

Lexical semantic change detection (LSCD) aims to identify whether the words change their meaning over time, or not. LSCD is usually divided into two subtasks: graded change discovery and binary change detection. Graded LSCD is a subtask of ranking the intersection of (content-word) vocabularies according to their degree of change between a diachronic corpus pair C1 and C2 (Kurtyigit et al., 2021). Binary LSCD is a subtask of identifying whether a target word lost or gained senses from the 1st set of its usage to the second, or not (Schlechtweg et al., 2020).

Previous shared tasks on lexical semantic change detection (LSCD) were developed for English, German, Latin, and Swedish (Schlechtweg et al., 2020), Italian (Basile et al., 2020), and Russian (Kutuzov and Pivovarova, 2021). This one was in Spanish (D. Zamora-Reina et al., 2022). Spanish is a fusional Romance language of the Indo-European language family with rich morphology and a lot of national varieties. So far, LSCD in shared tasks were developed for three Romance languages, three German languages, and one Slavic language. Only two of them are analytical (English and Swedish), while others are fusional.

In this shared task we tested several methods. For graded change discovery we used BERT embeddings with clustering (Montariol et al., 2021). For binary change detection we used 3 methods. The first one was word embeddings again. Two others were grammatical profiling (Kutuzov et al., 2021), and grammatical profiling combined with permutation tests (Liu et al., 2021).

Though grammatical profiles by themselves yield worse performance than embedding-based method, they could be significantly improved by applying of additional significance tests.

2 Methods

2.1 BERT embeddings method

For this method we used a base version of BERT with 12 attention layers and a hidden layer size of 768. The exact pre-trained model was the one for Spanish [1] (Devlin et al., 2019). All parameters were set to the default as in the Transformers library ver. 4.14.1 (Wolf et al., 2020).

The method consisted of several steps. First, we split the corpora into train and test sets. The train/test ratio was 90/10. We used the lemmatized version of the corpora in this method. Then we took the pre-trained BERT model for Spanish and ran a fine-tuning process on the train set of the corpora using the test set for evaluation. The code we used for fine-tuning is provided as one of the examples in the Transformers library repository [2].

After fine-tuning the model we extracted the embeddings for the target words from the full corpora provided. The embeddings were extracted separately for two time periods. To generate a final embedding for each target word, the embeddings from all 12 attention layers of the BERT model were summarized. The embeddings for all entries of every target word were extracted this way.

As a result, we obtained two matrices for every

*Equal contribution, the authors listed alphabetically.

[1] We used the following model: https://huggingface.co/dccuchile/bert-base-spanish-wwm-uncased

[2] https://github.com/huggingface/transformers/tree/main/examples/pytorch/language-modeling

Proceedings of the 3rd Workshop on Computational Approaches to Historical Language Change, pages 193 - 197
May 26-27, 2022 ©2022 Association for Computational Linguistics

target word. One matrix represented one time period. The dimension of the resulting matrix was Nx768, where N is the number of occurrences of the target word in the corpus of particular time period.

The final step was clustering. We ran a *k*-means clustering algorithm on the rows of the resulting matrices. It should be noted that we also attempted to use the affinity propagation algorithm, but it proved unfeasible at this point, as the number of target words and the number of their embeddings was too large for the affinity propagation approach. So the final decision was to resort to the k-means algorithm which is much faster. The number of clusters was set as a hyperparameter which we tuned at the development phase. The development phase demonstrated that the results were the best when the number of clusters equaled to a multiple of 7 with the larger numbers showing better results. In order to find a balance between the clustering time and the results we decided that the number of clusters should be 28.

The resulting clusters presumably represented some gradations of word meanings. In order to calculate the graded change between the sets of clusters from two time periods, we used the average of the cosine distances between all pairs of the cluster centroids. The binary change was calculated by clustering the resulting graded changes into two clusters: the words that fall into the cluster with higher centroid value were considered as changed. The other words were considered as unchanged.

To detect binary gain/loss we took the cluster centroids calculated on one of the previous steps. Those centroids were clustered once again, but this time we used the affinity propagation method that determined the number of clusters automatically. The result clusters presumably represented the basic meanings of target words. After that we compared the number of resulting clusters for both time periods. If the number of clusters in the first period was larger than that in the second period, we assumed that this word lost a sense. If not, we assumed the word gained a sense.

As for the optional COMPARE task, our submission was identical to that for the main Graded task. We did not use any other method for that.

2.2 Grammatical profiling

All language aspects are strongly interconnected. It means that semantic changes may be tied with grammatical changes. Diachronically, it can be observed through lexicalization and grammaticalization in particular. In Spanish, the modern usage of the verb *andar* 'to go' can be a good example of grammaticalization:

De que Blasillo ***ande*** *al escuela me e holgado mucho* (16th c.).

'Since Blasillo has been **going** to school, I have been very happy.'

– *¿Y eso es todo el problema? —* ***Ándale****, exactamente eso.* (21th c.)

'And that's the whole problem? **Yes, yes** (lit. walk to it), that's exactly it.' (Company Company, 2008)

So here we can see that this verb changed its meaning while changing its form.

The idea of grammatical profiling is that semantic change can be discovered through significant changes in the distribution of morphosyntactic categories. This method is described in (Kutuzov et al., 2021) in detail, so here we explain only the main points. To get grammatical profiles, the frequency of morphological and syntactic categories for each target word were counted in both corpora, that were in advance tagged and parsed with UDPipe (Straka and Straková, 2017) [3]. Then, for each target word and for both morphological and syntactic dictionaries, a list of features was created by taking the union of keys in the corresponding dictionaries for the two time bins. After that, feature vectors $\vec{x_1}$ and $\vec{x_2}$ were made. Each dimension of these vectors represented a grammatical category and the value it took was the frequency of that category in the corresponding time period (Kutuzov et al., 2021). Then, the cosine distance $cos(\vec{x_1}; \vec{x_2})$ between the vectors were calculated to estimate the change in the grammatical profiles of the target word [4]. These distances can be used for graded change discovery. For binary detection, the top *n* target words were classified in the ranking as 'changed' (1) and others as 'stable' (0).

2.3 Grammatical profiling enhanced with permutation-based statistical tests

Earlier statistical significance tests were applied to semantic change detection methods based on contextual word embeddings (Liu et al., 2021). Permutation-based statistical testing can be applied when data is limited. We used permutation tests to improve the results obtained with grammatical

[3]We used the following model: spanish-gsd-ud-2.5-191206.udpipe

[4]The code is available at https://github.com/glnmario/semchange-profiling

profiling, as the aim of the permutation test is to discover whether the observed test statistic (i.e. the cosine distance) is significantly different from zero (Liu et al., 2021). Permutation tests reassigned group labels (time periods) to all observations by sampling without replacement.

For binary change detection we calculated the default distance between grammar profiles. Then, we took sentence indices from the first and the second corpus for every target word and permute them by randomly splitting them between two time periods. If the number of possible permutations were less than 1000 we used all permutations. Then we calculated cosine distance between grammar profiles generated after shuffling. So, we have 2 sets of distances: the original cosine distance between grammar profiles and the permutated cosine distances between grammar profiles.

Let us assume, there were 5 permutations, so we got 5 distances, e.g., 0.1, 0.7, 0.4, 0.15, and 0.2, and the original cosine distance was 0.3. We took only those permutated cosine distances that were larger than the default cosine distance. In this example, these are 0.7 and 0.4 (two values). So, we divided the number of these larger permutated distances by the number of permutations. In this example, this is 2/5. This result is a p-value (Liu et al., 2021).

If the number of permutations were greater than 1000, the procedure was the same, but we corrected the p-value for every digit capacity, i.e., we took the first significance threshold as 0.05 and step-by-step reduced it till 0.005 (Liu et al., 2021). In other words, we first randomly selected 1000 permutations and computed p-value. If this was larger 0.05, we stopped the procedure, otherwise took more permutations for more precise estimations.

As a result, we had the cosine distance between grammar profiles and the p-value for every target word. For binary change detection we sorted these values both by the distance and the p-value and labeled top *n* target words as changed.

3 Results

The submission results are presented in Table 1.

Clustering turned out to be the best one among all our methods. In graded change discovery it was proved to be better than both baselines and took the 3rd place in the leaderboard.

Grammatical profiling demonstrated the worst results among three methods we used (see Table 1).

Graded			
	COMPARE	Spearman	
Clusters	0.558	0.553	
Baseline	0.561	0.543	
Grammar	—	*0.390*	
Binary			
	Precision	Recall	F1
Clusters	0.567	**0.607**	**0.586**
Grammar	0.714	0.357	0.476
Stats	**0.750**	0.429	0.545
Baseline	0.846	0.393	0.537
Gain			
	Precision	Recall	F1
Clusters	0.192	0.357	0.250
Baseline	0.400	0.143	0.211
Loss			
	Precision	Recall	F1
Clusters	0.421	0.320	0.364
Baseline	0	0	0

Table 1: Submission results: *Clusters* means embedding clustering method, *Grammar* means grammatical profiles and *Stats* means grammatical profiles combined with a permutation test. Grammatical profiling for graded discovery was made after the competition.

However, the results indicate that it was significantly improved by applying a permutation test. It should also be noted that grammatical profiling with a permutation test demonstrated the best precision among all participants and was only outperformed by the baseline. We also applied grammatical profiling for graded change discovery after the competition. The result was worse than baseline (see Table 1).

The clustering method was our only method that was applied to the optional Gain/Loss task, however, it did not show good results. While this method surpassed the baseline numbers, it proved to be significantly inferior to the other methods participating in the task. We assume that it happened because we approached the Gain/Loss task as a separate task. The better approach might have been to somehow use the results we received on the main Binary task in order to calculate the gain/loss values.

There is another problem with the method that we can think of. The method assigned a gain/loss label for the word if the number of clusters in two time epochs differs even by one. Perhaps a better approach would have been to decrease the sensi-

word	change graded	change graded golden	change graded difference
actitud	0.369	0.925	0.556
propiamente	0.473	0	0.473
fallecimiento	0.468	0	0.468
viernes	0.447	0	0.447
trato	0.490	0.051	0.439
distribuir	0.438	0	0.438
banco	0.514	0.925	0.411
canal	0.607	1	0.393
variedad	0.392	0	0.392
socialista	0.391	0	0.391

Table 2: BERT-based predictions compared with the gold standard.

word	change graded	change graded golden	change graded difference
marco	0.018	1	0.982
prima	0.118	1	0.882
actitud	0.115	0.925	0.810
indicativo	0.202	1	0.798
canal	0.240	1	0.760
disco	0.167	0.915	0.748
pendiente	0.096	0.781	0.685
corriente	0.072	0.753	0.681
banco	0.246	0.925	0.678
cólera	0.098	0.741	0.643

Table 3: Grammatical profiles predictions compared with the gold standard.

tivity of the method and to ignore the insignificant differences between the number of clusters.

4 Discussion

Table 2 presents the top 10 words with the largest difference between BERT-based predictions and the gold standard. Closer inspection shows that there are two error types. According to the standard, some words (*actitud, banco*) changed a lot, while our prediction for these words appeared to be much lower. Meanwhile, there were words that did not change, however, our model labeled them as changed (*propiamente, fallecimiento, viernes, distribuir, variedad, socialista*). Interestingly, that within the top 10 words, the model fell into errors on the side of changing more often.

Table 3 presents the top 10 words with the largest difference between grammatical profiling predictions and the gold standard. Our prediction for these words was much lower than the gold standard. Some incorrect predictions are the same with the incorrect predictions obtained with the BERT-based method (*actitud, canal, banco*). A likely explanation is that these words have a complicated semantic structure and more than one meaning.

5 Conclusion

Further studies need to be carried out in order to evaluate the combination of profiling with statistical significance testing for other languages. Although the BERT-based method demonstrated the best results, more detailed error analysis is still required.

Acknowledgements

This research was supported in part through computational resources of HPC facilities at HSE University (Kostenetskiy et al., 2021).

References

Pierpaolo Basile, Annalina Caputo, Tommaso Caselli, Pierluigi Cassotti, and Rossella Varvara. 2020. Diacr-ita @ evalita2020: Overview of the evalita2020 diachronic lexical semantics (diacr-ita) task. In *EVALITA*.

Concepción Company Company. 2008. The directionality of grammaticalization in spanish. *Journal of Historical Pragmatics*, 9(2):200–224.

Frank D. Zamora-Reina, Felipe Bravo-Marquez, and Dominik Schlechtweg. 2022. Lscdiscovery: A shared task on semantic change discovery and detection in spanish. In *Proceedings of the 3rd International Workshop on Computational Approaches to Historical Language Change*, Dublin, Ireland. Association for Computational Linguistics.

Jacob Devlin, Ming-Wei Chang, Kenton Lee, and Kristina Toutanova. 2019. BERT: Pre-training of deep bidirectional transformers for language understanding. In *Proceedings of the 2019 Conference of the North American Chapter of the Association for Computational Linguistics: Human Language Technologies, Volume 1 (Long and Short Papers)*, pages 4171–4186, Minneapolis, Minnesota. Association for Computational Linguistics.

P. S. Kostenetskiy, R. A. Chulkevich, and V. I. Kozyrev. 2021. HPC resources of the higher school of economics. *Journal of Physics: Conference Series*, 1740(1):012050.

Sinan Kurtyigit, Maike Park, Dominik Schlechtweg, Jonas Kuhn, and Sabine Schulte im Walde. 2021. Lexical semantic change discovery. In *Proceedings of the 59th Annual Meeting of the Association for Computational Linguistics and the 11th International Joint Conference on Natural Language Processing (Volume 1: Long Papers)*, pages 6985–6998, Online. Association for Computational Linguistics.

Andrey Kutuzov and Lidia Pivovarova. 2021. Three-part diachronic semantic change dataset for Russian. In *Proceedings of the 2nd International Workshop on Computational Approaches to Historical Language Change 2021*, pages 7–13, Online. Association for Computational Linguistics.

Andrey Kutuzov, Lidia Pivovarova, and Mario Giulianelli. 2021. Grammatical profiling for semantic change detection. In *Proceedings of the 25th Conference on Computational Natural Language Learning*, pages 423–434, Online. Association for Computational Linguistics.

Yang Liu, Alan Medlar, and Dorota Glowacka. 2021. Statistically significant detection of semantic shifts using contextual word embeddings. In *Proceedings of the 2nd Workshop on Evaluation and Comparison of NLP Systems*, pages 104–113, Punta Cana, Dominican Republic. Association for Computational Linguistics.

Syrielle Montariol, Matej Martinc, and Lidia Pivovarova. 2021. Scalable and interpretable semantic change detection. In *Proceedings of the 2021 Conference of the North American Chapter of the Association for Computational Linguistics: Human Language Technologies*, pages 4642–4652, Online. Association for Computational Linguistics.

Dominik Schlechtweg, Barbara McGillivray, Simon Hengchen, Haim Dubossarsky, and Nina Tahmasebi. 2020. SemEval-2020 task 1: Unsupervised lexical semantic change detection. In *Proceedings of the Fourteenth Workshop on Semantic Evaluation*, pages 1–23, Barcelona (online). International Committee for Computational Linguistics.

Milan Straka and Jana Straková. 2017. Tokenizing, POS tagging, lemmatizing and parsing UD 2.0 with UDPipe. In *Proceedings of the CoNLL 2017 Shared Task: Multilingual Parsing from Raw Text to Universal Dependencies*, pages 88–99, Vancouver, Canada. Association for Computational Linguistics.

Thomas Wolf, Lysandre Debut, Victor Sanh, Julien Chaumond, Clement Delangue, Anthony Moi, Pierric Cistac, Tim Rault, Remi Louf, Morgan Funtowicz, Joe Davison, Sam Shleifer, Patrick von Platen, Clara Ma, Yacine Jernite, Julien Plu, Canwen Xu, Teven Le Scao, Sylvain Gugger, Mariama Drame, Quentin Lhoest, and Alexander Rush. 2020. Transformers: State-of-the-art natural language processing. In *Proceedings of the 2020 Conference on Empirical Methods in Natural Language Processing: System Demonstrations*, pages 38–45, Online. Association for Computational Linguistics.

GlossReader at LSCDiscovery: Train to Select a Proper Gloss in English – Discover Lexical Semantic Change in Spanish

Maxim Rachinskiy[△] **Nikolay Arefyev**[◇,▽,△]

[△]National Research University Higher School of Economics / Moscow, Russia
[◇]Samsung Research Center Russia / Moscow, Russia
[▽]Lomonosov Moscow State University / Moscow, Russia
myurachinskiy@edu.hse.ru, nick.arefyev@gmail.com

Abstract

The contextualized embeddings obtained from neural networks pre-trained as Language Models (LM) or Masked Language Models (MLM) are not well suitable for solving the Lexical Semantic Change Detection (LSCD) task because they are more sensitive to changes in word forms rather than word meaning, a property previously known as the word form bias or orthographic bias (Laicher et al., 2021). Unlike many other NLP tasks, it is also not obvious how to fine-tune such models for LSCD. In order to conclude if there are any differences between senses of a particular word in two corpora, a human annotator or a system shall analyze many examples containing this word from both corpora. This makes annotation of LSCD datasets very labour-consuming. The existing LSCD datasets contain up to 100 words that are labeled according to their semantic change, which is hardly enough for fine-tuning.

To solve these problems we fine-tune the XLM-R MLM (Conneau et al., 2020) as part of a gloss-based WSD system on a large WSD dataset in English. Then we employ zero-shot cross-lingual transferability of XLM-R to build the contextualized embeddings for examples in Spanish. In order to obtain the graded change score for each word, we calculate the average distance between our improved contextualized embeddings of its old and new occurrences. For the binary change detection subtask, we apply thresholding to the same scores.

Our solution has shown the best results among all other participants in all subtasks except for the optional sense gain detection subtask.

1 Introduction

LSCDiscovery (D. Zamora-Reina et al., 2022) is a shared task on Lexical Semantic Change Detection (LSCD) in Spanish. In general, LSCD is the task of automatically analyzing differences between word senses in two corpora. In the shared task, these two corpora represent two time periods (1810-1906 and 1994-2020), and the participants are asked to analyze changes in the meaning of words over time, or diachronic change.

There are two main subtasks in the shared task: graded change and binary change detection. In the first subtask, the participants are asked to rank a list of words according to the magnitude of change in the relative frequencies of their senses (measured by the Jensen–Shannon distance between the probability distributions over senses automatically inferred by the organizers from the pairwise human annotations). In the second subtask, for each given word the systems should detect if the sets of its senses appearing in the old and the new corpus are different, i.e. if any new senses have appeared or any old senses are not in use anymore.

Despite the success of recurrent and Transformer-based neural networks pre-trained as language models (LM) or masked language models (MLM) on large corpora in a wide variety of NLP tasks, they cannot be applied to the LSCD task in a standard way. Most datasets used to fine-tune such models for different NLP tasks contain tens or hundreds of thousands examples, each of these examples is a text fragment not longer than several hundred words that contain all information required to make a correct prediction. In LSCD one example is a word, however, inspecting many occurrences of this word in both old and new corpora is required to draw correct conclusions about changes of its meaning. This requires a model that can extract information from many word occurrences and somehow aggregate it to produce the final prediction. Also, this makes creating labeled datasets for the task extremely labour-consuming, resulting in typical datasets containing less than 100 labeled words per language (Schlechtweg et al., 2021; Kutuzov and Pivovarova, 2021), which is hardly enough for fine-tuning.

Alternatively, in Laicher et al. (2021) the con-

Proceedings of the 3rd Workshop on Computational Approaches to Historical Language Change, pages 198 - 203
May 26-27, 2022

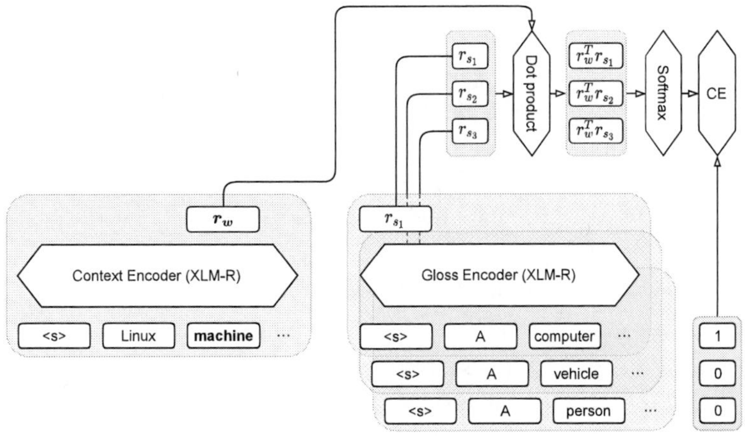

Figure 1: The multilingual gloss-based WSD model based on the BEM architecture.

textualized embeddings calculated by a pre-trained MLM without any fine-tuning were applied to solve the LSCD task. They found that the largest signal in these embeddings corresponds to the grammatical form, not to the meaning of words. This is known as the grammatical or orthographic bias of the contextualized embeddings and prohibits their direct application to the LSCD task.

The main idea behind our solution is that fine-tuning on some task that requires understanding word senses and at the same time ignoring word forms shall help to get rid of grammatical bias in the contextualized embeddings. A suitable task shall also have a large dataset for fine-tuning. In our solution of the LSCD task, we fine-tune a pre-trained MLM as part of a gloss-based WSD system, i.e. a system that can select the most appropriate gloss for a given word in a given context. Our WSD system is based on the architecture proposed in Blevins and Zettlemoyer (2020), however, we replace English BERT with multilingual XLM-R to make our system multilingual. We train the system on English WSD data only, then apply it to the texts in Spanish exploiting zero-shot cross-lingual transferability of XLM-R to obtain the contextualized embeddings for Spanish words.

Despite not using any labeled data in Spanish, the described method of fine-tuning XLM-R results in such contextualized embeddings that are directly applicable for lexical semantic change detection in Spanish. Our solution based on these contextualized embeddings has achieved the best results among all other participants in both main subtasks, and also in all optional subtasks except for the sense gain detection.[1]

2 Background

Our solution is inspired by the BEM (Bi-Encoder Model) system developed by Blevins and Zettlemoyer (2020) to solve the Word Sense Disambiguation (WSD) task in English. While WSD is essentially a classification task requiring to annotate each occurrence of polysemous words with one of their senses described in WordNet (Miller, 1995) or other sense inventory, a huge number of senses in WordNet (more than 100K) and zero or very few examples for most senses and words in the labeled training sets make standard classification approaches not applicable. Instead of treating senses as atomic classes, in BEM they are represented with their glosses from WordNet. Two encoders are introduced: the gloss encoder to build embeddings for glosses, and the context encoder to build contextualized embeddings for word occurrences. These encoders are trained jointly such that for each word occurrence among all glosses of this word a gloss describing its meaning in the given context can be selected by the similarity between the corresponding contextualized embedding and the gloss embeddings.

The original BEM system employs English BERT (Devlin et al., 2019) as both gloss and context encoders. The system is trained on the English WSD dataset SemCor (Miller et al., 1994). We replace English BERT with multilingual XLM-R (Conneau et al., 2020). XLM-RoBERTa (XLM-R for short) is basically the multilingual version

[1]Reproduction code: `https://github.com/myrachins/LSCDiscovery`

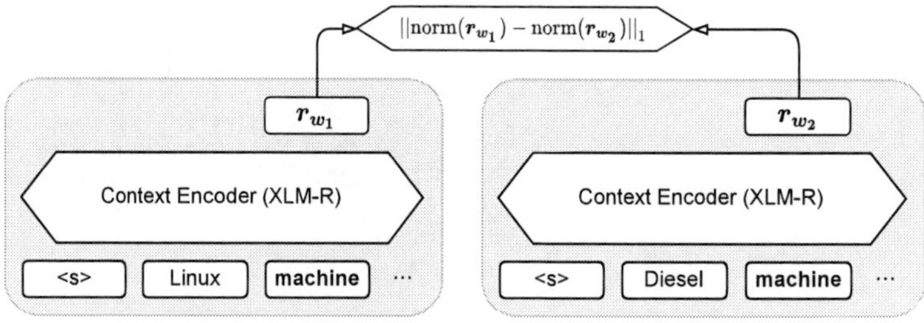

Figure 2: Employing the context encoder for distance estimation.

of RoBERTa (Liu et al., 2019), and RoBERTa is BERT (Devlin et al., 2019) with several improvements in the training procedure. All of these models essentially train the encoder of the Transformer-based machine translation system (Vaswani et al., 2017) with Masked Language Modeling (MLM) objective, i.e. to restore some words in a text fragment from nearby words (see Devlin et al. (2019) for technical details). In contrast to BERT and RoBERTa pre-trained on English texts only, XLM-R is pre-trained on 2.5TB of texts in 100 languages. Surprisingly, this allows not only processing texts in all of these languages but also demonstrates zero-shot cross-lingual transferability, meaning that after fine-tuning XLM-R to solve some classification task on English texts only, it often can solve the same task for texts in other languages reasonably well (Conneau et al., 2020).

Our approach to the LSCD task was initially developed during our participation in the RuShiftEval-2021 shared task on LSCD for the Russian language (Kutuzov and Pivovarova, 2021) and described in Rachinskiy and Arefyev (2021b). However, in RuShiftEval-2021 only a graded change detection task was proposed and the only metric was Spearman's correlation with the gold COMPARE score, which is the average similarity between word occurrences in two corpora (Schlechtweg et al., 2018). The LSCDiscovery shared task in Spanish offers a more thorough comparison of competing approaches by introducing both the graded change and the binary change detection subtasks. It also replaces the gold COMPARE scores with the gold Jensen-Shannon distance between the sense distributions inferred by the organizers, though calculating the gold COMPARE scores as an additional metric as well. Also in RuShiftEval-2021 our best solution was a linear regression model that used different distances between the contextualized embeddings as features and was trained on additional labeled data in Russian. This resulted in consistent but not very large improvement compared to simply using the raw distance between the contextualized embeddings. Thus, for the LSCDiscovery task, we decided to use the simpler solution that also does not require any labeled data in Spanish.

3 System overview

The architecture of our gloss-based WSD system is shown in figure 1. The architecture and the training procedure are borrowed from Blevins and Zettlemoyer (2020), except for the English BERT replaced with multilingual XLM-R in both context and gloss encoders. As usual for XLM-R, the input texts are surrounded by the special tokens <s> and </s>. To obtain the contextualized embedding for a word in context, the outputs at the positions of the target word are taken from the last layer of the context encoder. If the target word was split into subwords by the XLM-R tokenizer, then mean pooling is applied to the corresponding outputs. For each sense of the target word described in WordNet, the corresponding gloss is encoded by taking the output from the last layer of the gloss encoder at the position of the special <s> token.[2] The dot product between the contextualized embedding of the target word and the gloss embeddings for each of its senses is calculated, then the softmax function is applied to obtain the probability distribution over word senses.

The whole system is trained by minimizing the cross-entropy loss between the predicted distribution over senses and the correct sense. Following Blevins and Zettlemoyer (2020), we trained the

[2]This is the standard way of obtaining an embedding for the whole input sequence from MLM models, which is also used in the original BEM model. Some reasonable alternatives are averaging the outputs at all positions, or prepending the target word to each gloss and averaging the outputs at the positions of subwords of the target word. In any case, we believe that fine-tuning is important for obtaining good gloss embeddings.

system on English SemCor (Miller et al., 1994), which is a large dataset consisting of more than 200K sense-annotated word occurrences. The glosses were taken from WordNet 3.0 (Miller, 1995). The SemEval-2007 (Pradhan et al., 2007) WSD dataset served as the development set to choose the final checkpoint. The large version of XLM-R was employed for both encoders. We trained the system for 10 epochs, which took 3 days on two V100 GPUs. The XLM-R model fine-tuned as the context encoder of this WSD system is called the Gloss Language Model (**GLM**) below to distinguish it from the standard XLM-R pre-trained with the MLM objective only.

After the WSD system is trained, in order to estimate the similarity in meaning between two occurrences of the same word, we normalize their contextualized embeddings (divide them by their L1-norm) and calculate the Manhattan distance as shown in figure 2.

3.1 Graded subtasks

For all graded change subtasks, given each target word the score is calculated by the following algorithm.

1. Retrieve all occurrences of the target word in any of its forms from both corpora provided. We employed the same Spanish lemmatizer that was used by the task organizers. Then sample up to 100 pairs of sentences with the first sentence from the old corpus and the second from the new one.[3]

2. For each pair of sentences, calculate the L1-distance (the Manhattan distance) between the normalized embeddings of two occurrences of the target word. In order to normalize the embeddings, we divide them by their L1-norm. This choice is motivated by the previous experiments (Rachinskiy and Arefyev, 2021a,b).

3. Calculate the average of the distances from the previous step. This is known as the Average Pairwise Distance (APD) (Giulianelli et al., 2020).

The APD scores calculated by the last step of this algorithm seem to be a reasonable approximation of the gold COMPARE scores because they both represent the average similarity between word occurrences taken from two different corpora. But they are likely sub-optimal as an approximation of the gold JSD scores. In the future work, it is worth developing some alternatives to specifically approximate JSD.

The most computationally expensive part of this algorithm is calculating embeddings for about 778K word occurrences (4385 target words, 88.68 pairs of occurrences per word on average) This took about 6 GPU-hours on a V100 GPU. Computing distances and final scores takes an insignificant proportion of the whole time.

3.2 Binary subtasks

To obtain binary change predictions, we apply thresholding to our graded change predictions. During the competition, we experimented with two thresholding strategies. First, based on the observation that 9 out of 20 words (45%) in the development set belong to the negative class, we set the threshold equal to the 45-th percentile of APDs for the 60 hidden words revealed after the first subtask (**Thres. revealed**). This results in the same proportions of predicted classes in the test set as the proportions of true classes in the development set.

Alternatively, we calculated the 55-th[4] percentile of APDs for all 4385 target words in the test set from the first subtask (**Thres. all**). The same binary predictions were submitted for all binary subtasks, which is likely suboptimal and is the subject for improvement in the future.

4 Results

Tables 1, 2 show our results compared to the baselines and to the best results of other participants. In the graded subtasks our solution achieves the best results among all participants. In the post-evaluation experiments, we compared the fine-tuned XLM-R model (GLM) with the original one (MLM). Evidently, fine-tuning XLM-R on the WSD task gives a huge boost in performance. Our APD scores have a much higher Spearman's correlation with the gold COMPARE scores than with the gold JSD scores, which supports our hypothesis that simple averaging of the distances between the contextualized embeddings is more suitable as an approximation of the COMPARE metric.

[3]In (Arefyev et al., 2021) it was observed that taking more than 100 pairs does not significantly improve the results, though this was observed for a different model.

[4]This should have been the 45-th percentile, but we made a mistake and calculated the 55-th percentile instead. In the post-evaluation period, we fixed this error (**Thres. all, fixed** method in Table 2).

Model	JSD	COMPARE
our submissions		
GLM norm L1	**.735** (1)	**.842** (1)
top3 other teams for each metric		
UsrD7	.702 (2)	.829 (2)
aishein	.553 (3)	.558 (4)
akutuzov	.508 (5)	.459 (5)
lscdiscovery baselines		
baseline1	.543 (4)	.561 (3)
baseline2	.092 (8)	.088 (6)
our post-evaluation experiments		
MLM norm L1	.505 (5*)	.511 (4*)

Table 1: Results for the graded subtasks, Spearman's correlation with the gold JSD and COMPARE scores. * denotes the ranks that we would have had if we had submitted only this result.

Model	bin. change	sense gain	sense loss
our submissions			
Thres. all	**.716** (1)	.491 (3)	**.688** (1)
Thres. revealed	.656 (4*)	.510 (3*)	.621 (1*)
top3 other teams for each metric			
dteodore	.709 (2)	.000 (8)	.000 (6)
rombek	.687 (3)	.490 (4)	.593 (3)
kudisov	.658 (4)	.520 (2)	.600 (2)
UsrD7	.655 (5)	**.591** (1)	.582 (4)
lscdiscovery baselines			
baseline1	.537 (9)	-	-
baseline2	.222 (10)	.211 (7)	.000 (6)
our post-evaluation experiments			
Thres. all, fixed	**.722** (1*)	.483 (4*)	.667 (1*)

Table 2: Results for binary subtasks, F1-scores. * denotes the ranks that we would have had if we had submitted only this result.

For the binary change detection and the sense loss detection subtasks our solution also outperforms all other participants. However, for the sense gain detection subtask our solution shows F1-scores of 0.483-0.510, which is about 10 points of F1-score worse than the best result in the competition. Notice that we did not specifically address the optional sense loss and sense gain detection subtasks, instead, we reused the predictions from the main binary change detection subtask.

5 Conclusion

In this paper, we presented a solution for both Graded and Binary Change Detection. Our solution achieves the best results among all participants in both graded change detection subtasks, as well as two out of three binary change detection subtasks. The key component of our solution which is shown to be very important is fine-tuning of a masked language model as part of a gloss-based WSD system.

Acknowledgements

We are grateful to our anonymous reviewers. This research was partially supported by the Basic Research Program at the HSE University and through computational resources of HPC facilities at HSE University (Kostenetskiy et al., 2021).

References

N. Arefyev, M. Fedoseev, V. Protasov, D. Homskiy, A. Davletov, and A. Panchenko. 2021. Deepmistake: Which senses are hard to distinguish for a word-in-context model. In *Computational linguistics and intellectual technologies*, 20, page 16 – 30, Russian Federation.

Terra Blevins and Luke Zettlemoyer. 2020. Moving down the long tail of word sense disambiguation with gloss informed bi-encoders. In *Proceedings of the 58th Association for Computational Linguistics*.

Alexis Conneau, Kartikay Khandelwal, Naman Goyal, Vishrav Chaudhary, Guillaume Wenzek, Francisco Guzmán, Edouard Grave, Myle Ott, Luke Zettlemoyer, and Veselin Stoyanov. 2020. Unsupervised cross-lingual representation learning at scale. In *Proceedings of the 58th Annual Meeting of the Association for Computational Linguistics*, pages 8440–8451, Online. Association for Computational Linguistics.

Frank D. Zamora-Reina, Felipe Bravo-Marquez, and Dominik Schlechtweg. 2022. Lscdiscovery: A shared task on semantic change discovery and detection in spanish. In *Proceedings of the 3rd International Workshop on Computational Approaches to Historical Language Change*, Dublin, Ireland. Association for Computational Linguistics.

Jacob Devlin, Ming-Wei Chang, Kenton Lee, and Kristina Toutanova. 2019. BERT: Pre-training of deep bidirectional transformers for language understanding. In *Proceedings of the 2019 Conference of the North American Chapter of the Association for Computational Linguistics: Human Language Technologies, Volume 1 (Long and Short Papers)*, pages 4171–4186, Minneapolis, Minnesota. Association for Computational Linguistics.

Mario Giulianelli, Marco Del Tredici, and Raquel Fernández. 2020. Analysing lexical semantic change with contextualised word representations. In *Proceedings of the 58th Annual Meeting of the Association for Computational Linguistics*, pages 3960–3973, Online. Association for Computational Linguistics.

P. S. Kostenetskiy, R. A. Chulkevich, and V. I. Kozyrev. 2021. HPC resources of the higher school of economics. *Journal of Physics: Conference Series*, 1740:012050.

Andrey Kutuzov and Lidia Pivovarova. 2021. RuShiftEval: a shared task on semantic shift detection for Russian. In *Computational linguistics and intellectual technologies: Papers from the annual conference Dialogue*.

Severin Laicher, Sinan Kurtyigit, Dominik Schlechtweg, Jonas Kuhn, and Sabine Schulte im Walde. 2021. Explaining and improving BERT performance on lexical semantic change detection. In *Proceedings of the 16th Conference of the European Chapter of the Association for Computational Linguistics: Student Research Workshop*, pages 192–202, Online. Association for Computational Linguistics.

Yinhan Liu, Myle Ott, Naman Goyal, Jingfei Du, Mandar Joshi, Danqi Chen, Omer Levy, Mike Lewis, Luke Zettlemoyer, and Veselin Stoyanov. 2019. Roberta: A robustly optimized bert pretraining approach.

George A. Miller. 1995. Wordnet: A lexical database for english. *Commun. ACM*, 38(11):39–41.

George A. Miller, Martin Chodorow, Shari Landes, Claudia Leacock, and Robert G. Thomas. 1994. Using a semantic concordance for sense identification. In *Proceedings of the Workshop on Human Language Technology*, HLT '94, page 240–243, USA. Association for Computational Linguistics.

Sameer Pradhan, Edward Loper, Dmitriy Dligach, and Martha Palmer. 2007. SemEval-2007 task-17: English lexical sample, SRL and all words. In *Proceedings of the Fourth International Workshop on Semantic Evaluations (SemEval-2007)*, pages 87–92, Prague, Czech Republic. Association for Computational Linguistics.

Maxim Rachinskiy and Nikolay Arefyev. 2021a. GlossReader at SemEval-2021 task 2: Reading definitions improves contextualized word embeddings. In *Proceedings of the 15th International Workshop on Semantic Evaluation (SemEval-2021)*, pages 756–762, Online. Association for Computational Linguistics.

Maxim Rachinskiy and Nikolay Arefyev. 2021b. Zeroshot crosslingual transfer of a gloss language model for semantic change detection. In *Computational linguistics and intellectual technologies: Papers from the annual conference Dialogue*, 20, page 578 – 586.

Dominik Schlechtweg, Sabine Schulte im Walde, and Stefanie Eckmann. 2018. Diachronic usage relatedness (DURel): A framework for the annotation of lexical semantic change. In *Proceedings of the 2018 Conference of the North American Chapter of the Association for Computational Linguistics: Human Language Technologies, Volume 2 (Short Papers)*, pages 169–174, New Orleans, Louisiana. Association for Computational Linguistics.

Dominik Schlechtweg, Nina Tahmasebi, Simon Hengchen, Haim Dubossarsky, and Barbara McGillivray. 2021. DWUG: A large resource of diachronic word usage graphs in four languages. In *Proceedings of the 2021 Conference on Empirical Methods in Natural Language Processing*, pages 7079–7091, Online and Punta Cana, Dominican Republic. Association for Computational Linguistics.

Ashish Vaswani, Noam Shazeer, Niki Parmar, Jakob Uszkoreit, Llion Jones, Aidan N Gomez, Łukasz Kaiser, and Illia Polosukhin. 2017. Attention is all you need. In *Advances in Neural Information Processing Systems*, pages 5998–6008.

Author Index

Association for Computational Linguistics
209 N. Eighth Street
Stroudsburg, Pennsylvania 18360

ISBN 978-1-7138-6744-9

9 781713 867449

CURRAN ASSOCIATES INC.
proceedings.com